More
Twentieth Century
Dolls
FROM BISQUE TO VINYL

The Childhood Dolls of Mabel Louise Petry Anderton (1914-1972).

More Twentieth Century Dolls

FROM BISQUE TO VINYL

Volume One
A — H

Johana Gast Anderton

The next best thing to owning a doll is owning a good picture of it®.—J.G.A.

Wallace-Homestead
authoritative books on antiques & collectibles

First Printing October 1, 1974

Second Printing, Revised Edition 1979

Third Printing, 1981

Fourth Printing, 1983

The information contained herein does not constitute a statement of any legal rights or proprietary interests in or to any of the mentioned items. It is the intent of the author only to furnish descriptive information to collectors and dealers. Such information should not be construed as affecting or evidencing any actual copyright or patent rights or the absence thereof. The author has made every effort to be factual and accurate and any discrepencies are totally unintentional.

FRONTISPIECE

The dolls shown in the frontispiece are the much-loved and played-with childhood dolls of the author's late sister-in-law, Mabel Louise Petry Anderton, known to her family and friends as Louise. The larger doll is a twenty-two-inch Effanbee baby marked with the old script mark. It has tin sleep eyes, original mohair baby wig, open-closed mouth, and stationary composition shoulder head and lower arms from which the paint has fallen away in large sections revealing a "Can't Break 'Em" type material. The faded pink cotton body is excelsior-stuffed and the legs are hard-stuffed with cotton. The doll wears her original pale lavendar dress and bonnet as well as the former owner's white kid three-button baby shoes. In the toes of the slightly over-sized shoes were found bits of newspaper bearing a 1930 date; however, the doll dates from 1918. She came to the author with a well-preserved suitcase of carefully stitched and knitted garments.

The smaller doll is an Amberg Victory Doll and is fully described in AMB-23 elsewhere in this volume. She too is dressed in her original gown, a pale yellow organdy with lace trim.

These dolls are shown here in loving tribute to Louise.

- JGA

Library of Congress Catalog Card No. 74-84193

ISBN 0-87069-273-9

Unless otherwise credited,
all photographs, sketches, drawings, endpaper design,
cover design and layout are by the author.

Color Photography by Tony Barnes and Frances Hutchinson.

Printed in the United States of America

Published by

Wallace-Homestead Book Co.
1912 Grand Avenue
Des Moines, Iowa 50305

CONTENTS

Three-year-old Ihla Dugan, left, and her younger sister, Clella, pose for their 1910 portraits with a new doll, second prize in a Farmer's Alliance Store contest in Green, Kansas. Ref. COLOR-1-C.

Our Kathy—a real live doll.

Our Sheri with her doll.

DEDICATION

This book is dedicated to the hundreds of doll collectors all over the world who have so generously aided in its compilation and to my staff, especially to Cheryl Lynn and Kathy Wilk, for their unceasing effort and good cheer.

A very special word of appreciation is extended to Harry J. Guckert, Geyer-McAllister Publications, Inc., publisher of PLAYTHINGS magazine, and to PLAYTHINGS editor, Thomas X. Murn. Through the kindness and cooperation of these two men the author was provided access to the library and other facilities of the firm without which this book would have been something less than had been hoped.

Our Cheryl with her doll lamp.

In the rush of assembling the huge quantity of material collected for the first edition of this volume one of my special helpers was overlooked. Sheri Lynn came to New York at my urgent call to assist in handling the paperwork involved in my research and was of invaluable aid to me at that time. Sheri and the other two little girls shown here are grown, the mothers of young sons, and no longer in my employ.

THE PEOPLE CALLED DOLL COLLECTORS

—ACKNOWLEDGEMENTS—

When I wrote acknowledgements for TWENTIETH CENTURY DOLLS I was convinced I had witnessed the utmost in outpourings of generosity and cooperation. It is, however, with a genuine sense of awe that I begin here to express my appreciation for the help, courtesy, and thoughtfulness extended to me in preparation of this present volume.

No merchant could be more coldly calculating, no slave trader more suspicious of the condition of body and limb, no buyer more sharply aware of values than the knowledgeable doll collector. Yet it is perhaps the touching contact with yesteryear's children through the handling of their toys and dolls that often attracts an individual to the hobby. Such collectors feel a strong sense of their dolls' personalities and give them names as though they were real children. Dolls are groomed and costumed as carefully as any pampered child and curls coiffed with regularity.

Space alone prevents me from recounting the many incidents which point up the generous nature of doll collectors. Time after time I have been welcomed into a collector's home, made a part of the family, and been given the freedom to handle, examine, undress, and photograph valuable and beloved dolls. Often the condition of the entire house suffered in the process, for it was necessary to choose the largest room in which to photograph the dolls in order to allow an efficient traffic flow for the bringing in and out of large numbers of dolls.

It is one thing to have several hundred dolls neatly arranged on shelves, in cupboards, and in corners on stands. It is another situation to have the same number of dolls in various stages of undress and disarray lying about in stacks. I am sure many collectors spent days reassembling their displays after I was on my way to photograph yet another collection. On the bright side, many collectors told me they were delighted to have the excuse to handle their collections and more than a few discovered dolls they had quite forgotten in the process of sorting through an extensive accumulation.

Several doll clubs assisted by arranging for members to bring dolls to a special place for pictures or sent large packets of photographs which their members had taken. I am especially indebted to the members of the Amarillo Doll Association and the Puget Sound Doll Club. The Amarillo group were my gracious hostesses on two occasions and the Puget Sound club spent many hours photographing a large number of dolls for the book.

These people were especially kind in making their homes available to me or in other ways expressing their generous hospitality: Deet D'Andrade, Betty Gould, Gay Hendrix, Dorothy King, Nita Kinney, Jewell Parker, Patti Peticolas, and Betty Wiseman.

The following people have had a large share in the preparation of this book; without their kindness, consideration, and generosity it could never have come about: Susan Ackerman, Virginia Bailey, Yvonne Baird, Mrs. Don Barnes, Hanna Brachear, Irene Brady, Joan Breckenridge, Shirley Burtchett, Mildred Busch, Dorothy Cagle, Editha Campbell, Georgia Van Wie Cannon, Mozell Carter, Betty Chaffin, Lois and Orian Collinsworth, Mrs. H. Crane, Terry Crocheron, Dayne's Dolls, Mary Denton, Jennie Edgar, Ruth Edge, Kelly Ellenburg, Toddy Erickson, Sally Esser, Gloria Ferrino, Joan Fleming, Lillian Floyd, Beth French, Evelyn Gaylin of The Gay World of Dolls Museum, Terri Lee and Jerre Gibbins, Hazel Griffin, Dee Hafner, June Hahn, Doris Harris, Ava Heinzel, Ora Henson, Terri Darlene Hoskins, Norma Hughes, Frances Hutchinson, Mrs. J. C. Janke, Jo Smith of Jo's Antique Dolls, Agnes Johnson, Doris Kaufman, Dorothy King of Dollcraft, Nita Kinney of Nita's House of Dolls, Sylvia Kittman, Mrs. Frank Krol, Anna Lear, Zelma Martinez of Zel's Wonderland, Marian Mason, Catherine McDowell, Barbara McLaughlin, Jackie Meekins, Marge Meisinger, Ruth Mello, Mercedes Morrow, Janice Naibert, Margaret O'Rourke, Verna Ortwein, Grace Otto, Jewel Parker, Nancy Perry, Anneruth Pfister, Nettie Mae Phillips of Momma Gran's Dolls, Margaret Pierce, Karen Potter, Guadalupe Quijas, Ralph Griffith of Ralph's Antique Dolls, Genevieve Reeves, Nancy Ricklefs, Sharon Ricklefs, Elizabeth Rickwartz, Edna Rogers, Alice Rothert, Mrs. L. W. Rush, D. Salvisburg, F. Salvisburg, L. Salvisburg, Janice Sanders of Camelot, Mary Sanders, Lois Sargent, Ann Schmidt, Hazel Schorlemmer, Pat Sebastian, Ruth Sheinwald, Nelda Shelton, Juanita Shuts, Orpha Siehl, Olive Siewertz, Betsy Slap, June Sloan, Gretchen Smith, John A. Snelleman, Lucile Spalding, Irene Stevenson, Ethel Stewart, Tom and Susie Stroud of Collector's House, Doretta Swift, Ann Tardie, Cassie Terry, Bessie Thompson, Betty Tinker, Charles Vandiver, Othello Van Dusen, Barbara Vogan, Dorothy Wampler, Mary Ward, Alice Wardell, Elma Warren, Ada Webb, Margaret Weeks, LaVelle Wess, Dorothy and Robin Ann Wilker, Margaret Winson of Madame Alexander Fan Club, Betty Wiseman, and Joan Young.

OTHERS WHO HELPED

In one instance after another busy people in the doll industry took time away from already crowded schedules to recount experiences, recall names, dates, and odd bits of information, and to provide valuable insights. Joe Reisch, former Effanbee salesman and still active in the toy business, gave several hours one afternoon and proved a gold mine of information. Milton Marcus, another old-timer and retiree, made a long commuter train trip from Long Island to reminisce into my tape recorder for five hours. Larry Dopelt and Mel Rosenbloom of Eegee were generous with lunch and much information on more than one occasion. Bruce D'Andrade drove over fifty miles of mountainous highways and gave up an entire Sunday to help. Bruce, a former sales representative for several toy companies, also loaned his extensive collection of toy company catalogs.

Estelle Smith of Vogue, who had been saving a huge assortment of professional glossy photographs of dolls dating back to the old Arranbee company "just in case", kindly furnished a view at the transition between the two companies and a large amount of illustrative material.

Roy Raizen, Betty Gould, and Arthur Keller of Effanbee were gracious and helpful, even providing a desk at which to work one afternoon. Mildred Friedman of Alexander, Joseph L. Kallus of Cameo, Harry Kislevitz, President of Colorforms, and Kim McKim of Kimport Dolls all were most helpful.

If any names have been omitted, it is merely an oversight in the face of the tremendous number of people who contributed to the book. It is my hope their numbers are few and that they have already forgiven me.

—J.G.A.

FOREWORD

In the early 1960s, a friend lured me to a series of garage sales which resulted in a collection of colored glassware now known as *Depression Glass.* When my personal notebook record of what I had learned about the glassware was published in 1969 as THE GLASS RAINBOW, *The Story of Depression Glass,* a new way of life began for me.

An interest in dolls had survived from childhood and when another friend made a gift of an *antique* bisque head doll, a new hobby was launched. Every available book about dolls in the library system was read and re-read. Very soon it became evident that many of the dolls which were available at garage sales, estate sales, and thrift shops were not mentioned in these books. Again the urge to collect information and make it available to other collectors began a file which was to become a book. Within a period of two years enough material was assembled to make possible the publication of TWENTIETH CENTURY DOLLS, *From Bisque to Vinyl.*

The response was overwhelming. Collectors from every part of our country wrote with offers of assistance in identifying even more of the dolls of our century. Many sent photographs, some issued invitations, others wrote asking for publication specifications in order that they might send photographs suitable for inclusion in a sequel to "TCD." The volume already had become the touchstone, the common reference, for doll collectors and dealers in correspondence and advertising about collectible and modern dolls.

As distribution of TCD continued, more and more collectors expressed a wish to become a part of my research project. The quantity of information and available examples of the old dolls seemed endless and it soon became apparent that a deadline must be set on all contributions. Even so, the size of the volume was increased on three separate occasions, two of which came after the final retail price was set.

Nettie Mae Phillips as a child posed with brothers and her bisque-head doll.

Duplications have been kept to an absolute minimum; however, where variations of dolls shown in TCD were discovered these have been included in the present volume. Additional information, conclusions based on later information, and references which have seemed of sufficient import to risk an accusation of duplication have all been thoughtfully incorporated into MTCD.

Every effort has been made to maintain the accuracy of all entries. Where older spelling differs from that in use today the former has been used. All names attributed to dolls have been varified in a number of ways; through catalogs, advertising, company records, and the memories of former employees.

References to *"bisc finish", American Bisque, Bisc, Bisk, Nubisc, Newbisc,* and similar terms will be found throughout the text. Such terms are tradenames owned by various companies and refer to painted composition parts. An example is the lignumfibro composition called *Real American Bisque* by the *New Toy Manufacturing Company* in 1915.

Reproduction dolls have been avoided; however, some re-issue items are shown when such re-issues contribute to the overall doll story and represent true historical points in that story. The *Shirley Temple* dolls of the 1950s and 1970s, for example, are not reproductions; they are *new issues* of a line of dolls which simply continue that line.

It is my hope that collectors and dealers alike may find this work of some assistance in cataloguing their collections and extending their knowledge of this most fascinating of hobbies.

—Johana Gast Anderton
October 6, 1974
North Kansas City, Missouri

DOLLMAKING IN EUROPE

The manufacturer of toys was an important industry in Europe in the last half of the nineteenth century and the first several decades of the twentieth, albeit an industry almost entirely dependent on foreign markets. Only about twenty-five per cent of the total goods manufactured remained in Europe, with the United States, then Great Britain ranking as heaviest buyers of European dolls and toys. Total production of toys in the German Empire, for example, in 1906 was $22,500,000, of which $5,561,750 went to the United States.

German manufacturers were anxious to ship to the U.S. for two important reasons. First, the market was expanding as rapidly as the young country was civilizing its westward reaches. Second, the *ad valorem* system exacted tariff based on value of goods rather than on weight as was the case in other countries. High duties were levied on the lightweight but expensive dolls while lesser amounts were exacted on the heavier but cheaper toys.

The German toy industry was grouped in various localities—the Saxon Ore Mountains where wooden toys were chiefly manufactured; the Thuringian Mountains where papier-mache, wooden, and leather toys were made; and finally, Nuremberg, where metal toys predominated. Some toys were also produced in Wurttemberg, in the Black Forest, and in Berlin and Hanover. From Stuttgart and Nuremberg the wholesalers obtained the finest goods, second only to those made in Paris; in Sonneberg, the middle quality, while the cheapest came from the Ore Mountains.

All the German toy centers had at least one thing in common—the toys were chiefly produced in the homes of the workmen. An exception was Nuremberg where the manufacture was almost entirely in factories. The making of toys in the homes resulted in a certain diversity in goods as well as helped to keep prices down. One reason for the development of the German toy industry was the bountiful supply of raw materials. Another was the need, in a largely agricultural society, for occupation and income during the long winter months. Thus a huge industry was built up based on the skilled hands and economic needs of the farming community.

Prior to 1820 only wood and leather had been employed in the manufacture of dolls. Papier-mache was discovered in that year by a Sonneberg modeler and the industry was revolutionized. Doll manufacturing began to assume conspicuous proportions in 1850 when papier-mache parts were given a glowing wax coating which resulted in a finer, more natural-looking product. The more expensive bisque heads were made almost entirely in factories.

One of the largest factories was established early in the nineteenth century at Waltershausen by John Daniel Kestner. In the beginning the small shop made memorandum slates from paper pulp, then

Young Girls Sewing Dolls' Dresses in a Factory in Sonneberg.

A Family of Four Generations Making Toys in Their Home.

gradually increased its output to include wooden pop-guns, wood limb dolls, and other items. Dolls were first produced in about 1815 and were improved over a period of time; first wood limb dolls with wood or paper pulp heads; then the wood bodies were replaced with paper pulp versions. About 1845 the first dolls wearing chemise, shoes, stockings, and hood were placed on the market. Next, on a very small scale, muslin and kid dolls were turned out.

The Kestner Doll Factory at Walterhausen.

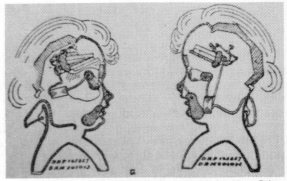

The Sleeping Eyes Created by Herr Stier.

The Porcelain Factory at Ohrdruf.

Cutting Kid Bodies in the Kestner Factory.

Adjusting Wigs at the Kestner Factory.

Filling Kid Bodies in the Kestner Factory.

Decorating Kestner Heads.

Moulding Jointed Kestner Dolls.

*Applying Enamel
to Paper Pulp Bodies.*

About 1860 a marked improvement was introduced in the form of porcelain heads and limbs as well as paper pulp doll heads and limbs with wax covering. At this time, too, the Papa-Mama dolls were introduced and Kestner invented the sleeping doll with movable eyes.[1] Early in its history the Kestner factory had started its home industry system with workmen furnishing various doll parts to be assembled at the main factory. When the porcelain factory was acquired at Ohrdruf it was possible to manufacture the doll in its entirety at the factory whereas other factories secured their porcelain heads elsewhere and assembled the dolls in their plants. Kestner also made celluloid heads in his own factory. These were noted for their finish which did not include the usual aniline colors that faded in a short time leaving a colorless, lifeless head.

Waltershausen was located in the dukedom of Sachsen-Coburg-Gotha at the foot of the Thuringian forest. Ohrdruf, where the porcelain parts were manufactured, was located on the Ohra, "about one and one-half hours from Waltershausen".[2]

Germany and other countries of Europe might have retained their hold on the world doll and toy market had not the fires of war burned so fiercely over those lands causing both England and America to look within for sources of such products. The September, 1939 issue of *Toy Trader and Exporter* carries a Turtle Mark advertisement with a *pasted-on* label which reads CANCELLED.

By July and August of 1940 full page ads offering dolls heads and toy tea sets were being offered by English firms, including the Howard Pottery. Accent in such times seems always to be on war toys— planes, uniforms, etc. Few dolls were offered; little girls must have had to "make do".

In the April, 1941 *Toy Trader* we read that "in the great cause of wartime charity the Princesses Elizabeth and Margaret have presented five of their treasured dolls to the "Relief for England" commission for exhibit and ultimate sale in the U.S. One of the dolls is dressed in a replica of an evening gown worn by the Queen on her visit to the U.S. in 1939. Another has a white organza dress copied from that which Her Majesty wore at the garden party at the White House."

By January, 1942 the toy shortage had indeed taken its toll among the children of England, and "out of the debris of shattered, bombed-out homes of England firemen fashioned toys for Britain's children in nursery schools." This practice seems to have caused no little concern among toy manufacturers who feared the idea would spread and who had quite enough problems already what with wartime labor and material shortages. In addition there was a most active "Second-Hand Toy" market flourishing in England both during and directly after the war which added to the anguish of the manufacturers. One cannot but wonder how many *antiques* might have been brought out and used as play dolls and toys during this depressing time.

[1] A similar claim has also been set forth for one Herr Stier who used glass eyes and a lead weight. Stier also may have been responsible for the first "real" eyelashes.

[2] PLAYTHINGS Magazine, April, 1906.

DOLLMAKING IN AMERICA

As we have seen, prior to World War I the majority of dolls sold in the United States were imported. Germany, Austria, France, England, and Japan were important sources of dolls and toys. As a result of the breakdown in relations with Germany, as well as lack of materials available for such manufacture during the war, a concerted effort began in the United States to build up the American toy industry.

Hundreds of small operations opened their doors across the nation with the main force located in the New York City area. This if not to say there were *no* doll manufacturers in business prior to 1914; much of the industry, however, had been directed toward *assembling* dolls from parts received from overseas.

For example, bisque heads and celluloid hands might be imported to be assembled with an American-made cloth body. Such dolls were then appropriately wigged (most often with imported wigs), costumed, and packed in boxes bearing the label of the American plant. Bisque heads were sometimes produced with the American company name incised in the bisque along with the trademarks of the foreign manufacturer.

Early in the century a few young companies had begun to make strong bids for a share of the expanding U.S. market. Among these was the *E.I. Horsman Company* which eventually was responsible for the first commercial all-American bisque head doll. The efforts of these American companies were greatly underscored by the patriotic outcry against *"Hun toys"* after the outbreak of war.

Such feelings were carried to what, from the distance of years, might seem great extremes. For example, in October, 1919, PLAYTHINGS reported on the arrival of a shipment of 4,000 cases of German toys in New York on the Holland-American steamer *"Nieuw Amsterdam"*. There was widespread public demand that the toys not be placed in the hands of American children. Many organizations, particularly among women, adopted resolutions and appointed committees for the purpose of preventing distribution of these toys.

Under such pressures and dispite the fact the toys had been bought and paid for in the spring of 1914 prior to the declaration of war, Butler Brothers refused to accept the shipment which had been in storage in Holland for four years. The shipment was abandoned to the custom house officials and Walter Scott, vice-president of Butler Brothers issued a statement: "Butler Brothers have set themselves against the German propoganda designed to reintroduce into America the German-made toys and china."

Scott further stated that Butler Brothers had for a number of years encouraged American manufacturers to supply goods such as those formerly imported. Although there was some opposition to the movement to reject the shipment, most houses bowed to public opinion and suffered the often considerable loss.

Filling the Molds With Can't Break 'Em Composition.

Meanwhile, whether because of or in spite of the war, the American doll industry was growing. Alfred E. Fountain, his son Alfred, Jr., and David Zaiden, among others, were working to perfect their own formulae and techniques. New machinery was being designed and manufactured, often on the site where it would be used. Electricity was being employed to speed the operation of many of the new machines with a resulting increase in production capacity.

Humidity continued to be a problem; it was often necessary to close down doll manufacturing operations entirely during rainy seasons or unusually wet years. Only new materials and modern air conditioning, yet to come, could cope with the drying problems suffered by the industry. Some of the composition materials were dried in electric ovens, but those depending on air drying were constant victims of weather. More than one old-time doll manufacturer has related to the author the anguish suffered when cases of stored doll parts were opened to reveal flaking, peeling finishes. Often entire shipments were rejected by distributors and returned to the factories.

Nevertheless the industry flourished and successes followed closely upon each other. The Amberg factory is a case in point. In the May, 1912 PLAYTHINGS, an employee of Amberg stated that the unbreakable doll might be traced directly to the day when the *Teddy Bear* became so popular. From the *Teddy Bear* grew the *Teddy Doll,* a *Teddy Bear* with an imported bisque or celluloid face, manufactured in the Amberg plant. From the *Teddy Doll* came the fur body doll with an unbreakable head—*"Sunny Jim"* released in the fall of 1909. *"Dolly Strong"* followed shortly thereafter, along with *"Baby Blue"* and *'Rosebud".* Then the fur body evolved into velvet followed by a sateen body dressed in removeable button romper suits or dresses.

Vats and Kettles Where Compositions Were Cooked.

Presses for Forming Dolls and Novelties From Wood Pulp or Other Composition. Machines Manufactured by M.A. Cuming & Company, New York.

Smoothing and Sanding a Can't Break 'Em Head.

The Toy Industry Point of View Was Often Expressed in Cartoons.

In 1910 Amberg offered their first 50-cent numbers; *"Samson"*, heralded as *"Uncle Sam's First Born"*, was an entirely unbreakable, fully jointed baby which was never widely advertised because of the popularity of several other dolls in the line. By 1912 the molds for *"Samson"* had been broken.

1910 also marked the appearance of the cork-stuffed body with unbreakable head and hands. *"Bobby Blake"*, *"Dolly Drake"*, *"Swat Mulligan"*, *"Little Brother"* and *"Little Sister"*, *"The School Boy"* and *"School Girl"*, *"Sassy Sue"*, *"Little Fairy"*, *"Sis Hopkins"*, *"Spic"* and *"Span"*, a dog and cat, and other animal characters with stuffed bodies and composition heads all were included in the line. *"Dorothy Dainty"* was also a star of this show.

1948 proved to be the year of transition—the year the long-standing reign of the composition doll was finally broken forever. Heavy rains in 1947 and 1948 had caused serious setbacks in doll production and the manufacturers were desperately seeking an alternative to the old materials. Plastics had been developed for military use during World War II and were beginning to find their way into civilian production. Vinyl was being used only by a few giant corporations, however, and it was a closely guarded secret.

Hard plastic was available in limited supply but the change-over was an expensive project. The steel molds used for composition were unusable with the new plastics. The composition was poured into the molds and the parts were baked or dried, depending upon the particular handling of the individual formula, then the molds were opened and parts were placed on racks for aging. An injection mold was needed for hard plastic and master molds were maintained from which production molds could be renewed. Some companies went out of business during these years, weakened by the losses suffered during the wet years and unable to finance a change-over.

An Artist Applies Finishing Touches to a Can't Break 'Em Head.

Cork Stuffing Department Where Bodies Were Filled With Cork.

Operating Room Where Bodies and Dresses Were Sewn.

Coloring Department Where Heads Were Given Flesh Tint.

The new hard plastic, however, proved a boon to the industry; heads were made in two parts then glued together, but there was no humidity problem, no peeling, flaking, or crazing. As vinyls were made available in larger quantities, the doll industry was among the first to recognize its possibilities. With vinyl even the small companies could market a profit-making quality doll. All the small details requiring undercuts in the ears, the nose, the eyelids, which had been avoided with earlier materials were now possible. Vinyl parts were removed from the mold while still warm and pliable; the material pulled away from undercuts with ease, revealing all the lifelike details so long desired. In addition, the expensive hand buffing and finishing were largely eliminated.

At first, war work precision machinery was converted to dollmaking purposes for these were the years of the Korean conflict. One long-time executive stated that everyone had his own "Rube Goldberg" inventions to produce the vinyl and plastic dolls. In the trade a "Rube Goldberg" was a put-together machine—anything to get the job done—which often assumed somewhat comic appearances.

The last major change in production methods came in the 1950s. The first 36" dolls had been too heavy and too costly. To make large dolls lighter and less expensive the blow molding techniques used for making detergent and bleach bottles were employed. This method allowed for a thinner wall section and was used for bodies and limbs only. Blow molding is not suitable for heads since it does not achieve the detail desirable to create life-like faces.

Although space has not allowed more than a casual review of the industry in the United States, one has only to walk through a toy department anywhere in the country today to be able to gauge the achievements of the past seventy-four years.

POTPOURRI

A number of cross-overs, that is molds being used by first one company and then another, have been noted in the text. There is another example of this multiple use of molds in the example of Canadian dolls. Eegee and Horsman dolls may be found with both Regal and Reliable marks. Molds are sometimes loaned "on a friendly basis" when principles have an interest in both the American and Canadian companies. In other instances, there is a licensing agreement as has been noted in the case of the *Canadian Shirley Temple* dolls. *Willie Talk* from Horsman also has a Canadian counterpart; Regal's *Stoneage Baby* has its American cousin.

Several companies have closed their doors in the past few years, among them *Topper, Transogram, Remco, Jolly, Jouette (Bee-Jay),* and *Hol-ee.* In other cases, doll companies have become a part of larger corporate enterprises. *Lakeside* was purchased by *Leisure Dynamics* and is still in production. *Amsco* is now a division of *Milton Bradley.*

Neil Estern, a sculptor who did a bust of the late John F. Kennedy, also creates dolls. Among these are *Flowerkins, Puppetrina, Patti Playpal,* and the *Gemettes.*

Eegee's 1974 entries, *Sassy* and *Pouty,* both have character faces. The report is that nine out of ten men like *Sassy* best while nine out of ten women like *Pouty* best.

The foam body and limbs of *Softina,* introduced in 1965, presented a real manufacturing problem. The process was slow and costly; in addition, forming the vinyl skin over the molded foam body was technically difficult.

Three dolls were offered by *Curtiss Publishing Company* as subscription premiums in the 1930s. They were a 15" *Sonja Henie* in white silk skating costume trimmed with white fur; a 14" *Deanna Durbin* in suede shoes, a belted dress, jacket with patch pockets, wearing a *Deanna Durbin* button; and a 13" *Snow White* in pink silk dress, velvet cloak, and high heel slippers with rosette trim.

Continually coming to the fore in interviews with doll people is the name *Bernard Lipfert.* In seventy years of creating dolls this man earned an enviable reputation for his genius. *Shirley Temple, Patsy, Dy-Dee, The Dionnes, Baby Coos, Toni, Pebbles, Bam-Bam* and a host of others sprang from his talented fingers.

Many stories of his eccentricities are told. He lived in Brooklyn and it is said that if you wanted a Lipfert head you must drop by his cluttered studio, play pinochle with him for an hour or so, always lose, and then order your doll head. For $50 or $500 he made designs for his clients—anything the customer wanted. Lipfert maintained a huge file of drawings, photographs, baby pictures, and magazine clippings from which he drew inspiration.

He was most skillful at "knocking off" his own designs in such a way that problems involving copyrights were kept at a minimum, which fact may account for some of the look-alikes we collectors often puzzle over.

Three little dolls from Germany, all in original costumes, found in an estate were either the possessions of one little girl or of three sisters. All three have bisque heads, papier mache bodies, stick legs, and blue glass sleep eyes. Left to right: **A.** 13½", marked **DEP / R6 / OA; B.** 14½", marked **ARMAND MARSEILLES / 390 / A-20-M; C.** 15", marked **Made in Germany / Armand Marseille / 390n / DRGM 246 / AOM.** *(Courtesy Nita Kinney, Nita's House of Dolls)*

HOW TO FIND DOLLS IN THIS BOOK

With few exceptions, each individual doll shown in this book has a number key shown with the photograph and repeated at the beginning of the descriptive paragraph. An extensive General Index lists these dolls in as many different ways as it was possible to consider them. Dolls from larger companies are grouped under the name of the manufacturer and shown in approximate chronological order. Letter marks, ie. **X** or **W**, etc., have been included alphabetically in the General Index. Number marks are listed separately. In addition, dolls are shown to illustrate types of materials from which dolls are made. Some dolls are listed by their "given names".

If the reader already owns TWENTIETH CENTURY DOLLS, this present volume will be found to be a most complimentary tool in the study of dolls. For ease of reference, the TCD identification system has been continued. For example, the Horsman section ends with HORS-32 in TCD and begins with HORS-33 in MTCD. Also, since TCD ends with page 464, this volume begins on page 465. The MTCD index lists all entries presently found in TCD plus thousands of new listings for MTCD so that one General Index serves both volumes, much as an encyclopedia made up of several volumes contains a General Index for all volumes in the set.

There are a number of reasons for continuing in this manner. Advertisers often refer to TWENTIETH CENTURY DOLLS in describing dolls for sale and collectors use the keys as reference. Such continuity will serve to avoid confusion in such references.

Several new categories have been added, others have been combined, and still others have been broken down into separate categories. A section on *Display Dolls*, another on *Novelties*, and a third on *War Dolls* are among the many new divisions. Classifying the personality and portrait dolls separately has proved not only difficult but almost impossible at times. For this reason, the two sections have been combined under the designation *Personality Dolls* and the key PERS has been used.

Where many of the German bisque dolls had been previously categorized under *German* (GER) or *Bisque* (BISQ), the listings have been made, wherever possible, under the manufacturer's name. Largely, the unidentified dolls remain under the two general classifications. Sections of *Advertising, Comics, Disney,* and other types found in TCD are continued and expanded in this volume and a large number of additional company listings have been included.

THE PICTURES IN THIS BOOK

The many pictures in this book have been gathered from a number of sources. As mentioned elsewhere, the author has personally photographed thousands of dolls throughout this country. In addition, many collectors have contributed both professional photographs and snapshots of their dolls. Further, a large number of pictures have been made from old catalogs, trade journals, magazines, and company files.

As a result, a wide range of quality may be seen in the reproductions in this book. Generally, the author feels that in the case of interesting or important dolls, a poor picture is better than no picture. Although poor quality photographs have been kept to a minimum, the author opted for inclusion of a few that ordinarily would not have been considered because of their quality in order to present at least a minimal record of the dolls involved.

THE VALUE OF DOLLS

Since this book is intended as a permanent reference work no price guide is included; it is the opinion of the author that such guides are usually out of date before they come off the press. In addition there is perhaps no other category of antique or collectible items more difficult to price accurately than dolls. While it is true that the increasing number of both antique shows and doll shows has contributed to a certain stabilizing of the market, there are other aspects to consider. With few other collector items are there so many vagaries to be considered in evaluating a given item: Is the wig original, a replacement, in poor condition, or simply not there? Is it (or was it?) of mohair, caracul, or human hair? Are the eyes new, old, broken, stabilized, crazed ? Are they tin, celluloid, glass (threaded, paperweight, blown), painted, side-glancing, flirty? Is the mouth open, closed, or open-closed? Are there teeth, painted or otherwise? Is there a tongue; does it move? Are the ears pierced—which way? How is the head marked? Is it an unusual mark or rather more common? And on and on.

Without pursuing the matter further than the head of the doll the point is made. And there is always the possibility the purchaser must deal with the *sentiment* factor when attempting to bring a transaction to a satisfactory conclusion. Too often the assumed value of a doll increases in direct proportion to the closeness of the owner's relationship to its original owner.

For these reasons only original prices are occasionally given to point up comparative quality and how that quality was reflected in the original wholesale or retail prices of the dolls in question. Such original prices may also serve as a barometer concerning the prices of other dolls of similar quality in a particular time period. All of which brings us back again to what the author has repeatedly said and written: The collector must ask herself concerning any doll, *"Do I want this doll enough to pay the price?"*

If the answer is *yes,* the doll is worth every penny.

More
Twentieth Century
Dolls

FROM BISQUE TO VINYL

Volume One
A — H

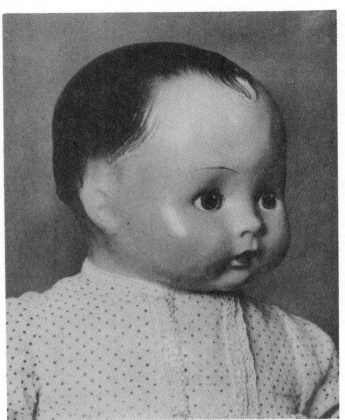

ABC-1.

 A.B.C. TOY

ABC-1. *Anette Baby.* 18"; molded-painted hair; painted blue eyes; closed mouth; composition flange-neck head, composition half limbs; original clothes. Marks: **ANETTE BABY/A.B.C. Toy** (with only one N in Anette) on head. *(Hahn Collection)*

ABC-1

ACME-1.

ACME TOY MFG.—CO.

ACME-1. *Boy.* Assorted sizes; molded-painted hair; painted eyes; closed mouth; composition head, stuffed body and limbs; Acme Toy Mfg. Co., NYC. *(Playthings, August, 1914)*

ACME-2. *Baby.* 17"; molded-painted yellow hair; painted blue eyes, lashes, unusually large pupils; closed mouth, heavy composition head and arms, slim, small hands, stuffed cloth body. Marks: **Acme Toy Co.** on head. *(Wardell collection)*

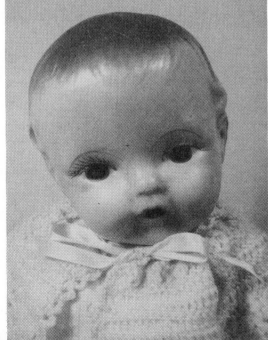

ACME-2.

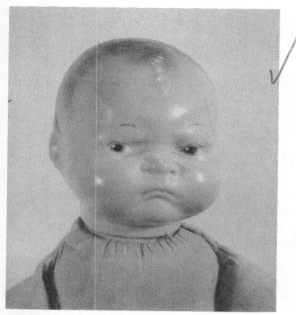

ACME-3.

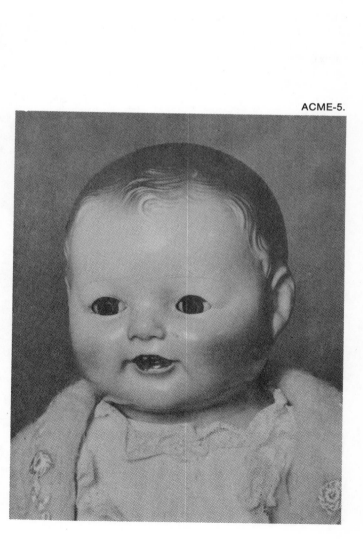

ACME-4.

ACME-5.

ACME-5.

ACME-3. *Grumpy-type.* 15"; molded-painted hair; painted eyes; closed mouth; composition head and guantlet hand, cotton-stuffed cloth body, cry box; grumpy expression, Bye-lo shaped head. Marks: **ACME/TOY CO.** on head. (Author's collection)

ACME-4. *Bye-lo type.* 14"; molded-painted hair; blue sleep eyes; closed mouth; composition head and hands, stuffed cloth body and limbs; original white dress, slip; ca. 1925. Marks: **TOY CO.** (Mason collection)

ACME-5. *Baby.* 19"; molded painted blonde hair; blue celluloid-over-tin sleep eyes, lashes; open-closed mouth, molded tongue, two painted upper teeth; composition stationary shoulderplate head and limbs; jointed hips and shoulders, stuffed cloth body; all original except booties; very good quality composition, shiny finish, deep rosy cheeks. Marks: **ACME TOY CO.** on shoulder plate. (Hahn collection)

ADVA-1.

ADV-A6.

ADV-B3.

ADVANCE DOLL AND TOY CO.

ADVA-1. *The Walking "Wabbit".* 18"; blue sleep eyes; closed mouth; body similar to Walkalon Doll (ref. TCD, p. 430); original bunny suit, shoes; original tag reads: **THE WALKING "WABBIT"**; includes mail-in offer for kit to change Wabbit into "Beautiful Walking Doll" for $2.00. Kit included wig and dress. The Advance Doll and Toy Co., West Haven, CT. *(Stewart collection)*

ADV-A7.

ADVERTISING DOLLS

The proliferation of advertising dolls only serves to underscore the increasing popularity of these dolls among collectors. Meanwhile the advertisers must be smiling to themselves at the manner in which they have duped the public into paying for their advertising. Collectors seem not to mind the usually nominal charge for advertising dolls, however, because they know that soon most advertisers will turn to other media leaving behind some very collectible dolls.

Sometimes these dolls are produced in extremely limited quantities (see TCD, p. 36, ADV-N1 and -N2). In other cases many thousands of dolls have been produced to fill the demand created by a major advertising campaign.

In still other instances the advertiser has published an entire *series* of dolls based on a trademark symbol. An example of the continuing promotion is the series based on the *Jolly Green Giant,* trademark of the Jolly Green Giant Company of Le Seur, Minnesota. Their numerous editions of the *Jolly Green Giant* have now been joined by *The Little Green Sprout ("Order him now before he grows up!").*

So long as public response indicates acceptance, advertisers will continue to utilize this excellent mode of publicity for their products, and collectors will be able to add interesting dolls to waiting collections.

ADV-A6. *Allergy Annie.* 15", lithographed cloth; came with coloring book; promotion used by Honeywell, "The Air Cleaner People".

ADV-A7. *Dolls of the World.* 8"; mohair wig; blue sleep eyes; plastic body; ca. 1972; promotion used by Atlantic Richfield. *(Janke collection)*

ADV-B3. *Babbitt Cleanser Boy.* 15"; molded-painted features; composition hands; all original; wears button that reads: *"Babbit's Cleanser"/"Babbit at your Service"* trademark of B.T. Babbitt Co.; sold for $1.00. *(Playthings, January, 1916)*

ADV-B4. *Bakery Girl.* Lithographed on cloth, flat cut sew and stuff doll.

ADV-B5. *Bazooka Joe.* 18"; lithographed on cloth; 1973; reads: **BAZOOKA JOE**® on front of shirt; promotion of Bazooka Bubble Gum.

ADV-B4.   ADV-B5.   ADV-B6.

ADV-B6. *Beta.* 10½"; with an 8" x 9" bedspread; lithographed cloth; comes with miniature shopping bag, ketchup, soap, mess kit, sponge; doll's dress reads: **Bad Doll,** original booklet reads: **"I'm a Bad Doll. I'm fun to play with."** Bedspread reads: **The Well Behaved Bedspread/Fiberglass/BETA.** *(Stewart collection)*

ADV-B7. *Betty Blue Bonnet.* 17"; rooted blonde synthetic wig; painted blue eyes, long plastic inserted lashes; open-closed mouth painted white teeth; fully jointed vinyl body, swivel waist, hi-heeled feet. Marks: **PerfeKta/Hong Kong.** *(Thompson collection)*

ADV-B8. *Jennie.* 22"; yarn wig; imitation rhinestone eyes; embroidered mouth; lithographed cloth body; instructions for making doll included; mail-in promotion on box of *Boraxo* cleaning product; 1974. *(Janke collection)*

ADV-B7.

ADV-B8.

ADV-B10.

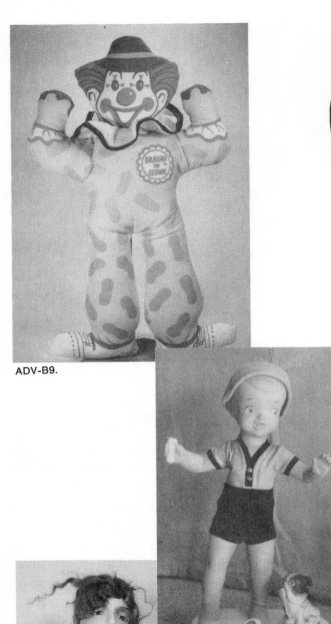

ADV-B9.

ADV-B12.

ADV-B11.

ADV-B9. *Bracho the Clown.* 18''; lithographed features and clothing, plastic clown collar; promotion for Brach's Candy. *(Rogers collection)*

ADV-B10. *Bonnie Breck.* 9''; rooted blonde wig; painted eyes; closed mouth; vinyl head and body, fully jointed, bendable knees; original clothes; original price $2.00; 1971. Cloth tag on dress reads: **BEAUTIFUL/BONNIE BRECK/MADE IN HONG KONG.** *(Stewart collection)*

ADV-B11. *Buster Brown Bed Doll.* 27''; mohair wig; painted eyes, applied lashes, painted mouth; stuffed sateen body, composition head. Marks: **BROWN bilt/SHOES/BUSTER BROWN** in oval on front of doll, picture of Buster Brown and Tigue over **BUSTER BROWN/SHOES** in oval on back.

ADV-B12. *Buster Brown Boy.* 26''; molded-painted hair; painted blue eyes; open-closed mouth; composition head and body; shirt, shorts, knit hat, molded-painted shoes, socks; 6½'' vinyl black and white dog, dog and boy on 3'' stand. Marks: **BUSTER BROWN®.** *(Courtesy Jo's Antique Dolls)*

ADV-B13.

ADV-C1.

Rag doll offer from C and H Brown Su

ADV-C2.

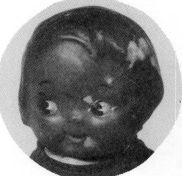

ADV-B12.

ADV-C3. *Colored Campbell Kid.* 11½; molded-painted black hair; painted black eyes; closed smile; composition head and hands, excelsior-stuffed body and legs; original clothes. *(Hughes collection)*

ADV-C4. *Campbell Kid.* 7"; molded-painted features, molded-painted rubber body; squeeker. *(Author's collection)*

ADV-B13. *Buster Brown.* 4"; all bisque; jointed arms; dressed in red. Marks: **Buster Brown Shoes.** *(Beard collection)*

ADV-C1. *C & H Sugar Kids.* 16"; lithographed features and clothes; sold for $1.00 plus C & H oval from brown sugar box for each doll. *(Hafner collection)*

ADV-C3.

ADV-C2. *C & H Sugar Kids.* Magazine offer for the rag dolls, expired December 31, 1973.

THE CAMPBELL KIDS

The Campbell Kids have been produced by Horsman for many years. Many drawings by Grace G. Drayton were copyrighted by the Joseph C. Campbell (soup) Company and the dolls were made to resemble this prolific artist's creations. Other examples of the Campbell Kids may be seen by consulting the Index.

ADV-C4.

ADV-C5.

ADV-C6.

ADV-C5. *Campbell Kids.* 10"; molded-painted brown and yellow hair; painted eyes; closed mouth; soft non-toxic vinyl, fully jointed; red and white shirts, pants, skirt, shoes, socks, vinyl lunch box, purse; $2.00 and two Chicken soup labels for each doll; offer expired May 31, 1972. *(Rogers collection)*

ADV-C6. *Campbell Kids.* 12"; yellow and orange yarn wig; lithographed features; 100% cotton bodies; chef's hats, kerchiefs, aprons, pink dress, blue pants, shirt, large "C" on hats. *1973 catalog illustration courtesy Sears, Roebuck & Co.*

ADV-C7. *Carnation Cry Baby.* 18"; rooted auburn synthetic wig; blue sleep eyes; open-closed mouth; fully jointed vinyl body; original clothes. (Horsman's Thirstee Baby). Marks: ©**HORSMAN DOLL INC./ 1962/No. 2000.** *(N. Ricklefs collection)*

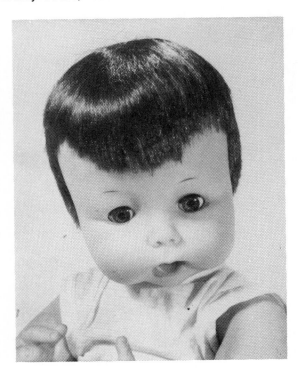

ADV-C7.

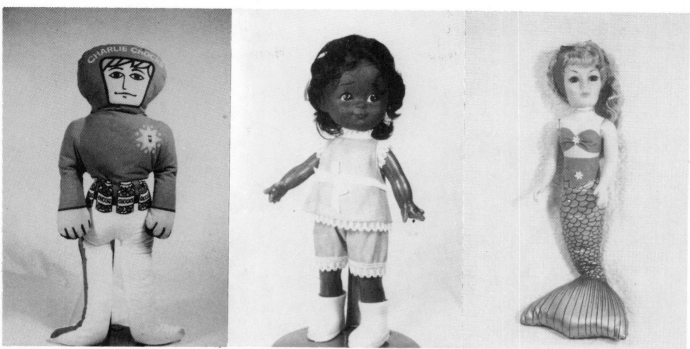

ADV-C8   ADV-C9   ADV-C10

Note: The photographs on this page, as well as hundreds of others through this book, are original photographs taken by the author in the homes of the owners of the dolls and are not old catalog pictures. The author travels widely in researching and photographing her books and relies heavily on the kindness and generosity of other collectors, for which she is most grateful. All catalog research throughout her work is carefully credited to the source.

ADV-C10

ADV-C8. *Charlie Chocks.* 20"; lithographed cloth; promotion for Chocks Vitamins. Marks: **CHARLIE CHOCKS** on head, **CHOCKS** on lithographed bottles around doll's waist. *(Stewart collection)*

ADV-C9. *Cheer Girl.* 10"; rooted synthetic wig; painted brown eyes; closed mouth; vinyl head, plastic fully jointed body; coral shirt, pants with trim, white vinyl boots; free doll with purchase of king-size box of Cheer detergent. Marks: **MADE IN HONG KONG.** *(Rogers collection)*

ADV-C10. *Chicken of the Sea Mermaid.* 20"; long blonde rooted wig; blue sleep eyes; closed mouth; vinyl head, arms, upper body, stuffed cloth fish body and tail; same head as used for Jeannie (ref. TCD, p. 346. *Courtesy Kimport Dolls)*

Fig. C-10: Mermaid Trademark of the Company. *(Courtesy Chicken of the Sea)*

fig. C-10

ADV-C11.

ADV-C12.

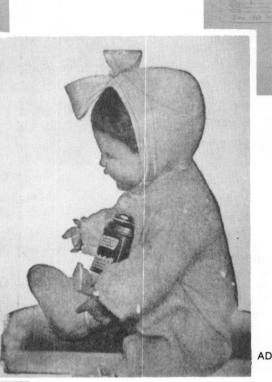

ADV-C13.

ADV-13a.

ADV-C11. *Chore Girl* 16"; lithographed cloth; promotion to advertise Chore Girl pot scrubbers. Marks: **CHORE GIRL** on front of doll. *(Stewart collection)*

ADV-C12. *Cooky.* 11"; rooted blond wig; black side-glance sleep eyes; closed mouth; vinyl head, arms, hard plastic body, legs; original clothes; Horsman 1968 promotion for Club Aluminum Cookwear. Marks: **H/14.** *(Siehl collection)*

With the doll came a letter that reads: *Dear Reader: Do you know why everyone calls me Cooky now??? I was walking along like a little doll when the Club Aluminum people discovered me and said, LOOKY LOOKY HERE COMES COOKY!" I said, NO NO MY NAME IS PEGGY. But they said, WE'RE GOING TO MAKE A STAR OF YOU AND GIVE YOU A NEW NAME. Then they took my picture with a beautiful pot cover for a hat and said, NOW YOU'RE COOKY THE CLUB ALUMINUM COVER GIRL! I just giggled. Yours truly (signed) Peggy I mean Cooky.*

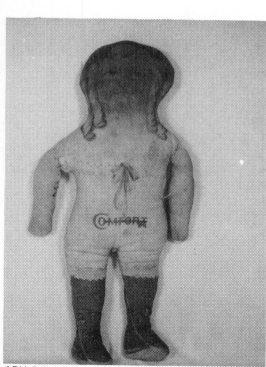

ADV-C14.

ADV-C15a.

ADV-C15.

ADV-C16.

ADV-C13. *Colgate Baby Bunting.* Mohair wig; painted eyes; painted mouth; composition head, hands, stuffed body, legs; each doll came with a full box or can of Cashmere Bouquet talcum powder. *(Playthings, May, 1917)*

ADV-C13a. Colgate trademark drawing from the August, 1917 issue of *Ladies Home Journal.* Drawing copyrighted in 1913.

ADV-C14. *Golden Locks.* 14"; lithographed cloth; molded bow on back of head; free gift from *Comfort Magazine* for a 25¢ subscription. Marks: **COMFORT** (with drawing of a skeleton key through the letters) **from AUGUSTA, ME.** on underwear.

ADV-C15. *Cracker Jack Boy.* Molded-painted hair; painted eyes; closed mouth; composition head and gauntlet hands, stuffed body and legs; wears sailor suit, cap, carries tiny box of Cracker Jack product. Cracker Jack label is on hat band. *(Playthings, January, 1917)*

ADV-C15a. Cracker Jack trademark from Playthings Magazine.

ADV-C16. *Rastus, the Cream of Wheat Chef.* 18"; lithographed cloth; (ref. TCD p. 27).

ADV-D1.

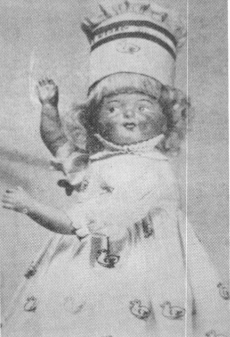

ADV-D1a.

ADV-D2.

ADV-F2.   F2a.

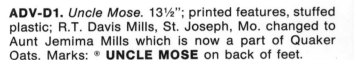

(Sunny Jim)
(Copyrighted)

ADV-F2-1

ADV-D1. *Uncle Mose.* 13½"; printed features, stuffed plastic; R.T. Davis Mills, St. Joseph, Mo. changed to Aunt Jemima Mills which is now a part of Quaker Oats. Marks: ® **UNCLE MOSE** on back of feet.

ADV-D1a. *Dolly Drake (Takes the Cake!).* 19"; golden curly wig; painted eyes; closed mouth; composition head and limbs, stuffed body; yellow dress with "drakes" printed on it, baker's hat, pantalettes, shoes, socks; sold for $1.00 retail, made by Reliance Novelty Co., NYC; trademark for Drake Brothers' Company Pound Cakes. *(Playthings, April, 1917)*

ADV-D2. *Dutch Boy Puppet.* 12"; molded-painted yellow hair; blue painted eyes; closed mouth; vinyl head, cloth puppet body; wears shirt and apron; promotion for Dutch Boy Paints. Marks: **Dutch Boy** on apron bib. *(Stewart collection)*

ADV-F2. *Facit Business Machine Man.* 24"; painted eyes; molded smile; heavy vinyl body and limbs, jointed neck and wrists; made in Germany, magnets attach to ceiling and doll is hung upside down in window display. Button on front reads: **FACIT. FACIT** and several numerals on hat. *(Author's collection)*

ADV-F2a. *Facit Business Machine Man.* 4"; brown painted hair; painted eyes; molded smile; fully jointed vinyl body, limbs; clothes painted in yellow, black trim, red buttons; from late 1960s. Marks: **MADE IN/ HONG KONG** on back, **FACIT** on hat. *(Author's collection)*

ADV-F2-1. *Sunny Jim.* 12"; composition head with painted features; white or baby blue fur stuffed bear body; made by Hahn & Amberg, NYC; *"Bright as the Sun, Cute as can be, I'm yours - "for fun", As you can see,"* ©. Promotion for "Force" cereal. *(Playthings, August, 1909)*

ADV-F3. *Benjamin Franklin.* 13"; lithographed cloth; yellow vest, black coat, red pants, glasses. Marks: **FRANKLIN LIFE/INSURANCE COMPANY** on back. *(Wiseman collection)*

ADV-F4. *Friendlee.* 16"; lithographed cloth, promotion for White Front Stores located in Seattle, WA. Marks: ® **1972 White Front, Inc.** *(Gibbins collection)*

ADV-G5. *Bandy.* 18"; painted eyes; painted closed mouth; composition head, wooden body, limbs, fully jointed limbs, elbows, knees, 1929. Marks: **GENERAL (GE) ELECTRIC/RADIO** on hat, **Art Quality** (picture of boy's head) **manu. by Cameo Prod., Inc./Port Allegany, PA/Des. & © by JLK. on foot;** on box end: script **GE** in circle **The/G-E-Radio/Bandmaster/Pub. No. 13-55.**

ADV-G6. *Sugar Bear.* Lithographed and felt features; stuffed fur cloth, blue shirt; Sugar Crisp cereal mail-in. Marks: **SUGAR BEAR** on shirt front.

ADV-G7. *Minx.* 10"; lithographed features, clothing, bow in hair; promotion for General Foods, Corp; Marks: **Minx** on shirt front, **1953 GENERAL FOODS CORPORATION** on back of belt.

ADV-F3.

ADV-F4.

ADV-G5.

ADV-G7.

ADV-G6.

ADV-G5.

ADV-G8

ADV-H1

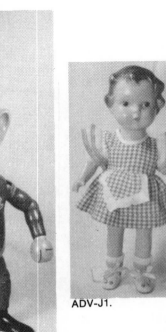

ADV-H2

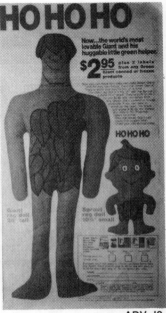

ADV-J1.

ADV-J2.

ADV-G8. *Gerber Baby.* 10"; molded-painted hair; painted blue eyes; open-closed mouth; soft vinyl, fully jointed; dressed in cotton sleeper. Marks: **The Gerber Baby/Gerber Prod. Co./19** © **72** on back, **Made in the British Crown Colony of Hong Kong** on tag on sleeper. *(Rogers collection)*

ADV-H1. *Heinz Baby.* 8½"; molded-painted hair, peak above forehead; painted side-glance eyes; closed smile; one-piece vinyl body, jointed at neck; molded diaper, shoes, socks; new dress; premium for Heinz Baby Food.

ADV-H2. *Hot Point Man.* 16"; painted eyes; molded-painted grin; composition head, body, wooden limbs, jointed neck, hips, shoulders, knees, elbows, ankles, wrists; wears hat made from Hot Point's emblem: large "H" with a triangle inside. Marks: **HOT POINT** across chest. *(Stewart collection)*

ADV-J1. *Jolly Joan.* 12"; molded-painted brown hair, blue bow; painted brown eyes; closed mouth; composition one-piece head and body, jointed arms, legs; original dress, replacement shoes, socks; ca. 1940, sold at cashiers booth at the Jolly Joan Restaurant in Portland, Oregon, dressed like the waitresses; Jolly Joan Restaurant now out of business. Unmarked. *(Wardell collection)*

ADV-J2. *Green Giant and Sprout.* 28", 10¼"; lithographed cloth; mail-in offer expired December 31, 1973.

ADV-J3.

ADV-K3.

ADV-K4.

ADV-K5-2.

ADV-J3. *Li'l Miss Just Rite.* 6¾"; rooted Saran pigtails; painted green eyes, black pupils; closed mouth; vinyl body and limbs, fully jointed; blue denim overalls, white cotton shirt, shoes; promotion for Just Rite Hamburger Co., Terre Haute, IN. Marks: **1965 R. Dakin & Co./Product of Hong Kong** on head, **Made in Hong Kong** on body, tag on overalls: **Dream Dolls/R. Dakin & Co./San Francisco/Prod. of Hong Kong**, tag on arm: **No. 2023/Pigtail Annie/SPECIAL**, reverse side: **Dream Dolls**, overalls read: **Lil Miss Just Rite.** *(Busch collection)*

ADV-K3. *Karo Princess.* 10¼"; hand painted features, soft colors; made of Lignumn fibre, "unbreakable"; promotion for Karo Syrup; made by American Ocarina & Toy Co. *(Playthings, 1919)*

ADV-K4. *Keebler Elf.* 6¾"; molded-painted vinyl jointed at neck; made by Chase Bag Co; offer expired August 31, 1974. Marks: © **1974 / KEEBLER CO.** on bottom of feet. *(Lynn collection)*

ADV-K5. *Goldylocks and the Three Bears.* 13½", 13", 12", 10"; lithographed cloth; Papa Bear holds box of Kellogg's cereal, Mama Bear and Johnny Bear hold cereal bowls that read: **Kellogg's.** Marks: **DADDY BEAR, MAMA BEAR, JOHNNY BEAR, GOLDYLOCKS** respectively on back of necks.

ADV-K5-1. *Toucan Sam.* 8"; lithographed cloth; write-in offer from Kellogg's cereal Fruit Loops; 1960s. Unmarked. *(S. Ricklefs collection)*

ADV-K5-2. *Tony the Tiger.* 13"; stamped cloth face, striped cloth tiger body; available for $3.00 from Kellogg's Sugar Frosted Flakes. Marks: **TONY / 1970 / "Kellogg Co."** on red scarf. *(Rogers collection)*

ADV-K5

ADV-K5-1.

ADV-K6.

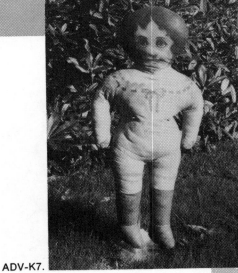

ADV-K7.

ADV-K7.

ADV-K8.

ADV-K6. *Mini People from Many Lands.* 3"-4½"; hand-carved beechwood figures; painted with non-toxic paints; clothing made from cardboard, nylon fur; Swiss Yodeler, Spanish-Main Pirate, Palace Guard, Venetian Gondolier, Wee Scotsman, English Policeman, Black Forest Man, John Bull; mail-in offer from Kellogg's cereals, 1970. *(Janke collection)*

ADV-K7. *Korn-Krisp.* 26"; lithographed cloth; **"My Name is Miss Korn-Krisp"** across lower waist in front. *(O'Rourke collection)*

ADV-K8. *Kresge Christmas Elf.* 4" head; molded-painted pink hair with green hat; painted black eyes; open-closed mouth; felt and cotton glove body. Marks: ©**1959 68 Kresge Co.** on neck. *(Wiseman collection)*

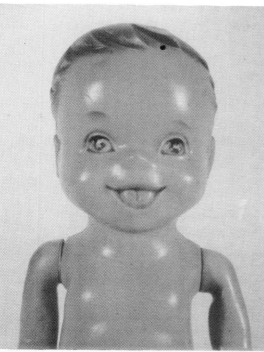

ADV-L6.

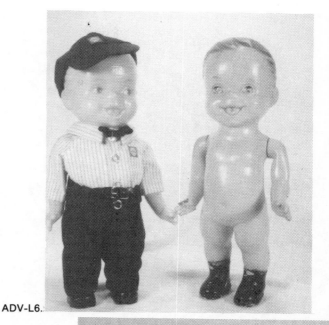

ADV-L6.

ADV-L6. *Lion Uniform Doll.* 13"; molded-painted hair. Older doll on right has brown painted eyes; all four new dolls examined have blue eyes. Mouth is open-closed with molded tongue. New dolls are lighter weight, thinner plastic, poorly molded and painted by comparison. Jointed shoulders only, painted-on shoes. Older uniform has cloth Texaco emblem stitched onto dark green uniform; new ones have paper Arco, Shell, Getty, and Citgo labels. Old Lion Uniform Company emblem is different than new one. Marks: Older doll is marked **LION** on back of body; new doll is marked **LION** on back and **MADE IN/HONG KONG** on neck. *(Author's collection, Courtesy Lion Uniform Co.)*

ADV-L7. *Lustre-Creme Starlet.* 7½"; dark brown synthetic wig; blue sleep eyes; closed mouth; fully jointed hard plastic; replacement clothes, painted-on shoes; came with a Lustre-Creme Shampoo booklet which included instructions for shampooing the doll's hair. Marks: **"Starlet" Lustre-Creme by Inez Holland House.** *(S. Ricklefs collection)*

ADV-L8. *Lustre-Creme Movie Star Doll.* 9"; blond synthetic wig; blue sleep eyes; closed mouth; fully jointed, hard plastic walker body with moving head; original pink dress, lace trim, white ribbon belt, vinyl shoes; also available was a 10-piece accessory set which included shampoo, brush, etc. Unmarked.

ADV-L7.

ADV-L8.

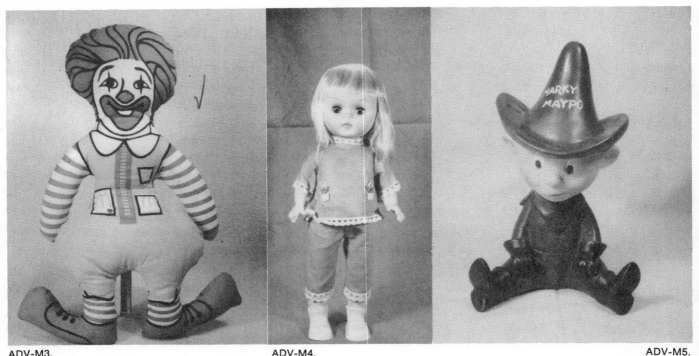

ADV-M3.   ADV-M4.   ADV-M5.

ADV-M3. *Ronald McDonald.* 16"; lithographed cloth printed in orange, yellow, white, black; distributed by McDonald Hamburger stands ca. 1971. Marks: **Ronald/McDonald** on back; picture on pockets of the *Golden Archs®*, a McDonald trademark. *(R. Anderton collection)*

ADV-M4. *Patti Flip.* 18"; rooted blonde wig; blue sleep eyes; closed mouth; soft vinyl head, fully jointed hard vinyl body, limbs; original green top, pants, lace trim; mail-in coupon from a margerine product. Marks: **K19** on head, **6514/KAYSAM** on body.

ADV-M5. *Marky Maypo.* 10"; molded-painted vinyl, hands hold onto a cereal bowl. Marks: **MARKY MAY-PO** painted on hat.

ADV-M6. *Betsy McCall.* 30"; rooted blonde Saran wig; amber sleep eyes; closed mouth; plastic body and head, hard vinyl hands and arms, magi-flex jointed; original clothes. Marks: **McCall Corp.** in a circle. *(Wardell collection)*

ADV-M6a. *Betsy McCall.* 1961 catalog illustration courtesy Sears, Roebuck & Co.

ADV-M6.   ADV-M6a.

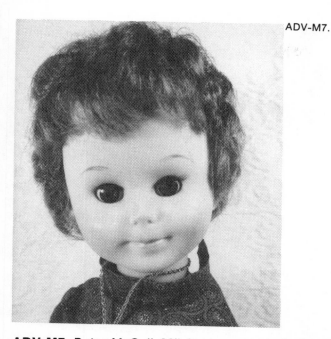

ADV-M7.

ADV-M7. *Betsy McCall.* 22"; brown rooted wig; brown sleep eyes; closed mouth; jointed limbs, wrists, ankles, waist, neck also turns to the side and bends forward.

ADV-M8. *Betsy McCall.* 11½"; red-brown rooted wig; amber sleep eyes; closed mouth; vinyl head, plastic body and legs, fully jointed; original clothes; 1964. *(Siehl collection)*

ADV-M9. *Betsy McCall.* 35"; brown rooted Saran wig; blue sleep eyes; closed melon grin; soft vinyl head, fully jointed vinyl limbs, plastic body; original clothes. American Character Doll Corp. Marks: **McCALL CORP./1959.** *(Stewart collection)*

ADV-M9.   ADV-M10.

ADV-M10. *Sandy McCall.* 36"; deeply molded-painted hair; blue sleep eyes; closed melon grin, soft vinyl head, fully jointed vinyl limbs, plastic body; original clothes, tag reads: **"I Am Your Life Size Doll SANDY McCALL".** Marks: **McCALL CORP./1959.** American Character. *(Stewart collection)*

ADV-M11. *Sandy McCall.* See ADV-M10 for description. *(Kaufman collection)*

ADV-M9.   ADV-M8.   ADV-M11.

ADV-M12.

ADV-M13.

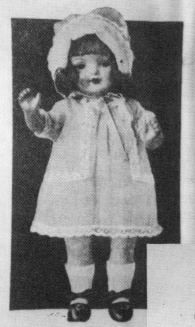

ADV-M14.

ADV-N3.

ADV-M12. *Wizard of Oz Characters.* 18" Strawman, 18" Tin Man, 16" Dorothy, 9" Cowardly Lion; lithographed cloth, bright colors; mail-in offer from MD Tissues.

ADV-M13. *Rag Girls.* 17"; yellow yarn wig; doll on left has one closed eye and one blue button eye; doll on right has two blue button eyes; lithographed cloth; original removable blouses, jumpers, lace trim; mail-in offer from MD Tissues.

ADV-M14. *Priscilla.* 14"; curly brown bobbed wig; blue sleep eyes, human hair lashes; closed mouth, all composition, fully jointed, doll walks when led; original pink organdy dress, lace trim, bonnet, bloomers, socks, patent slippers; ma-ma voice; came free with one new member subscription to Modern Priscilla Magazine. 1929.

ADV-N3. *Uneeda Kid.* Patent granted December 8, 1914 by special arrangement with the National Biscuit Co. *(Playthings, January, 1915.)*

ADV-N4. *Uneeda Kid.* 15"; molded-painted yellow hair; blue sleep eyes, closed mouth; jointed composition arms, jointed cloth hips, hard stuffed cloth body, composition head and lower legs with molded-painted black boots; wore rompers and fisherman's coat and hat of yellow sateen, carried a miniature package of "Uneeda" biscuits under his arm. Marks: **IDEAL** (in a diamond)/**U.S. of A.** *(Stewart collection)*

ADV-N5. *Uneeda Kid.* 11½"; painted eyes; closed mouth; composition head, gauntlet arms, lower body and legs, hard-stuffed upper body and upper arms; molded-painted yellow rainhat, painted black pants, boots; right arm is bent to hold miniature box of "Uneeda" biscuits. *(Naibert collection)*

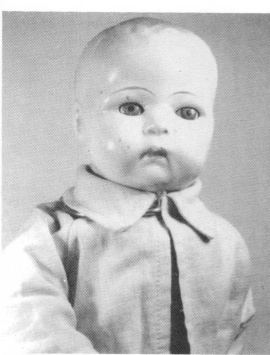

ADV-N4.

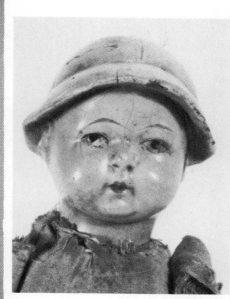

ADV-N5.

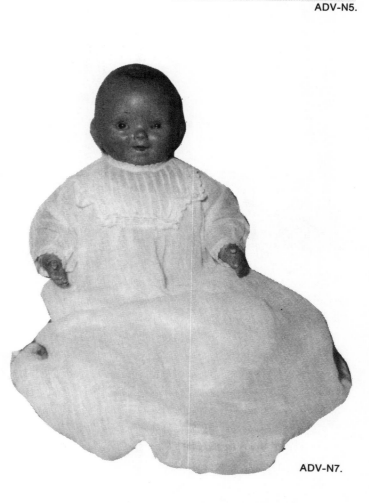

ADV-N5.

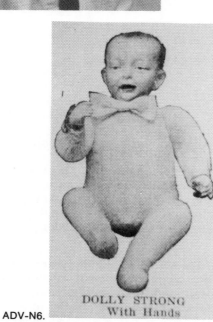

ADV-N6.

ADV-N6. *Dolly Strong, "The Naptha Soap Baby"* Molded-painted features; composition head, hands, stuffed plush body, limbs, fully jointed. Obtained by sending coupons to the company. Note resemblance to Kammer & Reinhardt #100 Baby; same head was used for Samson and Sambo, which see. Horsman. *(Playthings, April, 1910)*

ADV-N7. *Baby Bobby.* 18"; painted hair; intaglio painted blue eyes; closed smile; *Can't Break 'Em* head, composition hands, straw-stuffed cloth body and limbs; original dress, diaper; offered as premium for selling magazines; ca. 1900-1915. *(Cannon collection,* Needlecraft Magazine)

ADV-N7.

ADV-N8.

ADV-N9.

ADV-P5.

ADV-01.

ADV-N8. *Baby Mae.* 18"; curled wig; sleep eyes; closed mouth; "unbreakable" composition head, limbs; wears bloomer dress, lace trim, bonnet, socks, patent shoes; premium for eight subscriptions to Needlecraft Magazine; original paper tag reads: **IDEAL** (in a diamond)**/I CAN TALK/I " WALK/I " SLEEP.** *(Needlecraft Magazine, July, 1925)*

ADV-N9. *Neslings Baby and Crib Blanket.* 9" x 14" blanket, cotton knit, zipper and three buttons; Heubach bisque doll inside of blanket. Marks: **Minneapolis** with large letter **"M"** in centre of word/script **Neslings/KNIT SAFETY/CRIB BLANKET/PAT. NO. 2,151,434** on cloth tag on blanket.

ADV-O1 *Oster Super Pan.* 18"; lithographed cloth, bright blue and red colors; red cape ties around neck. Marks: **OSTER/SUPER/PAN** on shirt front. *(Rogers collection)*

ADV-P5. *Peter Pan.* 18"; lithographed cloth, bright orange, blue, red; purchased from Peter Pan Ice Cream Store in Topeka, KS. for $1.00 in 1972. Marks: **Chase Bag Co., Reidsville, N.C.** on paper sticker on back. *(S. Ricklefs collection)*

ADV-P6.   ADV-P8.

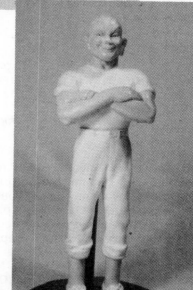

ADV-P7.

ADV-P9.

ADV-P6. *Phillips '66 Man.* 7"; molded-painted composition; one-piece body, nodder head on spring; carries gas nozzles in hands. **Phillips '66** emblem on front of body. Marks: **JAPAN** in an oval on blue and white paper label on base. *(Author's collection)*

ADV-P7. *Pickle Power.* One-piece molded-painted vinyl; wears yellow felt jacket with green pocket. Large cloth tag reads: **PICKLE/POWER** © **1967/RUSS BERRIE & CO., INC., PALISADES PARK, N.J./WALLACE BERRIE & CO., INC., VAN NUYS, CALIF.,** picture of two pickle heads, **"It's the Berries"** in a box. *(Stewart collection)*

ADV-P8. *Pizza Pete.* 7"; molded-painted hard plastic one-piece body; very large nose, hands folded across stomach. Marks: **PIZZA HUT/**® on stomach. *(N. Ricklefs collection)*

ADV-P9. *Storykins Cinderella and Coach.* 4"; rooted synthetic hair; painted eyes; closed mouth; plastic stationary arms and legs; pink velvet dress, lace insert in front, shoes, crown in hair; other dolls offered were: *Goldilocks,* with table, two chairs, Baby Bear, and a tea set and *Sleeping Beauty* with her four-poster bed; from Post Cereals; offer expired June 1, 1969. Mfr.: Hasbro. *(Author's collection)*

ADV-P10. *Mr. Clean.* 8"; two-piece molded-painted vinyl body, jointed only at waist, arms folded across chest; made for Procter & Gamble by Ideal ca. 1960.

ADV-P10.

ADV-P11.

ADV-R3.

ADV-S5.

ADV-P11. *Raisin Doll.* 15"; lithographed cloth; mail-in offer from Purina's Raisin Bran Chex cereal, 1973.

ADV-R3. *Roni Mac.* 11"; lithographed cloth. Marks: **AMERICAN BEAUTY/"RONI MAC"** on top of head. *(N. Ricklefs collection)*

ADV-S5. *Speedy Alka Seltzer.* 7½"; one-piece molded-painted vinyl body; carries large Alka Seltzer tablet. Marks: **SPEEDY** in red lettering on cap, © **MILES LAB.** on bottom of foot, **ALKA SELTZER** in molded letters on pill. *(N. Ricklefs collection)*

ADV-S6. *Selling Fool.* 15½"; molded-painted hair; painted eyes; painted closed grin; composition head and body, wooden limbs, ball-jointed shoulders, elbows, hips, knees; molded-painted clothes, radio tube hat. Taken from a figure conceived by Maxfield Parrish and executed by Joseph L. Kallus; used as selling promotion by RCA dealers, doll held placard in hands. Marks: **ART QUALITY MFG./CAMEO DOLL CO. N.Y.** on foot, **RCA RADIOTRONS** on hat and across chest; ca. 1926. *(Stewart collection)*

ADV-S6.

ADV-S7.

ADV-S8.

ADV-S9.

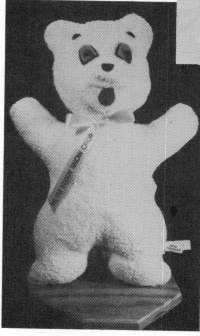

ADV-S9a.

ADV-S7. *Sandies Football Player.* 7"; painted eyes; painted smile; molded-painted composition body, spring in neck allows doll to nod; molded-painted black and gold football uniform, helmet, yellow **A** on shirt front; promotion of Sandies Hamburger stands. Marks: **SANDIES** painted on base. *(Author's collection)*

ADV-S8. *Leprechaun.* 15"; lithographed cloth; promotion for Shamrock Oil Company. *(Gibbins collection)*

ADV-S9. *Skookum.* 16"; molded-painted black hair; painted black eyes; molded closed smile; molded-painted composition head and hands; wears original clothes, red felt pants, blue felt shirt, feathers on head. Marks: **SKOOKUM/APPLE INDIAN/SKOOKUM PACKERS ASS./WENATCHEE, WASHINGTON.** *(Wiseman collection)*

ADV-S9a. *Teddy Snow Crop.* 14"; all terry cloth, felt features; 1972 promotion for Snow Crop Orange Juice. Blue ribbon around neck reads: **"HI, I'M TEDDY SNOW CROP".** Cloth tags stitched to side read: **HAND/WASHABLE** and **ALL NEW MATERIAL/POLLYURETHANE FILLED/© STUART INC., ST. PAUL, MIN.** *(Rogers collection)*

ADV-S10.   ADV-S11.   ADV-S12.

ADV-S13.

ADV-S10. *Sony Boy.* 8"; all vinyl molded-painted clothes and features; jointed at neck. Marks: **SONY** in red letters on shirt and **SONY CORP./JAPAN** on bottom of feet. *(Author's collection)*

ADV-S11. *Spic and Span.* Molded-painted hair, eyes; closed mouths; composition heads and hands, stuffed bodies; Dutch style clothes; promotion for Spic & Span cleaning product. Marks: **Spic & Span/AMBERG DOLL** on base. *(Playthings, February, 1912)*

ADV-S12. *Miss Sunbeam.* 17"; rooted blonde synthetic wig; blue sleep eyes; open-closed mouth with six teeth; fully jointed, vinyl head and limbs, plastic body; original clothes, promotion doll for Sunbeam Appliances. Marks: **Miss Sunbeam** on apron, **EEGEE** on head, **A** on body. *(N. Ricklefs collection)*

ADV-S13. *Elephant.* 6½" long; lithographed cloth; red blanket with yellow trim. Marks: **TODAY!/SUNSHINE/ANIMAL CRACKERS/AT YOUR/GROCER** on blanket.

ADV-S14 *Miss Supreme.* 15"; stamped oil cloth, ready to be embroidered. Marks: **MISS SUPREME** on waistband of dress. *(Wiseman collection)*

Apparently this design was used to advertise more than one product. Maxine Hiett has an uncut 100-pound sugar bag with this doll printed thereon; Celeste Cooley reports she has the doll in uncut condition advertising cookies; both products used the name **"Supreme."**

ADV-S15. *Bugs Bunny.* 11"; stuffed plush body; molded-painted vinyl head; talking ring, eight different phrases; promotion by GTE Sylvania, expired August 31, 1974.

ADV-T7. *Texaco Cheerleader.* 11½"; rooted long blonde wig; painted blue eyes; closed mouth; fully jointed vinyl; red knit top, white pleated skirt, also summer dress, red vinyl coat, white vinyl boots; promotion used by Texaco Oil Company, 1973. Marks: **T30/HONG KONG** on neck, **2/MADE IN/HONG KONG** on back. *(Author's collection)*

ADV-S14.

ADV-T7.

ADV-V2a.

ADV-S15.

ADV-V2. *Vermont Maid.* 15"; rooted long curls; blue sleep eyes; closed mouth; fully jointed vinyl; hi-heeled feet; green poplin jumper with separate white blouse; promotion by Vermont Maid Syrup, offered doll and clothes together or separately; expired July 31, 1964. Marks: **U22.** *(S. Ricklefs)* For illustration see next page.

ADV-V2a. *Vermont Maid.* Marks: **18.** *(D. Salvisburg collection)*

ADV-W1. *Carol Brent.* 15"; rooted wig in various colors; painted side-glance eyes; closed mouth; fully jointed vinyl; various costumes available. Carol Brent is a Montgomery Ward trademark. *1961 catalog illustration courtesy Montgomery Ward.*

ADV-W1.

VERMONT MAID DOLL AND WARDROBE ABOVE
(Doll and 3 extra costumes)
$4.25 Complete

Vermont Maid doll, exactly as shown at right (15 in. tall), plus 3 lovely extra costumes: acetate evening dress, smart cotton skirt and jacket, and for play— a knitted sweater and plaid pedal pushers!

WARDROBE MAY BE ORDERED SEPARATELY
for the girl who already has a Vermont Maid doll.
3 COSTUMES—$2.00
(Use handy coupon at right)

ADV-V2.

ADV-W2. *Dolly-Gram.* 6"; raffia wig; lithographed features; stuffed velvet body, felt hands; has pocket in front for message. Marks: script **Just/to/Say...** on pocket, **Dolly-Gram by / Western Union.** *(Author's collection)*

ADV-W3. *Boy.* 12"; painted hair, features; all composition one-piece body; molded-painted white towel with red border. Premium or trademark for Westinghouse Electric hot water heaters; square mark on towel where label has been removed. *(Perry collection)*

ADV-W4. *The Spearmint Kid.* Molded-painted curl; wriggly eyes; closed mouth; composition head and hands, cloth stuffed body, wooden legs; wears long hooded cape, pointed hat, carries spear; voice; promotion for Wrigley's Spearmint Gum; made by Baker and Bennet Co. *(Playthings, August, 1915)*

ADV-W2.

ADV-W3.

ADV-W4.

ADV-W3.

ADV-W5. *"The Spearmint Kiddo with the Wriggley Eyes."* 13"; molded-painted hair and mint leaves; wriggley eyes; painted open-closed mouth with teeth; composition head and hands, stuffed body and limbs; wears dress with arrows on front and around waist, shoes, socks; made by special arrangement with Wm. Wrigley, Jr. Co. by Louis Amberg & Sons; sold for $1.00 *(Playthings, December, 1912)*

ADV-W5.

ALEX-63a,b.

ALEX-64.

MADAME ALEXANDER DOLL COMPANY

Some of the most collectible American-made dolls of this century come from the Madame Alexander Doll Company. From 1923 through the present year, this company has turned out millions of quality dolls in costumes based on characters from literature, on the authentic national costumes of other lands, and on current fashions.

Most of the dolls are well marked; a very few are completely unmarked. These latter are sometimes difficult to identify when the original costumes are missing. Clothing is usually well-marked with sewn-in cloth labels, many of which give the name of the character represented.

As is true throughout the industry, this company uses several basic dolls which are costumed in numerous styles. For example, the same basic doll is used throughout the *International Series* and the *Dolls from Storyland Series.* At other times special heads have been created to represent certain celebrities or special characters.

ALEX-63a. *Oliver Twist.* 16"; blonde human hair wig; molded painted features; stuffed cloth; original clothes of aqua pique pants, orange flannelette jacket, royal blue picque cap, black patent shoes; ca. 1925. Marks: **OLIVER TWIST/MADAME ALEXANDER, NEW YORK.** *(Sheinwald collection)*

ALEX-63b. *Little Shaver.* 14"; blonde floss wig; molded buckrum face with painted features; wired stockinette body and limbs, black velvet shoes are part of legs; original clothes. Tag reads: **Little Shaver/Madame Alexander/New York/All Rights Reserved.** *(Sheinwald collection)*

ALEX-64. *Boy.* 20"; lambs wool wig; painted features; all stuffed cloth; head turns on built-up shoulders, jointed at shoulders and hips; original cotton clothes, leather shoes; ca. 1924. Marks: **MADAME ALEXANDER.** *(Otto collection)* Ruth Sheinwald reports she has the girl mate to this boy.

EARLY ALEXANDER RAG DOLLS

A rare find is this group of early, well-preserved rag dolls, most of which still boast their original costumes.

The doll in the white replacement dress and the doll wearing only original underwear are unidentifiable since their dresses have been lost. Both have blue-painted, side-glancing eyes and blonde mohair wigs. Construction is identical to Beth and Little Dorrit.

Opposite Page: Upper left: Back view shows original tags on dresses of ALEX-67 (left) and ALEX-66 (right).

ALEX-65. *Tippy Toe.* 18½"; blonde mohair wig; molded painted features; all stuffed cloth; ca. 1925. Unmarked. *(Tardie collection)*

ALEX-66. *Little Dorrit.* 16"; blonde mohair wig; molded painted features, brown side-glancing eyes; stuffed muslin body; all original green cotton dress with orange and white flowers, white organdy collar with orange ribbon, white binding on lower edge of dress, matching bonnet, one-piece organdy slip and pantaloons, shoes, socks; ca. 1930. Dress tag reads: **"Little Dorrit"/Madame Alexander/New York.** *(Tardie collection)*

ALEX-67.

ALEX-66.

ALEX-65.

ALEX-65-68.

ALEX-68.

ALEX-66.   ALEX-67.

ALEX-66.   ALEX-65.

ALEX-68.

ALEX-67. *Beth of Little Women.* 16"; red-brown mohair wig; brown painted eyes and rosebud mouth; stuffed muslin mask face; original off-white organdy dress with pink flowers, one-piece organdy slip and long pantaloons, white socks, black shoes; 1923-1930. Dress tag reads: **"Little Women"/Beth/ COPYRIGHT PENDING / MADAME ALEXANDER N.Y.** *(Tardie collection)*

ALEX-68. *Lady.* 24"; red-brown mohair wig; all stuffed muslin; molded features; painted blue eyes with very long lashes; painted closed mouth; very long arms and legs; original brown cotton skirt, beige velveteen jacket, turquoise scarf decorated with dogs, olive green grosgrain ribbon ties on jacket, long beige stockings, black leather shoes; 1930s. Dress tag reads: **MADAME/ALEXANDER/NEW YORK.** *(Tardie collection)*

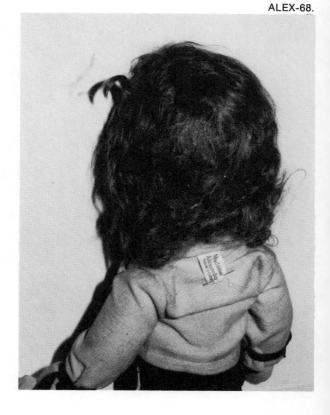

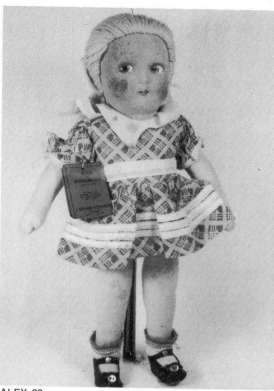

ALEX-69.

ALEX-69.

ALICE IN WONDERLAND DOLLS

One of the all-time favorite characters from fiction is *Alice*. The Alexander Doll Company has issued a number of *Alice* dolls over the years in various sizes.

ALEX-69. *Alice in Wonderland.* 16"; all cloth; felt mask face; painted blue eyes; yellow yarn hair with red hair band; red and white cotton dress and panties combination, red and white socks, black shoes; ca. 1923. Cloth tag on dress reads: **ORIGINAL/ALICE IN WONDERLAND / TRADE-MARK 304,488 / MADAME ALEXANDER N.Y.,** red paper tag has quote on one side from book beginning: **"Curiouser and curiouser"** and on the other side: **ALICE/IN/WONDERLAND/ TRADE MARK/(curiouser quote)/A MADAME ALEX-ANDER/CREATION/REG. U.S. PAT. OFF.** *(Weeks collection)*

ALEX-70. *Alice in Wonderland.* 22"; yellow yarn hair; painted blue eyes; painted closed mouth; pink cotton cloth stuffed with cotton; original red and white checked dress trimmed with red bias, white collar, attached bloomers, replacement red organdy pinafore, original shoes and socks; 1930s. Cloth tag on dress reads: **ORIGINAL/ALICE IN WONDERLAND/ TRADEMARK REG. U.S. PAT. OFF./MADAME ALEX-ANDER N.Y.** *(Busch collection)*

ALEX-70.

ALEX-71.

ALEX-71.

ALEX-71. *Little Shaver.* 16"; stuffed cloth; molded painted features; all original clothes; 1937. Cloth tag on dress reads: **LITTLE SHAVER/MADAME ALEXANDER/NEW YORK.** *(Wiseman collection)*

Artist Elsie Shaver painted the cover picture for the 1942 Neiman-Marcus Christmas catalog; Alexander's Little Shaver was featured in Neiman-Marcus' toy department that year.

ALEX-72.

ALEX-72.

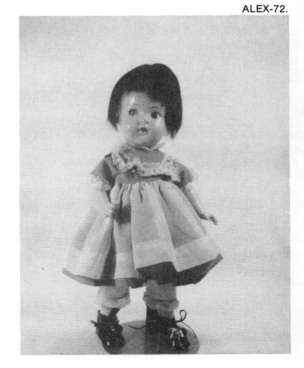

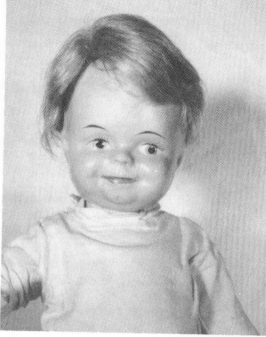

ALEX-74.

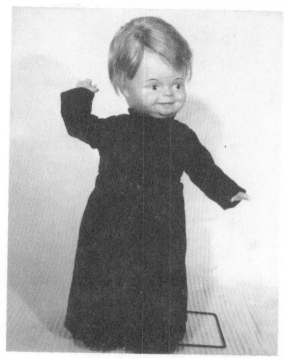

ALEX-74.

ALEX-73.

ALEX-72. *Snow White.* 13"; black bobbed wig; painted brown eyes; painted closed mouth; all composition fully jointed; faded red dress, white organdy sewn-on apron, lace trim with black ribbon lacing, rayon pantaloons, new black shoes; 1930s. Marks: **PR. ELIZABETH/ALEXANDER.** *(Courtesy Nita's House of Dolls)*

ALEX-73. *Pollera.* 7"; black mohair wig; painted blue side-glancing eyes; painted closed mouth; all composition, one-piece head and body, jointed shoulders and hips; all original white organdy dress with multi-colored embroidery and lace trim; 1930s. Marks: **MME./ALEXANDER** on back, original gold paper tag reads: **CREATED BY/MADAME/ALEXANDER/NEW YORK, N.Y./U.S.A.,** cloth tag on dress reads: **"POLLERA"/MADAME ALEXANDER/NEW YORK/ALL RIGHTS RESERVED.** *(Busch collection)*

ALEX-74. *Male Doll.* 14"; soft gray mohair wig; painted blue eyes; all composition, Patsy-type body; dressed in original black cassock of a priest, white shirt with original Alexander tag. *(D'Andrade collection)*

This unusual male doll may have been dressed not only in the cassock of a priest but in a doctor's white coat as well. This leads to speculation that the doll may have been used to represent Dr. Dafoe, the Canadian physician who brought into the world the famous Dionne Quintuplets.

Celia Lincoln has verified that this doll is, indeed, identified as Dr. Dafoe when associated with the Dionne Quintuplets dolls. In his book, THE COLLECTIBLE DIONNE QUINTUPLETS,[1] John Axe further verifies the identification.

[1]Axe, John, The Collectible Dionne Quintuplets, (Riverdale, MD, Hobby House Press, 1977)

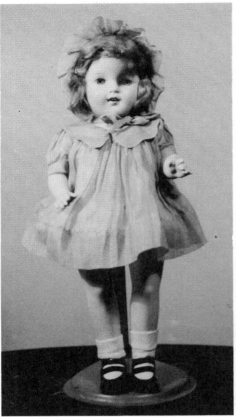

ALEX-76.

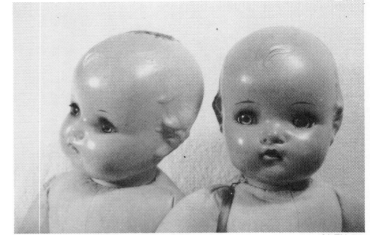

ALEX-75.

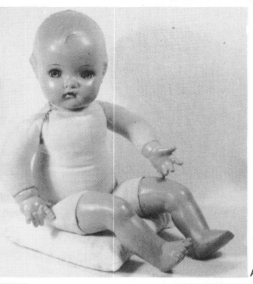

ALEX-75.

ALEX-77.

ALEX-77.

ALEX-78.

ALEX-78.

Note: The photographs on this page, as well as hundreds of others through this book, are original photographs taken by the author in the homes of the owners of the dolls and are not old catalog pictures. The author travels widely in researching and photographing her books and relies heavily on the kindness and generosity of other collectors, for which she is most grateful. All catalog research throughout her work is carefully credited to the source.

ALEX-75. *Identical Twins.* 21"; molded hair but did have wigs; blue sleep eyes, lashes; closed mouths; composition head, gauntlet hands, and lower legs, doll on left has pink cloth body, doll on right has unbleached muslin body; 1938-1940. Marks: **MADAME ALEXANDER** on back of head. *(Weeks collection)*

Jackie Barber of the Red Mushroom has an identical doll with brown eyes and the "rag mop" wig so typical of dolls produced by several companies, including Effanbee, during the war shortage years of World War 2.

ALEX-76. *Girl.* 19"; bright red wig; blue sleep eyes; open mouth with teeth; composition shoulder-plate and limbs, cloth body; all original blue organdy dress and bonnet, pink trim, replacement shoes; 1936. Unmarked but came in box marked **MADAME ALEXANDER.** *(Sheinwald collection)*

ALEX-77. *Betty.* 19"; human hair wig; light brown sleep eyes; painted closed mouth; all composition, jointed neck, shoulders, hips; original pink dress and bonnet, underclothes, shoes and socks; 1934. Marks: Gold paper tag on dress reads: **Betty/Madame Alexander/New York** in script. *(Rogers collection)*

ALEX-78. *Little Betty.* 13"; molded hair under blonde mohair wig; blue tin sleep eyes, hair lashes and painted upper lashes; rosebud mouth; all composition, fully jointed; original pink organdy petal dress, blue bow trim, attached underclothes; 1934. Unmarked. *(Perry collection)*

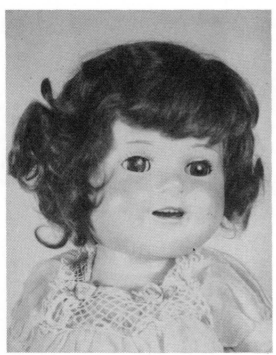

ALEX-79.

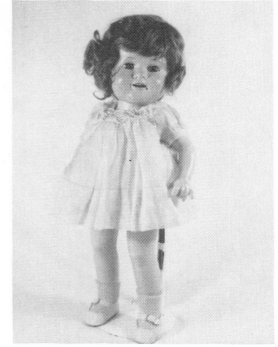

ALEX-79.

ALEX-79. *Baby Jane.* 16"; red-brown mohair wig; brown sleep eyes; open mouth with five teeth and red felt tongue; original pink organdy dress. Marks: **Baby Jane/REG/MME ALEXANDER** on head, paper tag reads: **UNIVERSAL STARLET/BABY JANE** (in script)**/MADAME ALEXANDER.** *(Edge collection)*

ALEX-80. *Cookie.* 17"; molded-painted brown hair; green sleep eyes; open mouth with two teeth, molded metal tongue; composition head and limbs, soft pink cloth body; original organdy dress and bonnet, shoes; paper tag reads: **"If you want me to look at you raise my left arm and I will turn my head from side to side; Raise my right arm and I will cry Mama,"** 2137371. Marks: **COOKIE/ALEXANDER DOLL** on paper tag. *(Wardell collection)*

ALEX-80.

ALEX-80.

ALEX-81.

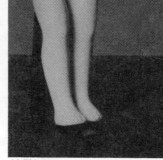

ALEX-81.

ALEX-82.

JEANNIE WALKER

In 1939, when Jeannie was introduced, she was billed as "a first-of-its-kind," and her walking mechanism was patented to protect its unique design. Although the dolls shown are fourteen-inch models, the author has photographed eighteen-inch examples as well.

ALEX-81. *Jeannie Walker.* 14"; light brown mohair wig; brown sleep eyes with lashes; painted closed tiny rosebud mouth; composition with a wooden crotch joined to body with a screw front and back, fully jointed; 1939. Marks: **ALEXANDER/PAT. NO. 2171281** on shoulders. *(Hahn collection)*

ALEX-82. *Jeannie Walker.* 14"; all original red and green plaid dress with pleated skirt, tam, lace trimmed panties and petticoat, Mary Jane shoes; tag on dress reads: **"JEANNIE WALKER/MADAME ALEXANDER N.Y. USA./ALL RIGHTS RESERVED.** See **ALEX-81** for description and marks. *(Cannon collection)*

ALEX-83. *Jeannie Walker.* 14"; in original box. See above for description and marks. *(Tardie collection)*

ALEX-83.

ALEX-84.

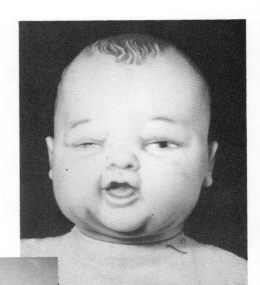

ALEX-85.

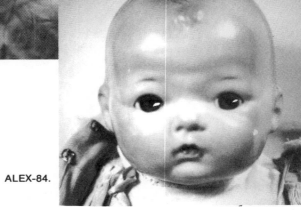

ALEX-84.

ALEX-87.   ALEX-88.

ALEX-86.

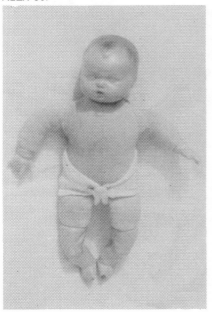

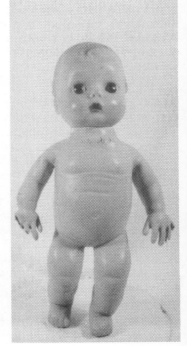

ALEX-89.

ALEX-89.

ALEX-90.

ALEX-84. *Pinky.* 20"; molded-painted hair; blue-green sleep eyes; painted closed mouth; composition head and limbs, stuffed pink cotton body; pink cotton dress and slip with lace trim, long pink georgette coat with attached hood trimmed in marabou, separate pink bonnet; 1940. Marks: **MME. ALEXANDER** on head, cloth tag on dress reads: **"PINKY"/Madame Alexander N.Y. U.S.A./ALL RIGHTS RESERVED.** *(Courtesy June Sloan Antiques)*

ALEX-85. *Crying Baby.* 17"; molded-painted hair; painted squinty blue eyes; open-closed mouth with molded tongue; old soft plastic or synthetic rubber head, rubber magic skin limbs, and kapok-stuffed cloth body with crier; ca. 1949-1952. Marks: **ALEXANDER** on head. *(Courtesy Kimport Dolls)*

ALEX-86. *Baby.* 10"; molded-painted brown hair; molded-painted permanently asleep eyes with lashes; painted bright red rosebud mouth; composition head, hands and lower legs, stuffed body and arms. Marks: **"ALEXANDER"** on head. *(Slap collection)*

ALEX-87. *Mama type.* 16"; molded hair with blonde mohair wig; blue sleep eyes with lashes; closed mouth; hard plastic head, magic skin limbs and stuffed pink cotton body with crier. Marks: **ALEXANDER** on head. *(Vandiver collection)*

ALEX-88. *Cherub.* 9½"; molded-painted hair; painted dark blue eyes; open-closed mouth; stuffed vinyl head and one-piece magic skin body; possibly a Butch or Little Genius. Marks: **ALEXANDER** on head. *(Vandiver collection)*

Originally identified only as *"Baby,"* according to Ruth Sheinwald, this doll, as *"Cherub,"* was dressed in white satin knee-length gown, white felt wings, and gold halo on a wire attached with a gold metal flower in back just under the Madame Alexander cloth tag. The name *"Cherub"* is not on the cloth tag, but on a separate 4-leaf clover paper tag on the wrist. Oddly enough, the under-dress is of red and white striped cotton. There is every possibility that this doll was dressed in other styles, in accordance with the Alexander policy of using a basic doll dressed in a multitude of styles.

ALEX-89. *W.A.V.E.* 14"; blond mohair wig; repainted blue side-glancing eyes; molded-painted closed mouth; fully jointed composition; original blouse and slip sewn to blue skirt, blue jacket has stripes and anchors, blue tie, blue and white hat with eagle emblem, white socks, black shoes and black leather purse; World War II era. Marks: **MME. ALEXANDER** on head, cloth tag on dress reads: **W.A.V.E./MADAME ALEXANDER / NEW YORK / RIGHTS RESERVED.** *(Allen collection)*

ALEX-90. *W.A.A.C.* 14"; blond mohair wig; blue sleep eyes; painted closed mouth; fully jointed composition; all original clothes; World War II era. *(Cannon collection)*

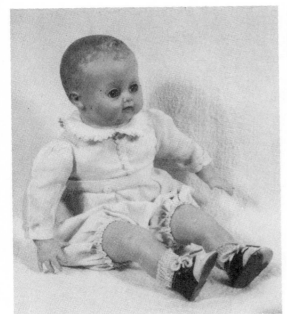

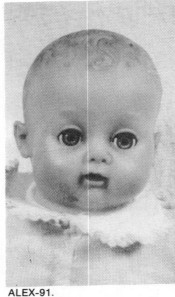

ALEX-91.

ALEX-92.

ALEX-91. *Butch.* 14"; molded-painted hair; blue sleep eyes with lashes; open-closed mouth with tongue; vinyl head and limbs, dimples in chin, elbows, and knees, stuffed cloth body; original pink and white romper suit; ca. 1940. Marks: **ALEXANDER** on head, cloth tag reads: **"BUTCH"/Madame Alexander N.Y. USA/All Rights Reserved.** *(Young collection)*

ALEX-92. *Toddler.* 18", 24"; deeply molded-painted hair; blue sleep eyes; open-closed mouth; vinyl head, hands, and lower legs, stuffed pink cotton body, squeeker; old, possibly original blue dress and white shoes; ca. 1948. Marks: **ALEXANDER** on head. *(Causey collection)*

ALEX-93a

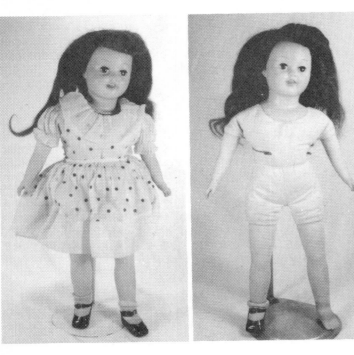

ALEX-93.

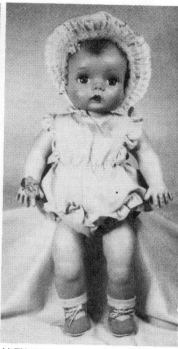

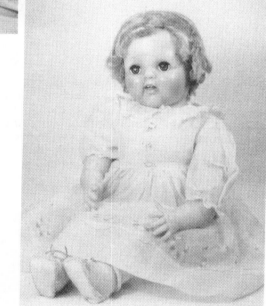

ALEX-94.

ALEX-94.

ALEX-95.

ALEX-95.

ALEX-93. *Girl.* 22"; human hair rooted into soft plastic; brown sleep eyes with lashes; open-closed mouth with molded-painted teeth and tongue; stuffed plastic head and limbs, stuffed pink cotton body; original white organdy dress with red flocked dots, white panties and slip with rayon socks, black patent slippers; note the nicely shaped legs. *(Author's collection)*

This doll, although not authenticated, bears such a striking similarity to verified Alexander dolls that it has been included in this classification. The quality of design and workmanship of the doll as well as the costume bespeak *Alexander.* In addition, unmarked Alexanders have been authenticated in the past (ref. TCD, p. 321-2).

ALEX-93a. *Debbie,* 22", by Fleischaker Novelty Company, Santa Monica, California, (also Venice, California). The two dolls shown, all original with original boxes, were purchased ca 1953-56. Marks on boxes read: **Debbie//$15.95//"The Doll With Rooted Human Hair"//Walks-Talks-Sleeps//Style No. 223// Fleischaker Novelty Co.,//Santa Monica, California.** Details of eyes, hair, and costume are also given. Dresses are of plaid rayon taffeta and checked cotton gingham, trimmed with white organdy. Dolls are completely unmarked. Photograph and information courtesy Mrs. Robert Lockard Atkins. Further, Pat Schoonmaker reports same doll in 1951 was called *"Little Girl (of Today)";* many were blondes. The author is indebted to these two collectors for this enlightening information.

ALEX-94. *Lovey Dovey.* 15"; deeply molded-painted brown hair; blue sleep eyes; painted closed mouth; stuffed magic skin body and limbs, hard plastic head; original romper suit and bonnet; ca. 1950. Marks: four-leaf clover-shaped paper tag on wrist reads: **Lovey Dovey** on one side, other side reads: **Madame Alexander/all rights reserved.**

ALEX-95. *Baby.* 22"; blond synthetic wig; blue sleep eyes; open-closed mouth with two inserted teeth and molded tongue; stuffed vinyl head and limbs, separate fingers, stuffed cloth body with crier; original pale pink organdy dress with pink and green embroidery, shoes; ca. 1954. Marks: **ALEXANDER** on head, tag on dress reads: **MADAME ALEXANDER, NEW YORK/ALL RIGHTS RESERVED.**

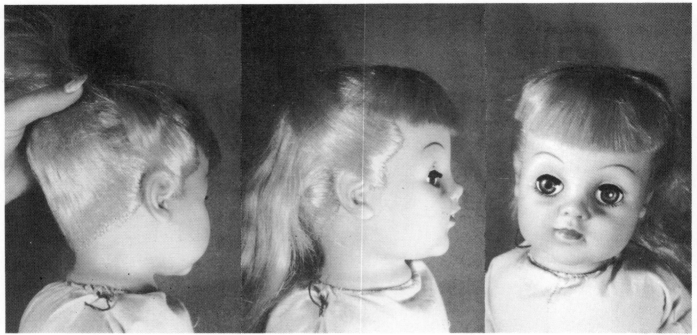

ALEX-96

A DOLL MYSTERY SOLVED

Occasionally a collector finds a doll with special personal appeal; such is the case with **ALEX-96.** The natural "little girl" profile and chin, the upturned nose and long blonde hair, all combined to evoke a picture of the author's beloved daughter. In addition, since the entire doll is stuffed, its weight makes it quite pleasant to hold.

Sentiment aside, however, the question of classification arises and must be dealt with. It was, therefore, with great delight that a near-twin to this doll was discovered in a collection being photographed during a research trip. That doll bore the clearly imprinted **ALEXANDER** mark on the back of the neck and wore its original clothes.

The only difference seemed to be the wig on the marked doll was glued-on while the unmarked doll boasted a beautifully rooted, although similarly styled, hair-do. The conclusion must be that the marked doll is a slightly earlier doll since the rooting technique is the newer of the two methods.

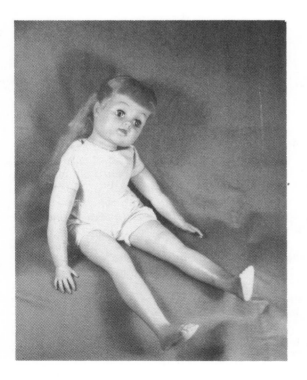

ALEX-96,-96-1. *Girl,* 27", long, thick, rooted yellow Saran wig; gray-blue sleep eyes, long thick lashes; soft vinyl stuffed heads and limbs, stuffed cloth bodies. Note the long, slim arms and legs. Old, possibly original blue organdy dress. ca 1954. Unmarked. *(Author's collection)*

ALEX-96-1a. *Alice in Wonderland,* 27", all original, dressed in typical Alice outfit, glued-on wig. It is entirely possible that we may expect to find this doll in various other costumes and identities. The majority of Alexander's dolls are often unidentifiable if the original clothing has been lost. We are indebted to Pat Schoonmaker, Doll Research Projects, for this firm identification and to John Schoonmaker for the photograph.

ALEX-96. ALEX-96-1.

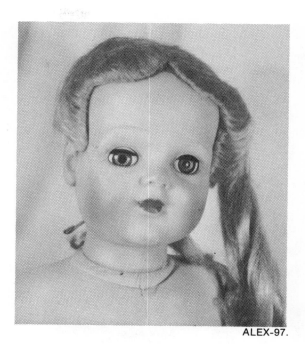

ALEX-97.

Reader Helen Porter writes that she has in her collection a doll with the same head as -99, but with a body like that of -96. Her doll is marked **ALEXANDER** on the back of the head.

ALEX-97. *Girl.* 27"; blond Saran wig; blue sleep eyes; closed mouth; stuffed vinyl head and limbs, stuffed cotton body; ca. 1954. Marks: **ALEXANDER** on neck. *(Gaylin collection)*

ALEX-98. *Girl.* 27"; all original red and white organdy dress, lace trimmed slip, bloomers. See above for marks and description. *(Busch collection)*

ALEX-98.

ALEX-96-1a.

ALEX-99.

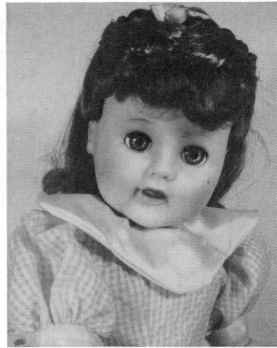

ALEX-100.

ALEX-99. *Boy.* 33"; molded-painted hair; painted black eyes; closed mouth; stuffed vinyl-rubber body and limbs, separate fingers. Marks: **ALEXANDER** on head. *(Phillips collection)*

ALEX-101.   ALEX-101.

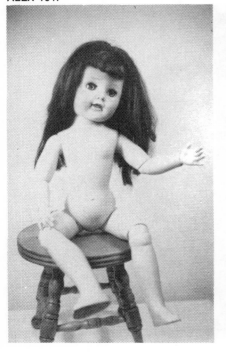

ALEX-100.

ALEX-102.

ALEX-102.

ALEX-103.

ALEX-103.

ALEX-100. *Madelaine.* 17"; red curled synthetic wig; blue sleep eyes; open-closed mouth with molded tongue; soft vinyl head, unusual hard plastic ball-jointed body and limbs; all original clothes; ca. 1954. Marks: tag on dress reads: **MADELAINE T.M./MADAME ALEXANDER/NEW YORK U.S.A.** *(Wess collection)*

ALEX-101. *Madelaine.* 17"; original pink organdy dress with black velvet ribbon and lace trim, pink rayon slip and panties. Marks: **ALEXANDER** on head. See above for description. *(Carter collection)*

ALEX-102. *Little Women.* 12"; blue sleep eyes; synthetic wigs; closed mouths; fully jointed plastic; all original clothes. Marks: tag on clothes read: **Louisa M. Alcott's LITTLE WOMEN/by Madame Alexander U.S.A./All Rights Reserved.** *(Griffin collection)*

ALEX-103. *Margaret Rose.* 17"; tosca human hair wig; blue sleep eyes with lashes; closed rosebud mouth; fully jointed hard plastic body; original pink dotted Swiss dress with two skirts and an overskirt, black velvet ribbon, roses tucked in on dress, pink taffeta panties and slip, long white stockings, black shoes; ca. 1950. Marks: **ALEXANDER** on head, tag on dress reads: **"Margaret Rose"/MADAME ALEXANDER N.Y. U.S.A./ALL RIGHTS RESERVED.** *(Author's collection)*

ALEX-105.

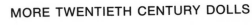

ALEX-105.

ALEX-105. *Nina Ballerina.* 14½"; red wig; blue sleep eyes; closed mouth; fully jointed hard plastic body and head; original white ballet dress, shoes; ca. 1951. Marks: tag on dress reads: **NINA BALLERINA.** *(Winson collection)*

ALEX-106.

ALEX-107a,b,c.

ALEX-106. *Alice in Wonderland.* 18"; blonde synthetic wig; blue sleep eyes; closed mouth; fully jointed hard plastic body and head; original checked cotton dress with white organdy pinafore, stockings, shoes; ca. 1951. Unmarked. *(Winson collection)*

ALEX-107a, b, c. Three examples of the modern shelf dolls:

-107a. 7½"; replacement synthetic brown wig; blue sleep eyes, closed mouth; fully jointed hard plastic; possibly original pink net ballerina dress, painted-on shoes; ca. 1952. Unmarked.

-107b. 8"; brown synthetic wig; green sleep eyes; closed mouth; hard plastic, jointed at neck, shoulders, hips, and knees; original plaid Scots dress, jacket, scarf, tam, socks with tassels, and shoes; ca. 1952. Marks: **ALEX** on back, tag reads: **1964 International Series.**

-107c. 7"; red braided wig; brown sleep eyes; closed mouth; fully jointed hard plastic; original black and silver dress, shoes and socks; ca. 1952. Marks: **Vogue Doll** on back. *(Mason collection)*

ALEX-108. *Binnie Walker.* 18"; blonde synthetic wig; blue sleep eyes; closed mouth; fully jointed hard plastic, standard walking mechanism; original red coat, 'leopard' skin hat and bag, hat box, shoes and socks; ca. 1954. Marks: **ALEXANDER** on back of head. *(Winson collection)*

ALEX-108a. *Winnie Walker.* 18"; dull blonde synthetic wig; blue sleep eyes; closed mouth; fully jointed hard plastic, standard walking mechanism; original blue dress with red and white striped sleeves; ca. 1954. Unmarked, has **Alexander** tag on dress. *(Winson collection)*

ALEX-108.

ALEX-109. *Maggie Walker.* 15"; auburn synthetic wig; blue sleep eyes; closed mouth; fully jointed hard plastic with standard walking mechanism; lavender dress with black belt; ca. 1954. Unmarked. *(Winson collection)*

ALEX-108a.

ALEX-109.

ALEX-112.

ALEX-111.

ALEX-110.

ALEX-113.

ALEX-113.

ALEX-115.

ALEX-114.

ALEX-110. *Cissette.* 9"; tosca wig; blue sleep eyes; closed mouth; vinyl head, fully jointed plastic body; original blue dotted dress, white collar, pink ribbon trim, petticoat, seamed nylon stockings; panties; earrings, flowered straw hat; ca. 1950s. Marks: **MME/ALEXANDER** on back, post card tag reads: **Cissette/MADE BY/Madame Alexander/A Thing of Beauty/is a Joy Forever,** tag on clothes reads: **"CISSETTE"/© MADAME ALEXANDER/NEW YORK, U.S.A.** *(Author's collection)*

ALEX-111. *Beth of Little Women.* 15½"; brown synthetic wig; blue sleep eyes; closed mouth; hard plastic jointed at neck, shoulders, hips, and knees; original pink dress with white organdy neck insert and sleeves, blue ric-rac trim; ca. 1955. Unmarked. *(Winson collection)*

ALEX-112. *Marmee of Little Women.* 15½"; black synthetic wig; original drop-shoulder dress in black rosebud print, black apron; see above for description. Marks: **ALEX** on head. *(Winson collection)*

ALEX-113. *Annabelle.* 20"; blond Saran wig; blue sleep eyes; closed mouth; fully jointed hard plastic; original sweater, skirt with ric-rac trim, white collar, shoes and socks, bow in hair; ca. 1955. Marks: script **Annabelle** on sweater, tag on dress reads: **Kate Smith's Annabelle/© Madame Alexander/New York U.S.A.** *(Wess collection)*

ALEX-114. *Nun.* 20½"; blue sleep eyes; closed mouth; fully jointed hard plastic; original authentic habit of the Order of St. Joseph; ca. 1955. Marks: **ALEX.** on head. *(Courtesy Nita's House of Dolls)*

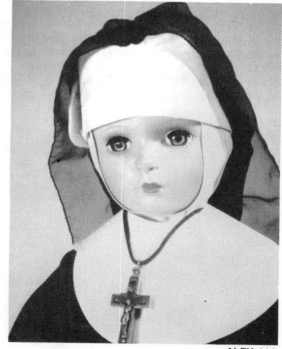

ALEX-114.

ALEX-115. *Baby.* 20"; molded-painted brown hair; blue sleep eyes; drink-and-wet mouth with molded tongue; soft vinyl head, hard plastic body and limbs, jointed at neck, shoulders, upper arms, and hips; possibly original checked dress; ca. 1955. Marks: **ALEXANDER** on neck. *(Wardell collection)*

ALEX-116.

ALEX-117.

ALEX-118.

ALEX-116. *Story Princess.* 15"; dark brown wig; blue sleep eyes; closed mouth; hard plastic, jointed at neck, shoulders, hips, knees; magenta taffeta and net dress, magic wand; shown on The Howdy Doody TV Show and The Perry Como TV Show; ca. 1956. Marks: **ALEXANDER** on head. *(Winson collection)*

ALEX-117. *Sleeping Beauty.* 9"; blonde synthetic wig; blue stationary eyes; closed mouth; fully jointed hard plastic, flat feet; all original long turquoise taffeta dress with gold trim, blue shoes; ca. 1957. Marks: **MME./ALEXANDER** on body. *(Busch collection)*

ALEX-120.

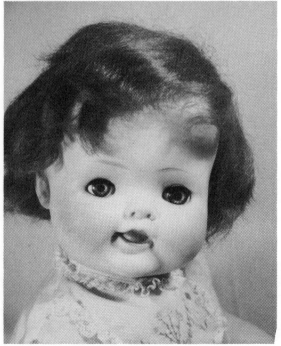

ALEX-119.

ALEX-121.

ALEX-122.

ALEX-123.

ALEX-123.

ALEX-118. *Kathy.* 21½"; molded-painted brown hair; brown sleep eyes with lashes; open drink-and-wet mouth; all vinyl fully jointed; all original, white dots on pink cloth romper suit, white hat, pink suede cloth slippers, pacifier and bottle; in original box; 1958. Marks: **MME/19©58 ALEXANDER** in circle on head, cloth tag on panties and top reads: **Kathy*/©** **MADAME ALEXANDER/*REG. U.S. PAT. OFF. N.Y. U.S.A.**, cloth wrist tag reads: **TO ALL LITTLE GIRLS EVERYWHERE** on front, inside are instructions on making the doll cry real tears by squeezing tummy, back reads: **Kathy/MADE BY/MADAME ALEXANDER/is/A GIFT TO CHERISH.** *(Author's collection)*

ALEX-119. *Kathy.* 20"; molded-painted hair; blue sleep eyes; open-drink and wet mouth; nine-jointed plastic body with soft vinyl head; original turquoise sunsuit and bonnet with white trim, sandals; (Note similarity of this doll's modeling and construction to AMER-9, TCD, p. 74). 1958. Marks: **ALEXANDER** on back of head, has original tags on clothes. *(Meekins collection)*

ALEX-120. *Girl.* 29"; rooted wig; blue sleep eyes; open-closed mouth with molded tongue; very heavy stuffed vinyl; 1958; believed by owner to be "Kathleen". Marks: **ALEXANDER** on head. *(Courtesy Nita's House of Dolls)*

ALEX-121. *Kelly.* 11½"; tosca synthetic wig; blue sleep eyes; closed mouth; fully jointed vinyl body; original pink checked dress, aqua pinafore, shoes and socks; 1958. Unmarked. *(Winson collection)*

ALEX-122. *Kelly.* 15"; rooted tosca wig; blue sleep eyes; closed mouth; fully jointed vinyl body, twist'n'turn waist; original rose taffeta dress with white sew-on apron, hat, shoes and socks. Marks: **MME/©/ALEXANDER** (in circle)/**1958** (with reversed 5) on head, **MME/19©58/ALEXANDER** in circle on back. *(Winson collection)*

ALEX-123. *Kelly.* 20½"; rooted tosca wig; blue sleep eyes; closed mouth; fully jointed vinyl with twist'n'turn waist; original red dress with blue striped pinafore. Marks: **ALEXANDER** on head, **19©58** in circle on upper back, **MME/©/ALEX** in circle on lower back. *(Winson collection)*

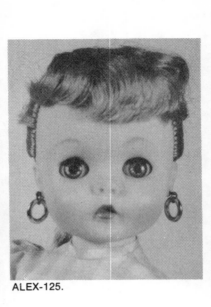

ALEX-125.

ALEX-125.

ALEX-124.

ALEX-124. *Pollyanna.* 15"; rooted blond wig; blue sleep eyes; closed mouth; hard vinyl body and limbs, soft vinyl head, fully jointed; original red and white dress, straw hat, red shoes with black spats. Marks: **MME/©/ALEX.** in circle **/1958** on head. *(Kaufman collection)*

ALEX-125. *Edith, the Lonely Doll.* 15"; rooted tosca wig; blue sleep eyes; closed mouth; fully jointed vinyl body with twist'n'turn waist; original pink and white checked dress with apron, shoes, socks, earrings. Marks: **MME. ALEXANDER/©** in circle on head, **©/1958** in circle on back of body. *(Winson collection)*

ALEX-126.

ALEX-127.

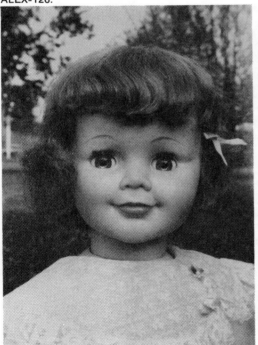

ALEX-126.

ALEX-128.

ALEX-128.

ALEX-129.

ALEX-130. *Walker.* 32"; Saran wig; brown sleep eyes with lashes; painted closed rosebud mouth; all hard plastic with walker mechanism; replacement clothes; ca. 1959. Marks: **ALEXANDER** on head, **A/MADAME ALEXANDER/DOLL** on back of body. *(Busch collection)*

ALEX-126. *Joanie.* 35"; rooted blonde wig; blue flirty sleep eyes; closed grin; very heavy vinyl body, soft vinyl head, walker mechanism; original white cotton dress with white cotton pinafore overskirt, two-layer slip, panties, beige shoes, socks. Marks: **ALEXANDER/19©59** on head, cloth tag sewn into waistline reads: **Joanie*/© MADAME ALEXANDER/*REG. U.S. PAT. OFF. N.Y. U.S.A.** *(Shutts collection)*

ALEX-127. *Sleeping Beauty.* 21"; yellow synthetic wig; blue sleep eyes; closed mouth; hard plastic body, head and legs, soft vinyl arms, jointed at neck, shoulders, elbows, hips, knees; original blue rayon satin gown with gold trim, crown of gold braid with rhinestones. Unmarked. *(Winson collection)*

ALEX-128. *Kathleen.* 24"; rooted blonde wig; blue flirty sleep eyes with long curly lashes; drink-and-wet mouth; fully jointed vinyl; original pink dotted dress, bow in hair, shoes, socks, bottle. Marks: **MME/19©59/ALEXANDER** in circle on head, original wrist tag. *(Winson collection)*

ALEX-129. *Janie.* 36"; thick rooted blonde Saran wig; blue sleep eyes; closed mouth; rigid vinyl body, fully jointed; original clothes. Marks: **ALEXANDER/1959** in arch on head, cloth tag on jumper reads: **Janie*/© MADAME ALEXANDER/*REG. U.S. PAT. OFF. N.Y. U.S.A.** *(Siehl collection)*

ALEX-130.

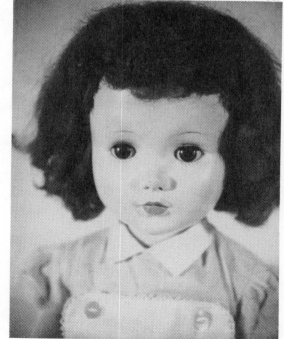

ALEX-132.

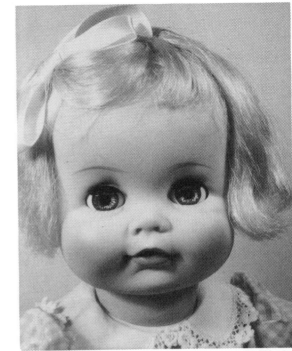

ALEX-132.

ALEX-131. *Cissy Debutante.* 20"; blonde wig; blue sleep eyes; closed mouth; hard plastic jointed at neck, shoulders, elbows, hips, knees; original brocade dress with ribbon sash, long white fingerless gloves, bracelets, earrings, jewels on dress, crown in hair; ca. 1960. Marks: **ALEXANDER** on head, original tag reads: **Cissy.** *(Kaufman collection)*

ALEX-131.

ALEX-133.

ALEX-133.

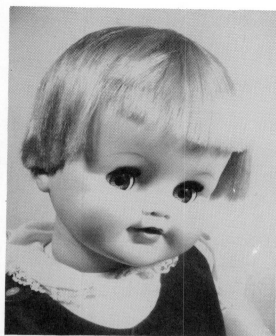

ALEX-134.

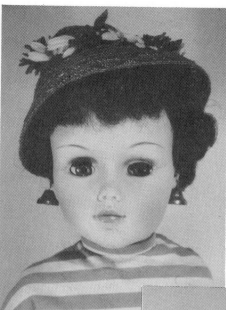

ALEX-135.

ALEX-136.

ALEX-136.

ALEX-132. *Baby Genius.* 21"; rooted blonde wig; blue sleep eyes; open-pierced mouth; fully jointed vinyl body; original checked dress and panties, shoes, socks. Marks: **ALEXANDER DOLL/19©60** on head, tag on dress reads: **BABY GENIUS/© MADAME ALEXANDER/REG. U.S. PAT. OFF. N.Y. U.S.A.** *(Wardell collection)*

ALEX-133. *Maggie Mixup.* 16"; rooted brick red wig; green sleep eyes; all vinyl, jointed at neck, shoulders, elbows, hips, and knees, freckles on cheeks; original aqua and white checked jumper, white blouse, dark stockings, shoes, straw hat; ca. 1960. Marks: **ALEXANDER** on head, **MME./ALEXANDER** on body. *(Winson collection)*

ALEX-134. *Timmy.* 29"; rooted blonde wig; blue flirty sleep eyes; open-pierced mouth; all hard vinyl, fully jointed. Marks: **ALEXANDER/19©60** on neck. *(Siehl collection)*

ALEX-135. *Mimi.* 30"; rooted dark brown wig; blue flirty sleep eyes with extra long curly lashes; closed mouth; hard plastic body and limbs, soft vinyl head and hands, jointed at neck, shoulders, wrist, hip, ankles; twist waist; original blue corduroy slacks, striped shirt, blue hat, black sandals, real bells on bracelet and earrings. Marks: **ALEXANDER/19©61** on head, original wrist tag. *(Author's collection)*

ALEX-136. *Mimi dressed as Heidi.* 30"; rooted blonde pigtails; original clothes; see above for description and marks. *(Siehl collection)*

ALEX-137.

ALEX-138.

ALEX-139.

ALEX-139.

ALEX-140.

ALEX-137. *Little Mary Sunshine.* 15"; rooted platinum wig; brown sleep eyes; drink-and-wet mouth; all vinyl jointed at neck, shoulders, hips; original Swiss lace white dress, shoes, socks. Marks: **ALEXANDER** on head, **MME. ALEXANDER/1961** on head, original wrist tag. *(Winson collection)*

ALEX-138. *Jacqueline.* 21"; rooted dark brown wig; brown sleep eyes with blue eye shadow; closed mouth; all vinyl, jointed at neck, shoulders, hips, knees; original green slacks, shirt, leather jacket, hi-heeled shoes. Marks: **ALEXANDER/19©61.** *(Winson collection)*

ALEX-139. *Baby Sweetheart.* 21"; rooted blond Saran wig; blue sleep eyes; open-closed mouth; vinyl and plastic body, fully jointed; all original pink and white dress and bonnet; mama voice. Marks: **ALEXANDER/19©61** on head, tag on dress reads: **MADAME ALEXANDER/NEW YORK/ALL RIGHTS RESERVED.** *(Kaufman collection)*

ALEX-141.

ALEX-142.

ALEX-143.

ALEX-144.

ALEX-140. *Smarty.* 12"; rooted plastic wig; blue sleep eyes; open-closed mouth; plastic body and limbs, fully jointed, soft plastic head; wears flowered nylon dress and bonnet, or artist's smock with paint brush and crayon in pocket. Marks: **ALEXANDER/©/1962** on head. *(Courtesy Sears, Roebuck and Co.)*

ALEX-141. *Smarty.* 12"; red rooted boy's wig; dressed in original shirt, jacket, shorts, shoes, socks and school book. Tag on shirt reads: **"SMARTY"/by MADAME ALEXANDER,** wrist tag reads: **SMARTY®/CREATED BY/MADAME ALEXANDER,** school book reads: **FIRST READER.** See above for description and marks. *(Wardell collection)*

ALEX-142. *Bunny.* 18"; plastic rooted wig; blue sleep eyes; open mouth with two teeth; fully jointed hard plastic, soft vinyl head; dotted Swiss cotton dress trimmed with organdy ruffles, party slippers, socks; holds arms out as if reaching; sold for $9.59. Marks: **ALEXANDER** on head. *(Courtesy Sears, Roebuck and Co.)*

ALEX-143. *Bunny Baby.* 17"; rooted blonde wig; blue sleep eyes; drink-and-wet mouth; rigid vinyl body and limbs, fully jointed, soft vinyl head; ca. 1962. Marks: **ALEXANDER** on head. *(Schmidt collection)*

ALEX-144. *Katie and Tommie.* 12"; rooted brown and blonde wig; blue sleep eyes; closed mouths; all vinyl fully jointed; boy wears blue jacket and pants, straw hat, striped socks, shoes; girl wears yellow taffeta dress, lace trim, rust-colored sash, white cap; 100th Anniversary Dolls for F.A.O. Schwartz & Co., 1962. Unmarked. Rocking horse reads: **100 YEARS IN TOYS/1862-1962** in gold. *(Winson collection)*

ALEX-145.

ALEX-147.

ALEX-148.

ALEX-146.

ALEX-149.

ALEX-149-1.

ALEX-150.

ALEX-151.

ALEX-145. *Baby.* 14"; rooted blonde or dark brown Saran wig; blue sleep eyes; drink-and-wet mouth; all vinyl fully jointed. Marks: **ALEXANDER DOLL CO. INC./19©62.** *(Wardell collection)*

ALEX-146. *Pamela.* 12"; three white wigs, one blonde wig and one brown wig; blue sleep eyes; closed; hard plastic fully jointed; in original box with six extra costumes, wears pink ballet dress; ca. 1963. Unmarked. *(Winson collection)*

ALEX-147. *Girl.* 17"; rooted blonde Saran wig; brown sleep eyes; drink and wet mouth; fully jointed vinyl; wears original red coat with sailor collar, red tam. Marks: **MME/19©64/ALEXANDER** in circle. *(Shelton collection)*

ALEX-148. *Janie.* 12"; dark brown rooted wig; blue sleep eyes; closed mouth; fully jointed vinyl, pigeon-toed stance; original white dress, slip, shoes and socks. Marks: **ALEXANDER/©/1964** on head, original wrist tag reads: **JANIE*/CREATED BY/MADAME ALEXANDER.** *(Winson collection)*

ALEX-149. *Little Shaver.* 12"; rooted pale blonde wig; painted blue side-glancing eyes; all vinyl, fully jointed; original lacey pink panties; came with toy telephone. Marks: **MME./ALEXANDER** in circle on head and body, **1964** on box. *(Winson collection)*

ALEX-149-1. *Little Orphan Annie.* 14"; rooted blonde wig; blue sleep eyes; closed sad-looking mouth; fully jointed vinyl, freckles on cheeks; original brown-flowered dress with white pinafore, shoes with spats. Marks: © **ALEXANDER 1965** on head. *(Winson collection)*

ALEX-150. *Little Orphan Annie.* 14"; original flowered dress, straw hat and shoes with spats; original dress tag reads: **Riley's Little Annie/by MADAME ALEXANDER/NEW YORK USA.** See above for description and marks. *(Wardell collection)*

ALEX-151. *McGuffey Ana.* 14"; rooted blonde wig; blue sleep eyes; closed mouth; all vinyl, fully jointed; all original clothes. Marks: © **ALEXANDER 1965** on head. *(Winson collection)*

ALEX-152.

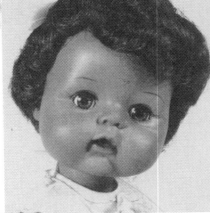

ALEX-152.

ALEX-154.

ALEX-153.

ALEX-153.

ALEX-155.

ALEX-155.

ALEX-152. *Baby Ellen.* 14"; rooted synthetic wig; brown sleep eyes; drink-and-wet mouth; soft vinyl head, soft satiny light brown plastic body and limbs, fully jointed; original black and white polka dot dress, knit booties, diaper and bottle. Marks: **ALEXANDER/19©65** on head. *(Rogers collection)*

ALEX-153. *Coco.* 20"; rooted blonde wig; blue sleep eyes; closed mouth; rigid vinyl jointed at neck, shoulder and waist, one-piece from waist down; flowered jersey dress, seamed stockings, extra hair piece and curlers, brush, comb and bobby pins; this doll was not manufactured for sale as Coco; however, body was used for *Melanie.* Marks: **ALEXANDER/©/1966** on head. *(Winson collection)*

ALEX-154. *Melanie.* 21"; rooted blonde long braids; dressed in original pale blue taffeta with lace edging, flowers in hair, cameo necklace. See **ALEX-153** for description and marks. *(Winson collection)*

ALEX-155. *Polly.* 18"; rooted black wig; black sleep eyes; closed mouth; all vinyl, fully jointed wired limbs; original aqua ballet dress, ballet slippers, flowers in hair, rhinestone earrings, ring on left hand. Marks: **ALEXANDER/19©66** on head, original tag reads: **POLLY*/CREATED BY/MADAME ALEXANDER.** *(Winson collection)*

ALEX-156.

ALEX-156. *Littlest Kitten.* 7½"; rooted blonde Saran wig; blue sleep eyes; closed mouth; fully jointed vinyl; all original blue dress and panties; ca. 1966. Marks: **ALEX. DOLL CO./©** on head, cloth tag reads: **"Littlest Kitten"/by MADAME ALEXANDER.** *(Mason collection)*

ALEX-157.

ALEX-160.

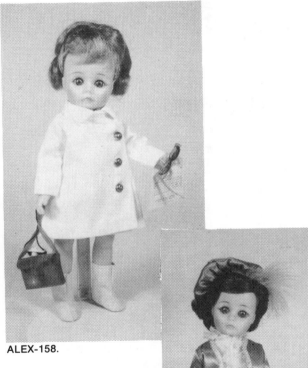

ALEX-158.

ALEX-159.

ALEX-157. *Alice in Wonderland, Tweedle Dum and Tweedle Dee.* 14", 10"; Alice has rooted blonde Saran wig; blue sleep eyes; closed mouth; hard plastic fully jointed body, soft vinyl head; all original clothes. Tweedle Dum and Tweedle Dee have molded-painted features; hard composition heads, stuffed felt bodies; wear red felt jackets, tan felt trousers, caps, shoes, and big white collars that read: **Dee** and **DUM**; ca. 1966. Marks: **ALEXANDER** on head, Tweedles have tag that reads: **OLD COTTAGE DOLL/MADE IN ENGLAND/REGISTERED TRADEMARK.** *(Sheinwald collection)*

ALEX-158. *Nancy Drew.* 12"; rooted red wig; blue sleep eyes; closed mouth; fully jointed vinyl; original white coat, green scarf, boots, purse, sunglasses and camera; based on character from Nancy Drew books by Carolyn Keene. Marks: **ALEXANDER/© 1963** on head, issued at a later date. *(Winson collection)*

ALEX-159. *Blue Boy.* 11½"; rooted dark wig; blue sleep eyes; closed mouth; all vinyl fully jointed; all original blue suit, shoes, hat, white ruffled shirt and white stockings; re-issued in 1973. Marks: **ALEXANDER/19©63** on head, cloth tag reads: **BLUE BOY** paper wrist tag reads: **A/MADAME/ALEXAN-DER/DOLL/BLUE BOY.** *(Swift collection)*

ALEX-160. *Maggie.* 17"; rooted long dark wig; sleep eyes; closed mouth; all vinyl, can sit or stand; *Elise* doll dressed in Scotch Plaid pleated full skirt, short green jacket with white collar and cuffs, straw hat and French-heeled shoes, 1973. *(Courtesy Madame Alexander Doll Co.)*

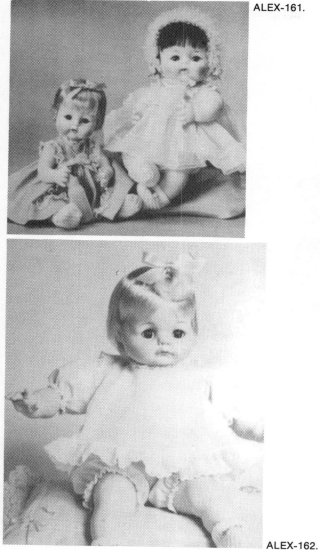

ALEX-161.

ALEX-162.

ALEX-163.

THE INTERNATIONAL DOLLS

These dolls, along with the Storybook series, have become Alexander classics. As is true of all the Alexander line, these diminutive representatives of far-away lands are meticulously and authentically costumed.

The same basic eight-inch doll is used for both the International Series and Storybook Series; glued-on wigs vary with the characterization; sleep eyes; closed rosebud mouth; fully jointed plastic; dressed according to the character.

Following are partial listings of dolls which have been issued in these two extensive series over the years.

ALEX-161. *Sweet Tears.* 9", 14"; fine rooted wig; sleep eyes; drink-and-wet mouth; fully jointed vinyl; wears christening dress and wool booties or checked dress, diaper, and booties, all come with bottle and pacifier; 1974. *(Courtesy Madame Alexander Doll Co.)*

ALEX-162. *Baby Precious.* 21"; rooted wig; dark sleep eyes; closed mouth; soft vinyl head, arms and legs, stuffed cloth body; wears pink cotton romper suit, white eyelet trimmed smock and white wool booties or pink cotton dress with lace panel on front, matching bloomers, bonnet, white socks and shoes; 1974. *(Courtesy Madame Alexander Doll Co.)*

ALEX-163. *Baby Lynn.* 20"; rooted short wig; blue sleep eyes; closed mouth; soft vinyl head, arms and legs, stuffed cloth body, cry voice; wears cotton dress, pinafore and bonnet or white organdy and lace dress with rosebud trim and slippers; 1974. *(Courtesy Madame Alexander Doll Co.)*

ALEX-164.

INTERNATIONAL SERIES

Argentina	Japan
Austria	Mexico
Belgium	Netherlands
Brazil	Norway
Canada	Poland
China	Portugal
Czechoslovakia	Rumania
Denmark	Russia
Finland	Scotland
France	Spain
Germany	Sweden
Greece	Switzerland
Hungary	Thailand
India	Turkey
Indonesia	Tyrol
Ireland	United States
Israel	Yugoslavia
Italy	

Top row left to right: No. 0779 — INDONESIA   No. 0785 — PORTUGAL   No. 0787 — TURKEY
Bottom row left to right: No. 0786 — RUMANIA   No. 0789 — YUGOSLAVIA   No. 0784 — NORWAY

Top row left to right: No. 0796 — SCOTTISH   No. 0795 — SPANISH   No. 0797 — HUNGARIAN
Bottom row left to right: No. 0794 — SWISS   No. 0799 — TYROLEAN BOY   No. 0798 — TYROLEAN GIRI

Top row left to right: No. 451 — MARY MARY   No. 453 — HANSEL   No. 454 — GRETEL
Bottom row left to right: No. 482 — RED RIDING HOOD No. 483 — BO PEEP   No. 452 — MISS FUFFET

Top row left to right: No. 435 — BRIDE   No. 440 — RED BOY
Bottom row left to right: No. 425 — SCARLET   No. 430 — BALLERINA   No. 431 — BETSY ROSS

ALEX-166.

All-2.

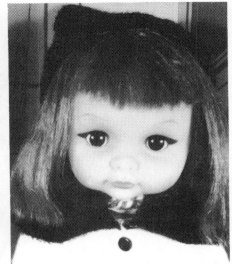

ALL-2.

ALEX-165.

STORYBOOK SERIES

Mary Mary	Betsy Ross
Red Riding Hood	Beth
Hansel and Gretel	Amy
Miss Muffet	Meg
Bo-Peep	Jo
Bride	Marme
Scarlet	Laurie
Red Boy	Alice
Ballerina	

ALL-1.

ALEX-166. *Janie.* 14", 20"; rooted synthetic curls; large sleep eyes; closed mouth; soft vinyl arms, legs and head, stuffed cloth body, cry voice; embroidered cotton dress with lace trim, matching bloomers, slippers with ribbons and socks; 1973. *(Courtesy Madame Alexander Doll Co.)*

ALLIED DOLL COMPANY

ALL-1. *Girl.* Painted features; composition head and limbs, soft body stuffed with cork; checked dress, shoes and socks. Mfr: Allied Doll Co., New York City. *(Playthings, June, 1919)*

ALLIED DOLL & TOY CORPORATION

ALL-2. *Wendy.* 14"; rooted red Saran hair; black sleep eyes; closed mouth; fully jointed hard vinyl; original coat and dress. Marks: **ALLIED DOLL & TOY CORP./BROOKLYN, N.Y.** © **1967** on original box, doll is unmarked. *(Mason collection)*

AMB-1.

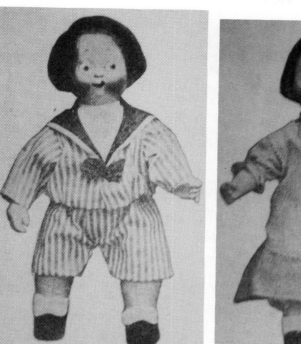

AMB-2.

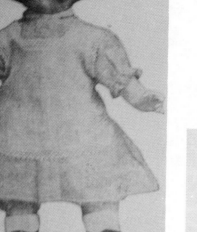

AMB-2a.

AMB-4.

LOUIS AMBERG AND SON

This firm both imported and manufactured dolls. (See DOLL MAKING Chapter). Louis Amberg was also known as an artist and designer of some of the dolls sold by his company.

AMB-1. *Papa-Mama Doll.* An example of the 1903 line had bisque head, human hair or mohair wig, glass sleep eyes, ball-jointed body, and a "voice". *From an advertisement in June, 1903, Playthings Magazine.*

AMB-2, 2a. *Bobby Blake and Dolly Drake.* Painted features; composition head and hands, cork-stuffed pink sateen bodies. "Made by special arrangement with and after designs by the artist and originator, G.G. Wiederseim (Grace G. Drayton), and by contract with the Fred. A. Stokes Co., publishers of the books of the same name." Wholesale prices of the dolls were $4.25, $8.50, and $12.50 per dozen. *(Playthings, May and June, 1911)*

AMB-3. *Sassy Sue.* Molded-painted hair; painted features with "Bisc" finish; composition head and limbs, stuffed body; striped dress with two detachable bows on head; sold for $8.50 per dozen; *"She of the Sweetly Satanic Smile"*, copyrighted, trademark registered. *(Playthings, September, 1911)*

AMB-4. *Swat Mulligan, "The Cute Baseball Kid".* Composition head, stuffed cloth body and limbs, painted features; sold for $8.50 per dozen; trademark registered; photo appears to be a K-Star-R #100 type character face. A *"Baseball Boy"* sold as late as 1914. There was a black version called *"Dixie Mascot"*. *(Playthings, February and March, 1911)*

AMB-3.

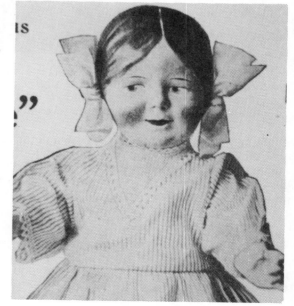

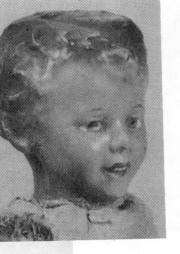

AMB-5.

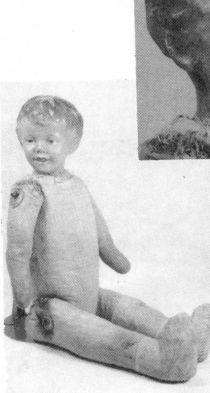

AMB-6.

43/133 "Little Sister"

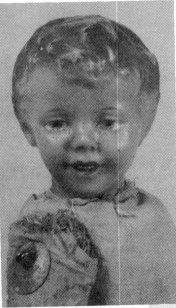

AMB-7.

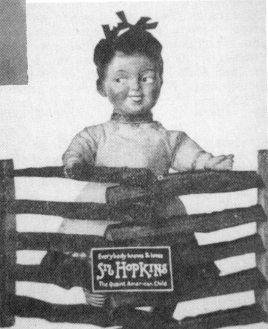

AMB-5. *Little Sister.* 14"; painted features; composition head, stuffed cloth body and limbs; blouse and pleated jumper. *(Playthings, March, 1911)*

AMB-6. *Character Boy.* 19"; deeply molded-painted hair; painted blue eyes; painted open mouth with four painted teeth; excelsior-stuffed unbleached muslin body, pink cloth arms and legs with pin and disc joints. Marks: ©/L A & S/1912. *(Hafner collection)*

AMB-7. *Sis Hopkins.* 14"; "Bisc" finish molded-painted composition head, arms and legs; hair ribbons; made by consent and approval of the originator, Rose Melville; copyright Louis Amberg and Son, 1911; trademark registered. *(Playthings, January, 1912)*

AMB-8.

AMB-8. *The Wonder Baby.* "Bisc" finish molded-painted composition head and hands, stuffed cloth body and legs; wears lace and ribbon-trimmed dress and bonnet. *(Playthings, June and July, 1913)*

AMB-10

AMB-9a, b, c. *Tiny Tots.* 13"; "Bisc" finish Hard-To-Break molded-painted composition head and hands, stuffed cloth body and legs; various costumes; childlike character expressions; *"They Stand Alone"*; sold for $8.00 per dozen. *(Playthings, August, 1913)*

AMB-10. *Louis Amberg* with two of his "Bisc-Faced" character dolls, the Tiny Tots. *From an article in October, 1913, Playthings.*

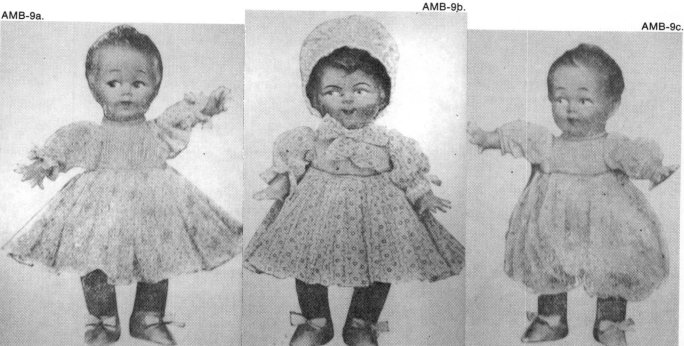

AMB-9a.   AMB-9b.   AMB-9c.

AMB-11.

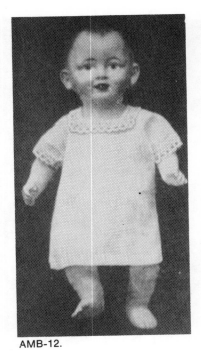

AMB-12.

AMB-13.

AMB-14a,b.

AMB-11. *Little Sweetheart.* From 16" to life size; "Bisc" finish molded-painted composition head and hands; stuffed body and legs; silk underwear, three-piece Angora wool suit, new in 1913. *(Playthings, January, 1913)*

AMB-12. *"Truest-to-Life" Babies.* 9"; "Bisc" finish molded-painted composition head, body and limbs; "Hard-to-Break" joints; sold for $4.50 per dozen. *(Playthings, January, 1913)*

AMB-13. *Miss Broadway.* 13"; "Bisc" finish molded-painted head and hands; cloth body and legs; wears a wrap and "Broadway hat"; sold for $1.00 each; copyright 1912, trademark registered. *(Playthings, January, 1913)*

AMB-14a, b. *Hail Columbia and Yankee Doodle.* 15"; "Bisc" finish molded-painted head and hands; stuffed cloth bodies and legs; dressed in stars and stripes; *"Every inch American";* sold for $1.00 each; copyright 1912, trademark registered. *(Playthings, January, 1913)*

AMB-15a,b.

AMB-17.

AMB-16a,b.

AMB-18.

AMB-15a, b. *Soldier Boy and Jack Tar, "Army and Navy Forever".* Molded-painted features; composition heads and hands, stuffed bodies and limbs; dressed in Army and Navy uniforms and carried American Flags. *(Playthings, May, 1914)*

AMB-16a, b. *Tango Tots.* Molded-painted features; composition heads and hands; stuffed cloth bodies and limbs; dressed in print dress and hat, and dark suit with white shirt and tie. *(Playthings, April and May, 1914)*

AMB-17. *Jim Dandy.* 18"; molded-painted composition head with "nonpeelable washable bisc finish heads"; stuffed body and limbs; in assorted dress styles; $54.00 per gross. *(Playthings, February, 1914)*

AMB-18. *Pouty Pets.* 12", 16"; with or without wigs; painted side-glancing eyes; closed mouth; composition head and hands, stuffed body; *"The Baby with the Come Hither Expression";* sold for 50ᶜ and $1.00. *(Playthings, January, 1915)*

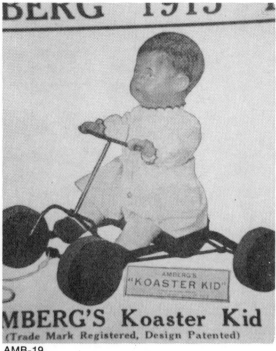

AMB-19.

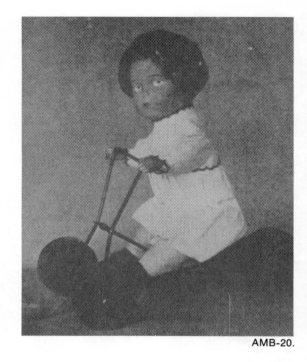

AMB-20.

AMB-19. *Koaster Kid.* Molded-painted composition head and hands, stuffed body and limbs; came with steel and wood 'koaster' with pull string; also available were Go-Cart Baby and Go-Cart Dolly with a steel collapsible go-cart; trademark registered, design patented. *(Playthings, April and May, 1915)*

AMB-20. *Koaster Kid.* Molded-painted composition head and hands, stuffed body and limbs; different head than AMB-19; mechanical doll propels itself on 'koaster'; sold for $1.00, trademark registered. *(Playthings, February, 1915)*

AMB-22.

AMB-21.

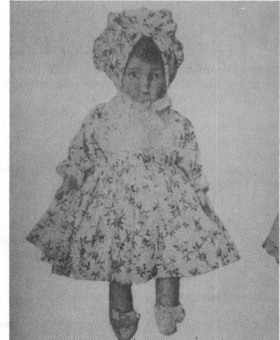

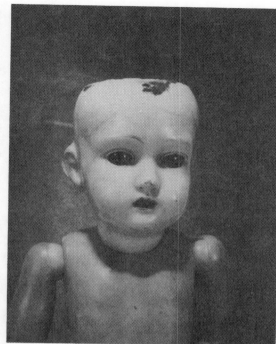

AMB-23.

AMB-23a.

AMB-24.

AMB-23.

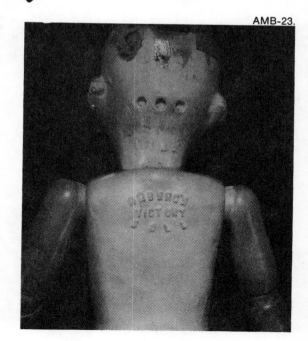

AMB-21. *Sweethearts.* With or without wigs; painted eyes; closed mouth; composition head and hands, cloth body, limbs; beautiful lace-trimmed dresses and bonnets; sold for 50ᵉ and $1.00. *(Playthings, January, 1915)*

AMB-22. *Pollyana the Glad Doll.* Molded-painted composition head and hands with "Bisc" finish, stuffed body and limbs; print dress and bonnet with lace trim, ribboned shoes; $1.25 retail. *(Playthings, October, 1917)*

AMB-23. *Victory Doll.* 15"; brown human hair wig; tin blue decal sleep eyes; open mouth with four teeth and felt tongue; composition head, wood and papier mache ball-jointed body; original white dress, slip, pantaloons, and shoes; 1917. Marks: **L.A.&S.** on head, **AMBERG'S/VICTORY/DOLL** on back. *(Author's collection; the childhood doll of the late Louise Petry Anderton)*

AMB-23a. *Victory Doll.* Four sizes; trademark registered; *"We have out-Germaned the Germans".* See above for description and marks. *(Playthings, December, 1917)*

AMB-24. *The "Amkid" Doll.* 17", 20", 24", 28"; mohair or human hair, blond or tosca wigs; painted eyes on the 17" and 20", moving "Fool Proof" eyes on all sizes; open mouth; imitation kid bodies stuffed with cork, composition heads, breast plate and forearms; jointed at neck, elbows, shoulders, hips and knees; "Fool Proof" eyes were patented. *(Playthings 1918)*

AMB-24.

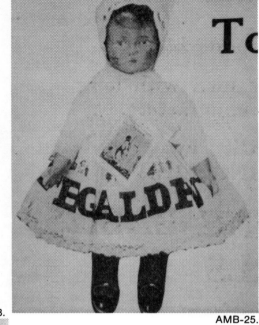

AMB-28.   AMB-25.

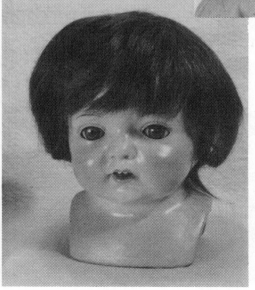

AMB-26.

AMB-27.

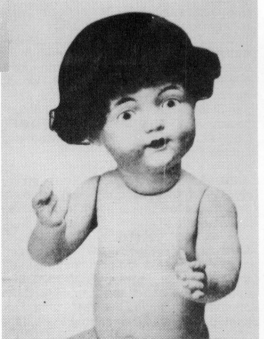

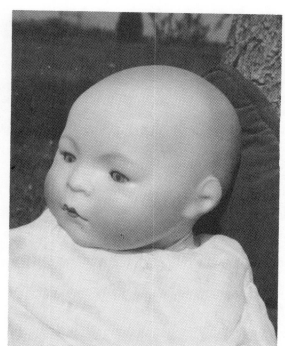

AMB-29.

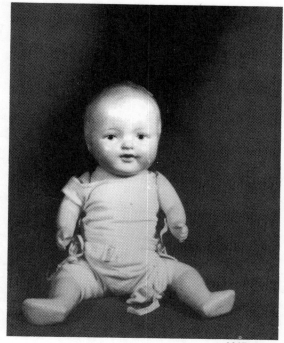

AMB-29-1.

AMB-29-1. *Vanta Baby.* 11"; molded-painted yellow hair; painted blue eyes; painted open-closed mouth, tongue, two teeth; fully jointed composition; original diaper and shirt. Marks: **AMBERG** on back; cloth tag on clothes reads: **VANTA** and **TRADE MARK / REGISTERED.** *(Author's collection)*

AMB-30. *Newborn Baby.* 12"; molded-painted yellow hair; painted blue eyes; closed mouth; composition flange head and gauntlet hands, cloth body and limbs; original lace-trimmed nightie; came in painted black cradle with mattress and pillow; ca. 1920s. Marks: (top line is indistinguishable)/**LOUIS AM-BERG** stamped on back. *(Warren collection)*

AMB-25. *The Educational Doll.* Molded-painted hair; painted eyes; closed mouth; composition head and hands, cloth body and limbs; wears dress and bonnet with letters of the alphabet and fairy tale characters on the skirt, Mother Goose Fairy Tale book comes with doll; design pat. #150.280, copyrighted by Amberg, 1916. *(Playthings, February, 1917)*

AMB-26. *Head.* 8"; replacement wig over molded hair; celluloid over tin eyes; open mouth with two teeth; composition head. Marks: **9/L.A.&S./19©18.** *(Author's collection)*

AMB-27. *Victory Character Baby.* Glued-on mohair wig; "fool-proof" sleep eyes; closed mouth; all composition jointed at neck, shoulders and hips; patented "Fool-Proof" eyes, *"you can dig your fingers into this eye and it won't twist out of position".* *(Playthings, December, 1918)*

AMB-28. *Mibs.* 16"; molded-painted hair; painted eyes; closed mouth; stuffed cloth body and limbs with molded-painted shoes; ca. 1921. *(Stewart collection)*

AMB-29. *Baby.* 26"; painted hair; blue glass sleep eyes; closed mouth; bisque head, composition hands, cloth body and limbs. Marks: **AMBERG & SON/GERMANY** on neck. *(Griffin collection)*

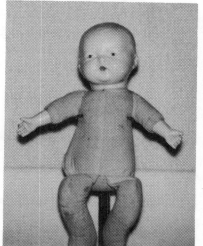

AMB-30.

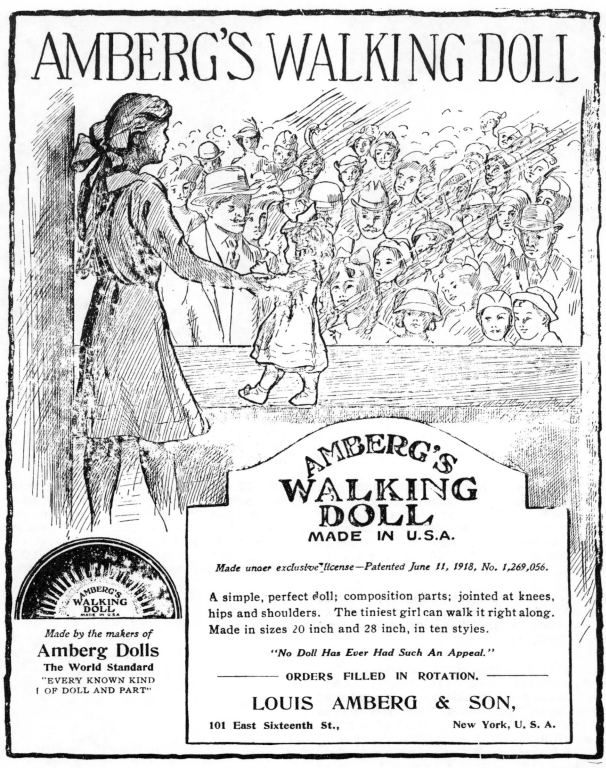

AMB-31.

AMB-31. *Amberg's Walking Doll.* Advertisement from *Crockery and Glass Journal,* August 7, 1919.

AMB-32. *Sunny Orange Blossom.* 13¾"; molded-painted "orange" head; painted blue eyes; closed mouth; composition head and limbs, stuffed cloth body; originally made sound when squeezed; patented by Otto Ernst Denivelle; originally dressed all in orange with name on ribbon across chest. Marks: ©/LA & S/1924 on head. *(Ortwein collection)*

AMB-32.

AMB-34.

AMB-33.

AMB-33. *Girl.* Molded-painted hair; painted blue eyes and upper lashes; closed mouth; all composition jointed at neck, shoulders, waist, and hips. Marks: **AMBERG/PAT. PEND./L.A. & S.©1928** on head. *(Wardell collection)*

AMB-34. *Boy and Girl.* 8"; molded-painted yellow hair; painted amber side-glancing eyes; tiny closed mouths; all composition jointed at shoulders and waist; boy dressed in original overalls, painted shoes and socks; 1928. Marks: tag on overalls reads: **AN AMBERG DOLL with/BODY TWIST/all its own!/PAT. PEND. SER. NO. 32018.** *(Stewart collection)*

AMB-35. The death of Louis Amberg on April 13, 1915, was reported in the May issue of Playthings that year. From a beginning as a clerk in the wholesale notions and specialty business he went on to establish, in 1890, the firm which became one of the largest jobbing and importing houses in the middle west. In 1898 the firm moved to New York as Amberg, Brill Co. In 1906 the importing end of the business was dropped and Mr. Amberg began to devote his entire energies to the manufacture of dolls and toys. About this time his son, Joe L. Amberg began to take an active interest in the firm and continued the business after his father's death. *(Playthings, May, 1915)*

AMB-35.

AMERICAN BISQUE DOLL CO., INC.

Established in 1919, the company had sales of $200,000 the first year. The *"American Bisque"* was, of course, a special patented composition.

AMER-21. *American Bisque Beauty.* Mohair or human hair wig; sleep eyes; painted closed mouth with two painted teeth; composition head and hands, stuffed body and limbs; ca. 1920. *(Playthings, February, 1920)*

AMER-21.

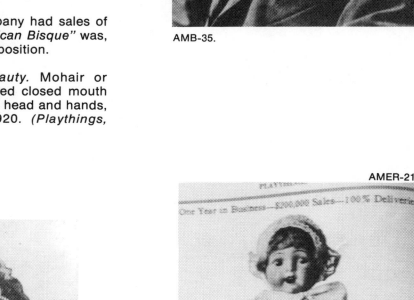

AMER-21.

AMERICAN CHARACTER DOLL CO.
AMERICAN DOLL & TOY (MFG.) CO.

An excellent example of the confusing aspects of researching any industry and its merchandise is to be found in the story of the "American" companies. First, manufacturing companies come and go with sometimes alarming frequency. This partner retires, that one buys the other out, or two companies merge. In the process the company name may be changed, sometimes only in a minor way; at other times the new company name may resemble in no way the former.

The American Doll and Toy (Mfg.) Co. was founded in 1892 by S.D. Hoffman. The January 1907 issue of *Playthings* states: ". . . exclusive of rag doll makers, there is only one doll manufacturer in the United States," in referring to the American Doll and Toy (Mfg.) Co. Hoffman owned the Can't Break 'Em process. At his death in 1909 the company and the process were sold to Aetna Doll and Toy Co. (Aetna made the Can't Break 'Em heads for Horsman), and these two companies later merged.

The American Character Doll Co. was founded in 1919 and used *Aceedeecee*, a phoneticism of the company's initials, as a trademark for its wood fibre composition heads. A little later they used *Petite* as their trademark.

The matter seems fairly simple at this point; however, sometime after about 1925, perhaps as late as the 1940's, American Character dolls began to appear in boxes marked American Doll and Toy Corp. Somehow we have circled upon ourselves. Since there is often little opportunity to trace the ebb and flow of the tides of private enterprise, we must leave it there at least for the time being.

For these reasons, all dolls identified as American Character, American Doll and Toy, or with the AM Doll mark have been grouped together and are shown in approximate chronological order.

AMER-22. *Fluffy Ruffles.* Can't Break 'Em head; painted features; composition hands; stuffed cloth body and limbs; assorted styles of clothing and wigs; distributed by George Borgfeldt and Co. Mfr.: AD&TMC. *(Playthings, May, 1907)*

The New York Herald had a comic strip by this name. For description of a bisque Fluffy Ruffles see Comics.

AMER-23. *Fluffly Ruffles.* Later version of same doll with inset glass eyes. Mfr.: AD&TMC. *(Playthings, December, 1907)*

AMER-22.

AMER-23.

AMER-24a,b,c,d.

AMER-24a, b, c, and d. Four examples of the Can't Break 'Em line for 1908. AD&TMC. *(Playthings, January, 1908)*

"Can't Break 'Em" DOLLS

AMER-25.

AMER-26.

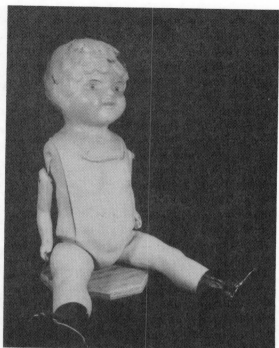

AMER-27.

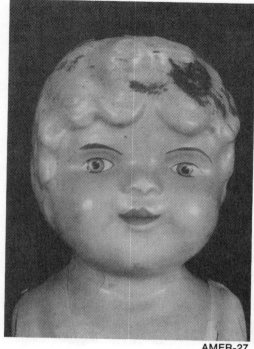

AMER-27.

AMER-28.

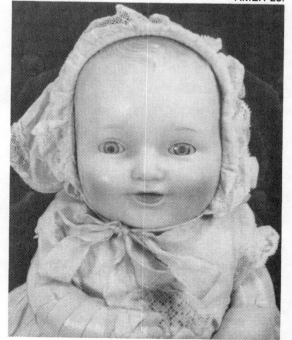

AMER-25. *Toddler.* Mohair wigs; sleep or stationary eyes; full composition and stuffed bodies; real baby faces painted with waterproof natural paints. The line was dressed in Rauser outfits; garments had buttons and buttonholes. Trademark: **MADE/IN/CHICAGO** in diamond. Mfr.: AT&DMC. *(Playthings, August, 1917)*

AMER-26. *Clown.* 25"; molded-painted white head and hair; decal eyes; closed red mouth; red spots on cheeks and eyes; excelsior-stuffed cloth body; original clown suit; ca. 1918. Marks: **AM DOLL.** *(O'Rourke collection)*

AMER-27. *Child.* 23½"; molded hair, evidence of glued-on wig remains; blue decal eyes; closed mouth; all composition, black painted shoes; ca. 1918. Marks: **AM. DOLL CO.** *(Rogers collection)*

AMER-28. *Baby Petite.* 16", 18"; inset green glassine eyes; molded-painted hair; open-closed mouth with two teeth; composition head and limbs with stuffed cloth body; original clothes; ca. 1925. Marks: **PETITE/AMER. CHAR. DOLL CO.** on head. *(Thompson collection)*

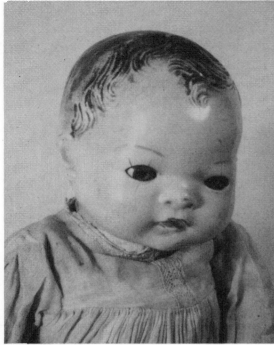

AMER-29.

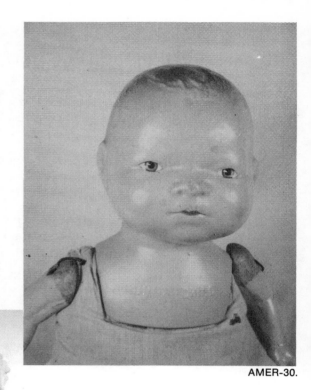

AMER-30.

AMER-32.

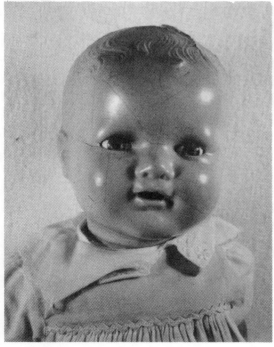

AMER-31.

AMER-31.

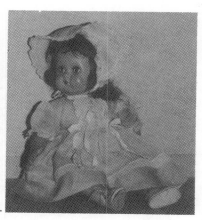

AMER-34.

AMER-33.

AMER-29. *Baby.* 16"; molded-painted brown hair; brown sleep eyes; closed mouth; composition head and gauntlet hands, stuffed cloth body and limbs; original dress; ca. 1925. Marks: **A.M. CHAR. DOLL.** *(Wiseman collection)*

AMER-30. *Honey Child.* 18"; molded-painted hair; painted blue eyes; closed mouth; composition stationary shoulder head and arms, arms jointed with wire; excelsior-stuffed cloth body and legs. Marks: **HONEY CHILD** on front of shoulder head. On another example this mark was found on back of the shoulder head: **1926/AM DOLL Co.** The front had the same mark as doll illustrated. Mfr.: ACDC. *(Edge collection)*

AMER-31. *Sally.* Molded-painted brown hair; tin blue sleep eyes; closed mouth; composition head and limbs, stuffed cloth body; original yellow cotton dress and bonnet; 1927. Unmarked. Cloth tag on clothes reads: **A Lovable Petite Doll/SALLY** with a line drawing of doll. Mfr.: ACDC. *(Wardell collection)*

AMER-32. *Baby.* 22"; molded-painted hair; brown sleep eyes with lashes; open mouth, originally had teeth; composition head, arms and lower legs; stuffed cotton body and upper legs; original dress; ca. 1930. Marks: **AM. CHAR DOLL** on head. *(Vandiver collection)*

AMER-33. *Baby Sue.* 19"; sprayed hair; blue sleep eyes with lashes; closed mouth; hard plastic head, latex magic skin limbs, cotton-stuffed pink cotton body; all original rayon organdy dress and bonnet, original price $9.98; ca. 1948-1950. Original silver paper tag reads: **Baby Sue/Latex Arms and Legs/HEAD OF LONG LIFE PLASTIC/PERFECT DETAIL/LIGHT WEIGHT/DURABLE,** front of tag reads: **AMERICAN CHARACTER** around a picture of little girl holding a doll. *(Causey collection)*

AMER-34. *Baby Sue.* 14"; glued-on wig; sleep eyes; closed rosebud mouth; hard plastic head, soft sticky plastic limbs, stuffed body; original pink organdy dress and bonnet, shoes; cry voice; ca. 1948-1950. Mfr.: ACDC. *(Campbell collection)*

NAMES OF DOLLS

Manufacturers who owned trademarks or copyrights on certain names issued dolls carrying those names time after time through the years, thus creating an atmosphere of tradition. *("Come to the Toy Fair and see "Our Carey" this year!")* When businesses were closed or sold, the trademarks, copyrights, and molds, as valuable property, were sold or leased to other manufacturers. Sometimes a name (or even a mold) was leased out or even just loaned "on a friendly basis". The latter takes place in the modern doll manufacturing world as well.

Thus we find a 1940-ish *Baby Sue,* then later a 1952 doll bearing the same name. Ideal, as an example, has been producing an almost unbroken line of Betsy Wetsy dolls for many years. The style of the line reflects improvements in production methods and materials as well as changes in taste and fashion. The latest *Betsy Wetsy* looks very unlike that pioneer of the same name.

AMER-35.

AMER-36.

AMER-37.

AMER-37.

AMER-36.

AMER-39.

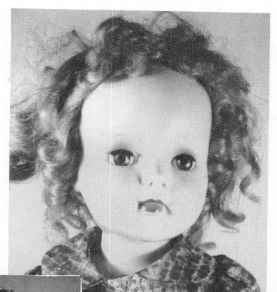

AMER-38.

AMER-40.

AMER-35. *Baby Sue.* 17"; molded hair with glued-on blond Saran wig; blue sleep eyes; open-closed smile with molded-painted teeth and tongue; soft vinyl head, sticky vinyl limbs, stuffed cloth body; all original cotton organdy dress and bonnet with pastel embroidery, real rubber baby pants have disintegrated; cry voice; sold for $10.98; ca. 1952. Marks: **AMER. CHAR. DOLL** on head. *(Author's collection)*

AMER-36. *Chuckles.* 21"; glued-on blonde Saran wig; blue sleep eyes with lashes, open-closed smile with molded-painted teeth and tongue; vinyl head and limbs, stuffed cloth body; cry voice; all original blue corduroy coat and bonnet, rayon dress, pink cotton slip and bloomers, shoes and socks; sold for $14.98. Marks: **AMER. CHAR. DOLL** on head. *(Author's collection)*

AMER-37. *Chuckles.* 18"; rooted blonde Saran hair; blue sleep eyes with hair lashes; open-closed smile with molded-painted tongue and teeth; soft vinyl head, stuffed non-sticky vinyl limbs, stuffed cloth body; cry voice; original white sheer dress and apron with blue embroidery; pink slip and panties trimmed with white lace, shoes and socks; original wrist tag; ca. 1952. Marks: **AMER. CHAR. DOLL** on head. *(Lynn collection)*

AMER-38. *Walker.* 24"; blond wig; blue sleep eyes; closed mouth; all hard plastic walker; ca. 1950. Marks: **AM. CHAR.** on head. *(Courtesy Camelot)*

AMER-39. *Girl.* 15"; blonde synthetic wig; blue sleep eyes; closed mouth; all hard plastic jointed at neck, shoulders and hips; ca. 1954. Marks: **A.C.** *(Griffin collection)*

AMER-40. *Walker.* 20"; brown replacement wig; blue sleep eyes; closed mouth; hard plastic walker body; ca. 1954. Marks: **A.C.** *(Mason collection)*

AMER-41.

AMER-41.

AMER-42.

AMER-43.

AMER-43.

AMER-41. *Sweet Sue.* 21"; glued-on blond Saran braids, extra chignon; blue sleep eyes; closed mouth; hard plastic walker body, head turns when walks; original pink satin overskirt, taffeta underskirt with net trim, flower and lace trim, pink satin shoes, pink knit socks; ca. 1954. Marks: **A.C.** on head. *(Author's collection)*

In 1954, a *Sweet Sue* girl in sizes 15, 18, 22, and 25" was dressed as *Annie Oakley.*

AMER-42. *Toni.* 20"; rooted Saran wig; blue sleep eyes with lashes; closed mouth; all vinyl fully jointed with swivel waist, hi-heel feet; all original clothes with wardrobe, earrings; ca. 1955. Marks: **AMERICAN/©/CHARACTER** in circle, original box marked **TONI.** *(Swift collection)*

AMER-43. *Chuckles.* Rooted Saran hair; blue sleep eyes with lashes; open-closed mouth with molded-painted tongue; all vinyl with jointed head, arms and legs; all original clothes; ca. 1958. Unmarked, original paper tag in shape of a rattle reads: **CHUCKLES.**

AMER-44. *Sweet Sue Walker.* 23"; rooted Saran hair; blue sleep eyes with rose highlights and lashes; closed mouth; plastic head, body and legs, soft vinyl arms, jointed at neck, shoulders, elbows, hips, and knees; original rose peach dotted organdy dress with taffeta underclothes; *"she bends knees and elbows, sits, kneels to pray, clasps her hands, walks"*; ca. 1955. Marks: **AMER. CHAR. DOLL** on head. *(Author's collection)*

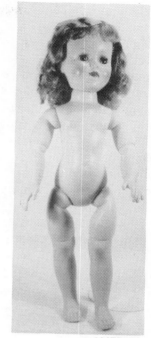

AMER-44.

AMER-44.

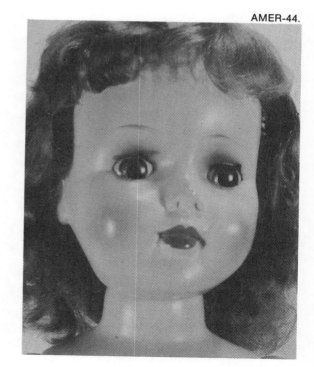

AMER-44.

AMER-45.

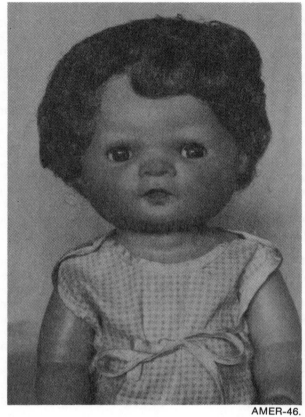

AMER-46.

AMER-48.

AMER-47.

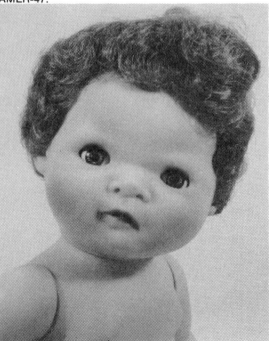

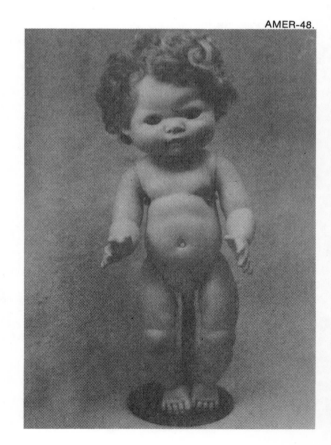

AMER-50.

AMER-45. *Girl.* 10"; dark brown rooted hair; blue sleep eyes; closed mouth; all hard plastic fully jointed, hi-heel feet; ca. 1958. Marks: **AMER. CHAR. DOLL CORP/©/1958** in circle on head, **AMERICAN/©/ CHARACTER** in circle on back. *(Courtesy Camelot)*

AMER-46. *Baby Toodles.* 14"; rooted hair; blue sleep eyes; closed mouth; all vinyl fully jointed; pink and white checked sunsuit. Marks: **AMERICAN CHARACTER DOLL, 1958** © on back of head. *(T. Hoskins collection)*

AMER-47. *Infant Toodles.* 16"; rooted Saran hair; blue sleep eyes; closed mouth; all vinyl fully jointed; cry voice; original pink pleated nylon dress and bonnet. Marks: **AMERICAN CHARACTER DOLL CORP./© 1958.** *(Author's collection)*

AMER-48. *Infant Toodles.* Undressed to show body construction. See above for description and marks. *(Bailey collection)*

TOODLE-LOO

This doll was introduced in 1961 and was carried in the Sears Christmas catalog that year listed as a 21" doll. Three photographed by the author all measured 18" long. Such catalog discrepancies may account for some of the puzzles doll collectors continually try to solve.

Toodle-Loo was designed to represent a three to four-month-old baby; *Butterball* was a six to eight-month-old. They were described as being made of a soft foam plastic called *"Magic Foam"*. This material is completely unlike the latest "foam" material such as that used for Mattel's *Baby Tender Love.*

AMER-49.

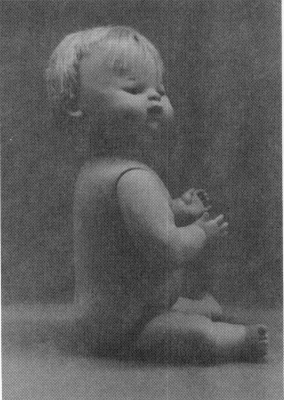

AMER-49. *Toodle-Loo.* 18"; rooted blond synthetic hair; painted brown eyes; closed mouth; fully jointed *"Magic Foam"* plastic body. Marks: **AMERICAN DOLL & TOY CO. 1961.** *(Perry collection)*

AMER-50. *"The New Tiny Tears".* 20"; rooted Saran hair; sleep eyes; drink-and-wet mouth; fully jointed vinyl body, same head as used for *Toodle-Loo;* cotton knit pants, sweater, cap, diaper, booties, bottle, pacifier and bubble pipe; waves "bye" when tummy is squeezed, blows bubbles when right arm is raised, comes in plastic car seat; sold as the *"New Tiny Tears"* in 1962. *(Courtesy Sears, Roebuck and Co.)*

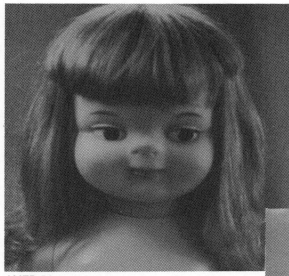

AMER-51.

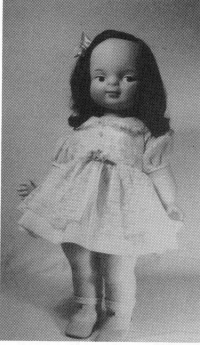

AMER-52.

AMER-53.

AMER-51.

CHUCKLES

These dolls are usually found with the front hair pulled back or standing upright. In restyling it may be helpful to know the original hair-do on most dolls was a side-parted, over-the-brow arrangement. This Chuckles is considered an important addition to a vinyl collection since she is quite unusual in appearance and construction.

AMER-51. *Chuckles.* 23"; rooted blonde Saran; painted brown eyes with molded lids and lashes; closed mouth; all vinyl, jointed at neck, shoulders, elastic strung legs. Marks: **AMER. DOLL & TOY CO./1961/©** in circle on head.

AMER-52. *Chuckles.* 23"; dark brown rooted Saran hair; original tag reads: *"Bright, new, pert Chuckles, the little girl doll with a different look."* See above for description and marks. *(Siehl collection)*

AMER-53. *Chuckles.* Also came with rooted red hair, painted blue eyes; original blue and white striped dress, pink and white cotton dress and bandana, white cotton capri pajamas or fruit-printed pinafore and bandana as shown. *(1961 Speigal Catalog)*

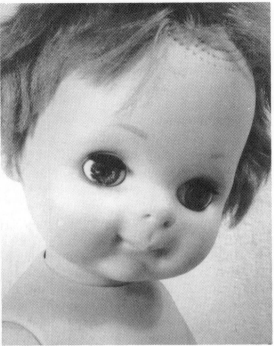

AMER-54.

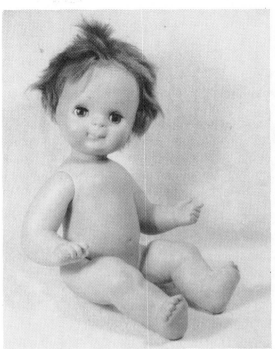

AMER-54.

AMER-55.

BUTTERBALL

Here is an example of a head being used on more than one doll. At first glance the two dolls shown may appear to be identical. There are, however, a number of differences in size, body style, and wigging. Look at the hands and feet of each doll. Molds are expensive; economically it is often necessary to use a head in many ways. This is even more the case with body parts.

AMER-54. *Butterball.* 19½"; rooted synthetic hair; blue sleep eyes; closed mouth with upper lip over lower lip; fully jointed vinyl body, note fat modeling. Marks: ©/1961/**AMERICAN DOLL & TOY CORP** in circle on head. *(Weeks collection)*

AMER-55. *Butterball.* 22"; rooted brown hair; blue sleep eyes; body is cloth over molded foam, battery operated voice says: *"I love Daddy," "I love Mommy", "So sleepy!"* and *"Baby so big";* zipper opening over molded cavity which holds batteries; vinyl head, arms and legs. Marks: **AMER. DOLL CO.** on head. *(Shutts collection)*

AMER-56.

AMER-59.

AMER-57.

THE WHIMSIES

Novelty dolls have a history dating back nearly as far as dolls can be traced. Continuing the tradition of such classics as Billiken etal, the Whimsies with their somewhat smirky smiles seem to romp along unruffled by the cares of life. A partial listing of the characterizations follows:

Polly the Lolly	Tillie the Talker
Miss Take	Bessie the Bashful Bride
Zack the Sack	Raggie
Simon (graduate)	Susie the Snoozie
Dixie the Pixie	Zero (football player)
Fanny (angel)	Lena the Cleaner
Hedda Get Bedda	Monk or Friar
(ref. TCD, p.305)	Girl Devil
Strong Man	The Tiny Whimsies
Wheeler the Dealer	

Dolls are 21"; one-piece stuffed vinyl body with molded head; molded-painted eyes; closed smile; assorted wigs and costume styles to suit characterization. Marks: **WHIMSIE/AMER. DOLL & TOY CO.** on head.

AMER-60a.

AMER-60b.

AMER-60c.

AMER-58a,b.

AMER-61.

AMER-56. *Monk or Friar. (Perry collection)*

AMER-57. *Wheeler the Dealer.* 1961 Montgomery Ward catalog illustration.

AMER-58a, b. *Polly the Lolly* and *Tillie the Talker.* 1961 Montgomery Ward catalog illustration.

AMER-59. *Lena the Cleaner.* Original tag reads *"Lena the Cleaner's frisky and bright, She looks pretty good for a gal that cleans day and night". (Perry collection)*

AMER-60a, b, and c. Illustrations from American Character brochures packed with dolls in 1960 and 1961.

AMER-61. *Tiny Whimsies.* 6"; assorted hair and clothes styles; painted eyes; closed smile; all vinyl; includes: *Pixie, Swinger, Granny, Minnie Mod, Jump'N, and Go-Go;* ca. 1961. Marks: **Made in HONG KONG** on head, **Whimsies/American Character, Inc.** on box. *(N. Ricklefs collection)*

AMER-62.

AMER-64.

AMER-64.

AMER-63.

AMER-65.

AMER-66.

AMER-67.

AMER-62. *Popi.* 10"; molded hair with three extra molded vinyl wigs; painted brown eyes; closed mouth; hard plastic, jointed arms and legs, body comes apart in three sections for easy dressing; ca. 1962. *(N. Ricklefs collection)*

AMER-63. *Girl.* 14"; rooted synthetic hair with growing hair feature; blue sleep eyes; closed mouth; fully jointed vinyl and plastic, button in stomach to make hair grow. Marks: **AM. CHAR. 63©** on head. *(Swift collection)*

AMER-64. *Baby Sue.* 17"; rooted Saran hair; blue sleep eyes; closed mouth; fully jointed vinyl body; original aqua cotton dress, bonnet and panties. Marks: **AMER. CHAR. DOLL/19©63** on head, original paper wrist tag. *(Author's collection)*

AMER-65. *Toddler.* 18"; rooted blonde hair; blue sleep eyes; closed mouth; soft head and arms, hard plastic body and legs, fully jointed; battery operated voice. Marks: **AMER. CHAR. DOLL/19©63** on head. *(Wardell collection)*

AMER-66. *Cricket, Tressy's Little Sister.* 9"; rooted blonde and growing hair; painted eyes; closed mouth; fully jointed vinyl with bendable legs; yellow dress; ca. 1965. *(Courtesy Spiegal Catalog)*

AMER-67. *Girl.* 13"; rooted blonde hair; painted brown eyes; open-closed mouth; vinyl head and arms, hard plastic body and legs, fully jointed; lower her arm and her mouth pouts. Marks: **AMER. CHAR. INC/19©66.** *(Wardell collection)*

Glamorous Pos'n Tressy

I have hair that grows, legs that pose, and a make-up face! Press a button to lengthen my hair, turn a key to shorten it. Apply my cosmetics (sold below) and wipe them off . . . over and over. I'm 11½ inches tall; jointed vinyl. I'm wearing a shift and high heels. Wire stand included.
35 J 3040. (12 oz.)......2.94

5 TRESSY OUTFITS
Swinging Sensation, Fireside Romance, Serendipity, Coffee Break and Polka Dots and Moonbeams (all shown). Dolls not included.
(2 lbs. 8 oz.)
35 J 3869....Set 5.98

AMER-67-1. *Glamourous Pos'n Tressy.* See illustration for complete description. Mfr: American Character, Inc. *(1966 Spiegels catalog illustration)*

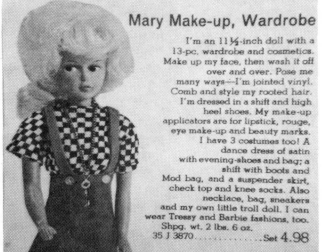

Mary Make-up, Wardrobe

I'm an 11½-inch doll with a
13-pc. wardrobe and cosmetics.
Make up my face, then wash it off
over and over. Pose me
many ways—I'm jointed vinyl.
Comb and style my rooted hair.
I'm dressed in a shift and high
heel shoes. My make-up
applicators are for lipstick, rouge,
eye make-up and beauty marks.
I have 3 costumes too! A
dance dress of satin
with evening-shoes and bag; a
shift with boots and
Mod bag, and a suspender skirt,
check top and knee socks. Also
necklace, bag, sneakers
and my own little troll doll. I can
wear Tressy and Barbie fashions, too.
Shpg. wt. 2 lbs. 6 oz.
35 J 3870 . . . . Set 4.98

AMER-67-2.

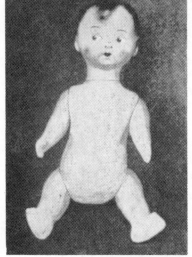

AMER-68.

AMER-69.

AMER-67-2. *Mary Make-up.* See illustration for complete description. Mfr: American Character, Inc. *(1966
Spiegels catalog illustration)*

AMERICAN GLUELESS DOLL CO.

AMER-68. *Character Baby.* 12", 14", 16", 18"; with or
without wig; painted side-glancing eyes; painted
mouth; socket joints, no elastic, *"No glue in head,
won't shrink. Guaranteed not to crack or peel. Can be
washed in hot water."* Mfr.: American Glueless Doll
Co., Brooklyn, NY. *(Playthings, January, 1918)*

AMERICAN OCARINA & TOY CO.

AMER-69. *"American Beauty".* 16", 17", 18", 19"; with
or without curly wigs and moving eyes; fully jointed
composition; daintily dressed; thirty different styles.
Mfr.: American Ocarina & Toy Co. *(Playthings,
August, 1919)*

AMER-71.

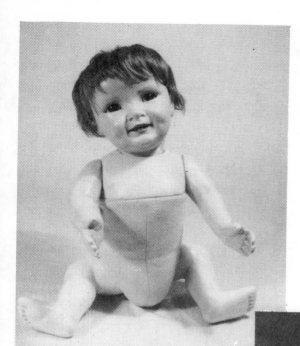

AMER-70.

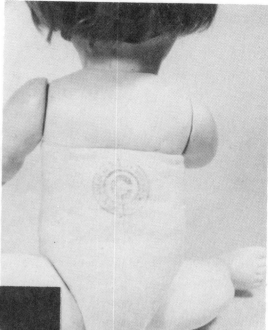

AMER-70.

AMER-70.

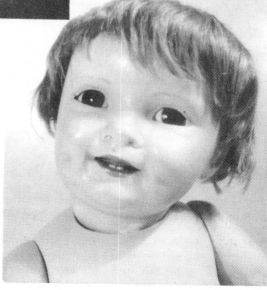

AMER-70.

AMER-70. *American Beauty.* 16''; mohair wig; stationery brown glass eyes; open mouth with tongue and two lower teeth; all composition, jointed at neck, shoulders and hips, body is covered with very soft padded covering. Marks: **AMERICAN BEAUTY DOLL/C** in a circle stamped on back. America Ocarina & Toy Co. *(Author's collection)*

AMERICAN PRODUCED STUFFED TOY CO.

AMER-71. *Kutie Kids.* 14½''; painted features; all composition jointed at shoulders only; girls dressed in sporting costumes of silk with fur trim or in silk *maline* and ribbons at $15.00 per dozen; boys dressed in knitted silk sweaters and caps at $14.00 per dozen. Mfr.: American Produced Stuffed Toy Co., New York. *(Playthings, October, 1918)*

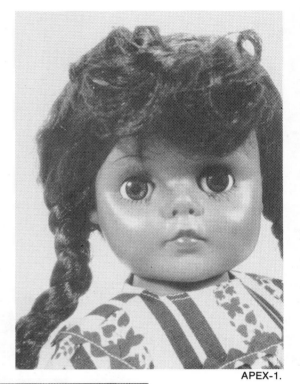

AMER-72a,b.

APEX-1.

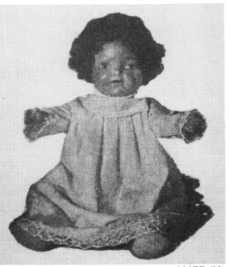

AMER-73.

ARC-1b.

ARC-1a.

AMER-72a, b. *Two girl dolls of 1918.* With or without wigs; painted eyes; painted mouth; composition head and hands, stuffed body and limbs; assorted styles of clothing; price 50ᶜ to $2.00. *(Playthings, April, 1918)*

AMER-73. *Baby.* Glued-on wig; painted eyes; closed mouth; composition head and hands, stuffed body and limbs; price 50ᶜ to $1.00. Mfr.: American Toy & Novelty Co., New York. *(Playthings, June, 1917)*

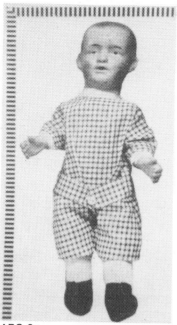

ARC-2a.

ARC-2b.

ARC-2.

APEX

APEX-1. *Negro Girl.* 22"; glued-on Saran wig; brown sleep eyes with lashes; closed mouth; brown stuffed vinyl, cry voice in head. Marks: **APEX** on head, **A** on lower back.

ARCADE TOY MFG. CO.

ARC-1a, b. *Boy and Girl.* Molded-painted hair; painted eyes; painted open mouth with teeth; composition heads and gauntlet hands, stuffed body and limbs; thirty styles price 25¢ to $1.00. Mfr.: Arcade Toy Mfg. Co., New York. (*Playthings, August, 1913*)

ARCY TOY MFG. CO.

ARC-2. *Composition girl doll head.* Arcy Toy Mfg. Co., New York. (*Playthings, 1915*)

ARC-2a, b. *Daddy Long Legs Girl and Boy.* Various sizes; painted features; composition head and hands, stuffed body and limbs. Mfr.: Arcy Toy Mfg. Co., New York. (*Playthings, January, 1915*)

ARMAND MARSEILLE

Dolls from this maker date back to the 1890s, although it is generally believed the firm is older. The factory, located in Koppelsdorf, Thur, was in the doll-making region of Germany and its output was as varied as that of nearly any other. Babies, toddlers, ladies, boys, characters, and nationally costumed dolls are all available to the collector today.

According to *The Toy Trader,* April, 1939, "*There are more than one hundred and fifty numbers in six size ranges, embracing hard bodies, soft bodies, dressed new born babies, and art dolls . . . this wonderful collection of 'Our Pet' series of dolls.*"

It is likely that most of the dolls described as being in the *'Our Pet'* series were not so marked. A photograph of more than forty 'numbers' in the line does indicate, however, that it included dolls such as that shown as **AM-26** and **AM-23** *(Just Me).*

AM-21.

AM-21.

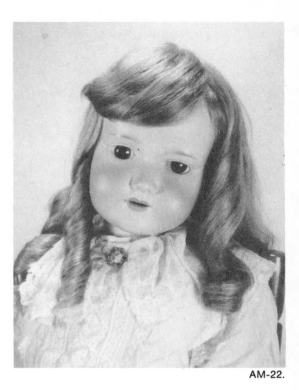

AM-22.

AM-21. *Our Pet.* 10"; replacement wig; blue sleep eyes; open mouth with two teeth; bisque head, fully jointed composition body and limbs; original red and white checked outfit and playpen with excelsior-stuffed mattress; from 1925. Marks: **TRADEMARK/A OUR PET M/REGISTERED/GERMANY/992/4/0,** tag on playpen reads: **MADE IN GERMANY/"OUR PET"/Registered/SECO** in pointed oval. *(Author's collection)*

AM-22. *Girl.* 42"; replacement wig; stationary brown glass eyes; open mouth, teeth; bisque head, ball-jointed wood and composition body; possibly original dress. Marks: **A.18M. / Germany.** See color plate 8-B. *(Author's collection)*

AM-23. *Just Me.* 7½"; original blonde mohair wig; sleep eyes; painted mouth; bisque head, elastic-strung composition, jointed at shoulders and hips; original white organdy dress and underclothes. Marks: **JUST ME/Registered/Germany/A 310/11/OM.** A 10" version of this doll is marked: **JUST ME/Registered/Germany/A 310/7/OM.** *(Meekins collection)*

AM-24. *Little Girl.* 14½"; replacement wig; blue glass sleep eyes; open mouth with four teeth; bisque head, papier mache body; original red cotton sateen lawn dress and hat with white lace trim; guaze pantaloons, red knit socks, new shoes. Marks: **Armand Marseille/300/A. 2/0 x M** on head. *(Author's collection)*

AM-23.

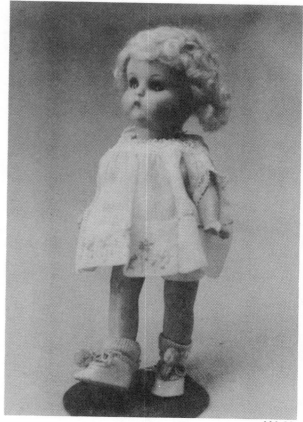

AM-23.

AM-24.

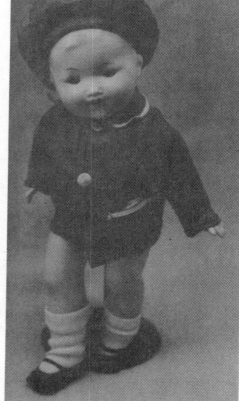

AM-25.

AM-26.

AM-25. *Negro Head.* 2½"; stationary brown glass eyes; red lips with four teeth; ca. 1894. Marks: **AM. 410/MADE IN GERMANY.** *(Parker collection)*

AM-26. *Boy.* 13½"; molded-painted light brown hair; blue glass eyes; open mouth with two teeth; all composition fully jointed; possibly original clothes. Marks: **A.M./Germany/352./1½ K.** *(Bailey collection)*

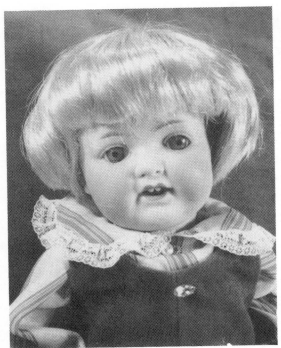

AM-27.

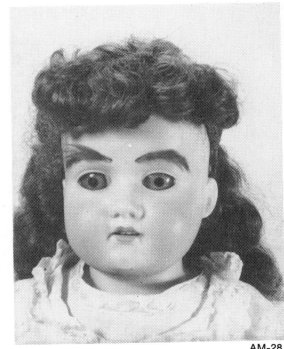

AM-28.

Fig-AM-28a.

AM-29.

AM-27. *Toddler.* 15"; new blonde wig; blue stationary glass eyes; open mouth two teeth; pierced nostrils; bisque head, composition body and limbs. Marks: **Armand Marseille/Germany/996/A/M.** *(Hutchinson collection)*

AM-28. *Miss Millionaire.* 23"; stationary blue glass eyes, fur eyebrows; open mouth four teeth; bisque head, kid body and limbs, universal hip joints, gussett knees and elbows. Marks: **AM/370** on head. Body: see fig. -28a. *(Hutchinson collection)*

AM-29. *Girl.* 27"; glass flirty sleep eyes; open mouth with two teeth and tongue; composition body and limbs. Marks: **Armand Marseille/Germany/990/A 14 M** on head. *(Griffin collection)*

AM-32.

AM-31.

AM-31.

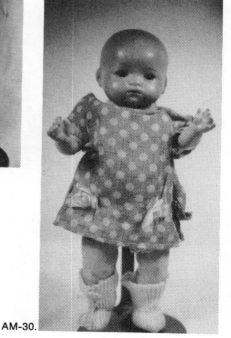

AM-30.

AM-30. *Dream Baby.* 8"; sprayed hair; stationary blue glass eyes; closed mouth; crude papier mache body and limbs; original clothes. Marks: **A.M./Germany/ 341/6/O.K.** on head. *(Courtesy June Sloan Antiques)*

AM-31. *Girl.* 16½"; replacement wig; grey glass eyes; open mouth four teeth; kid body and limbs, gusset knees; blue velvet dress, cotton underwear, black shoes. Marks: **Germany/DRGM. 201013/A 2/0 M** on head. *(Phillips collection)*

AM-32. *Lady.* 19"; replacement wig; blue stationary glass eyes; open mouth four teeth; bisque shoulder head and arms, kid body and limbs. Marks: **3200/AMO½DEP** on head. *(Hafner collection)*

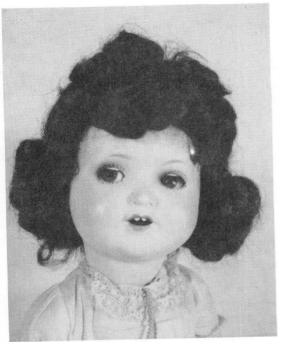

AM-33.

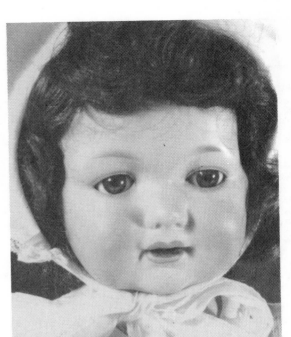

AM-34.

AM-33. *Girl.* 17"; flirty blue glass eyes; open mouth two teeth; bisque head; original white lawn dress; cry voice. Marks: **AM./966/3** on head. *(Shelton collection)*

AM-34. *Toddler.* 22"; new brown wig; blue glass sleep eyes; open mouth; bisque head, composition body and bent limbs. Marks: **G-327B/Germany/A 12-M.** *(Hutchinson collection)*

R&B-13.

ARRANBEE (R&B) DOLL COMPANY

This company, dating back to 1922, was purchased by Vogue Dolls, Inc. in 1958 and production was discontinued in 1960. Dolls with the marks **ARRANBEE, R&B,** or **R&B**-in-an-oval are now considered good collector's items.

R&B-13. *Bottletot.* 13"; molded-painted hair; blue sleep eyes; open mouth; all composition with celluloid with swiveled right hand; all original clothes and bottle. Unmarked doll, bottle is marked: **ARRANBEE/PAT. AUG. 10, 26.** *(Wiseman collection)*

Another Bottletot is listed on p. 71 (TCD, AMER-3-1) as an American Character doll since the catalog description indicates it to be *"a Petite Baby".* Petite was an American Character trademark for many years.

R&B-14.

R&B-15.

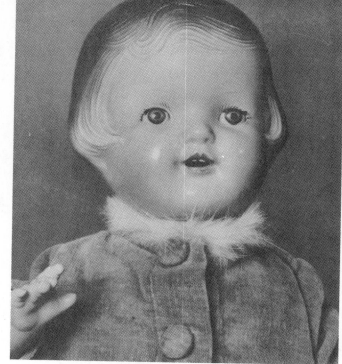

R&B-14.

Fig-R&B-14.

R&B ARRANBEE DOLLS NANCY'S WARDROBE ALL WOOD TRUNK

R&B-14. *Kewty.* 14"; molded-painted red-brown hair; blue tin sleep eyes; open mouth two teeth; all composition fully jointed; original clothes, five extra sets, trunk; ca. 1925-1930. Marks: **KEWTY** on shoulders, trunk marked: **"ARRANBEE'S NANCY"/NANCY'S WARDROBE,"** paper label in trunk reads: **R&B/ARRANBEE DOLLS/NANCY'S WARDROBE/ ALL WOOD TRUNK** in diamond. *(Hahn collection)*

R&B-15. *Dutch Boy.* 9"; molded-painted hair; painted eyes; closed mouth; all composition; original blue felt pants and hat, print shirt, red scarf and real wooden shoes; 1930s. *(Author's collection)*

THE NANCY STORY

Nancy is a name that recurs in the Arranbee history with regularity. R&B-6 (TCD, p. 92) shows a 12" Nancy which was patented March 17, 1930. A similar doll is R&B-14 shown here. This doll, however, is marked **KEWTY,** which serves to point up not only the multiple use of names but also the marketing of identical or similar dolls under different names.

Notice the difference in appearance created by different wigs. For example R&B-17, with curly blonde wig, is a real *Shirley Temple* double while the remaining Nancy dolls shown resemble the child star only slightly or not at all.

Body construction of the Nancy dolls of this period are identical to the Shirley Temple design, illustrating the "pirating" practices as common in the toy industry as in other areas of business. The Shirley Temple dimples are absent from the Nancy faces, however.

Nancy, of course, was only one of the dolls marketed to so closely resemble Shirley Temple as to confuse customers (ref, R&B-16a). Nancy is occasionally found in a Negro version. Another Shirley Temple look-alike is the Weiboldt *"Movie Queen"* which may be related to this.

R&B-16a,b.

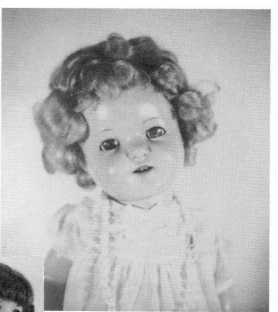

R&B-17.

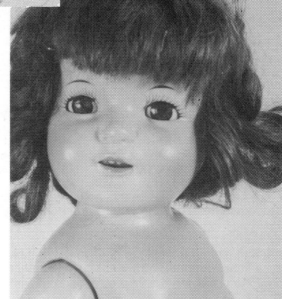

R&B-18.

R&B-18.

R&B-16a. *Nancy.* 17"; mohair wig; brown sleep eyes; open mouth with four teeth; fully jointed compsoition; original pink organdy dress, shoes, and socks. Marks: **NANCY** on head. *(McLaughlin collection)*

Doll was purchased in the 1940's as a gift for a niece by an aunt who thought it was a Shirley Temple. When the doll was recently contributed by the niece to the aunt's doll collection the true identity of the doll was discovered.

R&B-16b. *Shirley Temple.* 18"; blond mohair wig; brown eyes; open mouth six teeth; fully jointed composition; original clothes. Marks: **SHIRLEY TEMPLE/Cop. IDEAL/CO.** in arch on head, **SHIRLEY TEMPLE/18** in arch on shoulder, dress label reads: **Genuine/Shirley Temple/Doll/Registered Patent Off./Ideal Nov. Toy Co.** in square with **MADE IN U.S.A.** along right edge. *(McLaughlin collection)*

R&B-19.

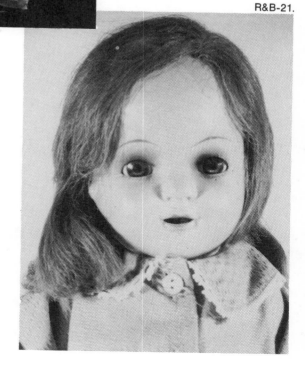

R&B-20.

R&B-21.

R&B-22a,b.

R&B-17. *Nancy.* 19"; all original dress. *(Busch collection)*

R&B-18. *Nancy.* 19"; original brown human hair wig; all original clothes. *(Author's collection)*

R&B-19. *Nancy.* 19"; completely original. *(Hafner collection)*

R&B-20. *Nancy.* 17"; original mohair wig. *(Wiseman collection)*

R&B-21. *Nancy.* 17"; original human hair wig. *(Wiseman collection)*

R&B-22a, b. *Nancy as Southern Belle.* 12", 17"; small doll has blonde mohair wig and blue sleep eyes; larger doll has tosca wig and brown sleep eyes; open mouths with four teeth; all composition jointed at necks, shoulders and hips; all original clothes; ca. 1940. Marks: Small doll has **13** on back; large doll is unmarked. Original tags read: **NANCY/R&B QUALITY/DOLL.** *(Sheinwald collection)*

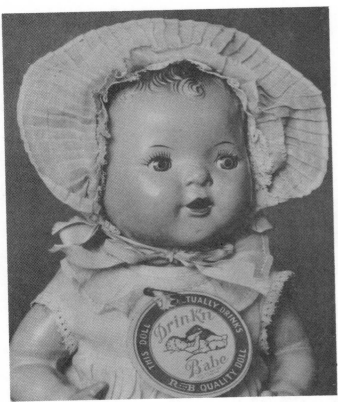

R&B-23.

R&B-23.

R&B-23-1.

R&B-23-1.

R&B-23-1.

R&B-23. *Drink'n Babe.* 14"; molded-painted curly brown hair; blue tin sleep eyes with painted and hair lashes; open mouth with felt tongue; all composition jointed at neck, shoulders and hips; completely original clothes plus an extra outfit; original trunk, nursing bottle, clothes pins, small milk bottle, bar of soap which reads: **SUNRUCO** on one side and **SOAP** on the other; ca. 1940. Marks: **DREAM BABY** on head and shoulders, original paper tag (see illustration) shows **PAT. U.S. PAT OFF/NO.1746568,** label in box reads: **DRINK'N BABE/THE DOLL THAT DRINKS LIKE MAGIC/AN R&B PRODUCT.** *(Hahn collection)*

R&B-23-1. *Nancy Lee.* 14"; glued-on blonde wig; blue sleep eyes; closed mouth; fully jointed hard plastic; original red and white checked taffeta dress, shoes and socks; ca. 1947. Marks: **R & B** on head, original box reads: **R&B/QUALITY/DOLL** (in circle)/**NANCY LEE.** *(Author's collection)*

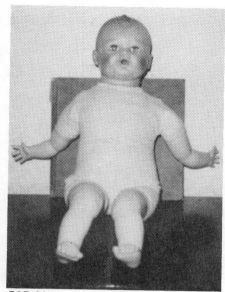

R&B-24.

R&B-25.

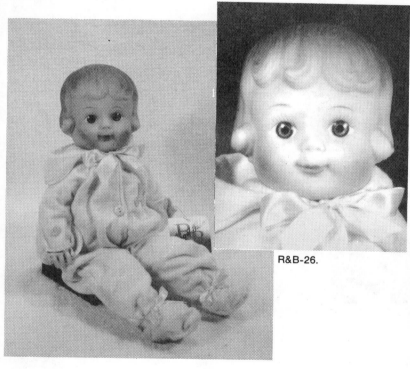

R&B-26.

R&B-25.

R&B-24. *Baby.* 22"; molded-painted hair; blue sleep eyes; molded synthetic rubber head and limbs, stuffed cloth body; cry voice; ca. 1947. Marks: **R & B** on head. *(Ackerman collection)*

R&B-25. *Little Angel.* 21"; molded-painted hair; blue sleep eyes with lashes; closed mouth; hard plastic head, soft vinyl limbs and stuffed pink cotton body; all original dress and bonnet, blue cotton slip; ca. 1947-1952. Marks: **R&B** on head, blue and gold paper tag reads: **LITTLE ANGEL/AN/R&B** (in circle)/**QUALITY DOLL.** *(Author's collection)*

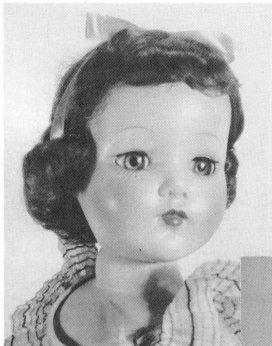

R&B-27.

R&B-27.

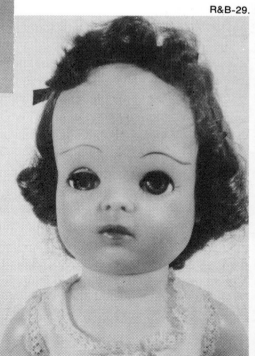

R&B-28.

R&B-29.

R&B-29.

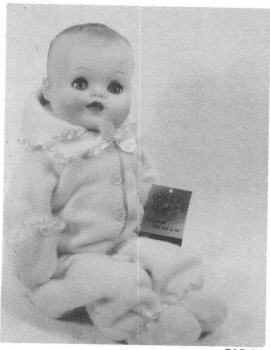

R&B-31.

R&B-26. *Angel Skin.* 13"; molded-painted hair; inset stationary blue eyes; closed mouth; stuffed soft vinyl head, stuffed magic skin body and limbs; all original in box; original price $2.98. Marks: **R&B** on head, original tag reads: **THE R&B FAMILY/Rock-Me, Nanette/Little Angel, Angel Face/Littlest Angel, Dream Baby/Baby Bunting, Angel Skin/Taffy,** box is marked 1954 (doll was advertised as early as 1947). *(Author's collection)*

R&B-27. *Nanette.* 21"; glued-on Saran wig; blue sleep eyes; closed mouth; fully jointed hard plastic; all original aqua embossed cotton dress; has walking mechanism; note resemblence to Nanette of 1954. Marks: **R&B** on head, **210** on shoulders, box is marked 1953. *(Author's collection)*

R&B-28. *Nancy Lee.* 15"; replaced wig; blue sleep eyes with very distinctive brows; closed mouth; fully jointed vinyl; ca. 1952. Marks: **ARRANBEE** on head. *(Wardell collection)*

R&B-29. *Nancy Lee.* 15"; glued-on Saran wig; blue sleep eyes with distinctive brows; closed mouth; stuffed vinyl head and limbs, unstuffed body, very heavy doll; in original box, came with hair curlers; original tag; ca. 1952. Marks: **ARRANBEE** on head. *(Author's collection)*

R&B-30. *Little Angel.* 16"; molded-painted hair; blue sleep eyes open-closed mouth; hard plastic head, soft stuffed vinyl limbs, pink cotton cloth body; original dress, shoes and socks. Marks: **R&B** on head. *(Author's collection)*

R&B-31. *Baby Bunting.* 15"; molded-painted hair; blue sleep eyes; open-closed mouth; vinylite plastic head, stuffed magic skin body and limbs; all original pink fleece bunting. Marks: **17BBS/R&B/D6** on head, box marked 1954, original tag reads: **Head is of Vinylite™ Plastic by Bakelite Company.** *(Author's collection)*

R&B-30.

R&B-32.

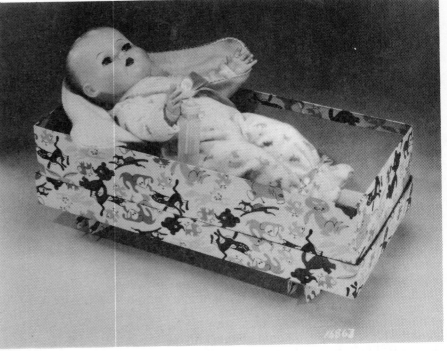

R&B-34.

R&B-35.

R&B-33.

R&B-37.

R&B-36. *Littlest Angel.* 11"; trademarked 6-29-54, registered 5-31-56 "The Surprise Doll, A Littlest Angel Doll." Littlest Angel was also available in a suitcase with wardrobe. Marks: **R&B 9.** (*Courtesy Vogue Dolls, Inc.*)

R&B-36-1. *Littlest Angel.* These dolls came in assorted suitcase wardrobe sets. (*Courtesy Vogue Dolls, Inc.*)

R&B-37. *Angel.* 17", 21"; rooted side-parted bobbed hair; sleep eyes; rosebud mouth; all fully jointed vinyl; clothes of assorted nylons and cottons; ca. 1956. (*Courtesy Vogue Dolls, Inc.*)

R&B-36-1.

R&B-36.

R&B-32. *Taffy.* 23"; rooted dark brown Saran hair; blue sleep eyes; closed mouth; hard plastic walker body, stuffed vinyl head; all original clothes; doll walks, sits, stands and turns head; ca. 1954. Marks: **R&B** on head, (*Author's collection*)

R&B-33. *Nanette.* 21"; rooted Saran hair; blue eyes; closed mouth; stuffed vinyl head, hard plastic walker body; all original red dress and hat, blue coat with fur trim, red buttons and shoulder bag; ca. 1954. Note resemblance to some Alexander dolls. Marks: **23ARV/R&B** on head, **210** on back, original tag reads: **The ARRANBEE Family-the most beautiful dolls in the world: Nanette, Nancy, Nancy Jane, Nancy Lee, Angel Face, Dream Baby, Little Angel, Angel Skin, Boy Doll,** in a box marked **Taffy.** Possibly different sizes had different names but were the same doll. (*Author's collection*)

R&B-34. *Sweet Pea.* All vinyl, ca. 1954. (*Courtesy Vogue Dolls, Inc.*)

R&B-35. *Little Dear.* 8"; rooted hair; blue sleep eyes; open-closed mouth; stuffed vinyl bodies; all original clothes; ca. 1956. (*Courtesy Vogue Dolls, Inc.*)

R&B-38.

R&B-39.

R&B-40.

R&B-41.

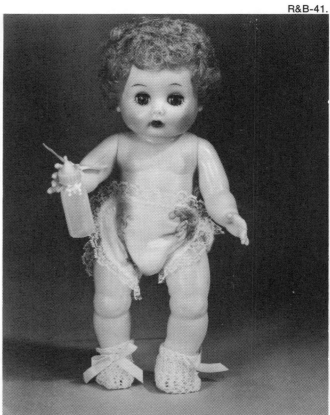

R&B-42.

R&B-43.

R&B-44.

R&B-38. *My Angel Walking Doll.* 36"; rooted long hair; sleep eyes; rosebud mouth; fully jointed polyethelene vinyl; assorted costumes; ca. 1956. Vogue later issued this doll as *Ginny* starting in 1960. They offered a 36" *Walking Ginny* carrying an 8" *Ginny* dressed in identical outfits which sold for $25.00 wholesale. *(Courtesy Vogue Dolls, Inc.)*

R&B-39. *Angel Face.* 16", 20", 25", 28"; poodle curled hair; sleep eyes; drink and wet mouth with tongue; polyethelene vinyl body; assorted costumes; ca. 1956. *(Courtesy Vogue Dolls, Inc.)*

R&B-40. *Angel Baby.* 16", 20"; molded-painted hair; sleep eyes; drink-and-wet mouth; fully jointed vinyl; pink taffeta pram suit or Christening dress with pink coat or blanket; ca. 1956. *(Courtesy Vogue Dolls, Inc.)*

R&B-41. *Sweet Angel.* 12"; rooted tosca, blonde, or dark poodle hair; sleep eyes; drink-and-wet mouth; fully jointed soft vinyl; assorted costumes; ca. 1956. *(Courtesy Vogue Dolls, Inc.)*

R&B-42. *My Angel.* With curly wig. See R&B-43 for description. *(Courtesy Vogue Dolls, Inc.)*

R&B-43. *My Angel.* 17", 26"; rooted Dutch bob on 17" doll, dark brown side part on 26" doll; sleep eyes; all vinyl toddler body; assorted nylon and cotton clothes; ca. 1957. *(Courtesy Vogue Dolls, Inc.)*

R&B-44. *Littlest Angel.* 11"; rooted blonde hair; blue sleep eyes, molded lashes; open-closed mouth; ball-jointed hard plastic; original white nylon dress flocked with red hearts, natural straw hat with flowers; 1954. Marks: **R&B / 9.** *(S. Ricklefs collection)*

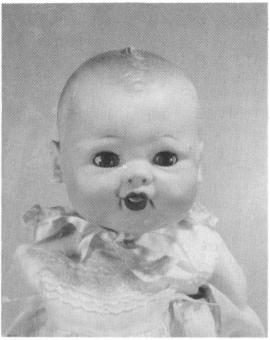

ARR-1.

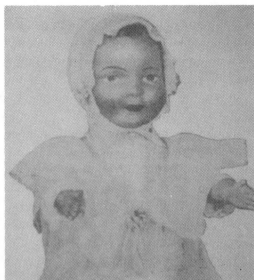

ART-1.

Patent applied for
AVRL-8a.

AVRL-8-1.

ARROW RUBBER

ARR-1. *Crying Baby.* 16"; molded-painted hair; blue sleep eyes; open-closed mouth with tongue; stuffed vinyl with squeeker; original white dress, bonnet, and pink booties. Marks: **ARROW RUBBER.** *(Author's collection)*

ART DOLL AND TOY CO. INC.

ART-1. *Nevvabrake Baby.* Molded-painted features; composition head and hands "with a 'Bisclike' finish"; "The composition form is owned by us exclusively," "wearproof and like the imported." Mfr.: Art Doll and Toy Co. Inc. *(Playthings, June, 1916)*

AVERILL MANUFACTURING COMPANY

Paul Averill Manufacturing Company, Averill Manufacturing Company, Georgene Novelties, or Madame Georgene Dolls - all a husband and wife team effort in dollmaking. From the variety shown here the collector can begin to comprehend the extent of the output of this manufacturer. Averill dolls indeed bridge the gap from bisque to vinyl - even though that vinyl may be a trifle tacky after nearly thirty years.

AVRL-8a-i. *Character Dolls.* From the pages of Playthings 1915-1916, these characters give a representation of the lines for those years. (See next page for remaining illustrations.)

AVRL-8-1. Madame Georgene Hendren Averill at the time her costumed characters were being introduced. *(Playthings, April, 1917)*

AVRL-8b.

"MADAME HENDREN"

AVRL-8c.

AVRL-8d.

AVRL-8e.

AVRL-8f.

AVRL-8g.

AVRL-8h.

AVRL-8i.

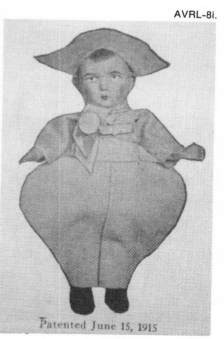

Patented June 15, 1915

AVRL-10a,b.

AVRL-12.

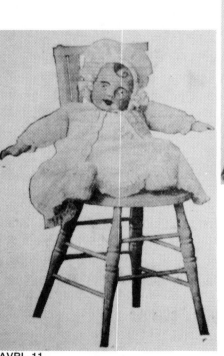

AVRL-11.

AVRL-9a,b,c.

AVRL-9a, b, c. *Indians.* -9a. 16", unmarked. -9b. 19", marks: **AM©CO.** on shoulder plate. -9c. 14", unmarked. These three, purchased as a set, are dressed in tan felt with colored tops. Brown composition hands and arms, brown cloth bodies and legs. All have tags reading: **MADAME HENDREN/MAY 9, 1916 PAT.** *(Sheinwald collection)*

AVRL-10a, b. *Papooses.* 7", 11"; these dolls are unmarked but match description of **AVRL-9a, b, c.** *(Sheinwald collection)*

AVRL-11. *"Life-like" Baby.* Three sizes; with or without wigs; sleep eyes; open-closed mouth; "real bisc heads", probably composition, patented voice exclusive with these dolls; with or without clothes; Patented June 18, 1918, Patent No. 1,269,363. *(Playthings, January, 1918)*

AVRL-12. *Dutch Character Girl.* Composition. *"Dressed in new and novel costumes created by Mme. Georgene Averill (formerly Madame Hendren)."* Mfr.: Paul Averill Inc. *(Playthings, February, 1920)*

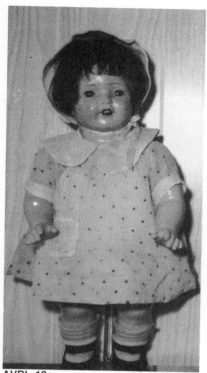

AVRL-14.

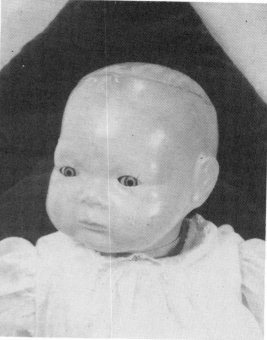

AVRL-15.

AVRL-13.

AVRL-16.

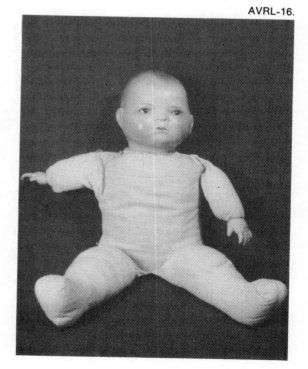

AVRL-13. *Girl.* 16"; original mohair wig; metal sleep eyes; open smile with four upper teeth; composition head and limbs, stuffed cloth body; all original white dress with blue polka dots, panties and slip combination, shoes and socks; ca. 1920. Marks: **"GENUINE MADAME/HENDREN DOLL"** on shoulders. *(Cannon collection)*

AVRL-14. *Baby Booful.* Four styles; wigs; stationary or sleep eyes; "feather-light" composition baby bodies, fully jointed or straight leg models. *(Playthings, January, 1920)*

AVRL-15. *Bye-lo Type.* 17"; Tin eyes; closed mouth; composition head and gauntlet hands, cloth body and limbs; ca. 1925. Marks: **A.M.C.Co.** on head, **GENUINE/MADAME HENDREN/DOLL/318/MADE IN U.S.A.** stamped on body. *(Henson collection)*

AVRL-16. *Bye-lo Baby.* 14"; painted hair; blue glass sleep eyes; closed mouth; paint over bisque head, stuffed cloth straight leg body, celluloid hands with the turtle-in-a-diamond trademark, cry voice; ca. 1925. Head has never been off the doll so is definitely original to this body. Marks: **Copr. by/Grace S. Putnam/MADE IN GERMANY** on head, **GENUINE/MADAME HENDREN/DOLL.614 (or 514)/MADE IN U.S.A.** stamped on body. *(Author's collection)*

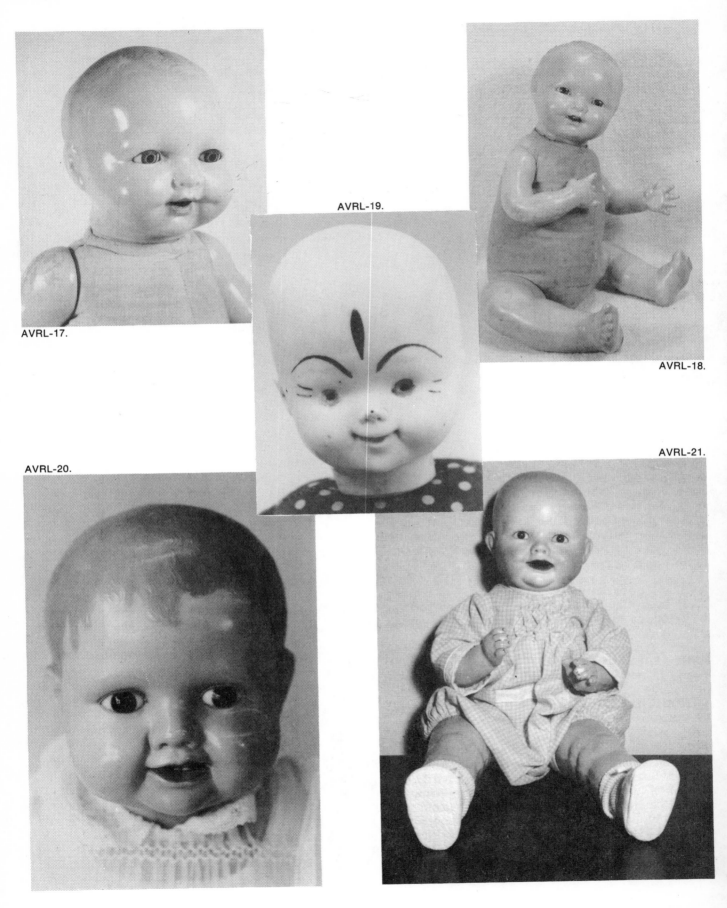

AVRL-17.

AVRL-19.

AVRL-18.

AVRL-20.

AVRL-21.

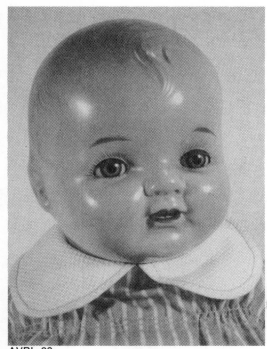

AVRL-22.

AVRL-24.

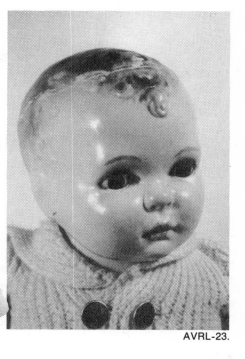

AVRL-23.

AVRL-17. *Baby.* 21"; molded-painted blonde; gray sleep eyes; open mouth; composition head and arms, stuffed cloth body and legs; ca. 1925. Marks: **MADAME HENDREN/DOLL** on head. *(Wiseman collection)*

AVRL-18. *Baby.* 18"; molded-painted, blue tin sleep eyes, no lashes; open mouth with two teeth; composition head and limbs, stuffed cloth body; cry box; ca. 1920s. Marks: **MADAME HENDREN/DOLL** on head. *(Author's collection)*

AVRL-19. *Clown.* 14"; originally had inset eyes; open-closed smile; stuffed red and white cloth body and black shoes; once wore hat; undated. Marks: **GEORGENE** incised on head. *(Perry collection)*

AVRL-20. *Bonnie Babe.* 16½"; molded-painted hair; brown stationary glass eyes; open-closed smile with two teeth; celluloid head, stuffed cloth body and limbs which can be positioned; ca. 1926. Marks: **BONNIE BABE/Reg. U.S. PAT OFF/Copyright by/Georgene Averill/Germany 34 (turtle mark).** *(Ortwein collection)*

AVRL-21. *Bonnie Babe.* Glass eyes; open mouth; bisque head, composition toddler body; owner's last childhood doll received for Christmas, 1926. Marks: **GEORGENE AVERILL / 7065 / 3652 / GERMANY**

on head. *(Cannon collection, photograph by the owner's son)*

AVRL-22. *Baby Hendren.* 19"; molded-painted hair; blue tin decal sleep eyes; open mouth with two teeth; composition swivel head and limbs, cotton stuffed body; cry voice; ca. 1930. Marks: **BABY HENDREN** on head. *(Young collection)*

AVRL-23. *Baby.* 23"; molded-painted hair; brown tin sleep eyes with lashes; closed mouth; composition head and gauntlet hands, hard-stuffed cloth body and limbs with stitched hip joints; ca. 1930. Marks: **©/A.M. Co., GENUINE/"MADAME HENDRON"/ DOLL/424/MADE IN U.S.A.** on body. *(Stewart collection)*

AVRL-24-27. *Rag Dolls.* 13" except -25 is 10"; all cloth; yarn hair; painted mask faces; all have original costumes except -25; these were produced during the 1930s and early 1940s. Marks: -25 and -27 are unmarked; -24 and -26 have tag reading: **A/GENUINE/(script) GEORGENE/DOLL/A Product of Georgene Novelties Inc./New York/Made in U.S.A.** (-25, *Mason collection*) (-27 *Young collection*)

AVRL-25.

AVRL-26.

AVRL-27.

AVRL-29.

AVRL-28.

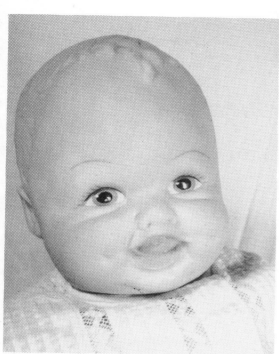

AVRL-30.

AVRL-31.

AVRL-28. *Baby Georgene.* 23"; curly blonde mohair wig; blue sleep eyes; closed mouth; composition head and limbs, cloth body; original shoes; ca. 1935. Marks: **BABY/GEORGENE** on head. *(Wiseman collection)*

AVRL-29. *Girl.* 20"; replacement wig; tin sleep eyes; open mouth; composition shoulder head and limbs, cloth body, voice box; replacement clothes, original clothes were rose crepe sleeveless dress with yellow taffeta coat and bonnet with pleated brim; ca. 1937. Unmarked. Tag reads: **Madame Hendren/Walking and Talking Doll** on front, **Swastika** emblem on back of tag. *(Sheinwald collection)*

AVRL-30. *Baby.* 26"; molded hair; painted blue eyes; open-closed mouth; sticky plastic head and gauntlet hands, cotton-stuffed cloth body and limbs; ca. 1945. Marks: **©/AVERILL** on head. *(Siehl collection)*

AVRL-31. *Georgene Doll.* 18"; yellow yarn hair; painted eyes with black button centers; painted mouth, oil cloth-type face, stuffed cloth body and limbs; red flounced skirt, bonnet, blue ribbons; ca. 1964. Marks: **"KIRGET"** on tag on clothes, paper tag reads: **AMERICA'S/BEST LOVED DOLLS/ARE MADE BY/"GEORGENE"/PENN. REG. NO15,** other side reads: **A "GEORGENE"/DOLL/Georgene Novelties, Inc./New York, N.Y./MADE IN U.S.A.,** label on box reads: **MADE BY/GEORGENE NOVELTIES, INC./NEW YORK CITY/MADE IN U.S.A., A/** (script) **GEORGENE/PRODUCTS** in plaque, **NO 5634/Color Red/GEORGENE DOLLS.** *(Kittman collection)*

BAB-1.

B

BABS MFG. CORP.

BAB-1. *Babs the Walking Doll.* 28"; "doll walks, dances, goes down stairs, etc. by means of a lateral sway and with the use of springs, elastics or other resilient means at the hips and knees which features are owned exclusively by this company." U.S. PAT NO. 1221970, 4-10-17. Mfr.: "Babs" Manufacturing Corp., Philadelphia. *(Playthings, 1917)*

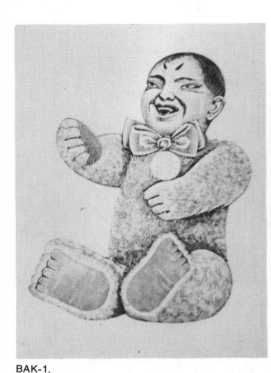

BAK-1.

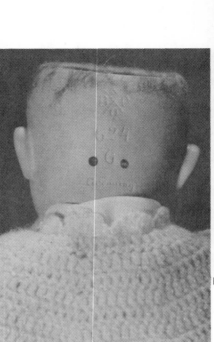

BAHR-1.

fig-BAHR-1.

BAW-1.

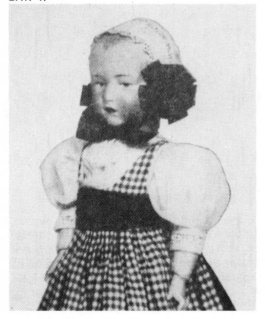

BAK-1. *Killiblues.* Stuffed body and limbs, composition head; registration applied for; sold for $1.00 retail. This is part of the *Billikin* craze. Each doll of this type had its own little good luck verse. Mfr.: Baker and Bennet Sales, Mfg., New York. *(Playthings, September, 1909)*

> *Here's some News:*   *Amidst the din*
> *I'm Kill-i-Blues!*   *Of hurried life*
> *That Color flies*   *I'll show you Glee!*
> *If at your knees*   *On land and sea*
> *I linger still.*   *My all is yours—*
> *So take me in*   *Depend on me.*
>   *—Killiblues.*

BAW-1. *Imported Doll.* Painted features, closed mouth, composition ball-jointed body; distributed by Bawo & Dotter. *(Playthings, March, 1910)*

BAHR-1. *Baby.* 15"; old human hair wig; blue sleep eyes; open mouth with two teeth; bent-limb composition body and head. Mfr.: Bahr Proschild. Marks: **B*P** (crossed swords) **0/624/G/Germany** on head. *(Hutchinson collection)*

BED DOLLS

These very popular dolls of the 1920s and 1930s are gaining in importance with the passing of years. They represent a unique approach to life, mirroring as they do an era which came to be known as *The Roaring Twenties.*

BED-2.

BED-1.

Several unusual Bed Dolls have come to the attention of the author. In addition, the Flapper classification has been included in this listing since the division is often obscure. For this reason dolls such as BED-1 have been included although obviously not suited to display on a bed.

These dolls were also known as Boudoir Dolls and there was much competition between the imported and American-made items.

An interesting feature of some is the hands. While most are rather simply done, the author has seen bed dolls with long, perfectly molded celluloid hands and others with exquisitely fashioned composition hands. One doll had composition hands of which the right hand had three fingers turned in with the forefinger and thumb arranged as though pointing.

BED-1. *Flapper-in-a-Swing.* 14"; molded-painted red-blonde hair; painted brown eyes; closed mouth; two-piece composition body, ball-jointed at waist, lower body and legs are one, upper body and head are one; jointed at shoulders; original silk and gauze dress with silk roses, painted shoes; 1920s. Marks: None in view; doll is sewn into dress which has never been removed. *(Author's collection)*

BED-2. *Baby Bed Doll.* 20"; glued-on blonde mohair wig; painted features; composition swivel head and arms, cloth body and legs; all original rabbit-fur-trimmed white satin dress. Note: This is not simply a cut-down adult doll but rather a very unusual *baby* face and body bed doll. Unmarked.

BED-3. *Bed Doll Mask Face.* 6"; painted pressed cloth. To illustrate how a mask face is made; note the buckram edge which will be turned back and carefully stitched down before the wig is applied. Marks: **7001 Patent Pending Wm. Glukin & Co., Inc., N.Y.C.** *(Courtesy Camelot)*

BED-3.

BED-4.

BED-5.

BED-5.

BED-6a.

BED-4. *Lady.* 28"; floss hair; painted features; stuffed cloth, face is stiffened cloth, head swivels; 1920s.

BED-5. *"Miss Paris".* 22"; blonde silk floss curls; painted blue eyes with highlights of red, green and white; painted mouth; stuffed stockinette body and head, plaster composition arms and legs; red, white, and blue faille dress with screen-printed pictures and captions of historic landmarks in Paris; ca. 1920s. Marks: Red, white and blue ribbon reads: **"Miss Paris"** and **"Souvenir de Paris"** in script. *(Author's collection)*

BED-6 a, b. *Two Bed Dolls.* 6a. Boudoir Doll. 27", mohair wig; composition head and limbs; multicolored dress and hat. 6b. V for Victory Doll. 30", long lashes; white wig; composition head and limbs. (1936 Hagn's Catalog)

BED-7. *Lady Bed Doll.* 27"; brown mohair wig; painted blue eyes; cloth body, composition head; original outfit; an unusually *bosomy* example. *(Courtesy Camelot)*

BED-7.

BED-8.

BED-6b.

BED-9.

BED-10.

BED-8. *Cigarette Smoker.* 29"; platinum mohair wig; painted side-glance eyes; painted mouth, open to hold cigarette; composition head, elongated stuffed turquoise sateen body and limbs; 1920s. Unmarked. This one always reminds me of my good friend, doll author, Jo Elizabeth Gerken. *(Author's collection)*

BED-9. *Cigarette Smoker.* 27"; mohair wig; painted blue eyes; painted red mouth; stuffed flesh-colored felt body, black cloth legs; brown velvet pants and coat lined in orange silk, lace camisole and pantaloons; black patent high-heeled shoes. Unmarked, possibly a Lenci creation. *(Henson collection)*

BED-10. *A Late Bed Doll.* 25"; rooted synthetic hair; inset stationary blue eyes with brows and lashes; closed mouth; brittle plastic shoulder head and limbs, stuffed cloth body, straight legs; all original white satin dress and hat with cheesecloth slip. Unmarked. *(Vandiver collection)*

BIJ-1a.

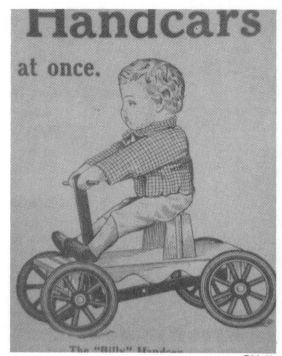

BIJ-1b.

BELL-1.

BELL-2.

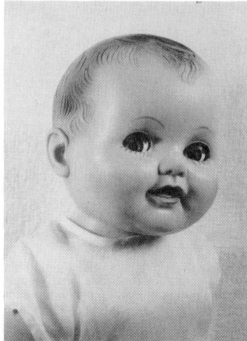

BEST-1.

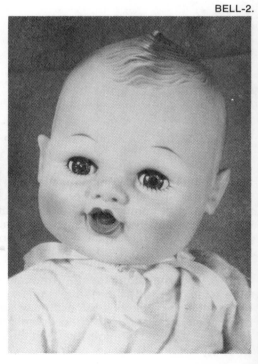

BELL-1. *Belle.* 18"; molded-painted hair; flirty blue sleep eyes, lashes; open-closed mouth; stuffed soft vinyl head, on replacement body; should have a magic skin body; ca. 1950s. Marks: **BELLE** on head. *(Author's collection)*

BELL-2. *Baby.* 19"; molded-painted hair; blue sleep eyes; open-closed mouth, tongue; fully jointed all vinyl; original white nightie, pink blanket and original box; 1950s. Unmarked. Mfr.: Belle Doll and Toy Corp., Brooklyn, NY. *(Mason collection)*

BEST-1. *The Bester Doll.* Six sizes, 16"-26"; molded and human hair wigs; inset eyes with or without lashes; open-closed mouth with teeth; fully ball-jointed body, extremely light weight; distributed by Morimura Brothers. Mfr.: Bester Doll (Mfg.) Co., Bloomfield, NJ. *(Playthings, December, 1918)*

BIJ-1a, b. *Jitney and Billy with Handcars.* Molded-painted hair; composition heads; stuffed cloth bodies and limbs; various costumes; doll 'operates' car when in motion. Mfr.: Bijou Doll Co., NY. *(Playthings, November, 1915)*

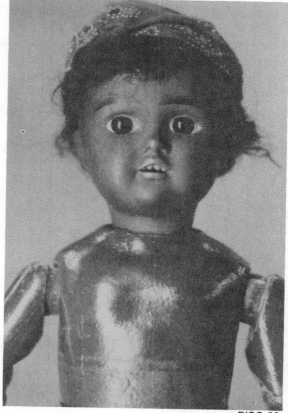

BISQ-30.

BISQUE DOLLS

The term 'bisque doll' usually conjours images of peaches-and-cream complexions, long curled wigs, and ruffled dresses. More and more collectors, however, are giving shelf space to the small nonentities made from the 1920s through the early 1940s. Such bits of porcelain of varying quality, painted to resemble flesh or fashion, are unbelievably varied in design. Although many are shown, it is probable the reader will find at least a few in her own collection which are not illustrated here. It is possible to classify these in loose categories, that is, to group them as to similarities of appearance and construction. Turn to CELLULOID to compare these bisque items with their less expensive brothers and sisters.

BISQ-30. *Negro child.* 11"; original black mohair wig covered with original turban; stationary brown glass eyes; pierced ears; open mouth with four upper teeth; nine-piece painted brown composition body with wooden joint reinforcements, bisque head, stringing attaches to the back of the crown with two clips. Marks: **227/Dep.** on head. *(Meekins collection)*

BISQ-31. *Girl.* 18"; human hair wig; blue sleep eyes; open mouth with five teeth; stick body, pale bisque head. Marks: **2** on head. *(Courtesy Nita's House of Dolls)*

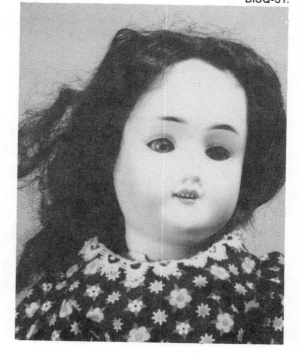

BISQ-31.

BISQ-32.

BISQ-33a.

BISQ-33b.

BISQ-34.

BISQ-32. *Toddler.* 10"; mohair wigs; brown sleep eyes; open mouth with teeth; bisque head, papier mache body and limbs; old, not original clothes. Marks: **Made In Germany/**(crossed banners)**/D. 6/0** on head. *(F. Salvisburg collection)*

BISQ-33a,b. A group of small bisque dolls. All molded-painted, jointed at neck, shoulders and hips; some wear original clothes. *(Courtesy Ralph's Antique Dolls)*

BISQ-34. *World War I Characters.* 4¼"; all molded-painted features; all bisque; molded-painted Aviator and Dough Boy uniforms; ca. 1917. Marks: **Nippon.** *(Ortwein collection)*

CATALOG REPRINTS

The author feels catalog reprints have a certain place in any research project. Since the quantity of tiny bisques alone makes them difficult to handle in a book of this nature, it seems well at this point to show the reader as many dolls as possible in the space available. The following pages have therefore been given over to reproduction of a number of listings from the catalogs of Butler Brothers, Wholesalers of General Merchandise, New York, for 1928 through 1935. These dolls, of course, are not limited to those years since most of them were available (as long as stocks lasted) well into the years of World War II. Other examples may be seen in the COMICS section. Note, the term 'China Dolls' in these old catalogs referred to the type known to collectors as bisque; that is, an unglazed porcelain. Wholesale prices have been included for the entertainment of the reader.

If a doll illustrated here matches except for size, bear in mind space did not permit the inclusion of all sizes in each model whereas the old catalogs listed each size separately.

BISQ-35. *Imported bisques.*

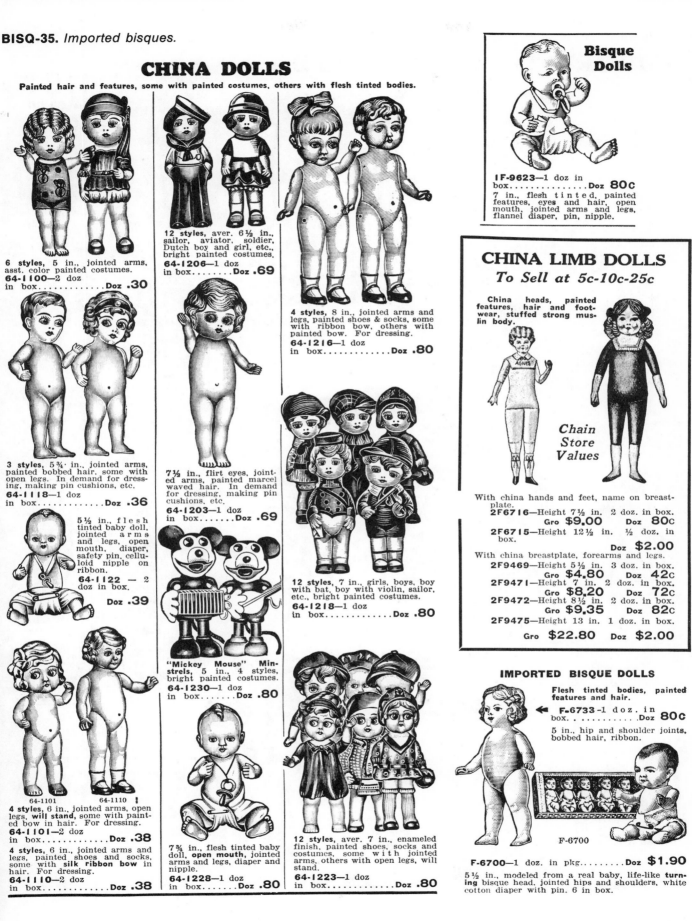

CHINA DOLLS

Painted hair and features, some with painted costumes, others with flesh tinted bodies.

6 styles, 5 in., jointed arms, asst. color painted costumes.
64-1100—2 doz in box.............Doz .30

3 styles, 5¾· in., jointed arms, painted bobbed hair, some with open legs. In demand for dressing, making pin cushions, etc.
64-1118—1 doz in box.............Doz .36

5½ in., flesh tinted baby doll, jointed arms and legs, open mouth, diaper, safety pin, celluloid nipple on ribbon.
64-1122 — 2 doz in box.
Doz .39

4 styles, 6 in., jointed arms, open legs, **will stand**, some with painted bow in hair. For dressing.
64-1101—2 doz in box.............Doz .38

4 styles, 6 in., jointed arms and legs, painted shoes and socks, some with **silk ribbon bow** in hair. For dressing.
64-1110—2 doz in box.............Doz .38

64-1101 64-1110

12 styles, aver. 6½ in., sailor, aviator, soldier, Dutch boy and girl, etc., bright painted costumes.
64-1206—1 doz in box.......Doz .69

7½ in., flirt eyes, jointed arms, painted marcel waved hair. In demand for dressing, making pin cushions, etc.
64-1203—1 doz in box.......Doz .69

"Mickey Mouse" Minstrels, 5 in., 4 styles, bright painted costumes.
64-1230—1 doz in box.......Doz .80

7¾ in., flesh tinted baby doll, **open mouth**, jointed arms and legs, diaper and nipple.
64-1228—1 doz in box.......Doz .80

4 styles, 8 in., jointed arms and legs, painted shoes & socks, some with ribbon bow, others with painted bow. For dressing.
64-1216—1 doz in box.............Doz .80

12 styles, 7 in., girls, boys, boy with bat, boy with violin, sailor, etc., bright painted costumes.
64-1218—1 doz in box.............Doz .80

12 styles, aver. 7 in., enameled finish, painted shoes, socks and costumes, some with jointed arms, others with open legs, will stand.
64-1223—1 doz in box.............Doz .80

Bisque Dolls

1F-9623—1 doz in box..............Doz 80c
7 in., flesh tinted, painted features, eyes and hair, open mouth, jointed arms and legs, flannel diaper, pin, nipple.

CHINA LIMB DOLLS
To Sell at 5c-10c-25c

China heads, painted features, hair and footwear, stuffed strong muslin body.

Chain Store Values

With china hands and feet, name on breastplate.
2F6716—Height 7½ in. 2 doz. in box.
Gro $9.00   Doz 80c
2F6715—Height 12½ in. ½ doz. in box.
Doz $2.00
With china breastplate, forearms and legs.
2F9469—Height 5½ in. 3 doz. in box.
Gro $4.80   Doz 42c
2F9471—Height 7 in. 2 doz. in box.
Gro $8.20   Doz 72c
2F9472—Height 8½ in. 2 doz. in box.
Gro $9.35   Doz 82c
2F9475—Height 13 in. 1 doz. in box.
Gro $22.80   Doz $2.00

IMPORTED BISQUE DOLLS

Flesh tinted bodies, painted features and hair.
← **F-6733**—1 doz. in box. ....Doz 80c
5 in., hip and shoulder joints, bobbed hair, ribbon.

F-6700

F-6700—1 doz. in pkg........Doz $1.90
5½ in., modeled from a real baby, life-like **turning** bisque head, jointed hips and shoulders, white cotton diaper with pin. 6 in box.

BISQ-36. *Imported bisques*

IMPORTED CHINA DOLLS Tinted bodies, painted features and costumes

2F9485—4 in., jointed arms. 2 doz. in box.....**Doz 42c**
Gro $4.80

2F9781—2¼ in. 1 gro. in box.
Gro 55c

2F9648—4½ in., jointed arms and legs. 2 doz. in box.
Doz 32c
Gro $3.60

2F9649—4½ in., jointed arms and legs, mohair wig. 2 doz. in box.
Doz 37c
Gro $4.20

2F9670—3¾ in., jointed arms. 3 doz. in box.
Doz 35c
Gro $4.00

2F9676—3½ in., jointed arms, gilt striped trunks. 2 doz. in box.
Doz 40c
Gro $4.55

2F9674—3½ in. jointed arms, painted bow in hair and dress. 2 doz. in box.
Doz 65c
Gro $6.75

2F9740—3 in., 2 styles silk costumes, jointed arms. Asstd. 2 doz. in box.
Doz 65c
Gro $7.40

2F9489—4¾ in., jointed arms and legs. 1 doz. in box.
Doz 75c
Gro $8.50

2F9643—4¾ in., jointed arms. 1 doz. in box. ..**Doz 78c**
Gro $9.00

2F9813—5¼ in., jointed arms, blue and pink velveteen costumes. 1 doz. in box.
Doz 78c
Gro $9.00

Imported China Doll—5¼ in., jointed arms, flesh color, painted features and hair.
2F9491—1 doz. in box.
Doz 77c
Gro $9.00

2F9650—5½ in., mohair wig, jointed arms and legs, painted shoes and stockings. 1 doz. in box.
Doz 79c
Gro $9.00

2F9494—5⅝ in., jointed arms. 1 doz. in box .....**Doz 80c**
Gro $9.00

2F9672—Dutch boy, 5¼ in., jointed arms, asstd. color costumes, shoes and stockings. 1 doz. in box.
Doz 80c
Gro $9.00

2F9677—5¾ in., jointed arms and legs, painted bathing costume, gilt striped trunks. 1 doz. in box.
Doz 80c
Gro $9.00

Jointed arms and legs, long white flannel slip, in white willow basket.
2F9691—3¾ in. doll, 6 in. basket. 2 doz. in box.
Doz 89c
Gro $10.15
2F9692—4 in. doll, 8 in. basket. 1 doz. in box.
Doz $1.75
Gro $20.00

2F9678—2 styles, 6¼ in., flirt eyes, painted marcel, some with bows, asstd. color painted bathing suit with animal designs, black trim. Asstd. 1 doz. in box.
Doz 80c
3 doz. lots. **Doz 75c**

IMPORTED CHINA DOLLS
Flesh color china bodies, painted features and hair, jointed arms.

2F9656—2 styles (boy, girl), 3½ in., jointed arms. Asstd. 2 doz. in box.
Doz 42c
Gro $4.80

2F9648—4½ in. 2 doz. in box.......**Doz 32c**
Gro $3.60

2F9643—4¾ in. 1 doz. in box.........**Doz 80c**
Gro $9.00

1F-9660—2 doz in box.........**Doz 35c**
2 styles, 5½ in., jointed hips and shoulders, asstd. painted and imitation hair wigs.

F-9647 — 2 doz. in box.
Doz 36c
5 in., jointed arms and legs, painted hair bow, slippers and stockings.

BISQ-37. *Imported bisques.*

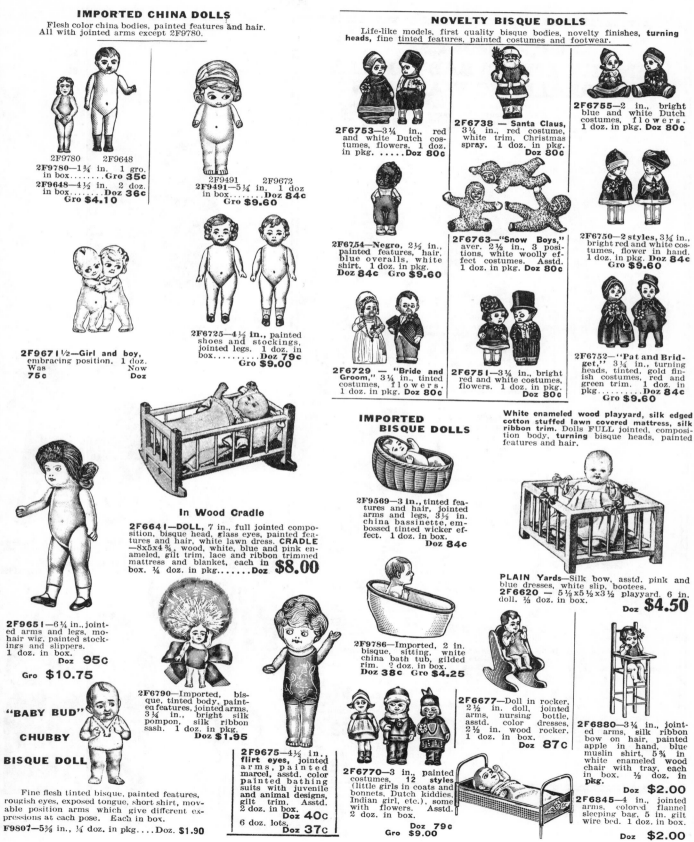

IMPORTED CHINA DOLLS

Flesh color china bodies, painted features and hair. All with jointed arms except 2F9780.

2F9780 2F9648

2F9780—1¾ in. 1 gro. in box........**Gro 35c**

2F9648—4½ in. 2 doz. in box........**Doz 36c** **Gro $4.10**

2F9491 2F9672

2F9491—5¼ in. 1 doz in box........**Doz 84c** **Gro $9.60**

2F9671½—Girl and boy, embracing position. 1 doz. Was **75c** Now Doz

2F6725—4½ in., painted shoes and stockings, jointed legs. 1 doz. in box..........**Doz 79c** **Gro $9.00**

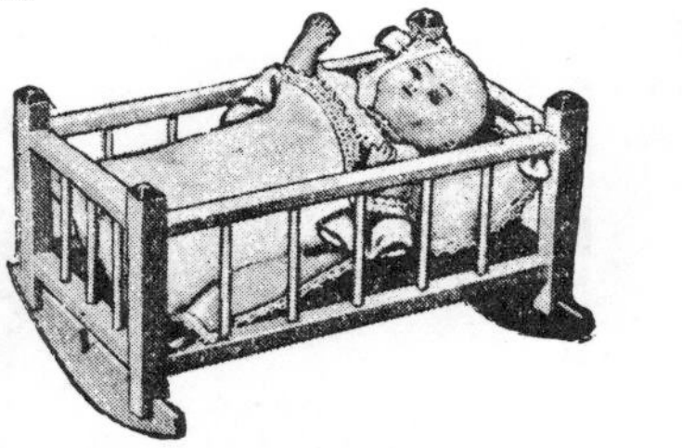

In Wood Cradle

2F6641—DOLL, 7 in., full jointed composition, bisque head, glass eyes, painted features and hair, white lawn dress. **CRADLE**—8x5x4¾, wood, white, blue and pink enameled, gilt trim, lace and ribbon trimmed mattress and blanket, each in box. ¼ doz. in pkg.......**Doz $8.00**

2F9651—6¼ in., jointed arms and legs, mohair wig, painted stockings and slippers. 1 doz. in box. **Doz 95c**

Gro $10.75

"BABY BUD" CHUBBY BISQUE DOLL

Fine flesh tinted bisque, painted features, rougish eyes, exposed tongue, short shirt, movable position arms which give different expressions at each pose. Each in box.

F9807—5⅜ in., ¼ doz. in pkg....Doz. **$1.90**

2F6790—Imported, bisque, tinted body, painted features, jointed arms, 3¼ in., bright silk pompon, silk ribbon sash. 1 doz. in pkg. **Doz $1.95**

2F9675—4½ in., **flirt eyes,** jointed arms, painted **marcel,** asstd. color **painted bathing suits with juvenile and animal designs,** gilt trim. Asstd. 2 doz. in box. **Doz 40c**

6 doz. lots, **Doz 37c**

NOVELTY BISQUE DOLLS

Life-like models, first quality bisque bodies, novelty finishes, **turning heads,** fine tinted features, painted costumes and footwear.

2F6753—3¼ in., red and white Dutch costumes, flowers. 1 doz. in pkg. .....**Doz 80c**

2F6738 — Santa Claus, 3¼ in., red costume, white trim, Christmas spray. 1 doz. in pkg. **Doz 80c**

2F6755—2 in., bright blue and white Dutch costumes, flowers. 1 doz. in pkg. **Doz 80c**

2F6754—Negro, 2½ in., painted features, hair, blue overalls, white shirt. 1 doz. in pkg. **Doz 84c Gro $9.60**

2F6763—"Snow Boys," aver. 2½ in., 3 positions, white woolly effect costumes. Asstd. 1 doz. in pkg. **Doz 80c**

2F6750—2 styles, 3¼ in., bright red and white costumes, flower in hand. 1 doz. in pkg. **Doz 84c** **Gro $9.60**

2F6729 — "Bride and Groom," 3¼ in., tinted costumes, flowers. 1 doz. in pkg. **Doz 80c**

2F6751—3¼ in., bright red and white costumes, flowers. 1 doz. in pkg. **Doz 80c**

2F6752—"Pat and Bridget," 3¼ in., turning heads, tinted, gold finish costumes, red and green trim. 1 doz. in pkg..........**Doz 84c** **Gro $9.60**

IMPORTED BISQUE DOLLS

2F9569—3 in., tinted features and hair, jointed arms and legs, 3½ in. china bassinette, embossed tinted wicker effect. 1 doz. in box. **Doz 84c**

White enameled wood playyard, silk edged cotton stuffed lawn covered mattress, silk ribbon trim. Dolls FULL jointed, composition body, **turning** bisque heads, painted features and hair.

PLAIN Yards—Silk bow, asstd. pink and blue dresses, white slip, bootees.

2F6620 — 5½x5½x3½ playyard. 6 in. doll. ⅓ doz. in box. **Doz $4.50**

2F9786—Imported, 2 in. bisque, sitting, white china bath tub, gilded rim. 2 doz. in box. **Doz 38c Gro $4.25**

2F6677—Doll in rocker, 2½ in. doll, jointed arms, nursing bottle, asstd. color dresses, 2½ in. wood rocker. 1 doz. in box. **Doz 87c**

2F6880—3¼ in., jointed arms, silk ribbon bow on hair, painted apple in hand, blue muslin shirt, 5¾ in white enameled **wood chair with tray, each** in box. ½ doz. in **pkg.** **Doz $2.00**

2F6770—3 in., painted costumes, **12 styles** (little girls in coats and bonnets, Dutch kiddies, Indian girl, etc.), some with flowers. Asstd. 2 doz. in box. **Doz 79c Gro $9.00**

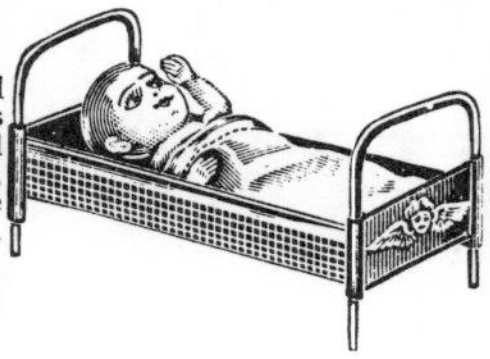

2F6845—4 in., jointed arms, colored flannel sleeping bag, 5 in. gilt wire bed. 1 doz. in box. **Doz $2.00**

BISQ-38. *Imported bisques.*

Very Newest!
"MARY ANNE" BABY DOLLS
IN REALISTIC WALKERS

Something BRAND NEW! Our own creation, and made exclusively for us. Bound to be a sensational success because they have everything that makes for success—child appeal, novelty—and absolutely practical. Imagine the delight of the little girls who see them. It's a shame someone didn't think of this interesting combination years ago.

Dolls are life-like, flesh tinted, TURNING heads, painted features and hair, FULL jointed except 2F6629, asstd. color dresses and rompers. **Walkers**—Realistic, sturdy, asstd. enameled colors, smoothly finished wood.

2F6629   2F6630   2F6631   2F6632

With Bisque Dolls—Painted eyes.

2F6629— 2¾ in. doll, jointed arms, white slip, 1½ in. walker. Asstd. 2 doz. in box.
Doz 85c

2F6630—4 in. doll, full jointed, asstd. pink, blue and white slips, 2⅝ in. walker. asstd. 1 doz. in box.
Doz $2.00

With Composition Body Dolls—Turning bisque heads, moving glass eyes except 2F6631.

2F6631—6¾ in. doll, white slip, diaper, 4¼ in. walker. Asstd. ½ doz. in box. **Doz $4.00**

2F6632—8 in. doll, 3 style dresses, 5¼ in. walker with seat, imitation leather strap, steel rollers, ribbon pull cord. Asstd. ¼ doz. in box. **Doz $8.00**

[WE FURNISH CAPITAL
See Terms
Bottom of
This Page]

2F6634   2F6635

With Composition Body Dolls—Turning bisque heads, **moving glass eyes**, walker with imitation leather strap, steel rollers, ribbon pull cord.

2F6633—8½ in. doll, 3 style dresses, 5¼ in. walker with seat, tray, counting frame with colored beads. Asstd. ¼ doz. in box.
Doz $11.00

2F6634—9¾ in. doll, 3 style dresses, bootees, 5¾ in. walker with seat, ribbon bow trim, each in box. Asstd. ¼ doz. in pkg. **Doz $15.00**

2F6635—12 in. doll, 3 style dresses, bootees, 6¼ in. walker with seat, counting frame with colored beads, ribbon bow trim. 1 in box. **Each $1.75**

2F6636—13½ in. doll, 3 style dresses, bootees, 7¾ in. walker with shaped seat, tray, counting frame with colored beads, ribbon bow trim. 1 in box. **Each $2.25**

2F6637—14¾ in. doll, 3 style dresses, bootees, 8½ in. walker with shaped seat, tray, counting frame with colored beads, ribbon bow trim. 1 in box. **Each $2.75**

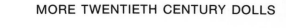

PENNY SOLID CHINA DOLLS

Painted features, blonde and brunette hair.

F9780—1¼ in., white unglazed, for cake favors. 1 gro. in box.
Gro. 50c

F9781 — 2½ in., white body. 1 gro. in box........Gro. 85c

F9780   F9781

6 styles, 7 in., girl with cat, boy with violin, sailor boy, etc., bright painted costumes.
64-1209—1 doz in box.**Doz .78**

12 styles, 6 to 6½ in., roguish eyes, some with painted bows in hair, others with silk ribbon collar, bright painted costumes.
64-1200—1 doz in box..............**Doz .60**

12 styles, aver. 6 in., asstd. boys and girls in bright painted costumes.
64-1124—2 doz in box..............**Doz .39**

6 in., flesh tinted baby doll, jointed arms and legs, open mouth.
64-1212—1 doz in box...............**Doz .75**

12 styles, 8 in., large eyes, some with open legs, bright painted costumes, **all will stand**.
64-1224—1 doz in box.**Doz .80**

BISQ-39. *Imported bisques.*

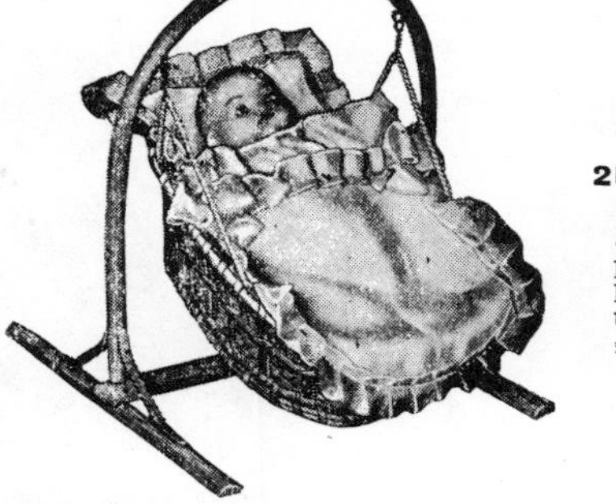

BABY DOLL IN SWING

2F6835—6½ in., true to nature doll, soft stuffed body, bisque baby head, flesh tinted, **sleeping eyes, painted features, press voice,** composition hands, 7½ in. pink lined willow basket, lawn pillow and coverlet, ribbon trimmed, 9 in. wood stand. 1/12 doz. in box....... Doz **$8.00**

DOLLS IN CRIBS

Ribbon trim white enameled wood cribs on metal wheels, cotton stuffed lace trim white lawn covered mattress, CONCEALED VOICE CRIES WHEN DRAWN ALONG FLOOR, ribbon pull string, all dolls with TURNING bisque heads, painted features and hair, MOVING GLASS EYES, composition hands, well stuffed cotton bodies, lace and ribbon trim white lawn dress, white socks.

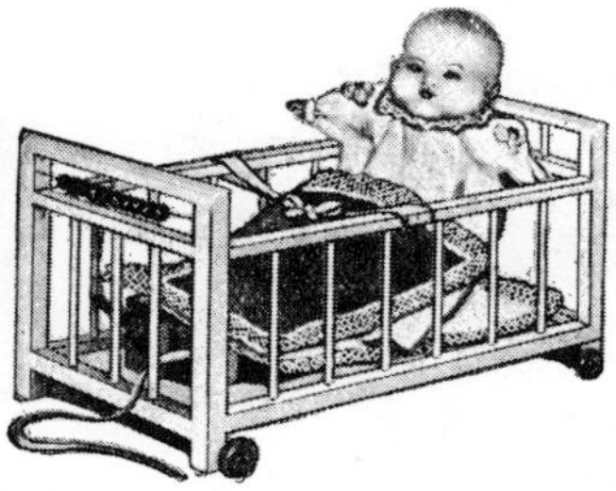

2F6610—8x4¾x4¾ crib, braid trim colored flannelette blanket, 6 in. doll, each in box. ¼ doz. in pkg. .... Doz **$8.00**

2F6611—8¾x5¼x5 crib with counting frame, lace trim colored flannelette blanket, 7 in. doll. 1/12 doz. in box...... Doz **$10.50**

2F6612 — 10¾x5½x5½ crib with counting frame, lace trim colored flannelette blanket, 8½ in. doll. 1/12 doz. in box. Doz **$12.50**

2F6613—12x6½x6 crib with counting frame, lace coverlet and pillow to match, 9 in. doll. 1/12 doz. in box. .... Doz **$18.00**

"LITTLE DARLING" DOLLS

IN HIGH GRADE FANCY BASKETS

Quality merchandise—an excellent gift item

Well made handled round baskets of fancy braid interwoven splint and straw, reinforced edges, hinged top with bamboo fastener, white and pink mull and cotton ribbon crepe lining, braid and ribbon trim, full jointed composition doll, TURNING bisque heads, flesh tinted, MOVING EYES.

2F6846—7 in. doll lace and ribbon trim white lawn dress, diapers, white socks, 7¼ in. basket, lace and ribbon trim flannelette cape with hood attached to cover. 1 in box. Each **$1.90**

WITH WIGS—Attractive dresses with bonnet to match, ribbon bow tie, lace trim underwear, white socks and slippers.

2F6847—9 in. doll, 10¼ in. basket, 2 additional outfits — blue flannelette jacket and bonnet, underwear, socks other lace trim batiste, cap to match, ribbon support on cover. 1 in box. Each **$3.75**

2F6848—11 in. doll, 12 in. basket, additional outfits — 2 flannelette dresses, braid and lace trim, white voile dresses, colored ribbon trim, bonnet to match, 2 sets lace trim white lawn underwear, ribbon support on cover. 1 in box. Each **$6.00**

DOLL IN BASKET CHAIR

With Extra Clothing Outfit

2F6817—11¼ in. wicker basket, lace trim felt effect covered seat, braid trim cotton crepe dress, bonnet to match, white lawn slip, socks and slippers, Red Riding Hood rubber cape and bathing cap, all attached to inside of basket, 8½ in. full jointed composition doll, **turning bisque head with wig,** painted features, **moving eyes,** braid trim rayon bathing suit. 1/12 doz. in box. Doz **$15.00**

BABY DOLL IN FANCY TRIMMED BASKET

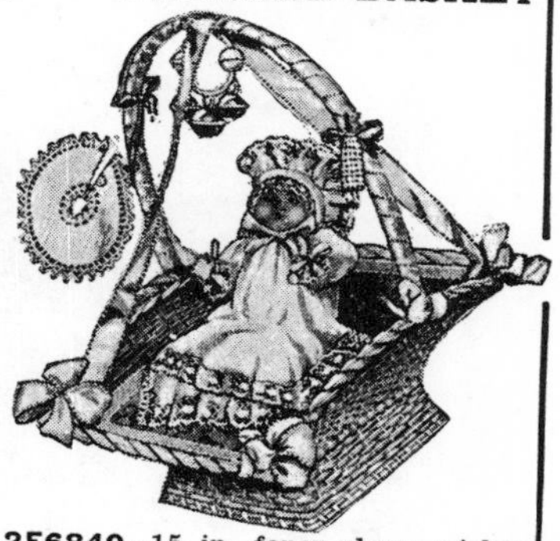

2F6849—15 in. fancy shape wicker basket, flowered lawn lining with ribbon trim, large ribbon wound handle, ribbon streamers and bows, celluloid ring bell rattle, knit covered nursing bottle, pacifier, lace trim flannelette bib collar. 11 in. full jointed composition baby doll, **turning** bisque head, flesh tinted, painted features and hair, **moving eyes, opened mouth showing 2 teeth, fine quality white** voile dress, lace and ribbon trim, bonnet to match, lace trim white lawn slip, flannelette diapers, white socks. 1 in box. Each **$3.90**

"NEWLY BORN" BABY DOLL

Live Baby Modeled

2F6800—8 in., well modeled life-like bisque head, flesh tinted, **sleeping glass eyes, baby voice,** painted features, cotton stuffed **body,** composition hands, ribbon trimmed white lawn dress. ½ doz. in box. Doz **$4.00** Gro **$45.00**

3 styles, 2½ in. jointed doll, 2½ in. cardboard shoofly, rocker and play yard. **64-1300**—2 doz in box........... Doz **.37**

CHARACTER BABIES

TURNING bisque heads, painted features, flesh tinted composition bodies, position limbs, jointed hip and shoulder, lace trim slips with ribbon bows.

2F6410 — 9 in. high, painted hair. ½ doz. in box. Doz **$2.00**

2F6412 — 12 in. high, **moving eyes,** open mouth showing 2 teeth, **mohair wig.** 1/3 doz. in box. Doz **$4.00**

BISQ-40. *Imported bisques.*

BABY DOLLS IN MOVING CARRIAGES

3 Sizes

With Voice

True-to-nature baby doll, flesh tinted bisque head, sleeping glass eyes, painted features and hair, well modeled composition body, white lawn slip, nipple on silk ribbon. In pink braided straw basket with pillow, strong mechanical clock work spring, runs straight while concealed voice cries "mamma." 1/12 doz. in box.

2F6690—8½ in. doll, 9 in. basket .... Doz **$18.00**

BABY DOLLS IN SULKIES

Full jointed composition baby dolls, bisque turning heads, moving eyes, painted features and hair, dresses in asstd. styles and colors, braid and lace trim, white lawn underwear, white bootees, pink, blue and white enameled wood & cardboard sulkies, gilt trim, ribbon safety strap, wood disc wheels, imit. rubber tires, 23 in. jointed wood handle.

2F6616—8 in. doll, sulky 4¾ in. high. 2 in box. Asstd. 1/6 doz. in pkg.
Doz **$8.00**

5c and 10c Sellers!

All Have Painted Features and Hair

6 styles, 3 to 4 in. jointed baby dolls with diapers and safety pins, asstd. nursing bottle, bath tub, rattle, etc. Each set in box.
64-1314—1 doz sets in box...... Doz sets **.80**

3¾ in. jointed doll, 4 in. asstd. color china bassinette, wicker effect, cotton filled, ribbon.
64-1320—1 doz in box....... Doz **.78**

4 in. jointed doll with diaper, 6 in. asstd. color wicker basket, cotton filled.
64-1324—1 doz in box...... Doz **.80**

"NEWLY BORN" SLEEPING BABY DOLLS IN FLOWER DECORATED BASKETS

Made Exclusively for Butler Brothers

True-to-nature, molded from real live babies, flesh tinted bisque heads, SLEEPING glass eyes, painted features and hair, well finished composition bodies on all except 2F6806, white socks. In white willow baskets—all except 2F6806—trimmed with small pink roses, buds and foliage and ribbon bows—lace trimmed pillows.

2F6806—5½ in. doll, baby voice, cotton stuffed body, blue or pink blanket, 8½ in. basket. 1/3 doz in box.
Doz **$4.00**
Gro **$45.00**

2F6810—8½ in. doll, lace trim long white lawn slip, 10¼ in. basket. 1/2 doz. in box.
Doz **$7.80**

2F6811—10¼ in. doll, lace trim long white lawn slip, silk bound pink or blue flannel blanket, 14 in. basket. 1/12 doz. in box.
Doz **$16.00**

Twins
2F6812—Two 8½ in. babies, lace trim long white lawn slips, basket 15 in. 1/12 doz. prs. in box.
Doz prs **$17.25**

2F6813—13 in. doll, long white lawn slip, lace and ribbon rosette trim, ribbon bound pink or blue flannel blanket, 16 in. basket. 1 in box.................Each **$2.25**

2F6814—15 in. doll, long white lawn slip, lace and ribbon rosette trim, ribbon bound pink or blue flannel blanket, 17½ in. basket. 1 in box.......... Each **$3.25**

BABY DOLLS IN PLAY YARD

White enameled wood play yard, silk edged cotton stuffed lawn covered mattress, silk ribbon trim. Dolls FULL jointed, composition body, **turning** bisque heads, painted features and hair.

PLAIN Yards—Play Yard, 5½ x 5½ x 3½ high, silk bow. **Doll**—6 in., asstd. pink and blue dresses, white slip, bootees.
2F6620—1/6 doz. in box.. Doz **$4.00**

WHEELED Yards—Moving eyes, opened mouth showing 2 teeth, lace trim white lawn dress, flannelette diaper, white socks.

2F6621—6¼ x 6¼ x 4¾ play yard, 7¼ in. doll, each in box. ¼ doz. in pkg. .... Doz **$8.00**

2F6622—7¼ x 7¼ x 5½ play yard, 8¼ in. doll, long dress, pacifier on string, metal bell rattle tied with ribbon on arm. 1/12 doz. in box.
Doz **$12.50**

DOLLS IN WICKER CHAIRS

A new line of baby dolls! Another appealing novelty combination sure to sell big. FULL JOINTED composition dolls, TURNING bisque heads, flesh tinted, MOVING GLASS EYES, lace and colored ribbon trim white lawn dresses, diapers, white socks, pacifier on ribbon, in asstd. color wicker chairs with table, ribbon trim, counting frame with colored beads, nursing bottle, celluloid rattle.

2F6605—6 in. doll, 5 in. chair, 3 in. table. 1/12 doz. in box.
Doz **$8.00**

2F6606—6½ in. doll, 5½ in. chair, 3¼ in. table. 1/12 doz. in box.
Doz **$9.50**

BISQ-41. *Imported bisques.*

3¼ In. High!
8 In Box!

It's almost unbelievable that so much merchandise can be offered to retail at 10c! You'll need a good stock of this number!

3¼ In.—No-two-alike in box, bright painted costumes, hair and features, shoes, socks, bow, etc.

64-1241—1 doz boxes in pkg.

Doz boxes .80

6 In Box

Wedding of the Dolls—3½ in., no-two-alike, painted features, hair, costumes, shoes and socks, asst. bride, groom, flower girl and boy, minister and church.

64-1256—1 doz boxes in pkg.........**Doz boxes .82**

Doll With Dog In Box

6½ In. — 2 styles, asst. color dress and slip, painted features and hair, jointed arms and legs, some with silk hair ribbon, china dog on ribbon leash.

64-1254—1 doz boxes in pkg.

Doz boxes .80

Each Pair In Box

3¾ In.—Bright painted, 6 styles, cowboy & girl, Indian & squaw, aviator & girl, sport boy & girl, Dutch boy & girl and Danish boy & girl.

64-1135—1 doz boxes in pkg.

Doz boxes .37

Doll With Dog In Box

4¾ In.—3 styles, silk dress, painted features and hair, some with painted ribbon bow, jointed arms and open legs, will stand, china dog on ribbon leash.

64-1125—1 doz boxes in pkg.

Doz boxes .39

6 In Box

2¾ In.—2 styles dolls, painted features, hair and bow, jointed arms, asst. color silk ribbon dresses.

64-1246—1 doz boxes in pkg...........**Doz boxes .80**

Doll in Trunk with Wardrobe

Painted features and hair, jointed arms, open legs, **will stand**, asst. color silk dresses, extra dress and bonnet, each in 5¾ x3 in. wood trunk with painted locks, hotel labels, etc., hook fastener.

64-1249—1 doz boxes in pkg.

Doz boxes .80

4 In Box

3½ In.—2 styles dolls, painted features and hair, jointed arms, asst. color silk dresses.

64-1251—1 doz boxes in pkg...........**Doz boxes .80**

5 In Box

U. S. Soldiers—3 to 4 in., Khaki painted uniforms, painted features, 5 styles in box, officer on horse and on foot, flag bearer and 2 body guards.

64-1280—1 doz boxes in pkg...........**Doz boxes .80**

5 In Box

2¾ In.—No-two-alike in box, bright painted costumes, features and hair.

64-1128—1 doz boxes in pkg...........**Doz boxes .39**

BORG-1.

BORG-3.

BORG-2.

BLO-1. *Answer Doll.* 10"; dark brown wig; blue sleep eyes; closed mouth; hard plastic; original clothes and box. Marks: **CINDERELLA / SIZE 01** on shoes, box is marked: **ANSWER DOLL / YES-NO / Manufactured by Block Doll, New York, N.Y.** *(S. Ricklefs collection)*

BLO-1.

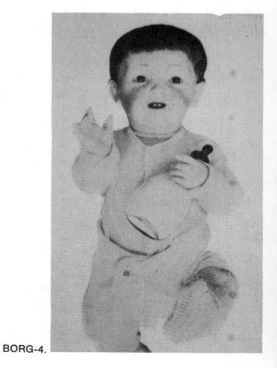

BORG-4.

BORG-6a-e.

GEO. BORGFELDT & CO.

This company, established in 1881, was responsible for a large number of the dolls so prized by collectors today. Both an importer and a manufacturer, Borgfeldt distributed American-made dolls as well. Here are a very few from his advertisements in Playthings.

BORG-1. *Multi-headed, imported doll;* January, 1910.

BORG-2. *Tiny Tots.* Composition heads and hands, stuffed body and limbs; 1911.

BORG-3. *Little Bright Eyes.* Side-glance glass eyes; stuffed body and limbs; U.S. and German Trademark Registered ©; 1911.

BORG-4. *Natural Baby.* Mfr.: Kestner; 1911.

BORG-5. *Fingy-Legs The Tiny Tot.* Painted composition head and hands, stuffed body and arms; knitted suit. "This patent covers the features in a plaything whereby the fingers of the person holding it form the legs of the doll, figure, or animal." U.S. Pat. #752607. May, 1912.

BORG-6a-e. *Jolly Kids.* **a,** *Babe;* **b,** *Harry;* **c,** *Carrie;* **d,** *Willie;* **e,** *Lilly.* Goo-Goo (flirt) eyes. From large line. 1913.

BORG-7. *September Morn.* All-bisque doll jointed at shoulders and hips. Doll based on figure in drawing by Grace G. Drayton which followed shortly the original September Morn painting which received world-wide acclaim. 1913.

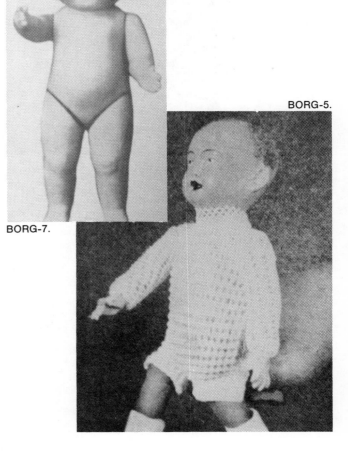

BORG-5.

BORG-7.

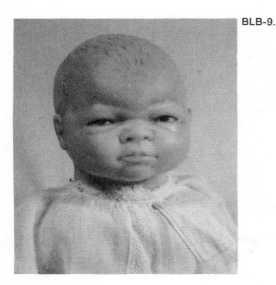

BLB-9.

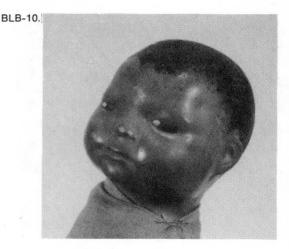

BLB-10.

BRU-1.

BRUCKNER DOLL

BRU-1. *Girl.* 20"; human hair wig; painted eyes; closed mouth painted teeth; stuffed body, American composition or papier mache. Marks: **2 / 3 / 8 / BRUCKNER DOLL / HOLYOKE MASS (in diamond) /** with picture of doll in center. *(O'Rourke collection)*

BYE-LO BABY

BLB-9. *Bye-lo Baby.* 15"; molded hair; painted blue eyes; closed mouth; sticky vinyl head and limbs, stuffed cloth body; original dress. Marks: ©**Grace Storey/Putnam** on head, dress tag reads: **BYE-LO BABY / NONE GENUINE WITHOUT SIGNATURE / Grace Storey Putnam.** *(Burtchett collection)*

BLB-10. *'Indian' Bye-lo.* 11"; painted black hair and eyes; composition head and gauntlet hands, stuffed body and limbs; hair has been retouched. *(Young collection)*

CAMEO EXCLUSIVE PRODUCTS

CAM-33. *Baby Blossom.* 20"; molded-painted blonde hair; black sleep eyes; closed mouth; composition shoulder head, arms and lower legs, stuffed body and upper legs; ca. 1927. Marks: **Des & Copyright/by J.L. Kallus/MADE IN U.S.A.** on shoulder head. *(Author's collection)*

CAM-34. *Little Annie Rooney.* 16"; painted black eyes; all composition body, jointed at shoulders and hips; ca. 1926. Unmarked. Patented by J. L. Kallus. *(Ethel Stewart collection, photograph by Nancy Perry)*

CAM-35. *Scootles.* 14½"; molded-painted hair; painted black eyes; closed mouth; fully jointed brown composition head and body; original peach romper, blue blouse and socks; 1930s. *(Ortwein collection, photograph by Jackie Meekins)*

CAM-36. *Betty Boop.* 12"; painted black hair and eyes; ball-jointed composition body; red molded-painted dress, panties, shoes; ca. 1932. Marks: **BETTY-BOOP / DES. & COPYRIGHT / by FLEIS-**

CAM-33.

CAM-34.

CAM-36.

CAM-35.

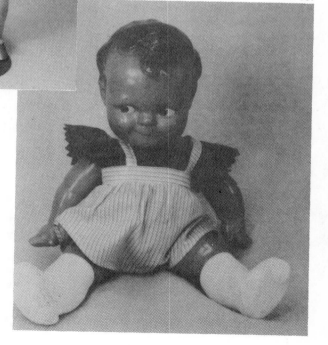

CAM-37.

CHER / STUDIOS in heart on front of dress; book is marked: **BETTY-BOOP in SNOW WHITE / ASSISTED BY / BIMBO AND KO-KO / MAX FLEISCHER PARAMOUNT TALKARTOON.** According to Mr. Kallus, Fleischer Studio copyrighted the animated cartoons; the articulated doll was designed, modeled, and copyrighted by Joseph L. Kallus. *(Stewart collection)*

CAM-37. *Joy.* Molded-painted curls with loop for ribbon; painted blue side-glance eyes; painted melon smile; segmented wood and composition construction; ca. 1932. Marks: **DES. & COPY'T/JOY/J.L. KALLUS** on label on chest. *(Stewart collection)*

CAM-41.

CAM-42.

CAM-38.

CAM-43.

CAM-38. *Pete the Pup.* 8"; molded-painted composition head with gray ears and red nose, painted eyes; segmented wood body also jointed at waist; painted red shirt, black pants, orange shoes; ca. 1932. Marks: **PETE THE PUP** on front, **Cameo** in small letters on nails on shoes.

Plans were for Mr. Kallus to draw a syndicated comic strip for King Features. The daily strips had been drawn and forwarded to King when J.V. Conley, King Features president, died and the project was abandoned.

CAM-44.

CAM-46.

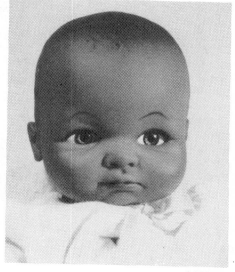

CAM-45.

CAM-41. *Kewpie.* 13"; molded-painted yellow; painted side-glance eyes; melon grin; fully jointed composition; original clothes; 1940s. Unmarked. Original box marked: **Kewpie doll/Design** and **copyright/by Rose O'Neill.** *(L. Salvisburg collection)*

CAM-42. *Cuddley Kewpies.* 9½", 7"; molded-painted wisp of hair on large doll; black side-glancing eyes; melon grins; vinyl faces, stuffed plush bodies and hats; large doll is musical; 1960s. Marks: **CAMEO©** under neck tag reads: **KEWPIE/by Rose O'Neill/ Cameo Doll Co.;** small doll unmarked. *(S. Ricklefs collection)*

CAM-43. *Baby.* 17½"; molded hair; inset blue eyes; closed mouth; soft vinyl head, magic skin limbs, stuffed cloth body; original clothes; 1950s. Marks: **CAMEO ©.** *(McDowell collection)*

CAM-44. *Sleep-Eyed Baby Mine.* 18"; molded-painted hair; blue sleep eyes with lashes; open-closed mouth; patented joints (same as Miss Peep, TCD, p. 132, CAM-27.); ca. 1961. Marks: **CAMEO ©** on body, **©/CAMEO** on head. *(Author's collection)*

According to Mr. Kallus, this doll was named after an old song, "Boy of Mine", from a movie starring Henry B. Wallthal. Baby Mine was only produced for one or two seasons.

CAM-45. *Colored Miss Peep.* 15"; molded hair; inset glassine brown eyes; closed mouth; soft-stuffed vinyl with patented joints; original clothes; ca. 1969. Marks: **USA53/CAMEO©** on head. *(Siehl collection)*

According to Mr. Kallus, the early Miss Peep had a cloth body and latex limbs.

CAM-46. *Scootles.* 14"; molded-painted hair; painted blue eyes; closed melon grin; fully jointed vinyl. Marks: **R7234 Cameo JLK** on head; paper tag reads: **"Scootles" / designed and copyrighted / by Rose O'Neill / A / CAMEO DOLL.** *(Mason Collection)*

According to Joseph L. Kallus, *Cameo* produced a wood pulp *Bye-lo* for *Borgfeldt* during the same period it was making the *Little Annie Rooney* doll (ref. CAM-18, TCD, pp. 126-7 and CAM-34, pp. 622-23). Mr. Kallus spoke of the difficulty of achieving a perfect opening for the tiny sleep eyes of this doll. Since wood pulp is not a fine-textured material, the edges of the eye opening had to be sanded carefully so the moving eye would not hang up on a minute protrusion. When questioned regarding the marks a collector might expect to find on a *Cameo* wood pulp *Bye-lo*, Mr. Kallus stated such a doll would carry only the usual *Bye-lo* markings.

CANADIAN DOLLS

CAN-1. *Negro child.* 13"; glued-on Caracul wig; flirty eyes; closed mouth; all vinyl, fully jointed; red hat and loincloth; purchased in Quebec in 1971. Unmarked. *(Edge collection)*

CAN-2. *Mounty.* 12"; molded-painted hair and eyes; closed mouth; all vinyl, fully jointed; dressed in all original Mounty's uniform; ca. 1972. Unmarked. *(Gibbins collection)*

CAN-3. *Young Sasquatch.* 8"; dark brown synthetic rooted hair; painted brown eyes; closed mouth; flocked vinyl body; plush loincloth; ca. 1972. Marks: **JAPAN** on head, **YOUNG SASQUATCH "souvenir" of Canada** on stand. *(J. Gibbins collection)*

YOUNG SASQUATCH - A LEGEND

With this unique doll came a folder printed with the following tongue-in-cheek message:

"SASQUATCH" is the Indian word for "Hairy Giant". Their place of domicile is reported to be the Harrison Lake area in British Columbia, about one hundred miles from Vancouver. It is there also where skeletons, burying places, and middens may be found.

Sasquatches have recently been getting more attention than ever, via the press, radio, and T.V. The Sasquatch tribe is primitive, shy and elusive, which may well be because no one is looking forward to meeting one or more of them on a lonely road late at night. Some are reported to be nearly eight feet tall.

It is only rarely that people have gotten to actually see them. However, the younger ones, like the one you now look at, do not seem to be afraid of strangers, and have been sighted more often. Indeed it was this that enabled our artist to make this likeness for you.

It is believed that Sasquatches are one of the few races that are still living by Nature's Law, completely shunning all contact with the rest of the world and living in very rugged terrain, in trees, and caves.

They have mastered the art of making fire and so are able to survive the winter's cold and cook some of their food. Once every four years, on the first full moon in July they light a giant fire on top of the impassable and almost completely isolated Mount Morris. All attempts of white men to reach the fire have failed so far.

The Indians called the Morris Valley "Saskahana" meaning "the place of the wild man".

Efforts to communicate with this mysterious race have been in vain but it is hoped that some day more will be learned about them."

Copyright 1968 by: Westcoast Sasquatch Distributors, Langley, B.C.

CAN-1.

CAN-2.

CAN-3.

CASC-1.

DOLLS

Cascelloid Limited, of Leicester, manufacture a complete range of dolls comprising soft bodied, dressed and undressed dolls, fitted with non-flam unbreakable heads, and also a range of hard bodied, fully jointed Baby Dolls, made from Plastex material. These are fitted with sleeping eyes and lashes. Included in the Plastex range are both dressed and undressed dolls, the one shown above being a 50cm. doll dressed in silk slip embroidered in pink and blue.

CASC-2.

CASC-3.

CASC-1, 2, 3. *Three "True-Life Dolls"* from Palitoy. Mfr.: Caselloid Limited, Leicester, England.

   -1. *Babyface.* 13", 17"; long separated fingers. *(The Toy Trader and Exporter, July, 1952)*

   -2. *Plastex Baby Doll.* See illustration. *(The Toy Trader and Exporter, April, 1940)*

   -3. *Polly Pigtails.* Puppet doll with plastic head and limbs and an empty body for the child's hand. *(The Toy Trader and Exporter, August, 1952)*

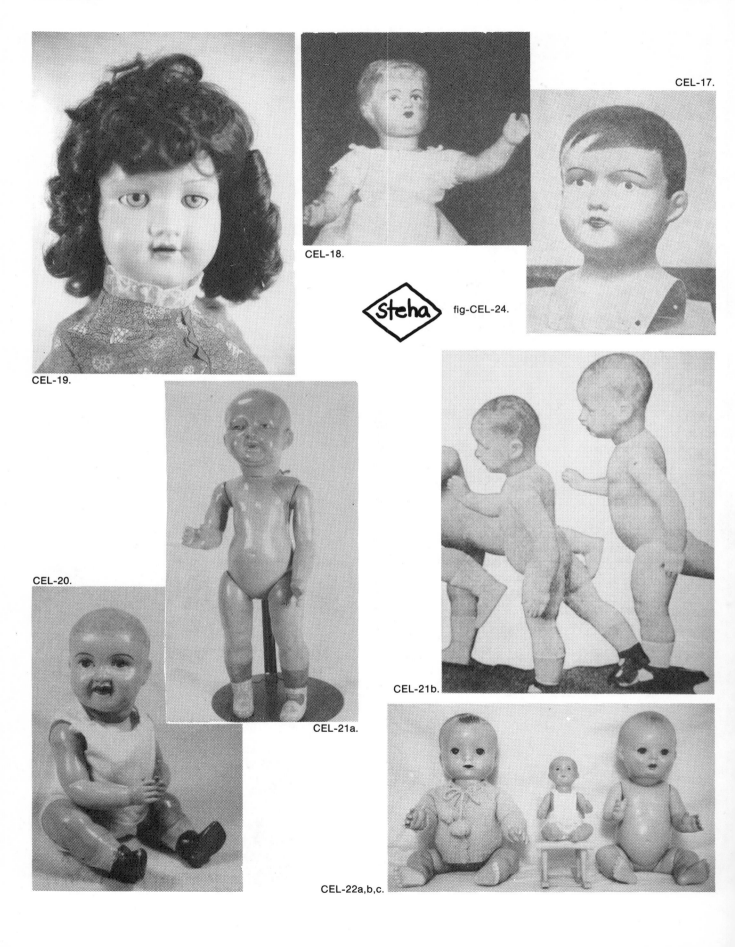

CEL-17.

CEL-18.

fig-CEL-24.

CEL-19.

CEL-20.

CEL-21a.

CEL-21b.

CEL-22a,b,c.

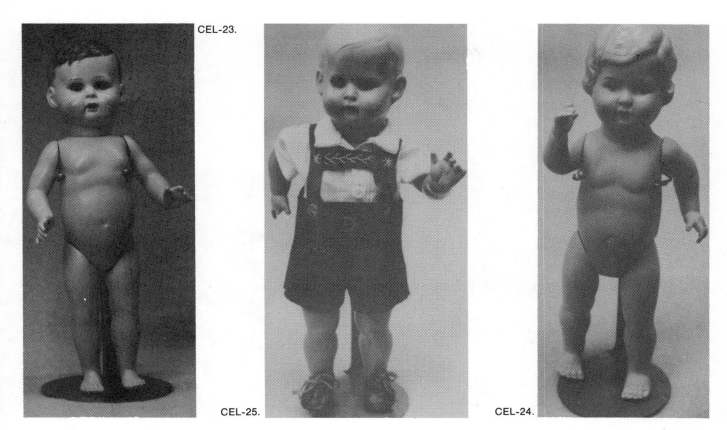

CEL-23.

CEL-25.

CEL-24.

CELLULOID DOLLS

As with bisque, the small imported celluloid dolls of the 1920s were available until the supply which had been in stock prior to the outbreak of World War II was depleted. Since distributors such as Butler Brothers often ordered dolls and toys from Europe and Japan by the shipload, ample stock may have been in the warehouses to carry through the first few years of conflict.

Again, in order to aid collectors in the identification of these small dolls, it seems well to show a large assortment. Those shown were being listed in the catalogs of 1926 through 1929.

The larger dolls shown present ample evidence of the fact that celluloid makes beautiful dolls; no other material gives quite the same effect. In addition, the variety seems virtually endless.

CEL-17. *Boy's head.* 5", 6"; molded-painted features. The company announced a new line of celluloid heads. Mfr.: Marks Brothers Co., Boston. *(Playthings, September, 1918)*

CEL-18. *Parsons-Jackson Toddler Girl.* All celluloid; serious "reposeful" face. Mfr: Parsons-Jackson Celluloid Collar Co. *(Playthings, March, 1913)*

CEL-19. *American-Made Girl.* 25"; replacement wig; blue painted eyes; open mouth six teeth; celluloid shoulder head, stuffed kid and cloth body and feet;

composition hands. Marks: **MADE IN/USA/MARKS/BROTHERS/CO./BOSTON/8** in shield on shoulder head. *(Author's collection)*

CEL-20. *Baby.* 10"; painted light brown hair; painted blue eyes; closed smile; fully jointed celluloid body with molded-painted shoes and socks. Marks: (picture of a stork)**/A4** on head, (picture of a stork)**/ TRADEMARK / THE PARSONS-JACKSON CO. / CLEVELAND, OHIO** on body. *(Stewart collection)*

CEL-21a, b. *Baby.*

a-An example of the straight-leg, all-celluloid Parsons-Jackson Toddler.

b-Advertisement from January, 1914 Playthings.

CEL-22a, b, c. *Three Celluloid Dolls.*

a. 13"; painted hair; blue inset glass eyes; open mouth two teeth; fully jointed. Marks: **MINERVA/GERMANY 5** on head, **MINERVA/MADE IN GERMANY 36** on body, small helmet-shaped mark on both. *(Schmidt collection)*

b. 7"; painted brown hair; painted blue eyes; fully jointed. Marks: **MOD-DEP** on head, **FRANCE/GNE** (in diamond)**/18** on body.

c. 14"; painted brown hair, blue sleep eyes; open drink and wet mouth. Marks: **MADE IN USA/IRWIN** (in circle).

CEL-26.

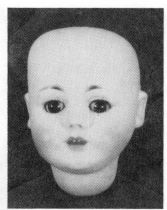

CEL-27.

CEL-28.

CEL-29.

CEL-30.

CEL-23. *Minerva Boy.* 13"; molded-painted hair; brown glass eyes; open-closed mouth with two painted teeth; fully jointed celluloid. Marks: (helmet mark)**/Germany/NO 4/30/o** on head, (helmet mark) **/Minerva/Germany/32** on body. *(Photograph by Jackie Meekins, Owner)*

CEL-24. *Minerva Girl.* 9½"; molded-painted blonde hair; painted blue eyes; open-closed with tongue; all celluloid jointed at shoulders and hips. Marks: (helmet)**/Minerva/23½/25/Germany** on head. *(Bailey collection)*

CEL-25. *Minerva Boy.* 11"; molded-painted blonde hair; blue glass eyes; closed mouth; fully jointed celluloid; all original lederhosen, shirt, suspenders and leather shoes. Marks: (helmet)**/No2/26/o** on head, (helmet)**/26/Germany/o/28.** *(Bailey collection)*

CEL-26. *Minerva Girl.* 14"; molded-painted blonde hair; blue glass eyes; celluloid; original black taffeta dress and shawl, apron and red patent shoes. Marks: (helmet)**/Minerva/Germany/5,** (helmet)**/Minerva/Germany/37.** *(Bailey collection)*

CEL-31.

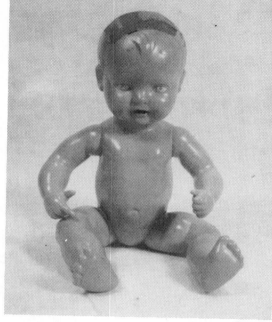

CEL-32.

CEL-32. *Baby.* 9½"; molded-painted hair; painted blue eyes; open mouth; all celluloid jointed at shoulders and hips; all original clothes. Marks: (turtle in diamond)/25. *(McDowell collection)*

CEL-27. *Head.* 4"; brown inset glass eyes; open-closed mouth two teeth. Marks: (Turtle mark) / **Achute-marke / 8 ½ / German / 1918.** *(Thompson collection)*

CEL-28. *Girl.* 15½"; molded-painted brown hair; blue glass eyes; open mouth four teeth; celluloid head, composition limbs, cloth body; all original white flowered muslin dress with red organdy ruffle. Mfr: Madame Hendren. Marks: **Germany/**(turtle mark)**/14** on head. *(Busch collection)*

CEL-29. *Girl.* 14½"; brown glass sleep eyes; open mouth four teeth; celluloid shoulder head, composition limbs, cloth body. Marks: (turtle in diamond)/**GERMANY/12/1926.** *(Gaylin collection)*

CEL-30. *Girl.* 15½"; molded-painted light brown hair; blue glass eyes; open-closed mouth with two upper teeth, six lower teeth; all celluloid jointed at shoulders and hips. Marks: (turtle in diamond)/**40.** *(Bailey collection)*

CEL-31. *Baby.* 9½"; molded-painted hair; blue painted eyes; open-closed mouth; all celluloid jointed at shoulders and hips; knitted pink and white wool suit; note similarity to Parsons-Jackson Baby. Marks: (turtle in diamond) / **SCHUTZ-MARK (square) / 24 / GERMANY.** *(Bailey collection)*

CEL-33. *Boy.* 10"; blonde wig; blue sleep eyes with lashes; open mouth with four teeth; all celluloid. Marks: **JDK/200/**(turtle mark)**/2/0** on head, (turtle mark)**/Germany/28½** on body. *(Hutchinson collection)*

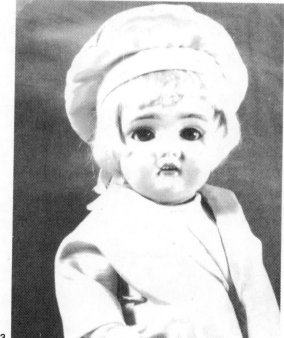

CEL-33.

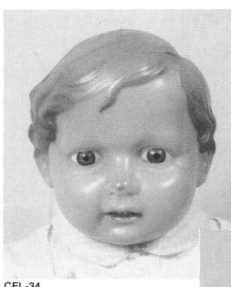

CEL-34.

CEL-36.

CEL-37.

FRANCE
fig-CEL-37.

CEL-35.

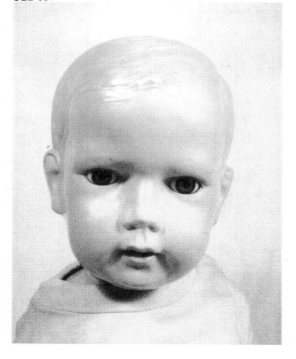

CEL-34. *Boy.* Molded-painted tan hair; stationary blue glass eyes; open mouth four teeth; celluloid head, composition limbs, cloth body with cry voice. Marks: turtle mark on head, body marked: **Genuine "Madame Hendren" Doll/1702/MADE IN USA.** *(Wess collection)*

CEL-35. *Boy.* 21"; molded hair; stationary blue glass eyes; open-closed mouth with upper teeth; all celluloid. Marks: (turtle in diamond)/**GERMANY/55/25** on head; (turtle in diamond)/**SCHUTZ MARKE/55/GERMANY/25** on body. *(Siehl collection)*

CEL-36. *Boy.* 14"; molded-painted hair; painted blue sleep eyes; closed mouth; all celluloid body. Marks: (plus sign in a circle)/**JAPAN** on back. *(Siehl collection)*

CEL-37. *Boy.* 22"; molded-painted dark hair; blue glass sleep eyes; closed mouth; all French celluloid. Marks: See fig. cel-37; marked head and shoulders. *(Hafner collection)*

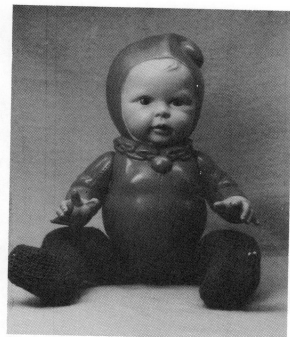

CEL-38.

fig-CEL-40.

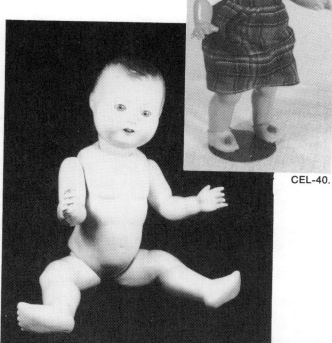

CEL-40.

CEL-41.

CEL-39.

CEL-38. *Baby.* 12" seated; molded lock of hair; painted blue eyes; closed mouth; all celluloid jointed at shoulders and hips; molded pajama suit painted red; entire doll painted red then paint was wiped from face and hands to give complexion. Marks: (clover leaf shape)**/MADE IN/OCCUPIED/JAPAN.** *(Photograph by Jackie Meekins, Owner)*

CEL-39. *Boy.* 6½"; molded-painted hair; painted blue eyes; closed melon grin, all celluloid jointed only at shoulders; blue knit suit possibly original. Marks: Fleur-de-lis with capital **J** in center**/MADE IN/OCCUPIED JAPAN.** *(Photograph by Jackie Meekins, Owner)*

CEL-40. *Girl.* 12"; molded-painted brown hair; painted blue eyes; closed mouth; fully jointed; original plaid dress, ribbon glued to hand, flannel slippers; ca. 1970. Marks: See fig. cel-40; marked on back. *(Mason collection)*

CEL-41. *Baby.* Molded-painted brown hair; blue glass eyes; open mouth with two teeth; all celluloid fully jointed. Marks: **MADE IN ENGLAND** on body, **SAROLD MANUFACTURING CO./MADE IN ENGLAND** printed in circle. *(Gaylin collection)*

CEL-43.

CEL-42.

CEL-42.

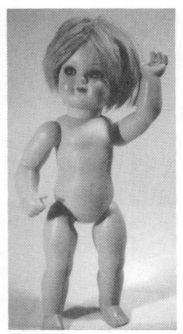

CEL-44.

CEL-44.

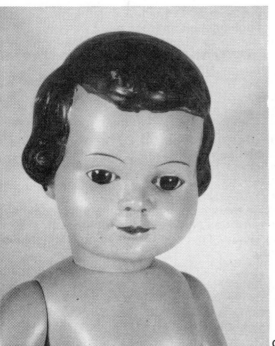

CEL-43.

CEL-42. *Dutch Lady.* 26"; molded-painted brown hair; blue sleep eyes; closed mouth; fully jointed celluloid; original dress and hat, wooden shoes; ca. 1950. Marks: (picture of stork)**/64, Holland** on instep. *(O'Rourke collection)*

CEL-43. *Girl.* 21½"; molded-painted dark hair; brown stationary glass eyes; closed mouth; fully jointed celluloid, painted nails. Marks: child seated with stork with superimposed **S.** *(Carter collection)*

CEL-44. *Girl.* 14"; blonde human hair wig; brown flirty eyes; closed mouth; fully jointed celluloid; all original red overalls with white animal print blouse. Marks: **GERMANY** on back, **K&W** in design, tag in overalls reads: **"Man Stobz"/38.** *(Busch collection)*

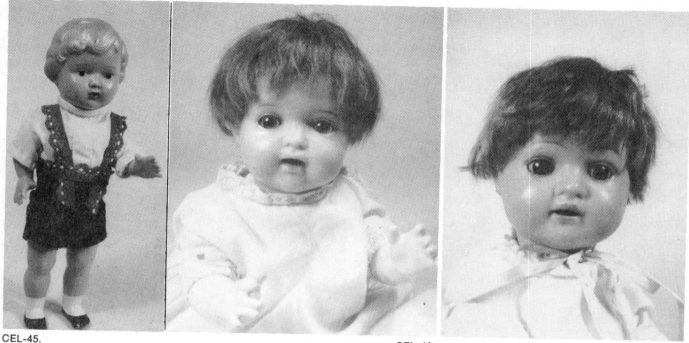

CEL-45.   CEL-46.   CEL-47.

CEL-49.

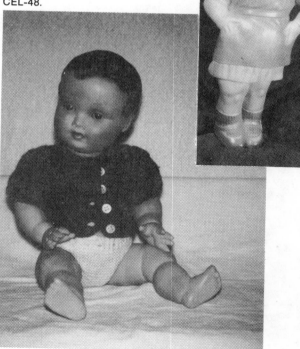

CEL-48.

CEL-45. *Boy.* 10"; molded-painted hair; blue painted eyes; closed mouth; fully jointed celluloid. Unmarked. *(Courtesy Camelot)*

CEL-46. *Baby.* 11½"; mohair wig; blue sleep eyes; open-closed mouth; fully jointed celluloid; old clothes. Marks: **K & W/W/298/2/**(turtle in diamond)/**Germany** in circle. *(Courtesy Nita's House of Dolls)*

CEL-47. *Baby.* 13"; human hair wig; brown sleep eyes; open mouth with two upper teeth; celluloid head, composition body and limbs. Marks: **SCHUTZ MARK/**(heart)/**S/36/GERMANY.** *(Stewart collection)*

CEL-48. *Toddler.* 17"; molded-painted black hair; brown flirty sleep eyes; closed mouth; all celluloid, jointed at neck, shoulders, hips, and waist. Marks: molded windmill/unintelligible name/**45** on back. *(Warren collection)*

Reader Susan Ackerman reports she has an identical doll with brown hair, stationary glass eyes, lashes, jointed neck, shoulders, hips and wrists. The unintelligible mark beneath the windmill is **FRANCE.**

CEL-50.

CEL-51.

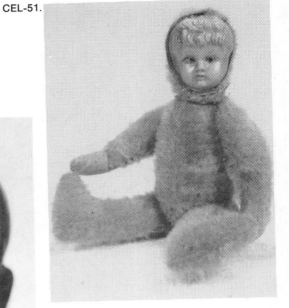

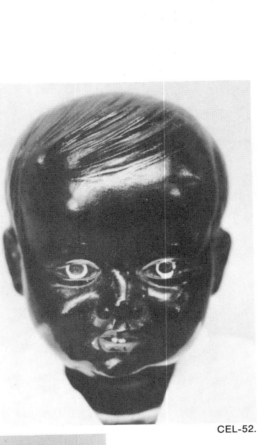

CEL-52.

CEL-52.

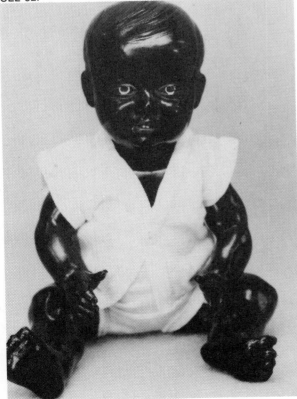

CEL-49. *Woman.* 5¾"; molded-painted hair; painted eyes; all celluloid; molded-painted clothes. Unmarked but someone has written 1928 on bottom of feet. *(Swift collection)* For illustration see preceding page.

CEL-50. *Eskimo.* Painted side-glance eyes; closed smile; celluloid face, stuffed cloth body and head, fully jointed, tall laced fur boots; ca. 1920; possibly Cliquot Club Eskimo doll. *(O'Rourke collection)*

CEL-51. *Doll.* 9"; molded-painted hair; painted eyes; celluloid mask face, newspaper-stuffed plush cloth body and limbs, fully jointed. *"The All Voice Doll'* was shown in 1912 Playthings in three sizes. *(Hafner collection)*

CEL-52. *Negro Baby.* 11"; molded hair; painted eyes with white outlines; open-closed mouth with two painted teeth; fully jointed black celluloid; replacement clothes. Marks: **30** on head and body with bird head. *(Ortwein collection)*

Celluloid Dressed Dolls

8¼ in., large roguish eyes, painted eyelashes, marcel waved hair, moving arms, asstd. percale dresses and underwear. **Chain store value!**

64-0989—1 doz in box.....................**Doz .87**

In Bag—5½x5 padded sateen bag, asstd. pink, blue, maize, etc., rayon overstitched edge, loop handle, stenciled dress design, inserted 3½ in. doll, with jointed shoulders. Asstd. 1 doz. in box.

1F5088 — White celluloid.
1F5089 — Black celluloid.......**Doz 89c**
Gro $10.50

Each with Musical Chimes

18 styles, 8 to 10½ in. high, school boy, bathing girl, boy with high hat, bell hop, clown, dude and dolls, some with movable arms and legs. Excellent variety of styles.

64-1066—2 doz. in box...................**Doz 1.20**

CELLULOID DOLLS

Heavy celluloid, painted features and hair unless otherwise stated, hollow featherweight bodies. In large demand for dressing, carriage trim and babies' baths.

F7161-62   F7172-74   F7168-69

Floating Dolls, fixed arms and legs.
F7161—3 in. 1 doz. in box.....Doz. 84c
F7162—6⅜ in., painted footwear. ½ doz. in box.................Doz. $2.15
Baby Models—Jointed arms and legs, stout bodies, elastic strung.
PAINTED HAIR—
F7171— 5   in. ½ doz. in box.....$2.00
F7172— 6¾ " ¼ "   "   4.25
F7173— 8¾ " 1/12 "   "   7.50
F7174—11¾ " 1/12 "   "   14.40
MOHAIR WIGS—   Doz.
F7168—6¼ in. ¼ doz. in box.....$4.25
F7169—8½ " 1/12 "   "   8.00

2F9466—8 in., jointed arms and legs. ½ doz. in box.
Doz $1.85
Gro $21.00

2F9396—6 in., jointed arms, asstd. color mohair wig. 1 doz. in box.
Doz $1.85
Gro $21.00

2F9637—7 in., pink and blue silk bloomers. ½ doz. in box.....**Doz $1.90**

Pickaninnies — Natural color, asstd. color dresses.
2F9514—2½ in. 3 doz. in box......**Doz 21c**
Gro $2.25

12 styles, aver. 6¾ in., asstd. boys' and girls', bright painted costumes, many with toys.
64-0962—1 doz in box............**Doz .78**

12 styles, aver. 5 in., bright painted costumes.
64-0810—2 doz in pkg............**Doz .39**

2 splendid assortments that give you an unusually large variety of styles without investing in large quantity! Bright colorful dolls . . . all popular fast selling styles that will SELL OUT CLEAN!

24 styles, 7 to 8½ in., asstd. Dutch boy and girl, bathing girl with parasol, boy with dog, Johnny Tucker, policeman, boy with sprinkling can, girl with mandolin, etc.
64-0968—2 doz in box......**Doz .80**

24 styles, 7½ to 8 in., asstd. boys, bathing girls, boy on hobby horse, girl and dog, tennis player, school boy and girl, etc.
64-0983—2 doz in box......**Doz .80**

12 styles, aver. 7 in., sailor, football player, aviator, baseball player, etc., bright painted costumes.
64-0974—1 doz in box............**Doz .78**

Animal Dolls with Blinking Eyes

4 styles, 7 in., asstd. cow, cat, teddy bear and elephant, bright painted costumes. **Chain store value.**
64-0995—1 doz in box............**Doz .84**

CELLULOID DOLLS

Painted features and hair, many with bright costumes.

Aver. 5¼ in., jointed arms and legs.
64-0806—2 doz in box........**Doz .35**

Negro dolls, 4½ in., 2 styles, jointed arms, asstd. color shirts.
64-0812—2 doz in box........**Doz .36**

12 styles, aver. 5 in., bright painted costumes.
64-0811—2 doz in pkg........**Doz .39**

6 in., flirt eyes, **jointed arms**, asst. color marcel waved hair.
64-0816—2 doz in box.
Doz .39

2 styles, 6 in., jointed arms and legs.
64-0819—2 doz in box....**Doz .39**

"Orphan Annie," 7¾ in., red dress, white socks, black shoes, movable arms.
64-0986—1 doz in box....**Doz .80**

2F9761—Rolling bead eyes, 4½ in., 6 styles, jointed arms, painted costumes. Asstd. 1 doz. in box.
Gro $9.00 Doz 79c

3 styles, aver. 7 in., asst. negro baby dolls and bell hops, bright costumes, some with jointed arms and legs.
64-0992—1 doz in box........**Doz .80**

Santa Claus, 7 in., 2 styles, painted red coat and hood, white beard, toys.
64-0980—1 doz in box........**Doz .80**

8½ in., 2 styles, **jointed arms and legs, open mouth,** linen diaper, nipple on silk cord.
64-0972—1 doz in box........**Doz .80**

Dressed dolls, 8 in., asst. dresses, large painted roguish eyes and marcel waved hair, some with painted ribbon in hair, jointed arms.
64-0990—1 doz in box........**Doz .80**

2F9386—3½ in., jointed arms, asstd. bright color silk chenille costumes. 2 doz. in box.
Doz 79c
Gro $9.00

2F9522—6 in., jointed arms, painted shoes and stockings. 1 doz. in box.
Doz 80c
Gro $9.00

1F-9668—2 doz in box..............**Doz 35c**
12 styles, aver. 5 in., asstd. boys, girls, aviator, Dutch girls, etc., **bright costumes. Will not rub off.**

12 styles, aver. 7 in., bright **painted costumes**, some with tennis racket, books, floral decorations.
64-0982—1 doz in box........**Doz .80**

9¼ In. High!

Jointed Arms!

A BIG DOLL with more than usual "eye-appeal" to sell at a popular price!

Large painted roguish eyes, asst. color painted marcel waved hair.
64-0978—1 doz in box.

Doz .80

25c CELLULOID DOLL ASSORTMENT

Excellent counter display! 12 different styles, attractive color costumes.

2F9371— Average 8½ in., 12 styles (asstd. school boy and girl, Indian with Tomahawk, boy with apple, girl with basket, bathing girls, etc.), painted features and hair, attractive color costumes. Asstd. 2 doz. in box. **Doz $2.00**

2F9804—8 in., asstd. bright color bathing costume, **folding Japanese parasol.** 1 doz. in box. **Doz $2.00**

F-9220—1 doz. in box. ....**Doz 80c**
6 styles, 4½ in., marcel hair, asstd. color marabou, feather and chenille dresses, some with headpiece to match, others with silver braid trim.

2F9527—6 in., jointed arms. 1 doz. in box .....**Doz 87c** **Gro $10.00**

2F9537—6 in., 3 styles, Asstd. 1 doz. in box.....**Doz 89c** **Gro $10.15**

2F9539—6 in., 4 styles (asstd. boys and girls), jointed arms, painted costumes. Asstd. 1 doz. in box. **Doz 89c**

Nursing Set—2½ in. doll, glass bottle with rubber nipple.

2F9410—2 doz. sets in pkg. **Doz sets 42c** **Gro sets $4.80**

Nursing Set—3 in. doll, full jointed, glass nursing bottle with rubber nipple, rubber pacifier, rattle.

2F9411—1 doz. sets in pkg. **Doz sets 84c** **Gro sets $9.60**

"Uncle Sam" — 6½ in., painted costume.
64-0821—1 doz in box.........**Doz .39**

Doll In Cradle—2 in. doll, 2½ in. cradle, pink and blue paper, silk ribbon.

2F9414—2 doz. in box. **Doz 80c** **Gro $9.00**

2F9399—3 in., full jointed, bottle, rocking chair, asstd. pink and blue enameled. 2 doz. in box.........**Doz 82c** **Gro $9.25**

Dolls' Bath Set—2½ in. doll, full jointed, white enameled metal bath tub, rubber sponge, wash cloth, hinged box.

2F9412—1 doz. sets in box. **Doz sets 80c** **Gro sets $9.00**

Doll In Bed—3 in. doll, jointed arms, 4 in. metal bed, pink and blue stitched flannel blanket, silk ribbon tied.

2F9800—1 doz. in box **Doz 89c** **Gro $10.15**

10c CELLULOID DOLL ASSORTMENT

14 styles—including our best selling numbers, bright colored costumes.

2F9370— Average 5½ in. 14 styles, (asstd. cowboys, football players, police woman, clown, bathing girls, boy and girl on scooter, etc.), painted features and hair, some with jointed arms and legs, bright color costumes. Asstd. 4 doz. in box. **Doz 80c**

CELLULOID DOLL NOVELTIES

Assortment—3½ to 4½ in. dolls, jointed arms and legs, imitation nursing bottles, asstd. color cardboard rocker, cradle, shoofly, baby walker, play yard and imitation peanut shell, some with ribbon trim.
64-0999—2 doz. in box.....................Doz .80

2F9604—5½ in., jointed arms. 1 doz. in box.
Doz 75c
Gro $8.50

2F9540 — 6½ in., jointed arms, painted shoes, 3 styles (asstd. bright color costumes). Asstd. 1 doz. in box. .....Doz 95c
Gro $10.75

2F9432—5 in., asstd. color painted sash, violin and bow, painted marcel wave hair. Asstd. 3 doz. in box.
Doz 42c

2F9428—4 in., jointed arms and legs. 2 doz. in box.
Doz 35c
Gro $4.00

"Newly Born"
2F9392 — 5 in., jointed arms and legs. 2 doz. in box.
Doz 75c
Gro $8.50

2F9532 — Average 5½ in., 6 styles, jointed arms. Asstd. 2 doz. in box
Doz 84c
Gro $9.60

2F9430—3½ in., jointed arms, red headband. 2 doz. in box.
Doz 32c

2F9413—1¼ in. doll, 1¾ in. cradle, pink and blue paper, silk ribbon. 3 doz. in box.
Doz 39c
Gro $4.45

2F9636—5¾ in., jointed arms, pink and blue silk bloomers. 2 doz. in box.
Doz 75c
Gro $8.50

2F9385 — 4 in., jointed arms, asstd. bright color crepe paper dresses and hats. 2 doz. in box.
Doz 75c
Gro $8.50

2F9792—3½ in., jointed arms, asstd. color silk chenille costume. 2 doz. in box.
Doz 79c
Gro $9.00

2F9633—4⅛ in., white fur ballet skirt, tinsel head band with feathers. 2 doz. in box.
Doz 79c
Gro $9.00

STAR VALUE

2F9388—4 in., jointed arms, asstd. color mohair wig. 2 doz. in box.
Doz 79c
Gro $9.00

2F9541—Santa Claus, 5 in., painted costume and shoes. 1 doz. in box.
Doz 79c
Gro $9.00

2F9793—3½ in., "Pickaninny," jointed arms, asstd. color silk chenille costume. 2 doz. in box.
Doz 79c
Gro $9.00

STAR VALUE

2F9790—3½ in. negro doll, jointed arms and legs, cardboard melon. 3 doz. in box.
Doz 79c
Gro $9.00

2F9399—3 in., jointed arms and legs, bottle asstd. pink and blue enameled rocking chair. 2 doz. in box.
Doz 79c
Gro $9.00

2F9393—5¾ in., jointed arms. 2 doz. in box.....Doz 80c
Gro $9.00

2F9434—6 in., jointed arms, red head band. 1 doz. in box.
Doz 84c
Gro $9.60

2F9756—4½ in., jointed arms, floral headband, asstd. blue, pink and red silk and lace dresses. 2 doz. in box.....Doz 84c
Gro $9.60

2F9531—Average 4 in., 6 styles (some jointed arms, others jointed arms and legs), bright 1, 2, and 3-color painted costumes. Asstd. 3 doz. in box.
Doz 42c
Gro $4.80

2F9422—5 in., 6 styles (some with jointed arms, others with jointed arms and legs). asstd. color painted plain, ribbon and floral trim bathing suits, some with caps. Asstd. 3 doz. in box.
Doz **45c**
Gro **$4.95**

F-9430 — 2 doz. in box.
Doz **35c**
3½ in., jointed arms, red head band.

F-9382—5¼ in. 2 doz. in box.
Doz **42c**
F-9383—7¼ in. 1 doz. in box.
Doz **84c**
"Playmates," bright painted costumes, shoes and hats. 6 styles, school boy and girl, tennis and basketball players, sport girl and boy.

F-9495 — 1 doz. in box.
Doz **75c**
6 in., flirt eyes, jointed arms, painted marcel.

F-9678 — 1 doz. in box.
Doz **78c**
2 styles, 6¼ in., flirt eyes, painted marcel, some with bows, asstd. color painted bathing suits with animal designs, black trim.

F-9714—2 doz. in box.
Doz **80c**
3¼ in., jointed arms and legs, in paper peanut shell.

F-9366—4 doz. in box.
Doz **84c**
32 styles, asstd. sizes 5¾ to 6¾ in., bright colors, asstd. boy scouts, sailors, cowboys, aviators, circus girl, school boy and girl, hunter, Dutch boy and girl, flirt doll and a good many others, many with jointed arms.

F-9394 — 1 doz. in box.
Doz **80c**
6½ to 6¾ in., flirt eyes, 6 styles, some with asstd. color bathing costumes.

F-9751 — 1 doz. in pkg.
Doz **80c**
5¼ in., asstd. color beads, 9 in. cord with celluloid button.

F-9393 — 2 doz. in box.
Doz **80c**
5¾ in., jointed arms.

F-9528—1 doz. in box ....Doz **80c**
6 to 6½ in., 6 styles, asstd. boys and girls, bright painted costumes, some with hats to match, others with painted ribbons and hair.

1F-9662—2 doz. in box.
Doz **35c**
3 styles, 5½ in., jointed arms. Used for making pin cushions.

MUSICAL CELLULOID DOLLS

Each with musical chime in body. 2 Styles— Clown and girl, heavy celluloid stock, painted features, costumes, slippers and socks.
2F9373 — 8 in. 1 doz. in box.
Doz **$2.10**
2F9374 — 9½ in. ½ doz. in box.
Doz **$2.25**

CELLULOID DOLLS WITH RATTLES

2F9372 — 9 in., 6 styles (dude, bell hop, clown, girl, etc.), jointed arms, bright painted costumes with caps and hats to match, will stand alone, rattles in body, some with small bells in hand. Asstd. ½ doz. in box.
Doz **$2.25**

Pink and blue paper cradle, silk ribbon tie. 2 doz. in box.
2F9413—1¾ in. cradle.
Doz **39c** Gro **$4.45**
2F9414—2½ in. cradle.
Doz **79c** Gro **$9.00**

15 DIFFERENT DOLLS

15 styles....including many of our best selling numbers....bright asstd. costumes on nearly every style.

2F9368— 6 to 6½ in., 15 styles (aviators, football players, sports, bride and groom, flirt, bathing and dolls in silk underwear, etc.), asstd. bright costumes, many with jointed arms. Asstd. 4 doz. in box.
Doz **95c**   Gro **$10.50**

CENT-2.

CENT-1.

CENT-3.

CENT-4.

CENT-6.

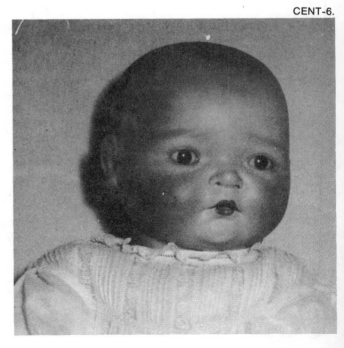

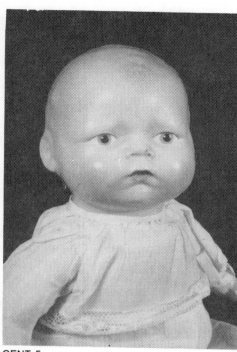

CENT-5.

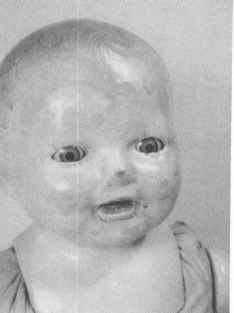

CENT-7.

CENTURY DOLL COMPANY

CENT-8.

CENT-1. *Girl.* Human hair wigs; sleep eyes; open-closed mouth with painted teeth; various costumes. Mfr: Century Doll Co., New York City. *(Playthings, October, 1919)*

CENT-2. *Girl.* 23"; brown human hair wig; blue tin sleep eyes; open mouth two upper teeth; stuffed cloth mama-type, composition shoulder head and limbs. Marks: **CENTURY/DOLL CO.** on head. *(Stewart collection)*

CENT-3. *Chuckles.* 12¼"; molded-painted hair; painted blue eyes; open mouth two teeth; composition shoulder head and limbs, stuffed cotton body; possibly original brown silk shirt with tan cuffs and collar, suede cloth lederhosen. Marks: **CHUCKLES/A CENTURY/DOLL** on shoulder head. *(Author's collection)*

CENT-4. *Chuckles.* 14"; molded-painted hair; painted eyes; open-closed mouth with teeth; composition head and limbs, stuffed cloth body. Marks: **CHUCKLES/A CENTURY/DOLL.** *(Cannon collection)*

CENT-5. *Bye-lo-type Baby.* 13"; molded-painted yellow hair; painted blue eyes; closed mouth; composition head and limbs, excelsior-stuffed cloth body; original clothes. Marks: **CENTURY DOLLS.** *(Gaylin collection)*

CENT-6. *Baby.* 18"; inset eyes; closed mouth; bisque head, composition hands and feet, cloth body and limbs. Marks: **CENTURY DOLL COMPANY/KESTNER GERMANY.** *(Cannon collection)*

CENT-7. *Chuckles.* 21"; molded-painted yellow hair; blue tin sleep eyes; open mouth; composition shoulder head and limbs, stuffed cloth body. Marks: **CHUCKLES/A CENTURY/DOLL** on shoulder head. *(Cagle collection)*

CENT-8. *Girl.* Painted composition features. "100 new numbers." "The Doll of the Century", "Every doll head from our own factory". Mfr: Century Doll Company. *(Playthings, April, 1916)*

CHI-11.

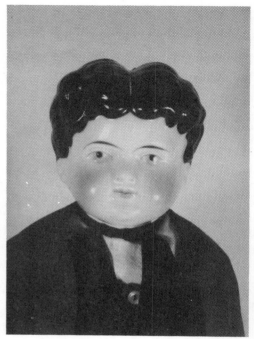

CHI-12.

CHI-13.

CHI-15.

CHI-14.

CHINA DOLLS

The variety of China heads available to collectors is diminishing in direct proportion to the number of those seeking the dolls. An intact long-standing collection either purchased or inherited would be a treasure indeed. Most collectors are not so fortunate as to come into the possession of such a collection and must garner additions one or two at a time. Few collections may exceed the variety of the one pictured in part on these pages. The side-part blonde boy is an important item; the pink lustre boy with brush mark hair is second to few.

China heads could well be termed 'button-box' dolls for often heads or limbs were stored there awaiting new bodies. Time and other interests sometimes prevented the restoration until a day when the button-box became part of an estate or garage sale. Collectors learn to look for dolls in every possible niche.

Sizes given here are for heads only unless otherwise specified.

CHI-11. *Lady.* 14"; molded-painted hair; painted blue eyes; all original cloth body, china shoulder head; original patent boots, redressed in 1947; doll brought to America in 1857. *(Parker collection)*

CHI-12. *Boy.* 5"; black hair with white part. *(Parker collection)*

CHI-13. *Boy.* 4"; blonde china head. Unmarked. *(Parker collection)*

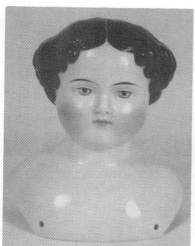

CHI-16.

CHI-17.

CHI-18.

CHI-19.

CHI-20.

CHI-22.

CHI-21.

CHI-14. *Boy.* 5"; blonde hair. *(Parker collection)*

CHI-15. *Lady.* 8"; dark hair, China shoulder head. *(Parker collection)*

CHI-16. *Lady.* 5¾" pink lustre China shoulder head; blue painted eyes; two sew holes front and back. *(Parker collection)*

CHI-17. *Scotch Boy.* 9½"; brush mark hair; painted blue eyes; pink kid body, pink lustre head; all original clothes; from the Seth Thomas collection. *(Parker collection)*

CHI-18. *Lady.* Light yellow hair; blue eyes. Unmarked. *(Parker collection)*

CHI-19. *Colored Head.* 2"; white eyes; red lips. *(Parker collection)*

CHI-20. *Head.* 1 11/16"; 2½" circumference; neck is ⅝" long. *(Lindermann collection)*

CHI-21. *Lady.* 3¾"; brown painted eyes; orange bracelets and earrings; China upper body with outstretched arms, China legs with gold molded-painted shoes. Marks: **GERMANY** with unintelligible number on lower edge. *(Parker collection)*

CHI-22. *Mme. Pompadour Dresser Doll.* Molded-painted China; a powder or pins box. *(Sheinwald collection)*

CHI-23.

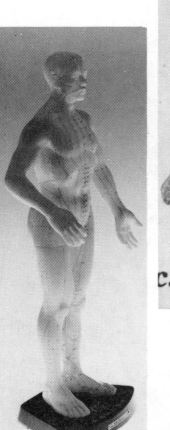

CHI-24.

COL-1.

COM-1a,b,c.

CHI-23. *Door of Hope Dolls.* China or wooden heads; cloth and wooden bodies; various costumes to fit characterizations, ca. 1917-1925.

The Door of Hope Mission was a home for refugees who became dollmakers. The wooden parts were hand carved and the clothes, which were made by girls of the mission, were exact reproductions of station, age and character of the person represented.

CHI-24. *Acupuncture Doll.* 22"; 361 acupuncture points, 14 meredian lines in Arabic numerals; comes in kit with enlarged ear model and hand model, needles encased in lucite block and booklet; sold for $90.00 in 1973. Mfr: Sobin Chemicals, Inc. Boston. *(Courtesy Antique Reporter, May, 1973, Johana Anderton on Dolls)*

COL-1. *Chubby-Kid.* 12"; with or without wig; painted eyes; wood fibre composition; distributed by Sears; also marketed as *The Columbia Twins, Columbia Jr., Miss Columbia,* and *O U Chubbikid!* (pat. pending); other companies made similar types. Mfr: Columbia Doll & Toy Co., New York City. *(Playthings, 1920)*

DOLLS FROM THE COMICS

A collection based on comic characters alone should be impressive. The comics have provided inspiration for many popular dolls of nearly every imaginable dollmaking material.

Dolls are classified alphabetically within the category according to the name of the strip whenever possible; late additions were classified by character name.

COM-A1a, b, c. *Action Boy.* 9"; molded-painted features; plastic body bends to all positions, dressed as L to R: *Robin, Super Boy,* and *Aqua Lad;* complete with accessories; Mfr: Ideal. *(1967 Sears, Roebuck and Co.)*

COM-A2. *Archie.* 18½"; all lithographed; orange hair; red shirt, orange and black bell-bottom pants; comic book came with doll. Marks: **Archie** on shirt front. *(Siehl collection)*

COM-A2.

COM-B5.

COM-B4c.

COM-B4a.

COM-B4b.

COM-B3.

COM-B3. *Bat Girl* and *Super Girl*. See illustration for description. Bat Girl, alias Barbara Gordon, was played by Yvonne Craig on the TV series. Also Wonder Woman and Aqua Woman; 1967. *(Courtesy Sears, Roebuck and Co.)*

COM-B4a, b, c. a. *Batman,* **b.** *Robin,* and **c.** *Bat Mouse.* 14", 16"; molded-painted vinyl heads; bodies rayon plush stuffed with cotton; appropriate costumes. *(1966 Spiegals Catalog)*

COM-B5. *Batman.* 5"; molded-painted features; vinyl head; cloth puppet glove. Marks: © **1966/NAT'L. PERIODICALS PUBS. INC./IDEAL TOY CORP/BM-P-H17** on head, **BATMAN** on glove. *(Wiseman collection)*

Bat Girl with extra costume

Bat Girl with helmet, cape, batarang, boots, bat gloves changes to Barbara Gordon in halter dress (not shown). Bendable plastic, she wears all 11½-in. doll fashions. Wt. 12 oz.
49 N 59917 . . . . $4.99

Super Girl with extra costume

Super Girl with cape, boots and Krypto dog changes to Linda Lee Danvers in halter dress (not shown). Bendable plastic, she wears all 11½-inch doll fashions. Shipping weight 12 oz.
49 N 59918 . . . . $4.99

Fearless Batman Troll
fights against crime
$1.99

COM-B6.

COM-B7.

COM-B9.

3 In Box
"Betty Boop, Bimbo & Bingo"—3 styles,
3⅛ to 3½ in., painted features and bright
costumes, asst. painted violin, accordion,
drum, bass-viol and horns.
64-1290—1 doz boxes
in pkg................Doz boxes **.84**

COM-B8.

BETTY BOOP DOLLS

The Greatest Sensation

Everybody knows
BETTY BOOP.
Constructed
of wooden seg-
ments with realis-
tic head molded of
wood fibre compo-
sition. Fully joint-
ed so that the doll
can be turned in
any position to im-
personate BETTY
BOOP of the
screen.

Produced in Green, Red
and Black. Packed each in
an individual lithographed
box. Stands 12 inches high.

No. 4D.
Per Dozen $12.00
Sample, each 1.25

COM-B10.

COM-B6. *Batman Troll.* 6"; rooted hair; inset eyes; molded vinyl troll body; felt Batman clothes; sold for $1.99 in 1967. Marks: **BATMAN** on clothes. *(Courtesy Sears, Roebuck and Co.)*

COM-B7. *Beanie.* 16½"; molded-painted yellow hair; painted blue eyes; open-closed smile with tongue; vinyl head and hands, stuffed clothes form body, molded shoes; talking ring; from "Beanie and Cecil" cartoon show; ca. 1960s. Marks: **MATTEL INC. TOYMAKERS** on shoe. *(Gaylin collection)*

COM-B8. *Betty Boop, Bimbo and Bingo.* See illustration for description. *(Butler Brothers, 1928 catalog)*

COM-B9. *Betty Boop.* 22"; all cloth, reinforced face; designed and executed by Patti and Deet. This is the first three-dimensional doll produced by Colorforms; licensed from King Features.

Shown here is one of four sample dolls hand-made by Deet and Patti. These identical samples were prepared for submission to manufacturers who then bid on the production of the item. By the time you read this, a new *Betty Boop* doll and a number of related items will be well on the way to market. *(Courtesy the Designers and Mr. Harry Kislevitz, President, Colorforms)*

COM-B10.*Betty Boop.* See illustration for description. *(Stack Manufacturing Co, 1936 catalog)*

COM-B11. *Bimbo Orchestra.* 3¾"; molded-painted bisque; yellow shorts, red shoes, green, red, magenta shirts; carry French horn, viola, concertina. Marks: **"BIMBO" ORCHESTRA/DES. & COPYRIGHT BY FLEISCHER STUDIOS/MADE IN JAPAN/GEO. BORGFELDT CORPORATION** on front of box; dolls marked: **"BIMBO © FLEISCHER STUDIOS"** on back, paper tag on bottom of feet reads: **"BIMBO"/DES. & COPYRIGHT/by FLEISCHER STUDIOS.** *(Author's collection)*

COM-B12. *Bimbo.* 6½", 9"; segmented wood body; enamel finish; painted features; wood knob tail; 9" doll has composition head. *"New 1932 Creations! Fast sellers at 50¢ and $1.00!"* *(Butler Brothers Catalog)*

COM-B13. *Mechanical Bonnie Braids.* 12"; single braid threaded through two holes; painted eyes; open-closed mouth, two lower teeth; molded-painted head and limbs, metal body, key wind control; ca. 1952. *(McLaughlin collection)*

COM-B11.

COM-B13.

Famous Movie Comics
Known to young and old

"BIMBO"

1F-2527—
6½ in., round wood head, flexible ears.

Doz
$4.00

1F-2528— 9 in., large composition head. **$8.00**
molded ears.
Doz
1/6 doz. in box.
Multiple jointed wood body, can be placed in many poses, asstd. color enameled finishes, painted hair and features, wood knob tail. Each in box.

COM-B12.

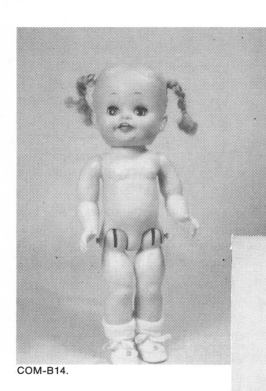

COM-B14.

COM-C2.

COM- C 4.

COM-B15.

COM-B14. *Bonnie Braids Toddler.* 13"; molded-painted yellow hair with Saran braids; blue sleep eyes; open-closed smile three molded-painted teeth; soft vinyl head, hard plastic walker body. Marks: **COPR. 1951/CHICAGO TRIBUNE/IDEAL DOLL** on head, **IDEAL DOLL/14** on body. *(Potter collection)*

COM-B15. *Bugs Bunny.* 10"; all felt and plush, stuffed; applied felt features; wired body; felt sombrero, cotton serape, fuzzy hat, red pants, green shirt. *(Author's collection)*

COM-C2. *Captain Action.* 12"; molded-painted features; completely posable hard plastic figure; wears *Captain Action* costume or *Batman* costume; comes with vinyl secret chamber carrying case; other *Captain Action* costumes available are: *Spiderman, Captain America* and *Superman* all with accessories; ca. 1967. Mfr: Ideal. *(Courtesy Sears, Roebuck and Co.)*

COM-C3a.

SNOWBALL

COM-C3b.

MIKE

FROM THE NEW YORK WORLD
"LADY BOUNTIFUL" SERIES

BLINK
SEND FOR NEW DOLL CATALOGUE

COM-C3c.

JANE

COM-C3d.

SKINNEY

COM-C3e.

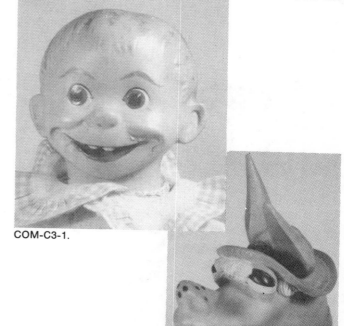

COM-C3-1.

COM-C5.

COM-C3a-e. *The Gene Carr Kids.* Molded-painted features; *Can't Break 'Em* heads, composition hands, soft, stuffed body and legs; various costumes; from the New York World *"Lady Bountiful"* Series. Includes: *Skinney, Blink, Snowball, Mike and Jane.* *(Playthings, June, 1915)*

COM-C3-1. *Jane or Mike, a Gene Carr Kid.* 14"; all original clothes. *(Stewart collection)*

COM-C4. *Casper the Friendly Ghost.* 9"; vinyl head with molded-painted features, stuffed plush body and limbs; ca. 1960s. Unmarked. *(Wiseman collection)*

COM-C5. *Charley Horse.* 10½"; rooted mane; painted eyes; molded-painted horse head with open mouth and two teeth; cloth puppet glove; from the Shari Lewis Television Show. Marks: © **1960 TARCHER/ PRODUCTIONS INC.** *(Wiseman collection)*

COM-D4.

COM-F4.

"Felix" Cat—Wood 3½ in., black & white enamel, leather ears, adjustable arms & legs, jointed tail.
1F2992—1 doz. in box.
Doz **$2.25**

COM-F5.

COM-F6.

COM-D5.

COM-D4. *Denny Dimwit.* 11"; molded-painted red hair and blue eyes; open-closed mouth with two painted teeth; his construction is like that of the *Swing-&-Sway* girl, Bobbi-Mae; molded-painted composition in three sections-head, body and legs-all hinged together on the inside with wooden pegs and metal crossbars; wears painted green peaked cap, red shirt, yellow coat, green mitts and brown shoes. Mfr: Wondercraft Co. NY. Marks: On box: **"DENNY DIMWIT, He Wiggles—He Waggles—He's Smart—He's Friendly. By permission of the Famous Artists Syndicate,** © **1948, The Chicago Tribune"**, and **"DENNY DIMWIT from WINNIE WINKLE, The Breadwinner, by BRANNER"**, box is decorated with panels from the cartoon strip. *(Sheinwald collection)*

COM-D5. *Dondi.* Molded-painted features; vinyl head and hands; no further description available. Central figure in comic strip and movie of same name. 1950s. *(Courtesy Nita's House of Dolls)*

COM-F4. *Felix the Cat.* See illustration for description. *(Butler Brothers, February, 1928)*

COM-F5. *Felix the Cat.* 13"; molded-painted features; all composition jointed at shoulders, chenille tail. Unmarked. *(Busch collection)*

COM-F6. *Baby Pebbles Flintstone.* 15"; rooted red hair; painted side-glance eyes; open-closed mouth; vinyl head and limbs, stuffed cloth body; original clothes and box; 1960s. Marks: © **HANNA BARBERA INC./IDEAL TOY CORP./FS14.** *(Wardell collection)*

COM-F7.

COM-F8.

COM-F11.

COM-F10.

COM-F7. *Baby Puss.* 10"; all molded-painted vinyl; painted green eyes; closed mouth with two teeth; yellow with black spots. Sabretooth housecat of *"The Flintstones".* Marks: © **HANNA BARBERA 1960** on head, **4** on bottom, box is marked: **KNICKERBOCKER TOY CO. INC., NEW YORK, N.Y./**© **HANNA BARBERA PROD.** 1961. *(N. Ricklefs collection)*

COM-F8. *Barney Rubble.* 10"; all molded-painted vinyl; green hair and toenails. From *"The Flintstones".* Marks: © **HANNA-BARBERA PROD./1960** on head. *(Author's collection)*

COM-F9. *The Flintstones and the Rubbles.* 10", 12"; all molded-painted vinyl; jointed heads. Includes Fred and Wilma Flintstone, Barney and Betty Rubble. (1961 Montgomery Ward Catalog)

COM-F10, 11. *Barney Rubble and Wilma Flintstone.* 16½", 20"; all lithographed cloth; purchased by the yard, sewn and stuffed; 1960s. *(Wiseman collection)*

COM-F12. *Fred Flintstone Hand Puppet.* 3"; molded-painted vinyl head, cloth puppet glove. Marks: ©/**HANNA BARBERA/PROD 1962 & TM/JAPAN** on head. *(Wiseman collection)*

COM-F12.

COM-F9.

Fluffy Ruffles Doll

COM-F13.

COM-J1a.

COM-J1b.

COM-H2.

COM-H1.

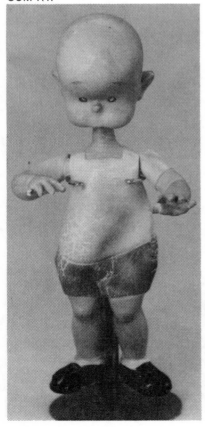

COM-K1.

COM-F13. *Fluffy Ruffles.* Bisque head, ball-jointed body; made in Germany by Samstag and Hilder Bros. and distributed by Geo. Borgfeldt and Co. New York Herald had a comic strip by this name (see AMER-22). *(Playthings, 1908)*

COM-H1. *Henry.* 8½"; molded-painted rubber; jointed arms; painted white shirt, red shorts and black shoes. Marks: **HENRY/COPYRIGHT 1934/CARL ANDERSON** on back. *(Photograph by Jackie Meekins, Owner)*

COM-H2. *Heckel (or Jeckel) Hand Puppet.* 5"; molded-painted vinyl, cloth glove. Marks: © **1960 TARCHER/PRODUCTIONS INC** on head. *(Wiseman collection)*

COM-J1a,b. *Joy and Gloom.* Composition and stuffed bodies. Creations of T.E. Powers, cartoonist for the New York American. The dolls were given wide publicity through the cartoons in newspapers all over the country. Sold wholesale $8.00 per dozen; copyrighted. *(Playthings, September, 1912)*

COM-L9a,b.

COM-L9c.d.

COM-L11.

COM-K1. *Abe Kabibble.* 16", 18"; composition head and hands, stuffed body and legs; appeared in six Hearst and twenty-four other daily papers; cartoonist was H. Hershfield. Mfr: Bleier Bros, New York. *(Playthings, February, 1915)*

COM-K2. *Krazy Kat, "The Gloom Chaser".* 20"; all stuffed felt; manufactured under exclusive arrangement with the originator, George Herriman, from the comic strip, patent #50088. *"When Krazy Kat is near there is nothing to fear".* Mfr: Averill. *(Playthings, November, 1916)*

COM-K2.

COM-L10.

COM-L9a, b, c, d. *The Dogpatch Family.* 14"; all molded-painted vinyl bodies with clothes; set includes Li'l Abner and Daisy Mae, Mammy and Pappy Yokum; sold for $3.79 each. These dolls were also made in another version with stuffed cloth bodies and limbs using the same vinyl heads. Marks: © **1957/Baby Barry Doll/25.** *(Alden's Catalog)*

COM-L10. *Little Audrey and Friends.* 9"; vinyl heads, stuffed plush bodies. The line included: Cinderella, Popeye, Olive Oyl, Donald Duck, Mickey Mouse, Pinocchio, Casper the Friendly Ghost, Dumbo, Pluto, Katnip, Merryweather, Goofy, Spooky Ghost and Jiminy Cricket. *(1961 Montgomery Ward Christmas Catalog)*

COM-L11. *Little Audrey.* 13½"; all molded-painted vinyl with painted blue side-glance eyes and red hair. Marks: ©/**HARVEY F.C.** on under side of skirt. *(Wiseman collection).* Ruth Sheinwald has a 13" *Lil Audrey* with jointed neck, shoulders, hips, and elbows with real ribbon in vinyl topknot. A Roberta doll, she carries roller skates as in the comic strip. Purchased 1960.

COM-L15.

"Orphan Annie" — 7¾ in., red dress, white socks, black shoes, movable arms.
64-0986—1 doz in box............**Doz .78**
Lots of 1 gro, **Gro 9.00**

COM-L12.

COM-L13.

COM-L16.

COM-L14.

COM-L12. *Little Orphan Annie.* 7½"; see illustration for description. *(Butler Bros., 1933)*

COM-L13. *Little Orphan Annie, Sandy, Lillums and Harold Teen.* All painted bisque; in original box. Mfr: Japan. **Copyrighted Famous Artists Syn./N. SHURE CO. Distributors CHICAGO, IL** on box. *(S. Ricklefs collection)*

COM-L14. *Little Orphan Annie and Sandy.* Papier mache or composition, fully jointed doll; this dog is different than other styles. *(Courtesy Nita's House of Dolls)*

COM-L15. *Little Orphan Annie.* 17"; all lithographed cloth stuffed; red yarn hair; red dress, black belt. *(1967 Remco catalog)*

COM-L16. *Little Orphan Annie.* 15½"; red rooted hair; roly-poly black eyes, these are the plastic eyes found on some novelty stuffed items; open-closed mouth; fully jointed plastic body; red dress, black belt, shoes and socks. An attempt by a TV-oriented company (Remco) to promote a non-TV doll, resulted in early cancellation of the item. Source also indicated the Remco *Kewpies* also (See REMCO) did not sell because of lack of television promotion. A Remco Kewpie may someday be a valuable addition to a Kewpie collection. *(1967 Remco catalog)*

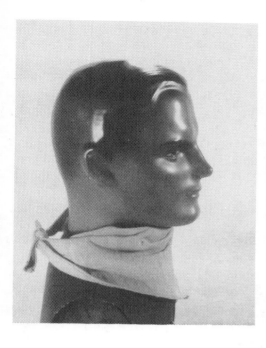

COM-L17.

Please turn to next page for description of these dolls.

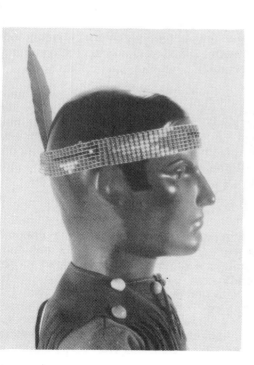

COM-L18.

COM-L19.

COM-L21.

COM-L20.

COM-L17. *The Lone Ranger.* 20½"; molded-painted black hair; painted brown eyes; closed mouth; composition swivel head, hands and boots, stuffed cloth body and limbs; all original green suede vest and cuffs, tan suede pants with picture of Lone Ranger and words: **Hi Yo Silver,** ©**The Lone Ranger Inc.,** tan hat with red-brown band and a star and **THE LONE RANGER** in rope script, working gun marked: **BIG CHIEF MADE IN USA.** Red paper tag reads: **THE LONE RANGER and TONTO/Manufactured by/DOLLCRAFT NOVELTY CO./SOLE LICENSEES/New York City** on one side, other side: picture of Lone Ranger, Tonto, and Silver reads: **LONE RANGER** in rope script, **OFFICIAL DOLL** and **copyright T.L.R.Co. Inc.** Doll is unmarked. *(Courtesy Remrey's Antiques)*

COM-L18. *Tonto.* 20½"; molded-painted black hair; painted brown eyes; closed mouth; dark red-brown composition swivel head, hands and feet, stuffed cloth body and limbs; all original "buckskin" shirt and pants with picture of Tonto and the words: **TONTO/The Lone Ranger's Pal;** real beaded headband with feather, moccasins, knife and gun marked: **BIG CHIEF MADE IN USA.** Original red paper tag (see COM-L17). *(Courtesy Remrey's Antiques)*

COM-L19, 20, 21. *The Lone Ranger, Tonto, and Butch Cavendish.* 9½"; molded-painted features; fully jointed action-figure plastic bodies; dressed in appropriate costumes with guns, holsters, boots, headgear. Also available are *Silver* and *Scout* with fully movable bodies, Tribal Tepee, and eight different adventure sets which supply all the necessary equipment for each episode. Mfr: Hubley Division, Gabriel Industries, Inc., 1973. *(Courtesy Hubley catalog)*

COM-M2.

COM-M3.

COM-N2.

COM-M2. *Moon Mullins.* 3¾"; painted black hair and eyes; closed mouth with hole for cigar; all molded-painted bisque; brown derby, black coat, red vest, yellow tie, black shoes; head mounted on spring to allow doll to "nod". Marks: **MOON MULLINS** on back, **GERMANY** on head. *(Ortwein collection, photograph by Jackie Meekins)*

COM-M3. *Jeff.* 3¼"; molded-painted features; all celluloid; painted black jacket, red bow tie. Marks: ©
1922/Germany. *(Ortwein collection, photograph by Jackie Meekins)*

COM-N2. *Nancy and Sluggo.* No description available.

Reader Ruth Sheinwald has an identical *Sluggo* with vinyl head marked © **S&P.** Her doll has red molded-on hat, one-piece body of magic skin, red and white striped shirt, blue pants, black jacket. Purchased in 1955; believed to be an Ideal doll.

COM-N3.

COM-N4.

COM-N5a,b,c,d.

COM-N5c.

COM-N3. *Nancy.* 15"; black yarn hair; painted black eyes; closed mouth; stuffed cloth body; black and white and red dress with yellow shoes. Unmarked. *(Thompson collection)*

Reader Ruth Sheinwald reports she owns the *Sluggo* mate to COM-N3, above. Although the doll is unmarked, it is all original and has a paper tag indicating it was manufactured by Georgene Novelties, Inc. She purchased her *Nancy* in 1961 and *Sluggo* in 1962. Georgene also made *Tubby Tom* and *Alvin* from the *Little Lulu* comics. Ruth also owns *Nancy* as shown in COM-N4, as well as the *Sluggo* to match.

COM-N4. *Nancy.* 20"; plush hair; lithographed cloth; tag on front reads: **NANCY/© 1972 UNITED/FEATURE SYNDICATE INC,** tag sewn into hip reads: **CELLULOSE FIBER/SYNTHETIC FOAM/STACEY LEE ORIGINALS/BROOKLYN N.Y./MASS T-10 PA (48 N.Y.).** *(Gibbins collection)*

COM-N5a-e. *The Nemo Series.* Two sizes; all painted bisque; sold for 25¢ and $1.00; from cartoon by Winsor McCay; includes: *Dr. Pill, Princess, Imp, Nemo and Flip.* *(Playthings, February, 1914)*

COM-N6.

COM-O3.

"OSWALD".
Movie Star

1F-2554 — ⅟₁₂ doz. in box. Doz   **$8.00**

COM-O2.

COM-O3-1.

COM-O4.

COM-N6. *Character Boy.* Molded-painted features; composition head, stuffed body. Note similarity to the *Gene Carr Kids* (COM-3a-e and -3-1). The character also bears a striking resemblance to *Alfred E. Newman,* the MAD Magazine "Mascot", as well as to *Funny Honey* (FRAN-1).

Doll on the right also has a composition head however, he is at present unidentified although definitely a character.

COM-O2. *Oswald Rabbit.* 16"; stuffed velour head and body; black and orange costume; has key-wind walking mechanism; from cartoons and comic strip. *(Butler Brothers)*

COM-O3. *Oswald Rabbit.* 17"; stuffed duvetyne head, ears and nose, velvet face, costume; key-wind walking mechanism allows doll to walk with swaying motion. Tag on shirt reads: **DARLING/TODDLER/WIND ME UP/AND I/WILL WALK.** *"New in '32".* (Butler Brothers, 1932)

COM-O3-1. *Oswald.* 15"; duvetyne face, soft stuffed duvetyne, terry cloth or percale body; ribbon collar reads: **OSWALD THE LUCKY/RABBIT;** sold for $3.90 per dozen: ca. 1932. *(Butler Brothers Catalog)*

COM-O4. *Our Gang.* Molded hollow bisque figures ready to paint with water colors; eight children and one dog; in original box with color card to show the colors to paint each character. Box marked: **HAL ROACH'S/OUR GANG/M.G.M./PICTURES.** *(Author's collection)*

COM-P7.

fig-COM-P8.

COM-P8.

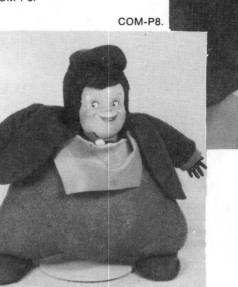

Cartoon Comics—Aver. 5 in., wood, elastic construction, **6 styles,** Pop-Eye, Moon Mullins, Orphan Annie, Humpty-Dumpty, etc., attractive color combinations.
63-8431—1 doz asst. in box ..**Doz .85**

COM-P11-1.

COM-P9

POPEYE

The greatest selling rubber toy on the market. Every child and even adults desire them. Made of rubber in bright colors. Put them on display and they sell themselves. Height 13 inches. Packed 1 dozen in package.

No. 40/15. Per Dozen............**$0.80**
Per Gross **9.00**

COM-P10.

GOB

Made of unbreakable w o o d composition, painted in bright colors. Has wooden pipe stuck in mouth. Height 15 inches. A very prominent character w e l l k n o w n by everyone. Pleases both the children and grown-ups.

No. 66/15. Per Dozen **$5.50**

JOE PALOOKA CHARACTERS

COM-P7. *Little Champ.* 14"; molded-painted yellow hair, blue eyes; fully jointed vinyl body; replacement clothes; Joe Palooka's son from the comic strip. *(Phillips collection)*

COM-P8. *Humphrey.* 16" tall, 18" wide; red plush hair; painted blue side-glance eyes; painted mouth; celluloid face, magic skin gauntlet hands, wool felt stuffed body; wears wool felt blue coat, orange and green body-pants, brown shoes, rubber bib, and blue felt hat. Unmarked. *(Author's collection)*

POPEYE AND FRIENDS

COM-P9. *Popeye.* See illustration for description. *(1936 Stack Mfg. Co. Catalog)*

COM-P10. *Popeye.* See illustration for description. *(1936 Stack Mfg. Co. Catalog)*

Also listed in same catalog was a 12" size at $3.50 per dozen.

COM-P-11. *Popeye.* 15"; all lithographed cloth. Unmarked. *(Gibbins collection)*

COM-P11.

COM-P15.

COM-P12.

COM-P13.

COM-P14.

COM-P11-1. *Popeye and Friends.* See illustration for description. *(1933 Butler Bros. catalog illustration)*

COM-P12. *Popeye.* 12½"; molded-painted foam on wire armature. Marks: © **1968/KING FEATURES/SYNDICATE INC/MFG. BY LAKESIDE/IND. INC./LIC. BY/NEWFIELD LTD./OF ENGLAND.** *(Wiseman collection)*

COM-P13. *Popeye.* 21"; molded-painted features, vinyl head and arms, stuffed cloth body and legs; removable clothes; talking ring, talks "like an old salt". *(1963 Wards Catalog)*

COM-P14. *Popeye.* 9"; molded-painted features; stuffed plush body and arms, vinyl head and hat, felt hands; blue and white body. Tag reads: **A GUNDERFUL CREATION T.M. REG. APPLIED FOR JAPAN** (in circle)/**Popeye** (script) in center, other side reads: **ALL NEW MATERIALS/GUND MFG. CO./360 Suydam St./BROOKLYN 37, N.Y./MADE IN JAPAN.** Ca. 1963. *(Photograph by Jackie Meekins, Owner)*

COM-P15. *Talking Popeye Hand Puppet.* 12"; molded-painted vinyl head, felt arms, cloth puppet glove with voice box inside, talking ring. *(Author's collection)*

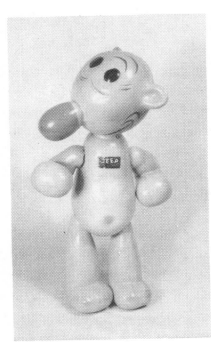

COM-P16.

COM-P17.

COM-P18.

COM-P16. *Jeep.* 13"; molded-painted wood; swivel head, jointed at shoulders and hips; red nose, blue spots on back. Paper tag on chest reads: **"JEEP"/1935/KING FEATURES SYN.** *(O'Rourke collection)*

COM-P17. *Olive Oyl.* 5¼"; segmented wood; painted orange skirt, blue, red, and white blouse, black shoes; painted features. Marks: **OLIVE OYL/©KFS.** *(Hafner collection)*

COM-P18. *Psyllium (Pus-Silly).* 10"; molded-painted hard rubber, with moving head; red grin; orange hair; blue eyes; faded blue pants, one white suspender with a black button, black shoes and hat. Marks: © - **1937/BY/THE SUN RUBBER CO./BARBERTON OHIO U.S.A.** on feet. *(Author's collection)*

COM-P19. *Psyllium and Popocatepetl.* 10"; all rubber with moving heads.

His mama named him Psyllium because it was such a cute name. (She found it in a Ward's Catalog!) Popo and the other boys called him Silly for short. Popo's real name is Popocatepetl; mama found it in a geography. Silly and Popo are always trying out new ideas. This picture was taken as they watched the corner cop's horse eating the display apples at the Grocery Store after Silly had obligingly pulled the basket over to the curb within easy reach. Won't they run when the Grocer Man chases them! (1937-1938 Ward's Catalog)

COM-P20a, b. *Puzzy and Sizzy.* 15"; molded-painted features; Puzzy has red hair and black eyes, Sizzy has blonde hair and blue eyes; all composition; appropriate clothes; copyright 1948 by Herman Cohn, Baltimore, Maryland (The House of Puzzy, Inc.). Marks: **PUZZY** (or **SIZZY**) ©/**H. of P., U.S.A.** *(Stewart collection)*

These characters were known as the *"Good Habit"* kids. Their images appeared on soap, hairbrushes, toothbrushes, and dozens of other grooming items for children decorated with decals produced by The Meyercord Co. of Chicago. The characters were based on a popular comic strip of the 1930s called *"Puzzy."*

COM-P19.

COM-P20b.

This Is
"Skippy"
I F-9694—
1 doz. in box.

Doz 78c
"Skippy," 5
in., jointed
arms, bright
costume.

COM-S3.

COM-R1.

"PUZZY"   "SIZZY"

COM-P20a,b.

COM-P20c.

COM-S4.   COM-S4.

COM-P20c. *Puzzy,* 15", all original, composition, red painted hair, large painted black eyes. *(Courtesy Barb Owens)*

COM-R1. *Rachel.* 3½"; all molded-painted bisque; swivel neck; from a comic strip by Frank O. King. *(Ortwein collection, photograph by Jackie Meekins)*

COM-S3. *Skippy.* See illustration for description. *(Butler Brothers, 1928)*

COM-S4. *Skeezix.* 14½"; lithographed, stuffed oil cloth; gusseted legs, arms stitched on separately; original blue chambray overall suit. *(Author's collection)*

COM-S5.

EVERYONE KNOWS THESE SCAMPS!

Comic Character Dolls From the Funny Papers

Every child in the country knows Smitty and Herby. They're one of the most popular comic strips and NOW here they are in dolls.

Here's Smitty Himself—

You'll like "Smitty," when you see how well he has been reproduced. Made from ravelproof material stuffed with 100% Prime Kapok—realistically colored.

No. **TA1174.** 14-in. "Smitty."
Each, 50c. Lots of 6, 46c. Net..**45c**
No. **TA1175.** 21-in. "Smitty."
Each, 90c. Lots of 6, 85c. Net..**83c**

—and Li'l Brother Herby

Steps right out of the picture to bring joy to the children. Made from hand applique ravelproof material and stuffed with light weight 100% Prime Kapok, realistically colored, too.

No. **TA1176.** 12-in. Herby. Each, 50c.
Lots of 6, 46c.
Less 2%, ·net................**45c**
No. **TA1177.** 19-in. Herby. Eeach, 90c.
Lots of 6, 85c.
Less 2%, net................**83c**

COM-S6a,b.

COM-S5. *Smitty.* 3¾"; molded-painted bisque; painted red cap, dark blue pants and coat, brown shoes. Marks: **Germany** on bottom of coat, **Smitty** across shoulders. *(Ortwein collection, photograph by Jackie Meekins)*

COM-S6a, b. *Smitty and Li'l Brother Herby.* See illustration for description. *(Butler Brothers, 1935)*

COM-S8.

COM-S7.

COM-S9.

"SNOOKUMS."

COM-S10.

COM-S11a,b.

COM-S11c,d.

COM-S7. *Napoleon alias Snookums.* 12''; composition head, stuffed plush Billiken-type body, sold for $8.50 per dozen. Mfr: Samstag and Hilder Bros., New York. *(Playthings, January, 1910)*

COM-S8. *The Newlywed Kid, Napoleon alias Snookums.* "The Newlyweds" cartoon, written by George McManus, was published in the New York World and other newspapers. *"The Newlyweds and Their Baby"* was a successful musical comedy of 1909 in which Sunny McKeen played the baby. *"He had the best looking mother and the worst looking father."* There was also a *Snookums* statuette. The cartoon strip and *Snookums* were popular through the 1920s. *(Playthings, December, 1909)*

COM-S9. *Newlywed Baby, Snookums.* Can't Break 'Em head composition hands, stuffed body and limbs. Mfr: Aetna Doll and Toy Co. *(Playthings, 1909)*

COM-S10. *Snoopy Astronaut.* 9''; molded-painted vinyl with original space suit, helmet, box; from the comic strip *"Peanuts"* by Charles M. Schulz, ® **UNITED FEATURES SYNDICATE, INC. 1969 / PRODUCED AND DISTRIBUTED BY/DETERMINED PRODUCTIONS, INC.** on box. Snoopy's dress consists of a regulation NASA fabric, safety life support system, bubble helmet, and World War I Flying Ace scarf. *(S. Ricklefs collection)*

COM-S11 a-d. *World's Greatest Super Heroes.* 8''; all molded-painted vinyl jointed at neck, shoulders, elbows, wrists, waist, hips, knees, ankles; wear stretch knit suits, plastic gloves, boots, capes, hats and masks: includes: *Batman, Robin, Aquaman, and Superman.* Marks: **N.P.P. INC./**© **1972** on head, **MEGO CORP./REG. U.S. PAT. OFF./PAT. PENDING/HONG KONG/MCMLXXI** on lower back, box reads: **NATIONAL PERIODICAL PUBLICATIONS, INC.** 1971. *(Author's collection)*

COM-S12.

COM-T7.

COM-S13.

COM-S15.

COM-S14.

COM-T8.

COM-T7.

COM-S12. *Superman* Head. 4"; all molded-painted vinyl. Marks: © **1965/NAT. PER. PUB. INC./SM-D-H13/IDEAL TOY CORP.** *(Author's collection)*

COM-S13. *Superman.* 16"; molded-painted vinyl head, rayon plush cotton-stuffed body and limbs; long red cape; (see B4 a-c for other super people). *(1966 Spiegel's Catalog)*

COM-S14. *Sweet Pea.* 11½"; molded-painted vinyl head and cap; large melon grin; stuffed cloth body and limbs; original long red dress; from *Popeye* cartoons. Marks: **386/D** on head; dress tag reads: **SWEET PEA/KING FEATURES SYNDICATE, INC/GUND MFG. CO.** *(Gaylin collection)*

COM-S15. *Sweetie Pie.* 9½"; molded-painted one-piece vinyl body; comic book character; holds identical tiny doll; 1950s or 1960s. Marks: **"Sweetie Pie"/A STERN TOY/**©**/N.E.A.** *(Author's collection)*

COM-T7. *Tom.* 20"; molded-painted vinyl head; open-closed mouth; stuffed blue and white corduroy body and limbs; from "Tom and Jerry" cartoons. Marks: **QUALITY ORIGINALS BY/MATTEL** ®**/TOM AND JERRY** © **METRO-GOLDWYN-MAYER, INC./**© **1965 MATTEL, INC. HAWTHORNE, CALIF./PAT'D IN USA/PAT IN CANADA, 1962/OTHER PATENTS PENDING/HEAD AND SEWN BODY MADE IN HONG KONG** on tag. *(Wiseman collection)*

COM-T8. *Trixie.* 8"; molded-painted vinyl; painted features and clothes; came holding cereal bowl; the baby character from the cartoon strip "Hi and Lois", © King Features Syndicate, Inc. drawn by Dik Browne. Marks: **N.F.** © **KFS** on seat. *(Wardell collection)*

COM-U1. *Uncle Wiggly.* 12½"; brown glued-on button eyes over painted eye outline; open-closed mouth with two painted teeth molded-painted vinyl head, stuffed cloth body, stitch jointed arms and legs; original felt hat, yellow felt jacket, white shirt, purple tie, blue cotton pants with red and white cuffs; ca. 1953; missing original cloth tag which read: **UNCLE WIGGLY.** *(Busch collection)*

COM-W1. *Wimpy.* 8¼"; all molded painted rubber; light blue tie, dark blue jacket, brown pants, and pink shirt; squeeker; from the Popeye cartoons. Marks: **KING FEATURES/SYNDICATE** on back. *(Author's collection)*

COM-W2. *Wimpy.* 3½"; molded-painted composition; feet are on rocker-type walker. Marks: **WIMPY/1920** (or 1930) **KING FEATURES INC/MADE IN USA/PAT. NO. 2140276** on right foot. *(Wiseman collection)*

COM-U1.

COM-W1.

COM-W2.

COM-W3.

COM-W4.

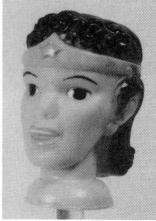

COM-W5.

COM-W7.

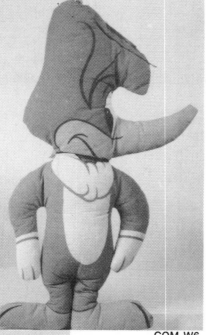

COM-Y1.

COM-W6.

COM-Y1.

COM-Y1.

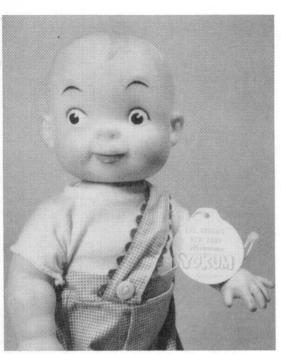

COM-Y2.

COM-Y3.

COM-Y3a.

COM-W3. *Wimpy.* 17"; molded-painted mask face; stuffed cloth body, pink felt ears; all original clothes. Unmarked. *(Potter collection)*

COM-W4. *Wimpy.* See illustration for description. *(1936 Stack Mfg. Co. Catalog)*

COM-W5. *Wonder Woman.* 4"; molded-painted vinyl head; comic book character. Marks: © **1966/NATL. PERIODICALS PUBS. INC./IDEAL TOY CORP.** *(Author's collection)*

COM-W6. *Woody Woodpecker.* 13½"; lithographed cloth, stuffed. Unmarked. *(Wiseman collection)*

COM-W7. *Woody Woodpecker Hand Puppet.* 16"; molded-painted vinyl head; cloth puppet glove. Marks: **QUALITY ORIGINALS BY/MATTEL ®/WOODY WOODPECKER ® &© by/Walter Lantz Productions, Inc./US PATS. 3,017,187 3,082,006 & 3,095,201/PAT'D IN CANADA 1962 OTHER PATS. PEND/HEAD AND SLEEVE IMPORTED FROM HONG KONG** on label, other side reads: **MATTEL, INC./M/TOYMAKERS.** *(Wiseman collection)*

COM-Y1. *Mammy Yokum.* 21"; molded-painted vinyl head, stuffed cloth body and limbs; all original clothes. Same head was used in an all vinyl version of the doll; from comic strip by All Capp. Marks: **BABY BARRY DOLL/© 1957** on head. *(Author's collection)*

COM-Y2. *Mysterious Yokum.* 11"; molded-painted features; soft vinyl head, stuffed magic skin body; squeeker; all original clothes, original price $2.98. Marks: ©/**U.F.S. INC./1953** on head, original tag reads: **LI'L ABNER'S/ NEW BABY /Mys—terious/YOUKUM/© 1953 UNITED FEATURES/ SYNDICATE, INC.** *(Potter collection)*

COM-Y3. *Yosemite Sam.* 7¼"; molded-painted plastic, fully jointed; painted features and legs; true to cartoon style, it has only three fingers and thumb. Marks: © **Warner Bros - Seven/Arts Inc. - 1968** on head, **R. DAKINS/COMPANY/PROD OF/HONG KONG** on left foot. *(Author's collection)*

COM-Y3a. *Yosemite Sam.* (1974 R. Dakin & Co. catalog illustration)

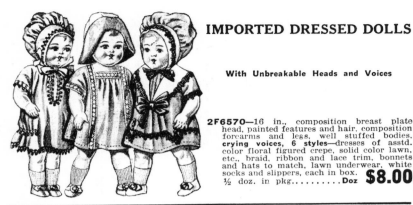

IMPORTED DRESSED DOLLS

With Unbreakable Heads and Voices

2F6570—16 in., composition breast plate head, painted features and hair, composition forearms and legs, well stuffed bodies, **crying voices, 6 styles**—dresses of asstd. color floral figured crepe, solid color lawn, etc., braid, ribbon and lace trim, bonnets and hats to match, lawn underwear, white socks and slippers, each in box. **$8.00** ½ doz. in pkg.........**Doz**

COMP-2.

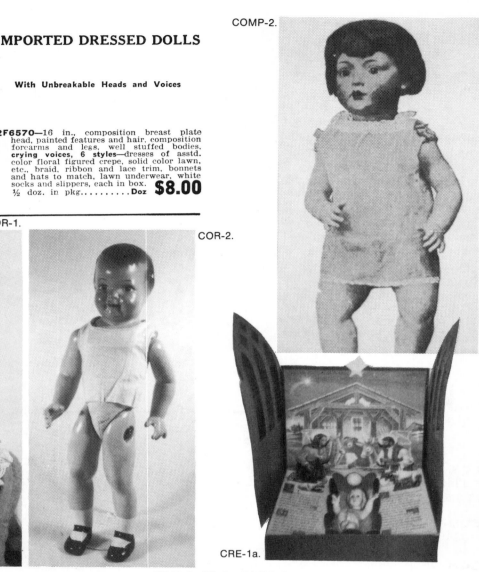

COMP-1.

COR-1.

COR-2.

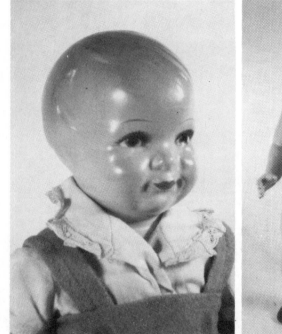

CRE-1a.

COMP-1. Examples of the imported composition dolls 1928-1932. See illustration for description. *(Butler Brothers, 1928)*

COMP-2. *Baby.* Human hair wig; sleep eyes; closed mouth; unbreakable composition ("paper compote"); jointed knees, elbows, and hands; *"will not burn".* Mfr: The Composition Novelty Co. *(Playthings, January, 1916)*

COR-1. *Grace Corry Child.* 13½"; molded-painted blonde hair; painted blue eyes with more eye "make-up" than usual; closed mouth, cloth body, composition shoulder head and limbs. Marks: ©/BY/**Grace Corry.** *(Wiseman collection)*

COR-2. *Grace Corry Boy.* 15"; molded-painted dark hair; painted eyes; closed mouth; composition head and limbs, stuffed cloth body; painted shoes and socks. Note unusual legs. Marks: ©/BY/**Grace Corry.** *(Wiseman collection)*

CRE-1. *Christ Child, Creche Doll.* 9"; molded-painted brown hair; painted brown eyes; open-closed mouth; molded body and diaper. Unmarked.

CRE-1a. *The Most Wonderful Story,* boxed set contained *Baby Jesus* doll, two-dimensional figures of *Mary* and *Joseph,* and the story. Quoted from the box: "Produced under the direction and guidance of religious leaders. 1958, Ideal Toy Corporation, Hollis, N.Y., made in U.S.A." Inside: "The Christmas Story taken from the Bible." On a paper envelope containing parts of the set-up: "This envelope contains one Cathedral Background Unit. Instructions for Assembly: Attach the 2 narrow side windows with 2 paper fasteners on each side. Paper fasteners are included in this kit. Open cover of Nativity Setting and place cutout of center window over top of lid. The 2 side windows will fall into place on the sides of the nativity setting." On the cover of the box is a triple-arched cathedral window and the words, "The Most Wonderful Story." The set was priced retail at $2.99. *(Photograph and information courtesy Pat Sebastian)*

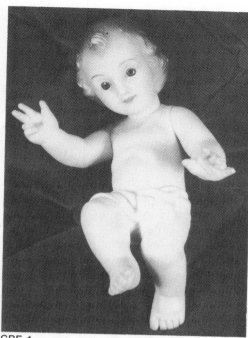

CRE-1.

CRE-2.

CRE-2.

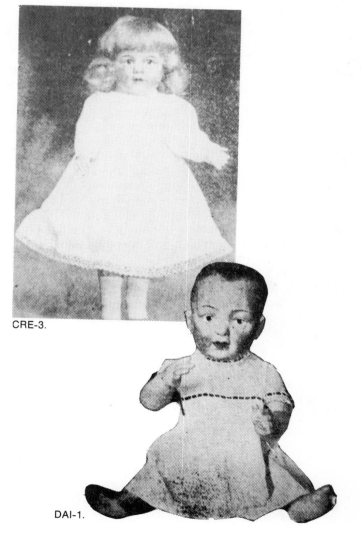

CRE-3.

CRE-2. *John the Baptist, Creche Doll.* 18"; carved-painted brown hair and beard; inset blown glass eyes; closed mouth; wooden papier mache body jointed at wrists only, body is painted blue under clothes, sandals are molded and painted; all original long white drawers and underskirt, faded old green satin robe with gold cape and lace trim; came from Italy. Unmarked. *(Cannon collection)*

CRE-3. Example of the 1919 line of one hundred styles of boys, girls, and babies made by the Crescent Toy Mfg. Co. *"H. Cohen, factory manager, has been manufacturing dolls for twelve years - he has a reputation for success."* Crescent Toy Mfg. Co., Brooklyn, NY. *(Playthings, January, 1919)*

DAI-1. *Dainty Doll Baby.* Molded-painted features; all composition head and body; retail price 25¢ to $1.00; *"Old timers with a new firm name".* Mfr: Dainty Doll Mfg. Co. NY. *(Playthings, March, 1917)*

DAI-1.

DAK-1.

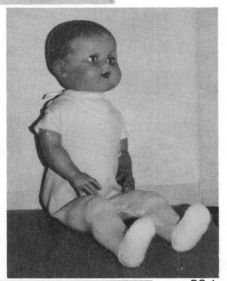

DC-1.

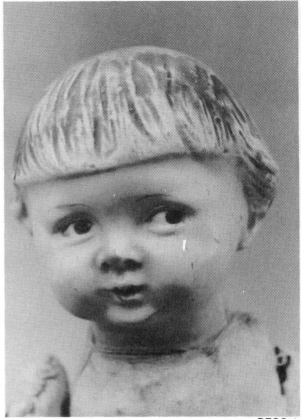

DECO-1.

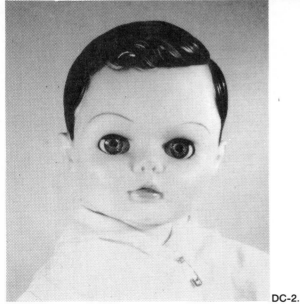

DC-2.

DAK-1. *Dream Doll.* 8"; orange yarn hair and beard; green eyes; stuffed cloth on wire armature; original blue coat, white pants, red and white striped shirt, yellow fisherman's hat, carries basket. Marks: **DREAM DOLLS/© R. DAKIN & CO./SAN FRANCISCO CALIF./PROD. OF JAPAN.** *(Vandiver collection)*

DECO-1. *Can't Break 'Em Boy.* 15"; molded-painted brown "Dutch" cut hair; intaglio brown eyes; closed mouth; composition head and gauntlet hands, excelsior-stuffed cloth body and legs, pin and disc jointed; 1910-1920. Marks: **DECO/134** on head. *(Perry collection)*

DEE AND CEE, CANADA

DC-1. *Baby.* 24"; painted hair; blue-gray sleep eyes with thick lashes; open-closed mouth; soft vinyl head, stuffed vinyl body and limbs; ca. 1950. Marks: **DEE CEE** on neck. *(Campbell collection)*

DC-2. *Mountie.* 15"; molded-painted black hair; blue sleep eyes; open-closed mouth; vinyl head, hard plastic body and legs; possibly original clothes; ca. 1950. Marks: **DEEANCEE.** *(Courtesy Nita's House of Dolls)*

DC-4.

DC-3.

DC-5.

DC-6.

DC-3. *Negro Baby.* 20"; brown sleep eyes; drink and wet mouth; soft vinyl head, rigid plastic body and limbs; tiny red earrings. Mfr: Dee Cee. *(Campbell collection)*

DC-4. *Boy.* 12"; molded hair and hat with feather; inset glassine side-glance eyes; open-closed Hummel-type mouth; very soft plastic jointed neck and shoulders; possibly original clothes; squeeker; ca. 1955. Marks: **DEE & CEE** on head. *(Courtesy Nita's House of Dolls)*

DC-5. *Girl.* 12"; rooted blonde hair; inset blue eyes with hard plastic lashes; open-closed Hummel-type mouth; fully jointed vinyl body, note unusual shape; ca. 1960. Marks: **DEE & CEE/MADE IN CANADA.** *(Courtesy Kimport Dolls)*

DC-6. *Eskimos.* 14", 16"; rooted straight black hair; painted black eyes; open-closed with four painted teeth; soft vinyl head, plastic body and limbs, fully jointed; fur-trimmed parka, snow pants and boots of white wool fleece, red and blue ric-rac trim; ca. 1960. Marks: **KOWEEKA ©/HUDSON BAY CO.** on head, **1-5/D & C** on lower back. *(McLaughlin collection)*

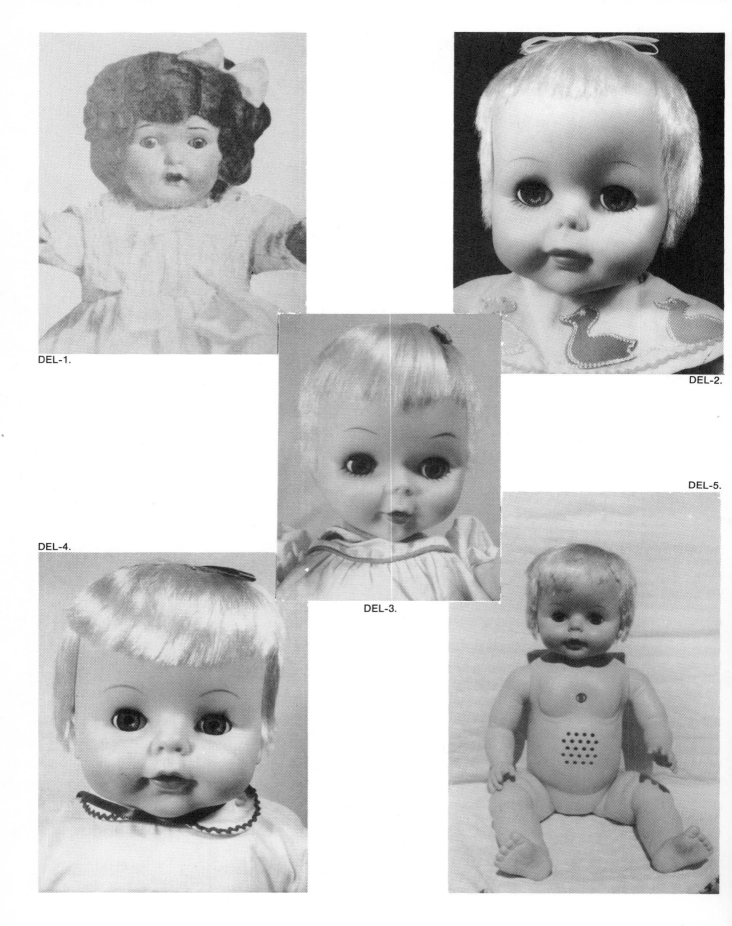

DEL-1.

DEL-2.

DEL-5.

DEL-4.

DEL-3.

DEL-1. *Baby.* Human hair or mohair wigs; sleep eyes; molded-painted composition; various costumes. Mfr: De Luxe Doll and Toy Co., New York. *(Playthings, January, 1919)*

DELUXE READING CORP.

TOPPER CORPORATION

Deluxe, a division of Topper, went out of business in 1972. Mechanically oriented dolls were always a specialty; their *Busy Baby* series is an example. Working models of these dolls may become interesting specimens in years to come.

DEL-2. *Tickles.* 20"; rooted blonde hair; blue sleep eyes; closed mouth; vinyl head and arms, hard plastic body and legs; original clothes; battery operated mechanism allows doll to cry, laugh when tickled and spanked. Marks: **19 ⓒ 63/DELUXE READING/75.** *(Wardell collection)*

DEL-3. *Baby Brite.* 13½"; rooted blonde hair; blue sleep eyes; open-closed mouth; vinyl head, hard plastic body and limbs; battery operated, push button and doll turns head and sleeps when lying down; push other button and she raises arms to be picked up. Came with complete set of white plastic furniture. Marks: **15/DELUXE READING CORP./ⓒ 1963 15ME#H** on head. *(Wardell collection)*

DEL-4. *Baby Boo.* 21"; rooted blonde hair; blue sleep eyes; open-closed mouth; vinyl head and limbs, hard plastic body; original red and white checked pants and white blouse; doll stops crying when the light is turned off or she is covered with a blanket, hugged, or given her pacifier. Marks: **111/DELUXE READING CO./ⓒ 1965.** *(Wardell collection)*

DEL-5. *Baby Boo.* Undressed view of doll shows construction. *(Photograph by Anneruth Pfister, Owner)*

DEL-6. *Little Miss Fussy.* 18"; rooted blonde hair; blue sleep eyes; open mouth with drink and wet feature; soft vinyl head and arms, hard plastic body and legs; original clothes; battery operated control allows doll to drink bottle, wet, and then fuss until diaper is changed. Marks: **K7/DELUXE TOPPER/1967.** *(Wardell collection)*

DEL-7. *Baby Catch-a-Ball.* 19"; rooted brown hair; blue sleep eyes; closed mouth with molded tongue; soft vinyl head, hard plastic limbs; silver bracelets on arms attract ball so doll appears to "catch" it, can also throw ball back to child. Marks: **2871/17EYE/PB2/75/DELUXE TOPPER/19ⓒ68.** *(Wiseman collection)*

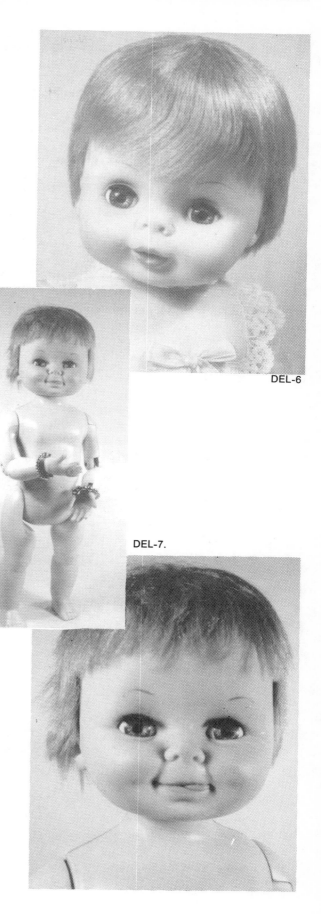

DEL-6

DEL-7.

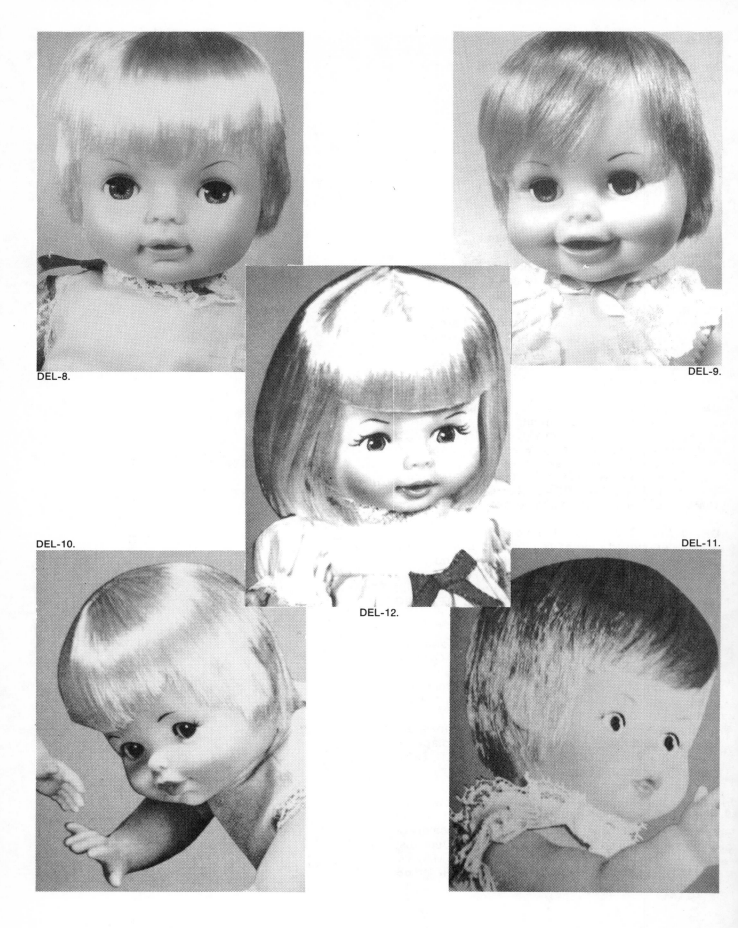

DEL-8.

DEL-9.

DEL-10.

DEL-11.

DEL-12.

DEL-13.

DEL-14.

DEL-15.

DEL-8. *Baby Peek 'N Play.* 18"; rooted blonde Saran hair; blue sleep eyes; open closed mouth; soft vinyl head and arms, hard plastic body and legs; original clothes; also came in black version; battery operated, raises hands to cover eyes, plays accordion, picks up bottle and drinks and raises arms to mommy. Marks: **72/DELUXE TOPPER/19©68.** *(Wardell collection)*

DEL-9. *Baby Party.* 10", 18"; rooted blonde hair; small doll has painted eyes; larger one has blue sleep eyes; open mouth; vinyl head and arms, hard plastic body and legs; redressed in copy of original clothes; battery operated, doll blows whistle and balloon, or blows out candles. Marks: **2770/17 EYE 39/DELUXE TOPPER.19©68.** *(Wardell collection)*

DEL-10. *Baby Crawler.* 7", 10"; rooted blonde hair; painted blue sleep eyes; open-closed mouth; soft vinyl head, hard plastic body and limbs, fully jointed with bent knees; wears two-piece crawl suit; 7" doll takes one "C" battery; 10" takes two "C" batteries. *(1969 Topper Catalog)*

DEL-11. *Baby Fussy.* 10"; rooted blonde hair; painted blue eyes; open-closed mouth; vinyl head, hard plastic body and limbs; original pink lace trim dress, diaper, shoes, bottle; drinks from bottle, then cries and kicks when wet until diaper is changed. *(1969 Topper Catalog)*

DEL-12. *Busy Baby Walker.* 10"; rooted blonde hair; painted blue eyes; open-closed mouth; vinyl head, plastic body and limbs, fully jointed; white dress with red trim, molded-on shoes; one "C" battery makes doll walk. *(1969 Topper Catalog)*

DEL-13. *Luv 'N' Care.* 18"; rooted blonde hair; blue sleep eyes; open mouth; vinyl head, hard plastic body and limbs, fully jointed; battery operated, try to feed doll, she cries and rubs tummy; put hot water bottle on tummy, she stops crying; cheeks glow with "fever" by means of a red light behind face, take temperature and give her a "pill", she stops crying. Marks: **DELUXE TOPPER.19©69.** *(Wardell collection)*

DEL-14. *Baby Ride-A-Bike.* 10"; rooted blonde hair; painted blue eyes; open-closed mouth; vinyl head, hard plastic body and limbs; fully jointed; dress, tights, shoes; battery operated, put doll on plastic bike, she pushes peddles to make bike move. *(1969 Topper Catalog)*

DEL-15. *Smarty Pants.* 18"; rooted blonde hair; blue sleep eyes; closed mouth; vinyl head, plastic body and limbs, fully jointed; original clothes. "Answers" questions; knows her right hand from her left and how many toes she has. Marks: **TOPPER CO./1971/©.** *(Wardell collection)*

DEL-16a.

DEL-16b.

DEL-16c.

DEL-16e.

DEL-16d.

DEL-16e.

DEL-16f,g.

DEL-16h,i.

DEL-16l.

DEL-16j,k.

THE WORLD OF DAWN

Though short lived, *The World of Dawn* was a doll universe, indeed. Six girls, Dawn, Angie, Glori, Dale, Longlocks, and Jessica, plus three boys, Gary, Van and Ron, were later (1971) joined by the girls of the *Dawn Modeling Agency*—Daphne, Denise, Melanie, Dinah, and Maureen. April and Kip (also 1971) were Dawn's *Drum Majorette* friends in costumes complete with boots and batons. Fancy Feet and Kevin came with *"Discos"*, a device on which they 'danced'.

"Dawn Head to Toe" (Longlocks, Dawn, or Angie) was a doll with three additional wiglets. *Dawn's Dress Shop* sported a three-way mirror. *Dawn's Country Place* included three separate room settings—Playroom, Bedroom, and Patio—all with furniture and accessories. Each *Model Agency* doll had its own fashion portfolio. A modern kitchen came fully equipped.

These dolls were made in huge quantities for a few years, are quite small, and the manufacturer is no longer in business. They would, therefore, be a wise addition to a comprehensive vinyl collection.

DEL-16a-n. *Dawn and Friends.* 6½"; rooted hair in various colors and lengths; painted eyes of various colors, thick synthetic hair lashes; closed mouths; all vinyl, jointed at neck, shoulders, waist, and hips, posable legs. Marks: © **1970/TOPPER CORP./HONG KONG** on lower back.

DEL-16m.

DEL-16n.

Dawn has blonde hair and blue eyes; Angie has black hair and brown eyes; Glori has red hair and green eyes; Dale is a Black girl with Afro and dark eyes; Jessica has short blonde hair and bangs; and Longlocks has dark hair that reaches below her knees.

a-Dawn	f-Ron	k-Denise
b-Angie	g-Van	l-Melanie
c-Glori	h-Dinah	m-Longlocks
d-Dale	i-Maureen	n-Jessica
e-Gary	j-Daphne	

DEL-17a.

DEL-17b.

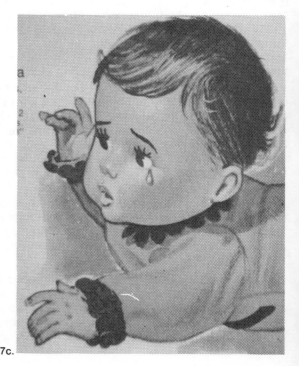

DEL-17c.

DEL-18.

DIS-15.

DEL-16-1.

Søren og Mette

DEN-1a,b.

DEN-1a,b. *Sexed Twins.* 11"; rooted synthetic blonde or dark hair; blue sleep eyes with lashes; drink and wet mouth but no lower opening so water must seep through hip joints; all vinyl, fully jointed; flannel diaper shirts only but large wardrobe available. Marks: *MADE IN DENMARK* on one side, **d.v.p. plastic** on other side; box is marked: **TVILLINGERNE/Soren og Mettel** on front and **Her ser du alt det toj, du Kan fa til tvillingerne** and **TOJ/TIL/SOREN/og/METTE.** *(Author's collection)*

DEL-16-1. *The Tom Boy.* 6½"; glued-on red mohair wig; painted features; all vinyl; original clothes. Marks: **33 / DELUXE READING CO. / © 1965** on head; **The Go-Go's (script) / TOPPER** (in oval) on plastic base. *(Shelton collection)*

DEL-17a, b, c. *Tear Drops.* 6"; *Belinda* wears a suit with pom-poms; *Cybil* wears a little suit with a kitty-cat on front; and *Ali* wears a suit with a flower decoration. Also planned was a Tear Drops'N'Crib set, a Tear Drops'N'Stroller, and a Tear Drops Sleep'N'Stroll set.

Here is an example of dolls that were never marketed although a complete work-up had been done on them including listing in a catalog (1972). These drawings are shown "just for fun"; in the writer's opinion they would have been most appealing little charmers. These three babies were Deet and Patti concepts.

DEL-18. *Gabbie.* Rooted blonde hair; blue sleep eyes; open mouth with drink and wet feature; vinyl head, plastic body and limbs; one-piece short romper; doll gurgles and coos, falls asleep and raises arms with help of battery control. *(1972 Topper Catalog)*

WALT DISNEY CHARACTER DOLLS

Any discussion of Disney dolls must begin with the character that started the cartoon maestro on his way - *Mickey Mouse.* As can be seen here, Mickey has been produced in almost endless variety of size, material, and style, but always with that certain something that marks him as a Disney creation. This is not to say the Disney dolls available are limited to Mickey. It is easy to imagine that nearly every character created by his genius has been translated into doll or puppet form.

There are a sprinkling of Disney characters elsewhere; consult the Index for their location.

DIS-15. *Mickey Mouse.* 13"; glued-on oil cloth eyes; painted mouth; stuffed black cloth body; real sheepskin chaps, molded-painted orange shoes, brass pistols, tan felt hat and rope. Holds small paper tag: **Mickey Mouse.** Mfr: Knickerbocker. *(Rebekka Anderton collection)*

DIS-18a-d.

63-8427 63-8426

63-8454 63-8453

"Mickey" and "Minnie Mouse" — Turned wood body, flexible arms, legs and tail, strong elastic construction, colored costumes, black & white features, can be set in all kinds of grotesque positions.

3⅞ In.
63-8426—Mickey Mouse
63-8427—Minnie Mouse
3 doz in box. **Doz .84**

5⅛ In.
63-8453—Mickey Mouse
63-8454—Minnie Mouse
1 doz in box. **Doz 2.10**

DIS-16.

DIS-19.

DIS-27.

DIS-17a-d.

"Mickey Mouse" Dolls

Here are Walt Disney's famous movie strip characters in imported china, to add a lot of life and color to your doll displays. They'll delight the hearts of every boy and girl who comes into your store . . . and SELL FAST!

4 Styles
"Mickey Mouse" Minstrels—5 in., bright painted costumes.
64-1230—1 doz in box........**Doz .80**

2 Styles
"Mickey and Minnie Mouse"—6 in., bright painted costumes.
64-1239—1 doz in box........**Doz .80**

MINNIE MOUSE

MICKEY MOUSE

NICK

A very prominent character known by everyone. Made of plastic composition, painted in natural colors. Very realistic. Height 12 inches. Packed one dozen in carton (No Less Sold).
No. 032/15.
Per Dozen...**$3.50**

DIS-25.

DIS-21.

NICK

Made of unbreakable wood composition, painted in bright colors. Face is painted in black and white. Silk ribbon bow around the neck. Height 12 inches. The most beloved character and the greatest seller of the day.
No. 67/15. Per Dozen **$4.50**

CARTOON and MOVIE CHARACTERS

3 In Box

"Mickey & Minnie Mouse"—3 styles, 3¼ to 3¾ in., painted costumes, asst. ball player, minstrel, soldier, flag bearer, nurse, etc.
64-1288—1 doz boxes in pkg................**Doz boxes .84**

DIS-20-1a-c.

Each Pair In Box

"Mickey and Minnie Mouse"—4⅛ in., 2 styles in box, painted costumes.
64-1286—1 doz boxes in pkg................**Doz boxes .84**

DIS-20a,b.

3 In Box

"Three Little Pigs"—3¼ in., painted costumes as featured throughout the country in the famous moving picture.
64-1284—1 doz boxes in pkg.
Doz boxes .84

DIS-22,23,24.

DIS-16. *Mickey Mouse.* 9"; molded-painted composition head and wooden body. Marks: ©/**WALT DISNEY** on back, **KNICKERBOCKER/TOY/CO. NYC** on lower back. *(Wiseman collection)*

DIS-17a-d. *"Mickey Mouse" Dolls.* See illustration for description. *(Butler Brothers, 1933 Fall Catalog)*

DIS-18a-d. *Mickey and Minnie Mouse.* See illustration for description. *(Butler Brothers 1933 Fall Catalog)*

DIS-19. *Minnie Mouse.* 10½"; molded-painted rubber; squeeker; painted panties, red and white dotted sundress. Marks: **WALT DISNEY PRODUCTIONS/THE SUN RUBBER CO./BARBERTON O. U.S.A.** *(Weeks collection)*

DIS-20a,b. *Mickey and Minnie Mouse.* See illustration for description. *(Butler Brothers 1928 Catalog)*

DIS-20-1a-c. *Mickey and Minnie Mouse.* See illustration for description. *(1928 Butler Bros. catalog illustration)*

DIS-21. *Mickey Mouse.* See illustration for description. *(Stack Mfg. Co. 1936 Catalog)*

DIS-22-24. *Three Little Pigs.* See illustration for description. *(Butler Brothers 1928 Catalog)*

DIS-25. *Mickey Mouse.* See illustration for description. *(Stack Mfg. Co. 1936 Catalog)*

DIS-26. *One of the Three Little Pigs.* 9"; painted brown eyes; painted grin; all composition, fully jointed; original clothes. Unmarked.

DIS-27. *Big Bad Wolf.* 3½"; molded-painted bisque; orange pants, green suspenders, red hat. Marks: **WALT DISNEY/MADE IN JAPAN** on back. *(Author's collection)*

DIS-28.

DIS-28. *Big Bad Wolf.* 26"; furry black head and chest; molded-painted face, stuffed cloth body and limbs, oilcloth feet; removable original clothes. *(Kaufman collection)*

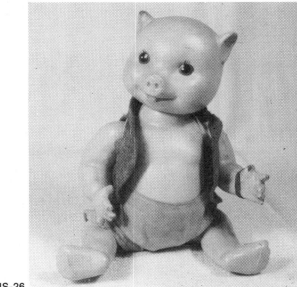

DIS-26.

DIS-29.

DIS-30.

DIS-31.

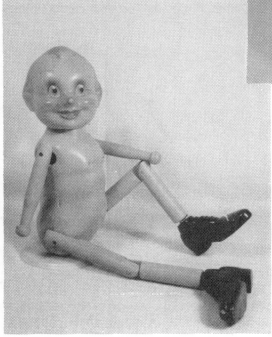

DIS-32.

DIS-33.

DIS-34.

DIS-35.

DIS-36.

DIS-29. *Panchito.* 15"; stuffed velvet and felt body over wire armature; oil cloth eyes on felt. Tag reads: © **Walt Disney Prod./Character Novelty Co./Licensee, South Norwalk, Conn.** (*Kaufman collection*)

DIS-30. *Dumbo.* Plastic disc eyes; stuffed plush body; music box. Marks: Tag on ear reads: **DUMBO/THE FLYING ELEPHANT/COPYRIGHT - WALT DISNEY PROD.**, other side reads: **GUND MFG. CO./I SWEDLIN LICENSEE/200 5th AVE. NYC 10 NY.** (*Wiseman collection*)

DIS-31. *Pinocchio.* 16½"; molded-painted yellow hair; painted blue eyes; nose has red tip; big red grin; composition head and body with wooden limbs jointed at knees, composition shoes. Unmarked. (*Burtchett collection*)

DIS-32. *Pinocchio Hand Puppet.* 5"; molded-painted vinyl head; lithographed glove. Marks: © **WDP - GUND ®/HONG KONG/691** on head, tag reads: **WALT DISNEY/CHARACTER/COPYRIGHT/WALT DISNEY PROD. PINOCCHIO** on glove. (*Wiseman collection*)

DIS-33. *Jiminy Cricket Hand Puppet.* 5½"; molded-painted vinyl head; lithographed glove. Marks: © **WDP - GUND ®/HONG KONG/689**, tag reads: **WALT DISNEY CHARACTER/COPYRIGHT/WALT DISNEY PROD, JIMINY CRICKET** on glove. (*Wiseman collection*)

DIS-34. *Jiminy Cricket.* 3¼" head; molded-painted features; composition head and hands, stuffed cloth body and limbs; original jacket. Marks: **JIMINY CRICKET / W.D.PR. KN. T. Co. / U.S.A.** on head. (*Burtchett collection*)

DIS-35. *Donald Duck.* 9½"; molded-painted features; composition and wood construction; original red coat and black and white hat. Marks: **WALT DISNEY'S MARIONETTES/"DONALD DUCK"/By MADAME ALEXANDER NY/ALL RIGHTS RESERVED** on head.

DIS-36. *Girl.* 15"; original mohair wig; round sleep eyes; closed mouth; fully jointed composition; could possibly be *"Rose Red"* who had sister called *"Rose White"*. Marks: **KNICKERBOCKER TOY CO./NEW YORK** on back, © **WALT DISNEY 1937** (or 1939). (*Sullivan collection*)

DIS-37.

DIS-38.

DIS-40.

DIS-39a.

DIS-39b.

DIS-39c.

DIS-37. *Stepmother.* 12"; gray mohair wig; painted black eyes; painted mouth with one tooth; composition head and limbs, stuffed cloth body; all original clothes. Marks: **WALT DISNEY'S MARIONETTES/ "STEPMOTHER"/(DISGUISED)/MADAME ALEXANDER N.Y. U.S.A.** on cloth tag.

DIS-38. *Grumpy, One of Seven Dwarfs.* 8"; all molded-painted rubber. Marks: **GRUMPY** on front of coat, © **WALT DISNEY PRO.** on coat tail. *(Wiseman collection)*

DIS-39a,b. *Sneezy and Sleepy, Two of the Seven Dwarfs.* 9"; molded-painted features, Sneezy has brown eyes; Sleepy has blue eyes; all composition; original red felt jackets, aqua felt pants, gold buttons. Marks: **SLEEPY** and **SNEEZY** on hats. *(Sullivan collection)*

DIS-39c. *Grumpy.* 9½"; mohair whiskers; painted features; one-piece composition with jointed arms; original clothes. Marks: © **Walt Disney / KNICKERBOCKER TOY CO.** (on back). *(Shelton collection)*

DIS-40. *Happy, One of the Seven Dwarfs.* 9"; molded-painted composition; original clothes. Marks: **WALT DISNEY'S MARIONETTES/"HAPPY"/MADAME ALEXANDER N.Y.** on cloth tag, with original play book.

DIS-41. Marionette set included the *Seven Dwarfs, Snow White, Prince Charming, Stepmother, Stepmother in disguise as the Wicked Witch, the Woodsman and a Maid.* Marks vary: **Doc, Happy** and **Dopey** have backwards numerals on heads; all others are marked **TONY SARG/ALEXANDER.** All have tags reading: **WALT DISNEY'S MARIONETTES/(name of character)/MADAME ALEXANDER N.Y.** *(Heinzel collection)*

DIS-42. *Snow White.* 21"; dark brown rooted hair, note hairline; blue sleep eyes; deep blood red mouth; early flexible vinyl body, fully jointed, bosom; original purple and yellow taffeta dress, gold shoes. Marks: **SNOW WHITE** on head, © **WALT DISNEY/PROD.** on right foot. *(Courtesy Nita's House of Dolls, Mahsem collection)*

DIS-42a. *Seven Dwarfs.* 8-8½"; molded-painted vinyl bodies; squeeker; painted red, blue or yellow clothes. Marks: Each doll has his name incised into right hip and © **WALT DISNEY PRD.** on back. *(Courtesy Nita's House of Dolls, Mahsem collection)*

DIS-42a. *Dopey.* From set illustrated. *(Courtesy Nita's House of Dolls, Mahsem collection)*

DIS-43. *Snow White.* Identical to doll shown in DIS-42. *(Wardell collection)*

DIS-42.

DIS-41.

DIS-42a.

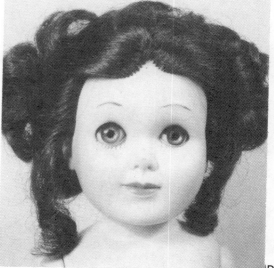

DIS-43.

DIS-45.

DIS-44.

DIS-47.

DIS-46.

DIS-44. *Dwarf from Set.* 7 to 8½"; all molded-painted vinyl; synthetic beards; moving heads. Marks: **HONG KONG** on neck, (must remove head to read mark). *(Hartwell collection)*

DIS-45. *Snow White and the Seven Dwarfs Charms.* ¾", 1¼"; molded-painted plastic; two different sets. Marks: **JAPAN.** *(Author's collection)*

DIS-46. *Mouseketeer Marionette.* 14"; molded-painted brown hair; blue eyes; composition head and hands, wooden body and limbs; black cap with ears, red cotton shirt, white pants; 1950s. Marks: **MOUSE-KETEER/ © WALT DISNEY PRODUCTIONS/MICK-EY MOUSE CLUB** on front of shirt. *(Photograph by Jackie Meekins, Owner)*

DIS-47. *Lady.* 3½"; molded-painted vinyl head; red and white polka dot puppet glove; from *"The Lady and The Tramp"*. Marks: © **W D P/LADY** on head. *(Wiseman collection)*

DIS-50.

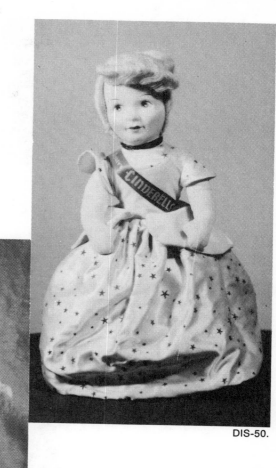

DIS-50.

DIS-48.

DIS-49.

DIS-48. *Tinkerbell.* 12"; blonde synthetic rooted wig; painted blue eyes; open-closed oval mouth; all vinyl jointed at neck, shoulders and hips; original green felt suit; painted green shoes with flowers, pink plastic wings covered with glitter. Marks: **WALT DISNEY PRODUCTIONS** on left foot, **13** on right foot. *(Busch collection)*

DIS-49. *Peter Pan.* 17"; molded-painted brown with green hat and red feather; painted brown eyes; smiling mouth; vinyl head and arms, green cloth body and legs; brown felt shoes, green felt shirt and brown belt; 1950s. Marks: **©/W.D.P./IDEAL DOLL** on head. *(Busch collection)*

DIS-50. *Cinderella.* 18"; blonde floss wig; painted features on mask face; cloth body; topsy-turvy two-headed doll; wears ball gown of pink velvet bodice and pink satin skirt with silver stars; scullery maid wears a white organdy blouse and apron and light blue cotton skirt; ca. 1951. Marks: Blue ribbon around body reads: **"Walt Disney's Cinderella".** *(Sheinwald collection)*

DIS-51.

DIS-51.

DIS-53.

DIS-52.

DIS-54.

Walt Disney's
Small World Dolls
8-inch friends in costumes
of far-away lands
$2⁹⁷ each

Adorable dolls in beautifully detailed

DIS-51. *Mary Poppins.* 36"; rooted black synthetic hair; blue painted eyes with rooted lashes; closed mouth; soft vinyl head, plastic body fully jointed; original clothes; 1960s. Marks: **PIN** on body, tag reads: **Walt Disney's Mary Poppins** with picture of doll, and a ribbon reading: **I CAN REALLY WALK.** *(N. Ricklefs collection)*

DIS-52. *Ko.* 13"; rooted black Saran hair; painted black eyes; closed mouth; fully jointed vinyl and hard plastic; gold felt long shirt; possibly a *"Small World"* doll. Marks: **K8** on head. *(Author's collection)*

DIS-53. *Cinderella.* 12"; molded-painted features; fully jointed vinyl body; rooted blonde hair; doll has two heads that interchange with the body; ball gown and scullery maid dress, pillow with glass slipper. *(Sears, Roebuck & Co. 1965 Catalog)*

DIS-54. *Small World Dolls.* 8"; molded-painted features; rooted or glued-on wigs; vinyl heads, plastic bodies; assorted costumes including French Can-Can girl, Dutch girl, South American girl, African girl, and Japanese girl, among others. *(Sears, Roebuck and Co. 1965 Catalog)*

DIS-55. *Ferdinand the Bull and Matador.* Ferdinand came in two sizes with black and gold art silk with velveteen face and horns. The Matador has a molded-painted composition head with stuffed cloth body and limbs and wears a velveteen hat, trousers, and cloak with felt jacket, epaulets and shoes. *"By arrangement with Walt Disney Mickey Mouse Ltd".* From Walt Disney's Silly Symphony Film, *"Ferdinand the Bull".* Mfr: H.G. Stone & Co. Ltd, London. *(Toy Trader and Exporter, 1939)*

DISPLAY DOLLS

Only on rare occasion is the average collector able to acquire a display piece. The writer was delighted, therefore, to be able to photograph an extensive collection of these figures for publication.

DISP-1. *Mechanical Victory Soldier.* 30"; came dressed as officers, privates, and Uncle Sam; doll salutes, turns head, points with finger, etc., as ordered; had eight-day clock movement; offered for manufacture by John M. Biggs Co, Chattanooga, TN, the inventor. *(Playthings, November, 1918)*

DIS-55.

DISP-1.

DISP-2a.

DISP-3-1.

DISP-2b.

DISP-2c.

DISP-2a,b,c. *Dancers and Musician.* Old Man 12", Girl 17", Man 18"; molded-painted hair on men, girl has yellow mohair wig; painted features; papier mache construction; authentic costumes of felt, wool, and real buttons; not tourist type, but used in business for display; made in Austria. Unmarked. *(O'Rourke collection)*

DISP-3. *Hans Christian Andersen.* 25½"; molded-painted black hair; painted blue eyes; papier mache construction; original clothes; made by artist for display in store in Denmark where doll was purchased; 1930s. *(O'Rourke collection)*

DISP-3-1. *Mechanical Man.* 16"; white wool yarn hair; painted blue eyes, lashes; closed smile; all composition; original clothes; man goes around, looks through telescope, bubbles come out end of telescope; electrified; speed can be regulated; purchased at Frederick & Nelson's Store in the 1940s. *(Stewart collection)*

DISP-4. *Trapeze Artist.* 7½" high, 13½" long; molded-painted one-piece composition; one-strap purple suit; knees attached to swing bar; loop in mouth for string or wire. *(O'Rourke collection)*

DISP-2c.

DISP-2a.

DISP-2b.

DISP-3.

DISP-4.

DISP-5.

DISP-5.

DISP-5.

DISP-6.

DISP-7.

DISP-7.

DISP-6.

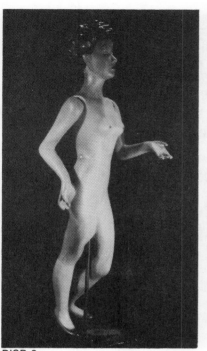

DISP-8.

DISP-8.

DISP-9.

DISP-10a,b.

DISP-5. *Farmer.* 25"; fur wig; blown glass eyes; open-closed mouth with teeth; papier mache; original felt clothes; doll nods head and rocks the dog he holds in his arms; his body is lined with newspapers from 1883 Germany. *(O'Rourke collection)*

DISP-6. *Mechanical Man.* 31"; fur wig; painted eyes; molded-painted grin and teeth; papier mache body, rubber hands and shoes, molded feet inside shoes; original clothes. Note: Distortion of face is actual; not because of camera angle. Former owner had doll in window in 1910. Doll originally wound with a key but it is now electrified; doll motions with right hand, left hand raises and lowers, and head moves to one side. *(O'Rourke collection)*

DISP-7. *Cop-on-the-Beat.* 22"; fur wig; blown glass eyes; open-closed mouth with teeth; German papier mache; original clothes; body is lined with old German newspapers. Doll winds like a clock and moves head from side to side and rolls eyes. *(O'Rourke collection)*

DISP-8. *Margit Nilsen Manikins.* 22"; molded-painted black hair, silk wigs sometimes applied; painted features; closed mouth; lasticoid body; 1940s. Used for studying dressmaking, milinery, dress design; photography, and window display. Used by Singer Sewing Machine Co., McCall Patterns; Harper's Bazaar Magazine; Traphagen School of Fashion in New York, The New England School of Art, and Lux Soap. *(Rogers collection)*

DISP-9. *Fashion Figure.* 31"; molded-painted features; composition with removable arms; original black and white checked Chanel suit, white blouse and pink taffeta slip; a pattern company display doll; 1950s. Unmarked. *(Author's collection)*

DISP-10a,b. *World War II Bride and Groom.* 16½", 17½"; groom has molded-painted features; bride has white silk floss curls, painted eyes and long lower lashes; one-piece hollow composition construction; white silk dress with train, slip with lace edging, white net veil and silk cap; man wears uniform of brown jacket with gold trim, light brown pants, brown hat and shoes; arms are bent so dolls can entwine arms: nail holes in shoes for wooden stand. Unmarked. *(Author's collection)*

DISP-12.

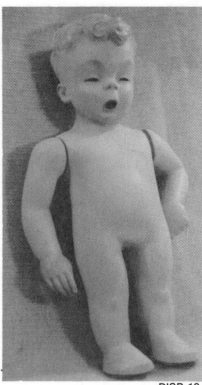

DISP-12.

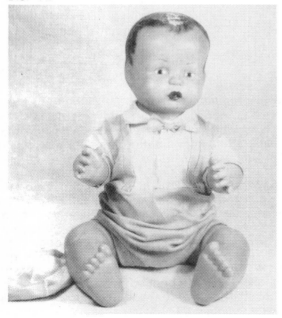

DISP-11.

DISP-11. *Baby.* 22"; molded-painted hair; painted blue eyes; open-closed mouth; one-piece plaster composition body and head, string strung arms and legs; dresses in real baby clothes; from Crosby's Department Store in Topeka, KS. Unmarked. *(Hafner collection)*

DISP-12. *Fisk Tire Boy.* 21"; molded-painted blonde hair, closed eyes with painted brown lashes; open-closed yawning mouth; composition body with jointed arms; redressed. Unmarked. *(Brady collection)*

The Fisk Tire Boy was created in 1906 by Burr E. Giffin. The Fisk boy was copyrighted on June 1, 1910, and registered as a trademark on July 21, 1914. He made his first appearance in the March 7, 1914, issue of The Saturday Evening Post. The Fisk Tire Boy carries a candle and a tire on one arm and is famous for the "Time to Re-Tire" slogan. All are registered trademarks of the Uniroyal Merchandising Company.

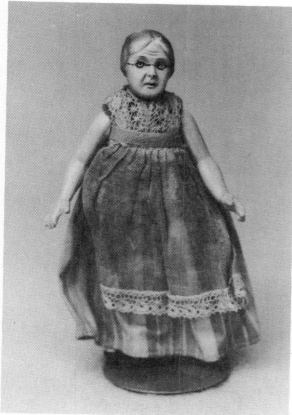

DOL-1.

"DOLLINDOLL" PRODUCTS for 1952

22 inch WALKIE-TALKIE—Synchronised Moving Head.

"WALKIE-TALKIES" with Synchronised moving head 16in. to 27in.
BABY DOLLS 14in. to 27in.
TEEN-AGE and CONTINENTAL STYLE DOLLS 16in. to 26in.
Delivery from Stock

ALL DRESSED OR UNDRESSED

Manufactured and Distributed by:—

DOLL INDUSTRIES LIMITED AND ASSOCIATED COMPANIES
148-150 HIGH ROAD, WILLESDEN, N.W.10
Telephone: WILlesden 0951 (3 lines) Cables: DILDOL, LONDON
Factories: LONDON, AYCLIFFE, SOUTH SHIELDS

16 THE TOY TRADER & EXPORTER for September, 1952

DOL-2.

DOLLHOUSE DOLLS

Although space does not permit listing the modern dollhouse families, the writer felt collectors would enjoy seeing this excellent older example of a dollhouse Grandmother.

DOL-1. *Grandmother.* 4¾"; molded-painted features including spectacles; fully jointed celluloid body; original painted long white stockings and black shoes, striped green and orchid, gold and beige cotton dress with lace trim, organdy apron. Marks: (helmet)/**GERMANY.** *(Ortwein collection, photograph by Jackie Meekins)*

DOLL INDUSTRIES, LTD

DOL-2. *Dollindoll "Walkie Talkie".* 16" to 27"; all hard plastic; synchronized moving head; dressed or undressed; also available were Teen-Age and Continental Style Dolls 16" to 26". Mfr: Doll Industries Limited, Willesden, England. *(Toy Trader and Importer, September, 1952)*

THE DOLL SHOP

DOL-3. *Dolly Dainty.* 14", 20", 26"; mohair or human hair wigs; sleep eyes; ball-jointed composition body; various costumes; also had the Bye-Bye Kiddie Walking doll. "The new F.A.M. Doll". Butler Brothers had Dolly Dainty as early as 1910 with bisque head, stationary glass eyes, fully jointed composition body. Mfr: The Doll Shop. *(Playthings, August, 1918)*

DOL-3.

DRA-1.

DRE-2.

DUCH-1.

DRA-2.

GRACE G. DRAYTON

DRA-1. *Googly.* 6½", 6¾"; molded-painted hair; blue glass eyes; closed melon grins; composition bodies, turning heads; painted clothes. Designed by Grace G. Drayton. Unmarked. *(Stewart collection)*

DRA-2. *Girl.* 13½"; molded-painted yellow hair; painted blue eyes; melon grin; composition head and limbs, cloth body, jointed limbs; original clothes. Marks: **99 DRAYTON/©**. *(Stewart collection)*

DREAM WORLD DOLLS

DRE-1. *Nun.* 11"; painted blue eyes; closed mouth; fully jointed composition; original black rayon habit, black bead rosary, gold crucifix. Marks: **DREAM WORLD DOLLS** (in script)**/REG. U.S. PAT. OFF./MAKE DREAMS COME TRUE** (over half-moon on cloud-shaped paper tag). Doll is unmarked. *(Vandiver collection)*

DUCHESS DOLL CORP.

DUCH-1. *Cowboy.* 7"; painted hair; sleep eyes; closed mouth; fully jointed hard plastic; original cotton and leather clothes. Marks: **DUCHESS DOLL CORP/DESIGN COPYRIGHT/1949** on back. *(Gibbins collection)*

EG-18a.

EG-18b,c.

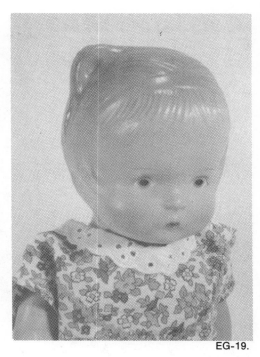

EG-19.

EEGEE

GOLDBERGER DOLL MFG. CO. INC.

One of the oldest doll manufacturing companies still in business, EEGEE's latest line seems as varied and interesting as anything presented in previous years. The company is making every effort to introduce innovative and appealing merchandise; note Honey Munch, the first baby doll with a ventriloquist head. Hopefully doll collectors will be able to influence Toy Department doll buyers in the coming years so that we may experience a 'come-back' of the character face and unique personality dolls.

EG-18a,b,c. Three dolls from the 1918 line advertised in the January and December issues of Playthings.

EG-19. *Patsy-type.* 15"; molded-painted hair, hairband, and hairbow loop; painted eyes; closed mouth; composition shoulder head and arms, excelsior-stuffed cloth body and legs, socks are part of legs; 1920s. Marks: **E. GOLDBERGER** on shoulder head. *(Young collection)*

EG-20. *Girl.* 13"; molded-painted hair and bow loop; painted blue side-glance eyes; closed mouth; composition head and body; old dress but not original; 1920s. Marks: **EEGEE** on body. *(Courtesy Nita's House of Dolls)*

EG-20.

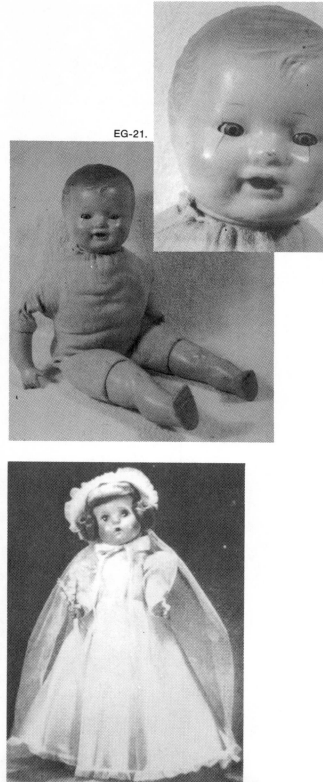

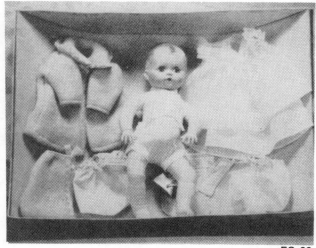

EG-21.

EG-23.

EG-22.

EG-22. *Layette Baby.* 14"; molded-painted hair; glassine sleep eyes with lashes; all latex body and limbs with hard plastic head; drink and wet feature; sold for $7.98 and $8.49. *(1948 EEGEE Catalog)*

EG-23. *Bride.* 15", 17", 19"; mohair wig; sleep eyes; rosebud mouth; fully jointed composition; white satin and net dress; sold for $6.98, $8.98 and $11.98; also came dressed as a Bridemaid selling for $5.98, $6.98 and $9.98 retail. *(1948 EEGEE Catalog)*

EG-24. *Boy.* Molded-painted hair; sleep eyes with lashes; closed mouth; fully jointed hard plastic; velvet pants with suspenders and cap; sold for $4.98; also came dressed as a girl. *(1948 EEGEE Catalog)*

EG-25. *Baby Doll.* 11"; molded-painted hair; painted eyes; open mouth with drink and wet feature; soft rubber head, crude rubber body and limbs; sold for $2.49; also came with a hard plastic head for $3.49. EEGEE's tradename for their rubber bodies was *"Luvable Skin"*. *(1948 EEGEE Catalog)*

EG-26a,b. *Baby Christine.* 15", 18", 21½"; with or without wigs; sleep eyes with lashes; open-closed mouth with teeth and tongue; hard plastic head, rubber limbs, cloth body; original organdy dress, petticoat, rubber pants, shoes and socks; same doll with wig (26b) sold for $1.00 more than doll without wigs which sold for $4.79, $6.98, and $7.98. *(1948 EEGEE Catalog)*

EG-27. *Baby.* 11", 13", 14", 17"; painted hair; sleep eyes with lashes; open drink and wet mouth; fully jointed hard plastic body. *(1948 EEGEE Catalog)*

EG-28. *Baby Cristine.* 14", 17", 20"; molded-painted hair; sleep eyes with lashes; open mouth with teeth and tongue; hard plastic head, latex body and limbs; doll wearing knitted shirt and pants sold for $3.49, $4.98 and $6.98; doll dressed in organdy dress, bonnet, underwear, shoes and socks sold for $4.49, $6.49 and $8.49. *(1948 EEGEE Catalog)*

EG-21. *Baby.* 18"; molded-painted hair; green tin sleep eyes; open-closed mouth, two painted teeth; composition head and limbs, rough cloth body. Marks: **E. GOLDBERGER** on head. *(Weeks collection)*

EG-26a.

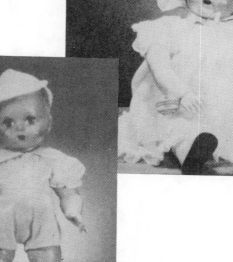

EG-26b.

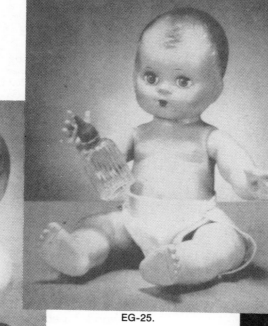

EG-24.

EG-27.

EG-28.

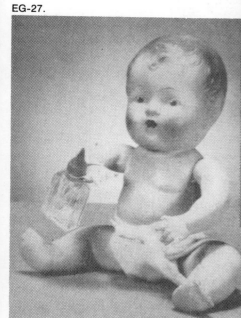

EG-25.

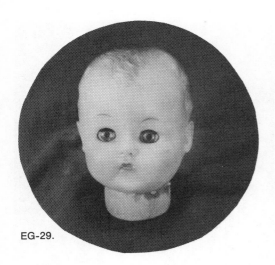

EG-29.

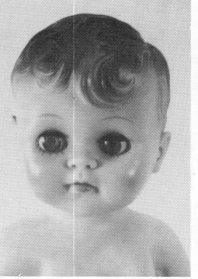

EG-30.

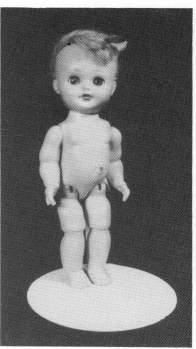

EG-32.

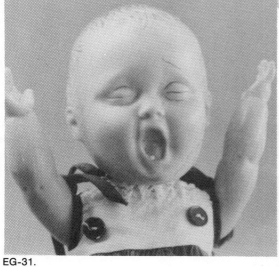

EG-31.

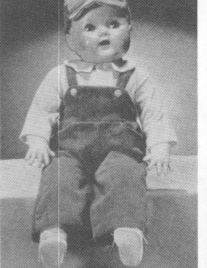

EG-34.

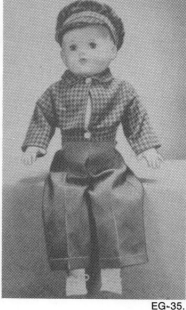

EG-35.

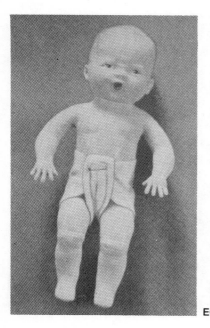

EG-33.

EG-29. *Head.* 5''; molded hair; blue sleep eyes; open-closed mouth with tongue; early vinyl head with wooden neck flange, originally had magic skin body; 1950s. Marks: **EE-GEE** on head. *(Lynn collection)*

EG-30. *Boy.* 14½''; molded-painted hair; blue sleep eyes; closed mouth; vinyl head, one-piece magic skin body; 1950s. Marks: **EE-GEE** on head. *(Terry collection)*

EG-36.

EG-38.

EG-38.

EG-37.

EG-31. *Baby Yawn.* 12"; molded-painted light brown hair; closed eyes; open-closed yawning mouth with one tooth; all vinyl; original red and white dress. Marks: **Y2/EEGEE** on head. *(Perry collection)*

EG-32. *Skater.* 11"; rooted blonde Saran ponytail and bangs; blue sleep eyes; closed mouth; soft vinyl head, hard plastic body jointed at neck, shoulders, hips and knees; originally wore dress and white roller skates; 1950s. Marks: **EEGEE** on head. *(Lynn collection)*

EG-33. *Baby.* 9½", 13", 16"; painted eyes; open-closed mouth; vinyl head, foam rubber-stuffed one-piece latex body and limbs; cry voice; dressed in various styles and also sold as twins in bunting. *(1951 EEGEE Catalog)*

EG-34. *Baby.* 25", 28"; molded-painted hair; sleep eyes with lashes; hard plastic head, foam-rubber-stuffed latex body and limbs; knitted shirt, long twill pants and cap, shoes and socks; sold for $10.98 and $13.98; cry voice. *(1951 EEGEE Catalog)*

EG-35. *Boy.* 25", 28"; painted hair; sleep eyes with lashes; closed rosebud mouth; hard plastic head, foam-rubber-stuffed latex body; checked corduroy Eisenhower jacket and cap, knitted shirt, long twill pants, shoes and socks; sold for $11.98 and $14.98. *(1951 EEGEE Catalog)*

EG-36. *Baby.* 13", 16"; molded-painted hair; sleep eyes; hard plastic head, foam rubber-stuffed latex body and limbs; dressed in various styles; cry voice. *(1951 EEGEE Catalog)*

EG-37. *Girl.* 16"; rooted Saran hair; sleep eyes with lashes; closed mouth; all hard plastic body and head; taffeta dress with metallic braid trim; sold for $7.95. *(1951 EEGEE Catalog)*

EG-38. *Boy.* 20"; molded-painted hair; blue sleep eyes with lashes; closed mouth; soft vinyl head and limbs, stuffed pink cotton body; replacement clothes; ca. 1956. Marks: **EEGEE/20** on head. *(Causey collection)*

EG-39.

EG-40.

EG-41b.

EG-41-1.

EG-41c.

EG-41a.

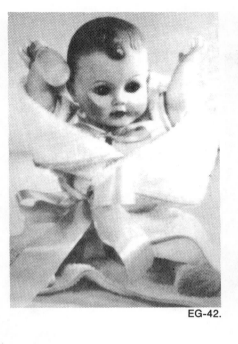

EG-42.

EG-43.

EG-39. *Baby.* 14½", 16", 20", 25", 28"; painted hair or glued-on Saran; sleep eyes with lashes; hard plastic swivel head, foam-rubber-stuffed latex body and limbs; cry voice; flocked nylon dress and bonnet with net trim; sold for $4.49, $5.98, $7.98, $11.98, and $14.98. *(1951 EEGEE Catalog)*

EG-40. *Karena Ballerina.* 21"; rooted hair; sleep eyes; closed mouth; hard plastic and vinyl, jointed at knees, ankles, neck, shoulders and hips, turns head when walked; ballet shoes, ballet dress of satin and net; note doll's box is like a stage. *(1958 EEGEE Catalog)*

EG-41a,b,c. *Little Debutantes.* 18", 19", 20"; rooted hair; sleep eyes; closed mouth; fully jointed vinyl with swivel waists, high-heeled feet, painted nails, "teen figure"; various costumes. *(1958 EEGEE Catalog)*

EG-41-1. *Miss Prim.* 13", 18", 28"; rooted Buster Brown style wig; sleep eyes; closed rosebud mouth; vinyl head, plastic body, jointed at head, shoulders, hips, elbows, knees; head moves as legs move; assorted nylon and cotton clothes; 13" size was all cotton-stuffed vinyl; sold retail for $3.98, $6.49, $13.98. *(1958 EEGEE catalog illustration)*

EG-42. *Baby Carol.* 11", 14", 16", 18", 20", molded hair or rooted wigs; sleep eyes; open drink and wet mouth; fully jointed vinyl; various costumes; sold for $3.98 to $9.98. *(1958 EEGEE Catalog)*

EG-43. *My Fair Lady.* 20"; same construction as *Debutante;* very fancy costumes such as beige satin dress or satin chromespun dress; EEGEE held the exclusive rights to make doll from the Broadway show of the same name. *(1958 EEGEE Catalog)*

EG-44. *Annette.* 36"; rooted long blonde hair; blue sleep eyes; closed mouth; all vinyl Patti Playpal type body with walk features; felt skirt, tee-shirt, long socks and shoes; also came with a short curly wig; assorted costumes. *(1961 EEGEE Catalog)*

EG-44.

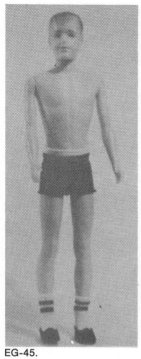

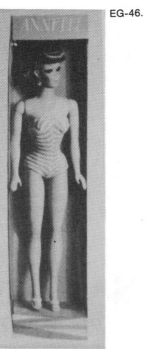

EG-46.

EG-45.

EG-47.

EG-48.

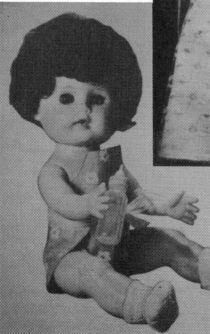

EG-49.

EG-50.

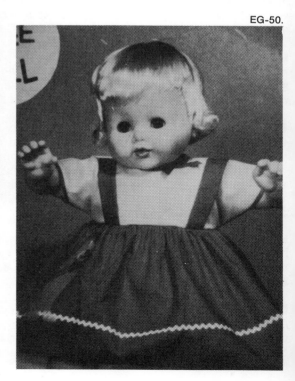

EG-51.

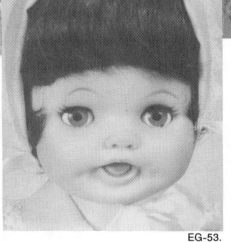

EG-53.

EG-52.

EG-45. *Andy.* 12"; molded-painted hair; painted eyes; closed mouth; fully jointed vinyl; wardrobe available; 11½" Annette's boyfriend. *(1963 EEGEE Catalog)*

EG-46. *Annette.* 11½"; rooted hair; painted eyes; closed mouth; fully jointed vinyl; wardrobe available; typical fashion doll. *(1963 EEGEE Catalog)*

EG-47. *Gemettes.* 15½"; rooted hair; sleep eyes; fully jointed vinyl; dressed in gem-like colored dresses to represent a gem stone; child's simulated jewel ring; includes: *Miss Emerald, Miss Amythyst, Miss Ruby, Miss Sapphire, Miss Diamond* and *Miss Topaz. (1963 EEGEE Catalog)*

EG-48. *Baby Darling.* 12", 16", 18", 20"; rooted curly hair; sleep eyes; drink and wet mouth; fully jointed vinyl; playsuit and bottle. *(1963 EEGEE Catalog)*

EG-49. *Charmer Bride Doll.* 20", 25"; rooted curly hair; sleep eyes with lashes; rosebud mouth; fully jointed vinyl; rayon dress with metallic overskirt. *(1963 EEGEE Catalog)*

EG-50. *Patticake.* 14", 20"; rooted pixie hair; sleep eyes; vinyl head and curved limbs, stuffed cloth body; assorted cotton and nylon dresses; claps hands, hug "mommy", and gurgles when tummy is pressed. *(1963 EEGEE Catalog)*

EG-51. *Tandy Talks.* 22"; rooted snowball bob; sleep eyes with lashes; smiling mouth with teeth; fully jointed vinyl; red and white checked polished cotton dress; talking string allows doll to say ten different things. *(1963 EEGEE Catalog)*

EG-52. *Princess Boudoir Doll.* 14"; rooted pastel hair; sleep eyes; closed mouth; fully jointed vinyl; nylon dress with ruffles, lace and ribbon over a rayon-covered wire hoop. *(1963 EEGEE Catalog)*

EG-53. *Baby Flora.* 18"; rooted brown hair; blue sleep eyes; open drink and wet mouth; fully jointed vinyl; assorted nylon and cotton dresses, shoes and socks; ca. 1963. Marks: **EEGEE18** on head.

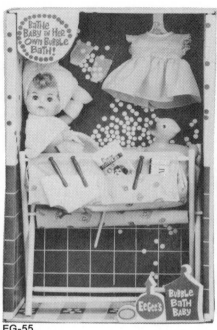

EG-58.

EG-56.

EG-55.

EG-54.

take my hand...
I walk with you

take my hand... I'LL WALK WITH YOU

EG-57.

EG-59.

EG-61.

EG-60.

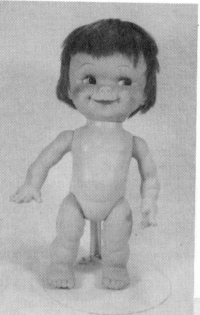

EG-62.

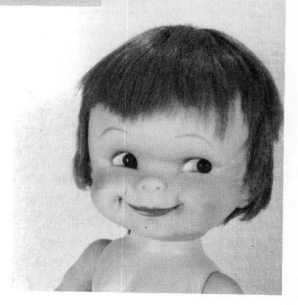

EG-54-60. 54. *Susan Stroller, Walking Doll;* **55.** *Bubble Bath Baby;* **56.** *Kiss-Me Doll;* **57.** *Susan Stroller Walking Doll,* with Stroller and Baby; **58.** *Sniffles;* **59.** *Sleepy Susan;* and **60.** *Kandi.* 1963. *(Courtesy Goldberger Doll Mfg. Co.)*

EG-61. *Baby Tandy Talks.* 20"; rooted pixie hair; sleep eyes; open-closed mouth with two upper teeth; fully jointed vinyl; straight leg version, red and white lawn dress with embroidered cat head; has pull string and says ten phrases. *(1963 EEGEE Catalog)*

EG-62. *Stoneage Baby.* 12"; rooted tosca hair; 3-D glassine eyes; closed mouth; fully jointed vinyl; doll came dressed in fur print diaper suit; 1963. See REGAL for an Eskimo version. Marks: **EEGEE/15C-3.** *(Author's collection)*

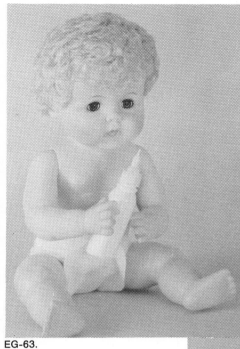

EG-63.

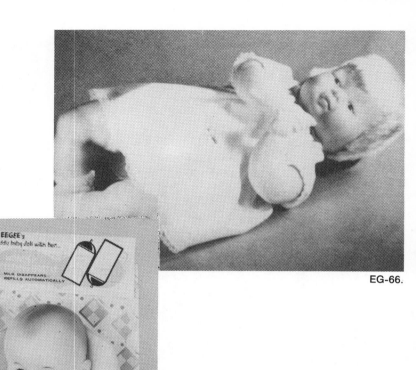

EG-66.

EG-64.

EG-65.

EG-63. *Sniffles.* Rooted curls; sleep eyes; open-closed mouth; fully jointed vinyl; diaper suit; 1963. *(Courtesy Goldberger Doll Mfg. Co.)*

EG-64. *I'm Hungry.* Molded hair; painted side-glance eyes; open-closed mouth; fully jointed vinyl; has bib with her name, plastic high chair, bottle; 1963. *(Courtesy Goldberger Doll Mfg. Co.)*

EG-65. *Cuddly Baby.* Molded hair; sleep eyes; open-closed mouth; fully jointed vinyl; 'magic' bottle, diaper, socks, blanket. *(Courtesy Goldberger Doll Mfg. Co.)*

EG-66. *New Born Bundle of Joy.* 14", 16", 20"; rooted synthetic hair in pixie cut; sleep and painted eyes; closed mouth; vinyl head and curved limbs, soft-stuffed cloth body; assorted baby outfits. She also came as *"Musical Baby"* with sleep eyes and a built-in music box. *(1963 EEGEE Catalog)*

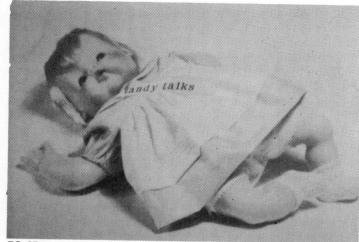

EG-67.

EG-68a.

EG-68b.

EG-68c.

EG-67. *Baby Tandy Talks.* 14", 20"; rooted pixie hair; sleep eyes; vinyl head, cotton-and-foam-stuffed soft body and limbs; assorted baby style clothes; pull string, says ten phrases; 1963. *(Courtesy Goldberger Doll Mfg. Co.)*

EG-68a,b. *Puppetrina.* 22"; blonde rooted synthetic wig; blue sleep eyes; open-closed mouth; vinyl head and arms, cloth body with hand puppet glove inside; came in red and white sailor dress. Marks: © **1963/EEGEE CO./PAT. PEND.** on head. *(Wardell collection)*

EG-68c. *Puppetrina.* All original doll. *(D'Andrade collection)*

EG-69.

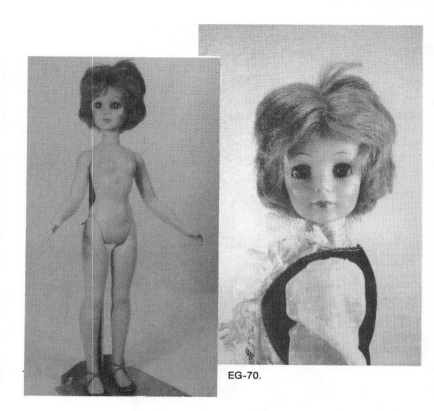

EG-70.

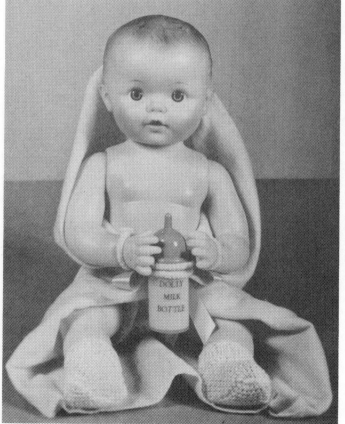

EG-74.

EG-69. *Baby Puppetrina.* 16"; rooted blonde hair; black sleep eyes; open-closed mouth; vinyl head and limbs, lightly stuffed cloth body with hand puppet glove; sailor dress. Marks: © **EEGEE CO./16-P** on head. *(Wardell collection)*

EG-70. *Charmer.* 21"; rooted Saran hair; blue sleep eyes; closed mouth; fully jointed vinyl. Marks: **8/©/EEGEE CO./1963/10** on head, © **1963/EEGEE CO.** on body. *(Author's collection)*

EG-71. *Mary Kate.* 10½"; rooted curly blonde hair; blue sleep eyes; open drink and wet mouth; fully jointed vinyl; original clothes; received on mail-in offer from Kellogg's cereal; 1960s. Marks: **10T/© EEGEE CO.** on head. *(Wardell collection)*

EG-72. *Baby.* 17½"; molded-painted brown hair; sleep eyes; open-closed mouth; fully jointed vinyl; possibly early Softina-type; redressed. Marks: **1964/© EEGEE CO.** on head. *(Wardell collection)*

EG-73. *Posi Playmate.* Rooted hair; sleep eyes; open-closed mouth; vinyl head, wired soft foam body; playsuit with pinafore decorated with kitten and ric-rac trim; came in box with swing. *(1965 EEGEE Catalog)*

EG-74. *Baby.* Molded-painted hair; inset eyes; open mouth with drink and wet feature; fully jointed vinyl; diaper, booties, blanket with magic bottle; possibly *Baby Susan* or *Baby Carol*; 1966. *(Courtesy Goldberger Doll Mfg. Co.)*

EG-73.

EEGEE
PoSi PlaymaTe

FEATURING
POSE N' PLAY
BENDABLE
ARMS & LEGS

BEND ME...
I STAY IN
ANY POSITION

SOFT, CUDDLY FOAM

EG-72.

EG-71.

EG- 75.

EG-76.

EG-78.

EG- 77.

EG-79.

EG-81.

EG-80.

EG-75-78. 75. *Susan;* **76.** *Sandi;* **77.** *Me and Me Too,* Charlot Byj-type girl and dog; **78.** *Shelly and Her Plush Puppy Fido,* also came with wig like 76; 1966. *(Courtesy Goldberger Doll Mfg. Co.)*

EG-79. *Posy Doll.* 13"; rooted synthetic blonde braids; large glassine eyes; closed smile; vinyl head, foam body and bendable limbs; printed flannel pajamas; packed in praying position in nursery display box. *(1967 EEGEE Catalog)*

EG-80. *Thumkins.* 5"; assorted Dutch and ponytail styled hair; painted eyes; all vinyl; six assorted dresses. *(1967 EEGEE Catalog)*

EG-81. *"Hello Dolly"* 11"; rooted synthetic side sweep hair-do; painted side-glance eyes; closed mouth; vinyl and plastic construction; print cotton dress and panties; plastic toy telephone. *(1967 EEGEE Catalog)*

EG-82.

EG-83a.

EG-83b.

EG-83c.

EG-83d.

EG-82. *Kandi.* Rooted hair; sleep eyes; closed mouth; vinyl head and limbs, stuffed cloth body; sunsuits and dresses; similar to Baby Dear; doll has music box and moves in time to music; 1967. *(Courtesy Goldberger Doll Mfg. Co.)*

EG-83. *Handee Poppet.* 24"; rooted hair in different colors; painted eyes with large lashes; open-closed mouth; vinyl head mounted on a turning post, child's hand holds post and other hand becomes the doll's hand; dressed as *Red Riding Hood, Alice in Wonderland, Gypsy, Cinderella* and *Bozo the Clown;* 1974. *(Courtesy Goldberger Doll Mfg. Co.)*

These are some of the latest *Padeet* dolls.

EG-84. *Bozo Ventriloquist Handee Poppet.* Same description as EG-83. *(Courtesy Goldberger Doll Mfg. Co.)*

EG-84.

EG-85.

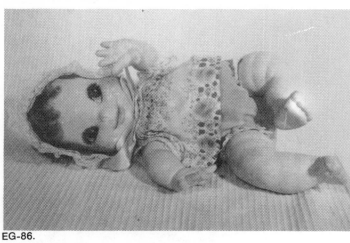

EG-86.

EG-86.

EG-85.

BABY LUV

Here is a rare opportunity to compare an artist's rendering of a doll with the actual production model. The head and limbs were modeled by Deet; the concept was completed by Patti and Deet.

EG-85. *Baby Luv.* 14"; rooted blonde hair; painted eyes with star-shaped high lights; open-closed mouth; vinyl head and limbs; pink cotton-stuffed floppy body; pink and white top, pants are part of body, elastic lace around legs, lace bonnet which was later deleted from doll. Marks: **14B.T./EEGEE CO./©** on head. *(Author's collection)*

EG-86. Original artist's model presented to EEGEE in 1970s. Made of Polyform by Deet D'Andrade. *(D'Andrade collection)*

F&B-55a,b.

F&B-56.

F&B-57.

EFFANBEE DOLL CORPORATION

This firm has recently come into the possession of two men who plan to continue the tradition first begun in 1910. Roy R. Raizen and Leroy Fadem are two young men who seem to reflect the enthusiasm of the founders, Bernard E. Fleischaker and Hugo Baum. Mr. Raizen is from an old toy industry family.

As may be seen by the variety shown here, Effanbee dolls present a true panorama of the growth of the American doll industry from 1910 to the present.

Photographs of the two founders shown here appeared in a 1920 issue of *Playthings* with an article titled *"A Romance of the Business World"*.

F&B-55a,b. Hugo Baum and Bernard E. Fleischaker. *(Playthings, 1920)*

F&B-56. *Foxy Teddy Bear.* Composition head and hands, stuffed Teddy Bear fabric; *"Another Teddy Bear Craze"*. *(Playthings, February, 1912)*

F&B-57. *Candy Kids.* Molded-painted hair; painted side-glance eyes; closed mouth; all composition; ca. 1915. *(Courtesy Nita's House of Dolls)*

F&B-58.

F&B-59.

F&B-60.

F&B-61.

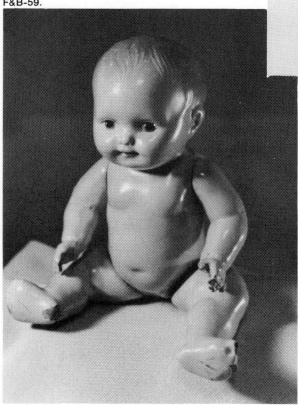

F&B-58. *Colored Grumpy.* 11½"; painted hair with floss braids; painted side-glance eyes; closed mouth; composition deep shoulder head and limbs, stuffed cloth body; these were manufactured from 1912 to 1939. Marks: **EFFANBEE/DOLLS/WALK-TALK-SLEEP** in oval. *(Author's collection)*

F&B-59. *Baby Huggins.* 9"; molded-painted yellow hair; blue eyes; closed mouth; fully jointed composition body; ca. 1913. Marks: **EFFANBEE.** *(Stewart collection)*

F&B-60. *Johnny Tu-Face.* Two sizes available; soft doll with composition body was made and distributed only a short time; this doll was not a commercial success and was quickly discontinued. The 1920s two-faced doll, known variously as *Soozie Smiles,* *Baby Surprise,* and *Surprise Baby* (ref. TCD, p. 306 MULTI-6,7), was a greater success commercially. *(Playthings, June, 1912)*

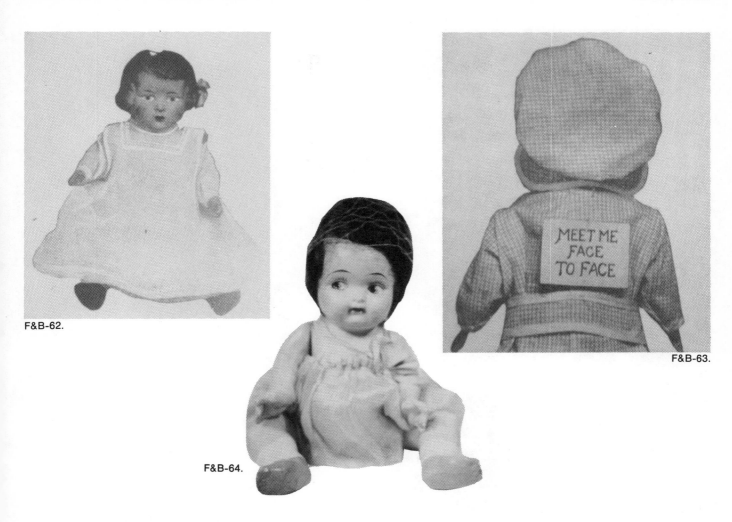

F&B-62.

F&B-64.

F&B-63.

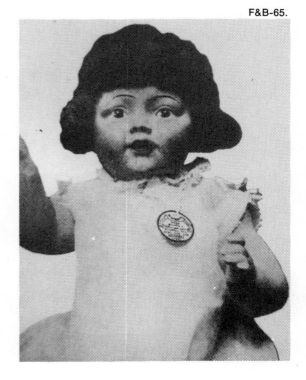

F&B-65.

F&B-61. *Baby Dainty.* 15"; human hair over molded hair; blue tin flirty eyes; closed mouth; composition shoulder head and limbs, cloth body; ca. 1913. Marks: **EFFANBEE/BABY DAINTY.** *(Stewart collection)*

F&B-62. *The Tango Kiddies.* Red, blue, or green hair; painted eyes and mouth; composition head and hands, cloth body and limbs; sold for $1.00 retail. *(Playthings, April, 1914)*

F&B-63. *"My face will be your fortune".* An ad to lure buyers to the Effanbee sales rooms at Toy Fair time. *(Playthings, January, 1916)*

F&B-64. *Little Sweetheart.* 12", 14"; human hair wig; painted blue eyes; closed mouth; all composition body; pale green silk underslip and dress, blue Mary Jane slippers with pink bows, white socks, all painted on over molded feet; 1917-1919. Marks: **Effanbee** on shoulder. *(Harris collection)*

F&B-65. *Baby.* Mohair wig; sleep eyes; open mouth with teeth and tongue; fully jointed composition; note that paper tag on dress is same as label on kid-bodied doll, next page. *(Playthings, July, 1916)*

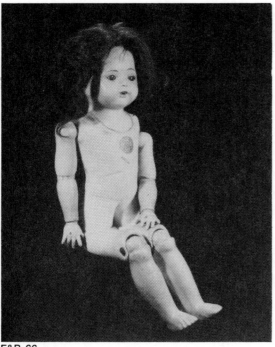

F&B-66.

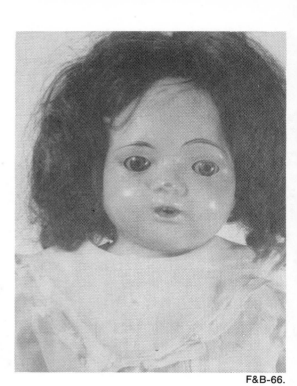

F&B-66.

Fig-F&B-66.

F&B-66.

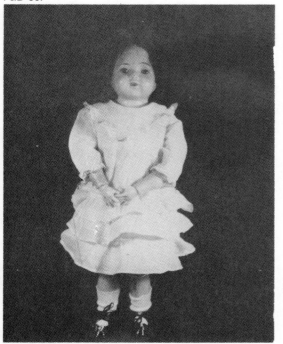

F&B-66. *Girl.* 20½"; human hair wig; blue tin eyes; open mouth with two molded teeth; composition head and ball-jointed arms and lower legs, soft kid body and upper legs; all original clothes except shoes and socks; 1914-1918. One of the finest early Effanbee dolls ever examined by this writer. Marks: See fig. F&B-66. *(Rogers collection)*

F&B-67. Baby. 16"; original mohair wig over molded hair; gray celluloid on tin sleep eyes; open mouth; fully jointed composition with jointed wrists. This doll is shown unidentified in a 1920 Effanbee advertisement reproduced in Kelly Ellenburg's book, *"Effanbee-The Dolls With The Golden Hearts".* It could be *"Cunning Baby"* advertised in Butler Bros. in 1918. 1918-1920. Marks: **Effanbee** on head and back. *(Author's collection)*

F&B-68. *Bathing Bud.* Painted features, all composition; one-piece silk bathing suit, head kerchief. *(Playthings, June, 1918)*

F&B-69. *A Dolly Dumpling Group.* A series of bedtime story booklets about *Dolly Dumpling* were written by a new Effanbee salesman, J. C. Ruben, in 1918. Shown is an illustration from the cover of one issue. *(Playthings, February-March, 1918)*

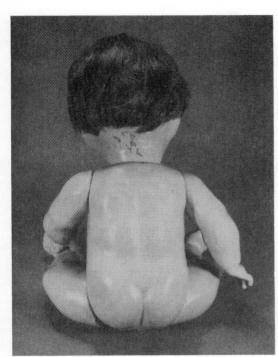

F&B-67.

F&B-68.

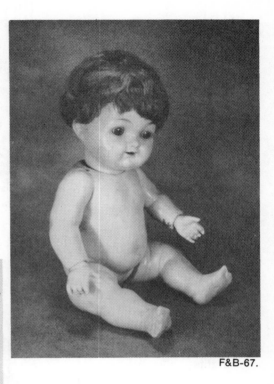

F&B-67.

F&B-67.

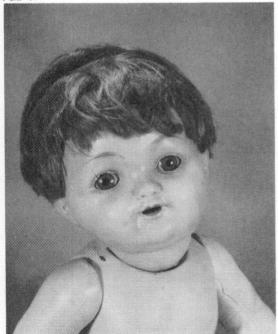

F&B-69.

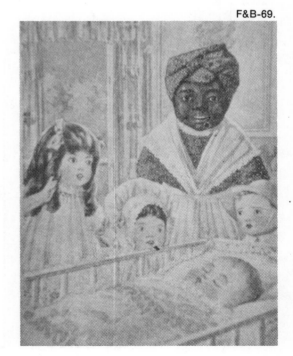

"EFFANBEE" DOLLY DUMPLING DOLLS

The latest newcomer in the doll world—"Effanbee" creation. 14½ in., modeled composition breast plate, heads and composition hands, painted features and hair, cork stuffed chubby bodies, position limbs, concealed hip and shoulder joints. Each in fancy box with "Dolly Dumpling" illustrated litho booklet.

F7756—3 styles, "Little Girl," colored lawn, flowered novelty voile and checked gingham dresses, short waists, full plaited skirt, lace trim or bias bound square necks and sleeves, French bonnets to match costumes, lace trim panties, white socks. ¼ doz. in pkg.

Doz. **$12.00**

F7756

F7757—2 styles, "Romper Babies," solid color linene and flowered novelty rompers, bias trim square neck and sleeves, 1 with belt and elastic knees, turnback bonnets to match costumes, white socks. ⅙ doz. in pkg.

Doz. **$12.00**

F7758—Baby, white lawn dress, full skirt, insertion headed lace edge flounce, square lace neck and trim sleeves, lace trim white lawn bonnet with ribbon strings, lace trim panties, white socks. 1/12 doz. in box.

Doz. **$12.00**

F7757

F&B-70. From the pages of 1918 Catalogs of Butler Bros. come these sketches and descriptions. A careful seamstress could duplicate many of these original outfits.

F7758

"BABY DAINTIES"

Composition breast plate, heads and composition hands, painted features, open mouth and pacifier, full mohair wigs, cork stuffed bodies, concealed hip and shoulder joints

F7914   F7915-17

F7914 —"Effanbee," 15 in., white lawn baby dress, lace trim neck, yoke, sleeves and bottom of skirt, ribbon and lace trim cap, lace trim panties, white socks. 1 in box.

Each, **$1.20**

"Effanbee"—Fine white lawn dress, lace trim neck, yoke, sleeves and bottom of skirt, lace and ribbon bow trim caps to match, ribbon strings, crocheted booties. 1 in box.
F7915—18½ in., lace trim chemise............Each, **$1.75**
F7916—21½ in., lawn underwear.............   "   **2.75**
F7917—24 in., lawn underwear...............   "   **3.65**

FRENCH BABY DRESSED DOLL
With Moving Eyes

"Effanbee" quality, composition head and hands, painted features, bobbed mohair wig. Extra value at this price.

MOVING EYES

F7539—15½ in., flowered lace stripe material, solid color lawn cross-over collar with tie strings forming sash, French bonnet to match costume, lawn underwear, white socks, colored slippers. 1 in box.

Each, **$1.75**

"OUR BABY" DOLLS—In Short Slips

Excellent values—"Effanbee" quality. Well modeled composition heads and hands, painted features and hair unless specified, well stuffed bodies, hip and shoulder joints. There will be a large demand for these.

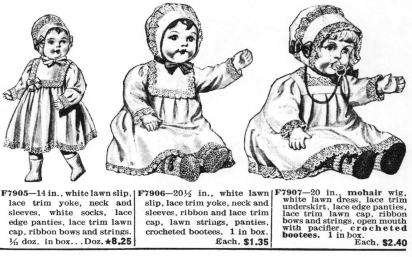

F7905—14 in., white lawn slip, lace trim yoke, neck and sleeves, white socks, lace edge panties, lace trim lawn cap, ribbon bows and strings. ½ doz. in box..Doz. ★**8.25**

F7906—20½ in., white lawn slip, lace trim yoke, neck and sleeves, ribbon and lace trim cap, lawn strings, panties, crocheted bootees. 1 in box.

Each, **$1.35**

F7907—20 in., mohair wig, white lawn dress, lace trim underskirt, lace edge panties, lace trim lawn cap, ribbon bows and strings, open mouth with pacifier, crocheted bootees. 1 in box.

Each, **$2.40**

F&B-70.

"CUNNING BABY" DRESSED DOLL
With Moving Eyes

"Effanbee" quality. Composition head and hands, painted features, bobbed mohair wig.

MOVING EYES

F7538—15½ in., white organdie dress, lace inserted yoke and skirt, lace trim, lace edge jacket effect, ribbon rosette, lace trim underwear, ribbon rosette on lace straw hat, white socks, colored slippers. 1 in box.

Each, **$2.00**

F7575

Worsted Jacket & Cap

Hand knit 2-color worsted jacket and cap with ribbon rosettes, bootees, lace trim dress, bib with baby pin, white lawn underwear.
F7575—17 in.. Each, **$3.25**

Baby

White lawn dress, full skirt, insertion headed lace edge flounce, square trim lace neck and lace trim sleeves, fancy bonnet, lace trim ties, white socks.

F7758—½ doz. in box.
Doz. **$12.50**

"Baby Catherine"

Short **mohair** wigs, moving eyes, white organdie short baby dress, lace and rosette trim, lace trim petticoat and panties, fancy bonnet, white socks, pink or blue **leatherette bootees**, pacifier on ribbon. 1 in box.

		Each
F7563—13	in...	**$2.25**
F7564—14½	" ...	**3.25**
F7565—18	" ...	**4.25**
F7566—21	" ...	**6.00**

French Baby

15½ in.. "Effanbee" quality, bobbed mohair wig. flowered dress. solid color trim. French bonnet. lawn underwear. white socks. colored slippers.
F7539—1 in box. Each, **$1.95**

F7539

F7576

3 Styles

"Little Girl." colored lawn. flowered novelty voile and checked gingham dresses. short waists. full plaited skirt, lace trim or bias bound square necks and sleeves. French bonnets to match costumes, lace trim panties, white socks.
F7756—¼ doz. in pkg..........Doz. **$12.50**

2 Styles

"Romper Babies." solid color linene and flowered novelty rompers, bias trim square neck and sleeves, 1 with belt and elastic knees. turnback bonnets to match costumes. white socks.
F7757—⅙ doz. in pkg..........Doz. **$12.50**

White Lawn Caps

Puff crown, lace front, ribbon rosettes and tie strings, cap, dotted swiss dress, lace trim, ribbon run, bib, bootees, underwear.

F7576—20 in......Each,	**$4.25**
F7577—24 " ...... "	**8.00**

F&B-71.

F&B-72.

F&B-72.

F&B-71. *Riding Hood Bud.* All composition with painted features; cotton cloth costume with basket. Also same ad offered *"Valentine Bud"* in a crepe paper costume with parasol in pastel colors. *(Playthings, October, 1919)*

F&B-72. *Wolf.* 9½"; painted brown composition head on Patsy-type body; painted brown eyes; wears grandmother's night gown and cap. Unmarked. *(Stewart collection)*

F&B-73. *Baby.* 16½"; blonde mohair wig; dark blue sleep eyes; open mouth with molded teeth; composition head and hands, cloth body and limbs; possibly original suit and hood; ca. 1918. Marks: **Effanbee.** *(Wiseman collection)*

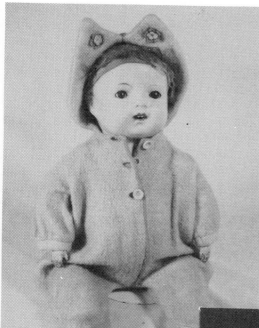

F&B-73.

F&B-74.

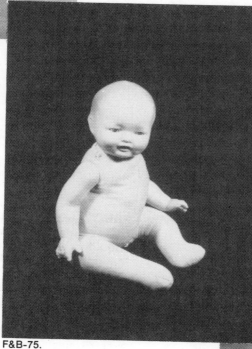

F&B-75.

F&B-76.

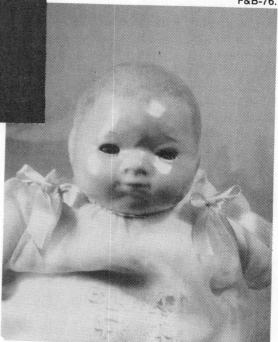

F&B-74. *Girl.* No description in advertisement. *(Playthings, January, 1920)*

F&B-75. *Bubbles.* 13"; molded-painted yellow hair; tin sleep eyes; open-closed mouth with two painted upper teeth; composition head and arms, cloth body and legs like *Baby Bumps;* ca. 1924. Marks: **EFFANBEE/BUBBLES.** *(Wardell collection)*

F&B-76. *Bye-lo type.* 12"; painted hair; blue sleep eyes; closed mouth; composition head, celluloid hands, cloth body and legs; 1925. Marks: **EFFANBEE.** *(Wardell collection, owner's childhood doll)*

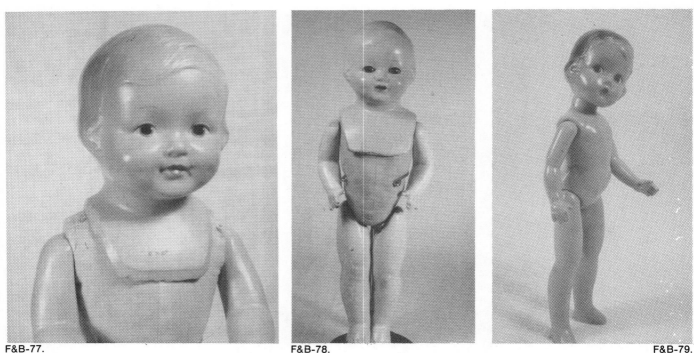

F&B-77.   F&B-78.   F&B-79.

F&B-80.

F&B-81.

F&B-77. *Early Patsy.* 16"; molded-painted blonde hair; painted blue eyes; closed mouth; composition shoulder head and limbs, *cloth* body; early 1920s. Marks: **EFFANBEE/PATSY** in oval. *(Griffin collection)*

F&B-78. *Early Patsy.* 14"; molded hair, unpainted; blue tin sleep eyes; open mouth four teeth; composition shoulder head and limbs, stuffed *cloth* body; 1920s. Marks: **EFFANBEE/PATSY/COPYR./DOLL** in oval. *(Stewart collection)*

F&B-79. *Girl.* 9¼"; molded-painted hair; blue painted eyes; closed mouth; all composition; 1920-1930s. Marks: **EFFANBEE/MADE IN U.S.A.** *(Young collection)*

F&B-80. *Boy.* 15"; painted blue eyes; red nostrils; open-closed whistler mouth with molded tongue; 1925. Marks: **FXB-NY.** *(O'Rourke collection)*

F&B-81. *Lovums.* 17"; molded-painted hair; blue sleep eyes; open mouth; composition shoulder head and limbs, cloth body; wind-up heart beats; ca. 1920s. Marks: **EFFanBEE/LOVUMS/©/Pat. No. 1283,558.** *(Edge collection)*

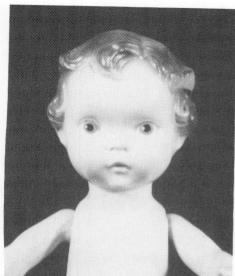

F&B-82.

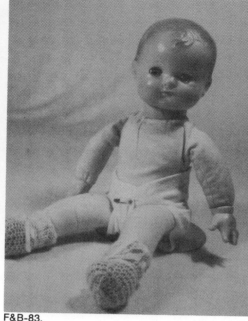

F&B-83.

F&B-84.

F&B-84.

F&B-82. *Girl.* 11¾"; molded-painted brown hair and blue bow; painted blue eyes; closed mouth; composition, jointed at shoulders and hips, Patsy-type body; ca. 1928. Unmarked. *(Gaylin collection)*

F&B-83. *Patsy Babyette.* 12"; molded-painted hair; blue sleep eyes; closed mouth; composition head and hands, stuffed pink cloth body and limbs; Marks: **EFFANBEE/PATSY BABYETTE.** *(Wardell collection)*

F&B-84. *Patsy Lou.* 22"; molded-painted hair; brown sleep eyes; closed mouth; composition, fully jointed; original clothes; 1929. Marks: **PATSY-LOU** on body, cloth label on dress reads: **NRA/** (picture of an eagle/**EFFanBEE/DURABLE/DOLLS** (in heart)/**MADE IN U.S.A.** *(Wardell collection)*

The National Industrial Recovery Act (NIRA) was passed by Congress in 1933 in response to President Roosevelt's congressional address of May 17, 1933. It was designed as an attempt to heal the economic wounds of a nation brought to its knees by the 1929 Stock Market crash and subsequent depression. The NRA (National Recovery Administration), by a separate executive order, was put into operation soon after the final approval of the NIRA, as the administering body for the new emergency law. The measure was to try to combat widespread unemployment and industries joined the effort on a volunteer basis. The tag sewn into the dress of F&B-84 is a reminder that the doll industry joined the national effort to put the country back on its feet.

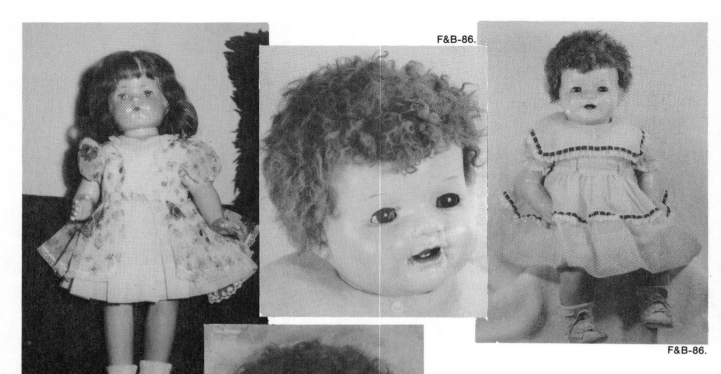

F&B-86.

F&B-86.

F&B-85.

F&B-87.

F&B-87.

F&B-85. *Patsy Lou.* 22"; human hair wig; green sleep eyes; closed mouth; all composition, fully jointed; ca. 1927; has *Effanbee* metal heart bracelet on wrist.

F&B-86. *Tousle Head.* 25"; lambswool wig; blue sleep eyes with hair lashes; open mouth with two teeth and tongue; composition head and limbs, stuffed cloth body; replacement child's clothes; 1928. Marks: backwards **500** on back of head. *(Author's collection)*

F&B-87. *Talking Tousle Head.* 28"; curly dark brown caracul wig; brown sleep eyes; open mouth with metal tongue and four teeth; composition head and limbs, cloth body with cavity for record box; same record unit as *Mae Starr* and *Dolly Rekord* (ref. TCD, p. 96, AVRL-1 and p. 433, W-T-9); records include *Now I Lay Me Down to Sleep, London Bridge* and *Brahms Lullaby.* Marks: **EFFANBEE/LOVUMS/©/PAT. NO. 1,283,558;** paper tag reads: **I Am Called TOUSLE HEAD 'cause My Hair is So Natural./AN EFFANBEE DURABLE DOLL/THE GOLDEN HEART LINE.** *(Kauffman collection)*

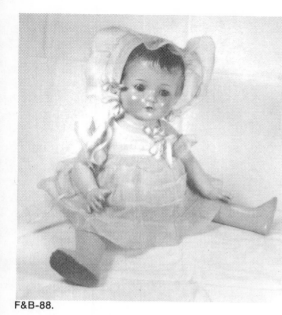

F&B-88.

F&B-89.

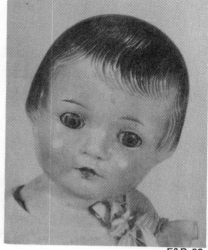

F&B-88.

F&B-90a,b.

F&B-88. *Patsy-type.* 18½"; molded-painted hair; sleep eyes; closed mouth; fully jointed composition; organdy dress and hood are original. Unmarked. *(Rothert collection)*

F&B-89. *Colored Patsyette.* 9"; molded-painted black hair; painted amber side-glance eyes; closed mouth; fully jointed brown composition; all original clothes. Marks: **EFFANBEE/PATSYETTE/DOLL.** *(Stewart collection)*

F&B-90a,b. *Patsy and Patricia.*
   a. *Patsy.* 14"; original auburn mohair wig over molded hair; golden brown sleep eyes with lashes; closed mouth; fully jointed composition; 1932. Marks: **EFFanBEE / PATSY** on head, **EFFanBEE / PATSY / DOLL** on back.

   b. *Patricia.* 15"; original blonde human hair wig over molded hair; blue sleep eyes with lashes; closed mouth; fully jointed composition; original shoes and socks; 1932. Marks: **EFFanBEE / "PATRICIA"** on back, **EFFANBEE / PATSY** on head, original metal heart tag reads: **EFFANBEE / DURABLE / DOLLS.** *(Weeks collection)*

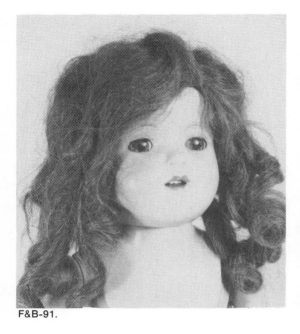

F&B-91.

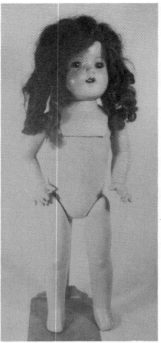

F&B-91.

F&B-92.

F&B-93a,b,c,d,e.

F&B-93e.   F&B-93a.

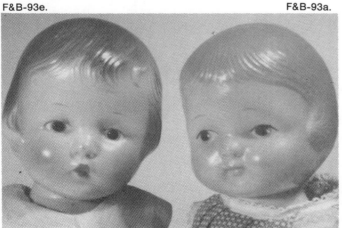

F&B-91. *Mary Ann.* 20"; brown human hair wig; gray sleep eyes; open mouth with teeth and felt tongue; composition shoulder head and limbs, stuffed cloth body; ca. 1930. Marks: **MARY ANN** on head. *(Wiseman collection)*

F&B-92. *Patsy-type Boy.* 11"; molded-painted brown hair; brown sleep eyes; closed mouth; composition toddler body; all original clothes; ca. 1930. Unmarked. *(Wardell collection)*

F&B-93a-e. *Patsy Junior and Friends.* Ca. 1930.

    a. 11"; blue painted eyes; original dress, unmarked.

    b. 11"; brown painted eyes; original **ARRANBEE** clothes. Marks: **EFFANBEE / PATSY JUNIOR.**

    c. 12"; blue painted eyes; original clothes. Marks: **ARRANBEE DOLL CO.**

    d. 12"; brown painted eyes; original clothes, tag reads: **A Lovable Petite Doll /** (picture of a doll) **/ Sally..** Marks: **SALLY / A PETITE DOLL** on body.

    e. 12"; blue painted eyes; original **ARRANBEE** clothes. Unmarked. *(Wardell collection)*

F&B-94.

F&B-95.

F&B-96.

F&B-94. *Colleen Moore Fairy Princess (Wee Patsy).* 5½"; molded-painted hair; painted eyes; closed mouth; composition, jointed at shoulders and hips; original clothes, molded-painted shoes and socks; 1930. Marks: **EFFANBEE / WEE PATSY** on back, pin on dress reads: **COLLEEN MOORE /FAIRY PRINCESS / AN EFFANBEE DOLL.**

F&B-95. *Babyette.* 12½"; sprayed dark hair; painted closed eyes with lashes; closed mouth; composition head and arms, stuffed pink cloth body and legs; 1930-1950. Marks: © **/ F&B / BABYETTE.** *(Stewart collection)*

F&B-96. *Patsy Baby.* 12"; molded-painted brown hair; blue sleep eyes; closed mouth; composition head, one-piece stuffed magic skin body; early 1940s. Marks: **EFFANBEE / PATSY BABY** on head. *(Wardell collection)*

F&B-97. *Suzette.* 11"; red mohair wig; brown painted eyes; closed mouth; composition, fully jointed; original cotton organdy print dress; 1930s. Marks: **SUZETTE / EFFANBEE / U.S.A.** on head; **SUZETTE / EFFANBEE / MADE IN / U.S.A.** on body. *(N. Ricklefs collection)*

F&B-98. *Tousle Head.* 23"; caracul wig; blue sleep eyes; open-closed mouth with four teeth; fully jointed composition; 1930s; came in assorted sizes. Marks: **24** on head. *(Griffin collection)*

F&B-97.

F&B-98.

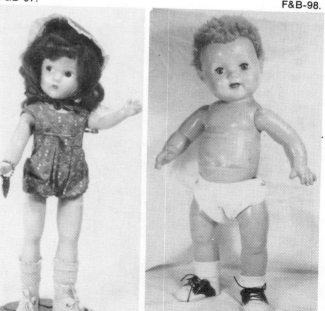

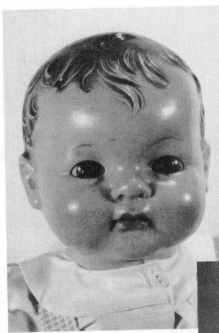

F&B-99.

F&B-100.

F&B-103.

F&B-102.

F&B-101.

F&B-104.

F&B-105.

F&B-102.

F&B-105.

F&B-99. *Sugar Baby.* Deeply molded, painted hair; brown sleep eyes; closed mouth; composition head and limbs, cloth body; 1936. Marks: **EFFANBEE / SUGAR BABY / TRADE MARK,** has metal heart bracelet. *(Author's collection)*

F&B-100. *Patsy Tinyette.* 8"; molded-painted hair; painted eyes; closed mouth; fully jointed composition; original clothes; 1933. Marks: **EFFANBEE / PATSY TINYETTE** on head; tag reads: **This is PATSY TINYETTE / Trademark Pat. Pend. / The Lovable Imp with tiltable / head and movable limbs / AN / EFFanBEE / DURABLE / DOLL;** box is marked: **Patsy Tinyette / An EFFanBEE Durable Doll.** *(Wardell collection)*

F&B-101. *Little Lady.* 22"; glued-on blonde floss wig; brown sleep eyes with lashes; closed mouth; fully jointed composition; all original black velvet and plaid taffeta gown with green sandals; 1939-49. Marks: **EFFANBEE / ANNE SHIRLEY** on back; gold paper heart tag reads: **"I am Little Lady / An Effanbee Durable Doll".** *(Author's collection)*

F&B-102. *Colored Anne Shirley.* 21"; human hair wig; brown sleep eyes; painted mouth; fully jointed composition; original clothes; 1935. Marks: **EFFANBEE / ANNE SHIRLEY** on shoulders. *(Photograph by Barbara McLaughlin, owner)*

F&B-103. *Anne Shirley.* 15"; original brown wig; blue painted eyes; closed mouth; fully jointed composition; original underclothes, redressed in copy of *Historical Series* dress. Marks: **EFFANBEE / ANNE SHIRLEY.** *(Mason collection)*

F&B-104. *Girl.* 21"; original human hair wig; flirty blue sleep eyes with hair lashes; closed mouth; fully jointed composition with separate fingers; hands like Dewees Cochran dolls, body like Little Lady series. Marks: **EFFANBEE** on back and head. *(Author's collection)*

F&B-105. *Dewees Cochran Girl.* 15"; original human hair wig; blue-gray sleep eyes with lashes; open-closed mouth with four teeth; fully jointed composition with separate fingers and pink nails; original blue and cerise taffeta dress, one-piece rayon slip and panties; cerise flowers on head band; 1936. Marks: **EFFANBEE / ANNE SHIRLEY** on body; has gold metal heart tag. *(McLaughlin collection)*

F&B-106.

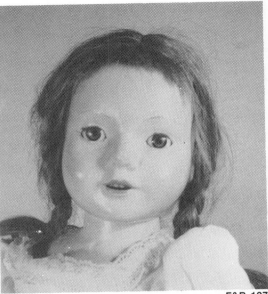

F&B-107.

F&B-108.

F&B-109.

F&B-106. *American Children.* 21"; blonde human hair wig; painted brown eyes; closed mouth; fully jointed composition; original pink voile dress with ribbon flowers, pink panties and slip, shoes and socks. This doll has been authenticated by Dewees Cochran as one of the dolls produced by Effanbee even though it is unmarked. The doll came with a paper tag that read: *Gloria Vanderbilt.* (Cannon collection)

F&B-107. *American Children.* 17"; human hair wig; brown sleep eyes; open mouth with four teeth; fully jointed composition; ca. 1936. Marks: **EFFANBEE/ANNE SHIRLEY** on body. *(Stewart collection)*

F&B-108. *American Children.* 21"; auburn human hair wig; painted blue eyes; closed mouth; fully jointed composition; original white blouse, red dress, blue vest, blue checked apron, panties, black shoes, socks; ca. 1937. Marks: **"EFFANBEE / AMERICAN / CHILDREN"** on head, **EFFANBEE / ANNE SHIRLEY** on body. *(Cannon collection)*

F&B-109. *Ice Queen.* 15"; original human hair wig; brown sleep eyes; open mouth with teeth; fully jointed composition; all original clothes; came with note from Dewees Cochran saying she had hand made the doll about 1938. Marks: **EFFANBEE** on head, **EFFANBEE / ANNE SHIRLEY** on back. *(Cannon collection)*

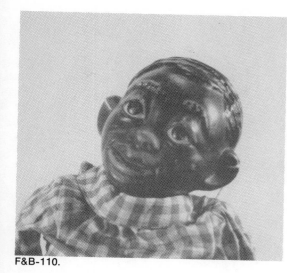

F&B-110.

F&B-110.

F&B-112.

F&B-111.

VIRGINIA AUSTIN

Puppeteer Virginia Austin designed and patented a number of puppets produced by Effanbee. *Lucifer, Liza Lee, Clippo the Clown, Emily Ann, and Poochie, the Dog* were among her creations. For a time she was *"Aunt Patsy"*, the personality created as part of the huge Patsy promotions. She also gave marionette demonstrations and founded the *"Clippo Club"* as part of the marionette promotion. She was, according to the account of one old-timer salesman, "the best demonstrator Effanbee ever had. If still living she would be in her nineties".

Puppets and marionettes were only made a very short time as they proved too costly and too much trouble. Effanbee also produced workshop puppets, theatres, and other accessories during this period.

F&B-110. *Lucifer.* 14"; molded-painted features; composition head, hands, and feet with wood and string marionette body; original red and white checked shirt, tan cotton pants; 1937. Marks: © / LUCIFER / V. AUSTIN / EFFANBEE. *(Author's collection)*

F&B-111. *Emily Ann.* 14"; molded-painted brown hair; painted blue eyes; closed mouth; composition head, hands and feet, wood and string marionette body; 1938. Marks: © / EMILY ANN / V. AUSTIN / EFFANBEE.

F&B-112. Virginia Austin demonstrating her famous marionettes. *(Playthings Magazine)*

F&B-113. *Clippo the Clown.* 14"; molded-painted features; composition head, hands, and feet, wood and string marionette body; original red and white polka dot clown suit; 1937. Marks: © / EFFANBEE / V. AUSTIN. *(Author's collection)*

F&B-113.

F&B-114.

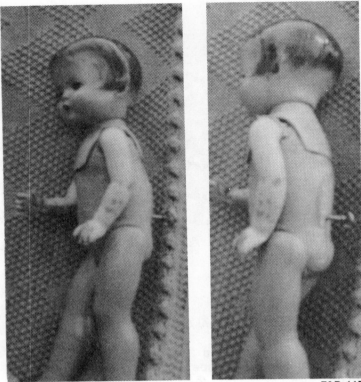

F&B-115.   F&B-115.

F&B-116.

F&B-114. *Pop Eye and Olive Oyl.* Molded-painted synthetic rubber heads, stuffed cloth bodies; original clothes, molded shoes. Marks: **1935,** both have original tags. *(Pfister collection)*

F&B-115. *Musical Patsy.* 17"; molded-painted hair; blue sleep eyes; closed mouth; composition shoulder head and limbs, cotton-stuffed body with music box in back that plays "Happy Birthday"; ca. 1940. Unmarked. *(Rogers collection)*

Original owner dated this doll as "approximately 35 years old". The mother brought out the doll for birthday celebrations; otherwise the doll was never played with. The right wrist shows evidence of a missing bracelet; bracelets have long been a trademark of Effanbee.

F&B-116. *Little Lady.* 18"; original blonde floss wig; blue sleep eyes with lashes; closed mouth; fully jointed composition body; original silver dotted and trimmed white dress, black velvet cape with red rayon lining; 1942. Marks: **EFFANBEE / U.S.A.** on head and back, original gold paper tag reads: **"A New Effanbee / Playmate".** *(Vandiver collection)*

F&B-117. *Babyette.* 11½"; molded-painted brown hair; painted closed eyes; closed mouth; composition head and hands, stuffed pink cloth body; ca. 1945. Unmarked. *(Gaylin collection)*

A person interviewed who knew Walter Fleischaker when he was a salesman for Effanbee reports the 1943 *Sleepy Baby* was named *Little Walter.*

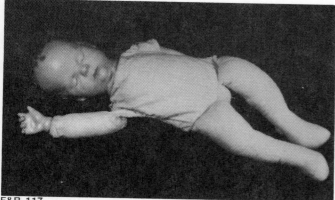

F&B-117.

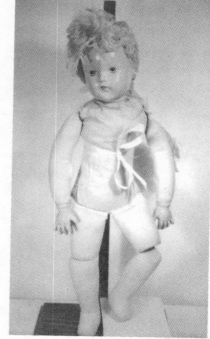

F&B-118.

F&B-119.

F&B-120.

F&B-118. *Little Lady.* 20"; yellow floss wig; painted blue eyes; closed mouth; composition head and hands, most unusual stuffed pink cotton body with jointed knees, ball jointed head; example of World War II material substitution production. Marks: **EFFANBEE / USA.** (Causey collection)

F&B-119. *Candy Kids.* 12"; molded-painted brown hair; blue sleep eyes with lashes; closed mouth; fully jointed composition body; original red dress and jumper suit with white trim and collars, red bonnet, crew hat, and shoes; 1946. Marks: **EFFANBEE.** (Author's collection)

F&B-120. *Twins.* 13"; molded-painted brown hair; painted blue eyes; closed mouth; sticky plastic head and limbs, cloth body; redressed; criers; ca. 1948. Marks: **EFFANBEE** on doll on right, left doll is un-marked. (Wardell collection)

F&B-121.

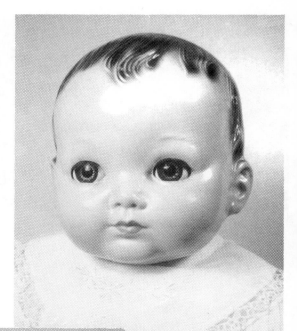

F&B-123.

F&B-122.

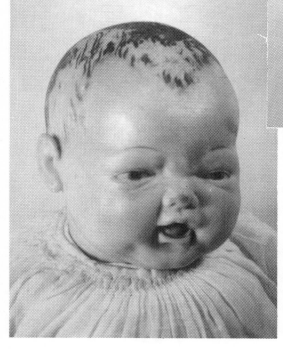

F&B-124.

F&B-121. *Patsy.* 14"; molded-painted hair; painted blue eyes; closed mouth; fully jointed composition; original clothes; 1946 re-issue. Doll is unmarked, box reads: **Patsy / An EFFANBEE DOLL / Copyright 1946 / Fleischaker & Baum Inc.** *(Wardell collection)*

F&B-122. *Character Baby.* 20"; molded-painted brown hair; painted blue eyes; open-closed mouth with molded tongue; early vinyl head and limbs, cloth body; ca. 1948. Marks: **EFFANBEE** on head. *(Wiseman collection)*

F&B-126.

F&B-127.

F&B-125.

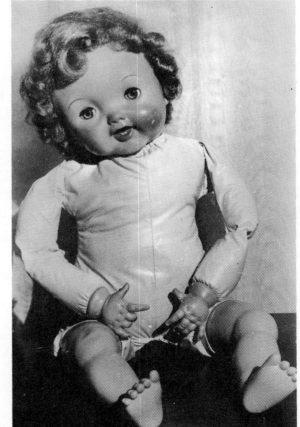

F&B-125.

F&B-123. *Baby.* 21"; molded-painted hair; flirty blue sleep eyes; closed mouth; composition head and limbs, stuffed cotton body; one of the *Mickey-Baby Bright Eyes-Tommy Tucker* clan; ca. 1943. Marks: **EFFANBEE / MADE IN USA.** *(Wardell collection)*

F&B-124. *Honey Walker.* 18½"; glued-on Saran wig; blue sleep eyes; closed mouth; fully jointed hard plastic walker body; original pink and white embossed cotton dress-panties combination, shoes and socks; 1952. Marks: **EFFANBEE** on head and back. *(Author's collection)*

F&B-125. *Cuddle-up.* 27"; rooted blonde hair; blue sleep eyes; open-closed mouth with two teeth; stuffed soft plastic head, hands, and legs, stuffed coated fabric body; original pink romper, blue fleece snow suit and pixie bonnet; ca. 1953. Marks: **EFFANBEE** on head. *(McLaughlin collection)*

F&B-126. *Rootie Kazootie.* 12", 19"; molded-painted features; open-closed mouth; stuffed vinyl head and hands, coated fabric body; has girl friend named Polka Dottie; 1954. Marks: **ROOTIE / KAZOOTIE / © / EFFANBEE** on head. *(Rickwartz collection)*

F&B-127. *Fluffy.* 8"; molded-painted hair; blue sleep eyes; closed mouth; fully jointed vinyl; ca. 1955. Marks: © **FLUFFY / EFFANBEE** on head. Some call this Katie. *(Author's collection)*

F&B-129.

F&B-129.

F&B-130a,b.

F&B-130a,b.

F&B-128.

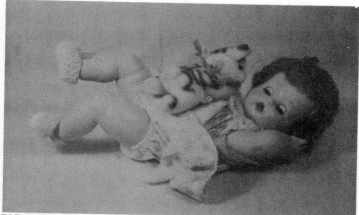

F&B-132.

F&B-132.

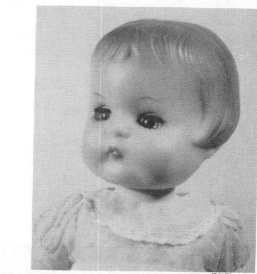

F&B-131.

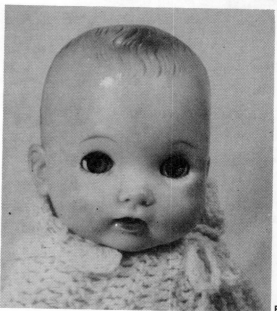

F&B-133.

F&B-128. *Candy Ann.* 20"; rooted brown Saran hair; blue sleep eyes; closed mouth; stuffed vinyl head and body, jointed at neck and shoulders; same hips as F&B-129; original organdy print dress with black velvet ribbon, white cotton panties, slip, straw hat; original price $11.95. Marks: **EFFANBEE** on head, gold paper heart tag reads: **I am your Candy Ann an Effanbee Durable Doll; 1955** on box and dress tag. *(Author's collection)*

F&B-129. *Candy Ann.* 20"; rooted blonde Saran hair; blue sleep eyes; closed mouth; stuffed soft vinyl with separate fingers; original white dress and underclothes, red velvet coat and hat; legs and body are one-piece with hip joint as a flattened section; 1955. Marks: **EFFANBEE.** *(Author's collection)*

F&B-130a,b. *Mother and Child.* 20"; 7½"; mother has rooted Saran hair; blue sleep eyes; closed mouth; soft vinyl head, hard plastic fully jointed walker body with jointed knees; all original clothes. Baby has molded hair; sleep eyes with solid plastic lashes; fully jointed soft vinyl; original soft "blanket" snowsuit. *Family of Three* included mother, baby, and 13" girl with ponytail. *Family of Four* or *Most Happy Family* included mother, baby, brother, *Mickey,* and sister, Fluffy. 1957-1959. Unmarked, gold metal heart tag on wrist; baby carries heart-shaped rattle. *(Author's collection)*

F&B-131. *Patsy-type.* 15½"; molded-painted hair; blue sleep eyes; closed mouth; vinyl head, fully jointed hard plastic body and limbs; ca. 1950s. Unmarked. Only vinyl Patsy from the original style ever seen by this writer. *(Wardell collection)*

F&B-132. *Twinkie.* 15"; rooted blonde hair; blue sleep eyes; drink and wet mouth; soft and hard vinyl jointed at neck, shoulders, hips, and knees. Marks: **EFFANBEE / © 1959** on head and body. *(Wardell collection)*

F&B-133. *Twinkie.* 16"; molded hair; blue sleep eyes; drink and wet mouth; vinyl head and body. Marks: **EFFANBEE** on head.

F&B-134.

F&B-135.

F&B-135.

F&B-137.

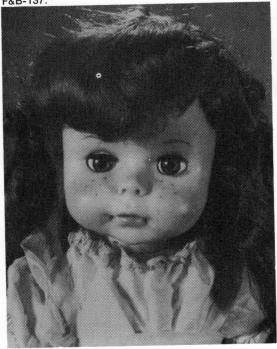

F&B-136.

F&B-134. *Baby.* 9"; rooted brown hair; brown sleep eyes; open-closed mouth; fully jointed vinyl and cloth body. Marks: **EFFanBEE / © 1962.** (*Thompson collection*)

F&B-135. *Mary Jane.* 30"; rooted hair; flirty blue sleep eyes; closed mouth; fully jointed plastic body; original clothes. Marks: **EFFANBEE / MARY JANE** on head, tag reads: **I am Mary Jane Your perfect Playmate / An Effanbee Durable Doll.** (*Kaufman collection*)

F&B-136. *My Fair Baby.* 22"; rooted hair; sleep eyes; drink and wet mouth; fully jointed vinyl; mama voice; ID bracelet. 14" newborn doll with molded hair; blue sleep eyes; drink and wet feature and clenched right fist was shown in the 1964 Wards Catalog. (*Montgomery Ward's 1960 Christmas Catalog*)

F&B-138.

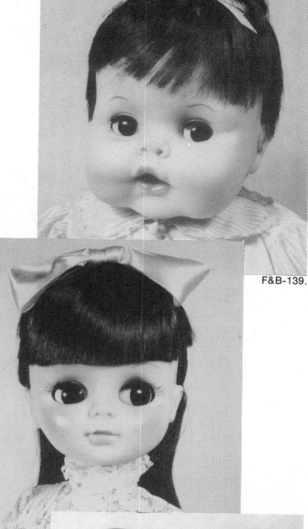

F&B-139.

F&B-140.

F&B-141a,b.

F&B-137. *Honey.* 18"; rooted blonde hair; blue sleep eyes; closed mouth; freckles; called *Suzie Sunshine* in 1964. Marks: **EFFANBEE / © 1961.** *(Mason collection)*

F&B-138. *Belle Telle.* 18"; rooted acetate hair; sleep eyes; open-closed mouth; vinyl head, fully jointed hard plastic body and limbs; hands made to hold telephone; cotton dress, panties, shoes, socks; con-cealed record player with record operates on one battery; says: *"My name is Belle Telle", "Please play with me", and "Please tell me a story",* etc.; sold for $13.45 with telephone. *(Sears Roebuck and Co., 1962)*

F&B-139. *Thumkin.* 18"; rooted brown hair; black sleep eyes; open-closed mouth; vinyl head and limbs, stuffed body; original clothes. Marks: **EFFANBEE / 19©65 / 9500 U 1.** *(Wardell collection)*

F&B-140. *Miss Chips.* 18"; rooted brown hair; black sleep eyes; closed mouth; fully jointed vinyl; original flowered dress and shoes. Marks: **EFFANBEE / 19©65 / 1700** on head; tag reads: **I am Miss Chips / An Effanbee Durable Doll.** *(Wardell collection)*

F&B-141a,b. *Half Pint,* also known as *½ Pint.* 11"; rooted blonde hair; black sleep eyes; closed grin; fully jointed vinyl; original clothes. Marks: **10ME / EFFANBEE / 19©66** on head; tag reads: **I am ½ Pint / AN / EFFANBEE© / DURABLE DOLL.** *(Wardell collection)*

F&B-142.

F&B-144.

F&B-143.

F&B-145.

F&B-142. *Colored Half Pint.* See above for description and marks. *(Siehl collection)*

F&B-143. *Bettina.* 21"; rooted brown hair; blue sleep eyes; open-closed mouth; vinyl head and limbs, stuffed pink cloth body; original clothes. Marks: **EFFANBEE / 19©67** on head, tag reads: **I Am Bettina / An Effanbee Durable Doll.** Another tag attached to clothes reads: **"This is Precious Baby".** Apparently marketed under both names.

F&B-144. *Baby Butterball.* 12"; rooted hair; blue sleep eyes; drink and wet mouth; fully jointed vinyl; original clothes. Marks: © **EFFANBEE / 1969 / 8569** on head and body; bracelet reads: **BABY;** pillow reads: **Effanbee Corporation;** tag reads: **I am Baby Butterball / An Effanbee Durable Doll.** *(Wardell collection)*

F&B-145. *Sweetie Pie.* 18"; rooted hair; blue sleep eyes; soft vinyl head and limbs, kapok-stuffed body; tilt doll and she cries. *(Sears, Roebuck and Co. 1969 Christmas Catalog)*

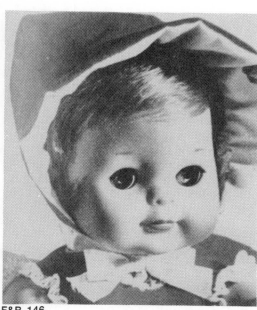

F&B-146.

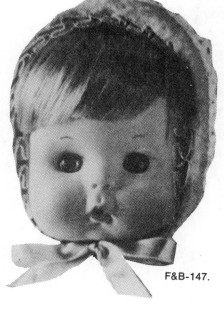

F&B-147.

EIS-1.

F&B-148.

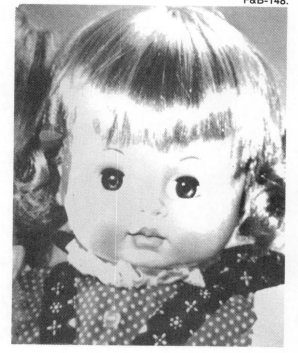

F&B-146. *Angel Baby.* 14"; rooted hair; sleep eyes; fully jointed vinyl body; available in white and black versions. This is called *Baby Face* in Effanbee's 1969 catalog. *(Sears, Roebuck and Co. 1968 Christmas Catalog)*

F&B-147. *Suzie Sunshine.* 18"; rooted hair; sleep eyes; drink and wet mouth; all vinyl; chinchilla cloth coat, hat, leggings and muff. *(Sears, Roebuck and Co. 1969 Christmas Catalog)*

Identical head on kapok-stuffed body with vinyl limbs dressed in white dress, pink coat and bonnet was shown as *Baby Button Nose* in the 1968 Sears Catalog. This same face appears on *"Sunny"* with sprayed hair in the 1973 collection; in the same catalog *Suzie Sunshine* is quite different.

F&B-148. *Sugar Plum.* 20"; rooted hair; sleep eyes; closed mouth; vinyl and kapok-stuffed cloth body; assorted organdy, batiste, and gingham outfits. *(1974 Effanbee catalog illustration)*

EIS-1. *Einco "Baby Dolly".* Three sizes; "special China heads", stuffed body and limbs. Mfr: Eisenmann & Co. Ltd., London. *(Toy Trader and Exporter, 1940)*

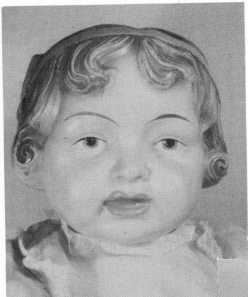

ELEK-1.

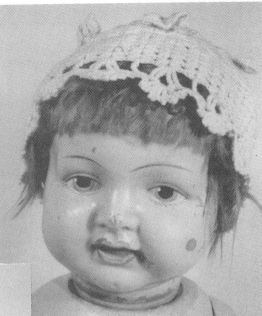

ELEK-2.

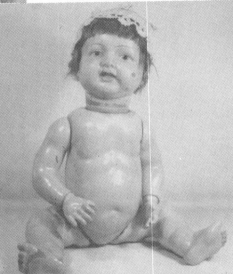

ELEK-5.

ELEK-3.

ELEK-4.

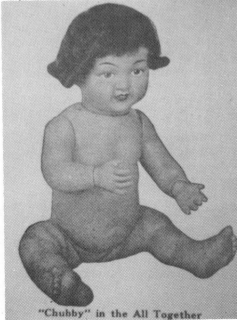

"Chubby" in the All Together

ELECTRA NOVELTY CO.

ELEK-7a,b.

ELEK-7c,d.

ELEK-6a,b.

ELEK-1. *Chubby.* 33½"; molded-painted hair with blue ribbon and bow; painted eyes; open-closed mouth; composition head and hands, excelsior-stuffed body and limbs; red nails; redressed. Marks: **ELECTRA INC. N.Y.** *(O'Rourke collection)*

ELEK-2. *Chubby.* 23"; mohair wig; painted blue eyes; open-closed mouth with upper teeth; fully jointed composition with jointed wrists. Marks: **ELEKTRA T&N CO. N.Y. / COPYRIGHT.** *(Burtchett collection)*

ELEK-3. *Chubby.* 24"; with or without wigs; painted eyes; open-closed mouth with teeth; fully jointed composition with jointed wrists; dressed or undressed; also called *Tootsie Wootsie* in an August 1916 ad. *(Playthings, April, 1916)*

ELEK-4. *Jolly Jumper Boy.* Composition head, stuffed body and limbs; two-piece suit. *(Playthings, January, 1912)*

ELEK-5. *Mother Hubbard's Dog.* 20"; stuffed body; composition shoes; Louis XIV style clothes; Patented September 26, 1911, #41,802. *(Playthings, June, 1912)*

ELEK-6a,b. *Amy and Laurie.* Composition head and hands, stuffed body and limbs. From Louisa May Alcott's *Little Women;* "This story has just been dramatized and is enjoying a sensational run at "The Playhouse" in New York". *(Playthings, October, 1912)*

Note the doll called *Amy* is a typical *Coquette*-type. These were made by various manufacturers; Ideal's was *Naughty Marietta;* New Toy Co. had *The Coquette;* and Effanbee also had *Naughty Marietta* but hurriedly changed to *Miss Coquette.* All were after the Heubach bisque *Coquette.*

ELEK-7a-d. Four dolls from the 1915 Elektra line which included boys, girls, and babies. *(Playthings, February, 1915)*

EMK-1.

ENG-1a,b.

EUG-1.

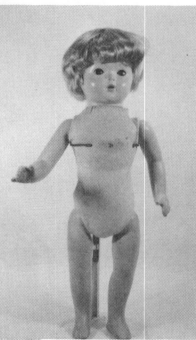

EST-1.

EST-1.

ENG-1c.

EMK-1. *Baby Marion.* Mohair or human hair wigs; sleep eyes; open-closed mouth with teeth; ball-jointed papier mache bodies; made in America. Mfr: Emkay Doll Mfg. Co., Brooklyn, NY. *(Playthings, December, 1917)*

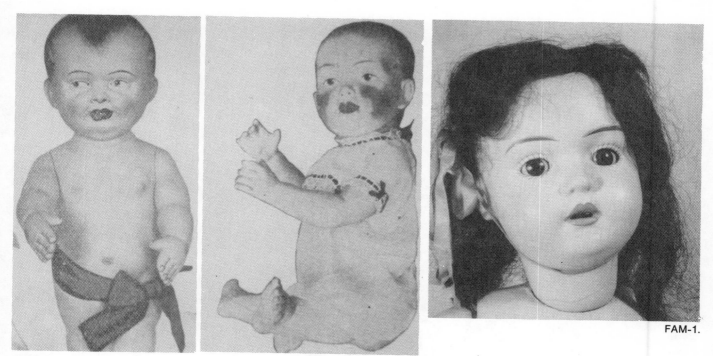

FAIR-2.   FAIR-1.   FAM-1.

ENGLISH DOLLS
(ENG-1a,b,c)

Here are three examples of English dolls of 1940 as advertised by M. Lowe (Birmingham) Ltd., manufacturers of dolls' clothing. Other English dolls are to be found by the name of the manufacturer. (*The Toy Trader and Exporter*)

EST-1. *Estrella.* 19½"; replaced wig over molded hair; dark pupils; open mouth with two teeth; composition head and limbs; excelsior-stuffed body. Marks: **ESTRELLA** on head. (*Author's collection*)

EUG-1. *Lorrie Lee.* 8¾"; rooted black Saran braids; painted black eyes; closed mouth; fully jointed brown vinyl; original clothes. Marks: **23 / LORRIE DOLL / 1969** on head; **MADE IN / HONG KONG** on back. (*Mason collection*)

F

FAIR-1. *The Eugenic Baby.* All composition. "Every dimple and curve of a young baby". Mfr: Fair Amusement Co., NY. (*Playthings, February, 1914*)

FAIR-2. *Babee, A Eugenic Doll.* Feather light composition; painted features; with or without wigs. Mfr: Fair Amusement Co., NY. (*Playthings, August, 1914*)

FAM-1. *Girl.* 20"; human hair wig; dark gray glass eyes; open mouth with teeth; fully ball-jointed composition, very pale bisque head with bright light red mouth. Marks: See fig. FAM-1. (*Stewart collection*)

FAM-2. *Sani-Doll.* Composition head and hands, stuffed body; painted features; expressive faces. Mfr: The Famous Doll Studio, Inc., NY. (*Playthings, March, 1917*)

FED-1. *Liberty Belle.* Wood pulp composition; pure silk clothes in red, white and blue. Mfr: Federal Doll Mfg. Co. Inc. (*Playthings, December, 1918*)

FAM
Doll
20"

Fig-Fam-1.

FAM-2.

fig-FISH-1.

FED-1.

Fisher-Price Toys ®

East Aurora, N.Y.

Assembled in
Mexico from
U.S. and Foreign
Components

REG. NO. PA. 274
All New Material

75% ACETATE
FIBER
25% OLEFIN
FIBER
SURFACE
WASHABLE

Reproduction of label
attached to toy.

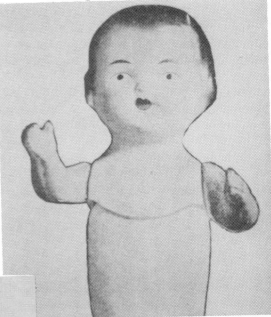

FED-2.

FISH-1.

FIB-1.

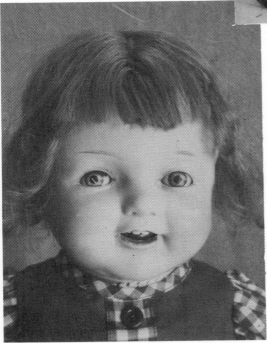

FED-2. *Roze.* Painted features; composition shoulder head and arms, cork-stuffed body and legs, pin and disc joints, arms are jointed to head with rubber. Mfr: Federal Doll Mfg. Co., New York City. *(Playthings, December, 1919)*

FIB-1. *Girl.* 28"; human hair wig; blue-gray tin sleep eyes with lashes; open mouth with four teeth and tongue; composition shoulder head, arms, and lower legs, new unbleached cotton body; ca. 1930. Marks: **FIBEROID** on head. *(Courtesy Jo's Antique Dolls)*

FISH-1. *The Fisher-Price Doll Family: Jenny, Audrey, Mary, Elizabeth, Baby Ann, and Natalie.* 13"; rooted wigs in various colors; painted eyes in blue or brown; closed mouths; vinyl heads and hands, movable heads, stuffed cloth bodies and limbs; removable skirts and overalls, 'pajama suits' never come off of dolls. Marks: On Jenny: **168380 / © 1973 / FISHER PRICE TOYS** on neck; for sewn-in cloth tag on doll, see fig-FISH-1. *(Author's collection)*

Fisher-Price would like you to meet our girls.

Jenny

Elizabeth

Baby Ann

Natalie

Mary

Audrey

These appealing little lapsitters were created with the same thoughtfulness and care that go into every Fisher-Price toy.

Soft huggable bodies to cuddle and coddle. Sweet faces and hands to wash up before supper and kiss before bedtime. Hair to comb, and clothing that fastens and unfastens easily. And every one of our girls has a personality all her own. Jenny is wistful. Elizabeth is a heartbreaker. Natalie, a dimpler. Mary looks trusting. Audrey has mischievous eyes. And Baby Ann is, well, a baby.

And now that you're acquainted, can they come over to play?

Look for Fisher-Price Dolls in your favorite Fisher-Price Toy Center.

©1974 Fisher-Price Toys, East Aurora, New York 14052. Division of The Quaker Oats Company.

FLEX-1.

FR-6.

FR-7.

FR-8.

FR-9.

FLEX-1. *Boy.* 11"; blonde floss Buster Brown style wig over molded hair; painted blue eyes; closed mouth; composition head, lead hands and extra large feet, stuffed body and limbs with wire armature; blue felt pants, yellow knit shirt. Marks: **FLEXO TOYS / PAT. APPLIED FOR** on both feet. *(Courtesy Nita's House of Dolls)*

FRAN-1. *Funny Honey.* 5"; rooted synthetic hair; painted features; one painted tooth; all vinyl; twists, turns, dances; jointed at neck and shoulders. Mfr: Frankonia Products, Inc. *(1965 Frankonia Products, Inc. catalog illustration)*

FRAN-1.

#4430 FUNNY HONEY

FRENCH DOLLS

Two magic words for doll collectors: French dolls. The tradition of fine doll making in France must originate in the basic French love for beautiful things. Whether in furniture, art, or dolls, the French artifact enjoys a reputation for artistic quality.

Here are shown a number of prize-winning dolls from a major collection as well as several from other smaller groupings.

FR-6. *Negro Man.* 18"; original caracul wig; large brown paperweight eyes; open-closed mouth; bisque head, papier mache body painted brown, applied ears. Unmarked. *(Courtesy Ralph's Antique Dolls)*

FR-7. *Girl.* 21"; original mohair wig; blue paperweight eyes; closed mouth; bisque head and gauntlet hands, ball jointed body. Marks: **A. MARQUE** on head. *(Courtesy Ralph's Antique Dolls)*

FR-8. *Long-faced Jumeau Girl.* 30"; braided wig; blue paperweight eyes; closed mouth; bisque head, applied ears, ball jointed hands; original red satin and moire dress trimmed in ecru lace. *(Courtesy Ralph's Antique Dolls)*

FR-9. *Lady.* 16"; original brown mohair wig; brown paperweight eyes; closed mouth; bisque swivel shoulder head, applied pierced ears. Marks: **E 16 J.** *(Courtesy Ralph's Antique Dolls)*

FR-10. *Lady.* 13"; brown human hair wig; painted gray eyes; closed mouth; celluloid construction, bisque head; all original clothes Marks: (picture of eagle) / **210 / 13** on head; (picture of eagle) / **FRANCE / 210** on back. *(Courtesy Camelot)*

FR-11. *Lady.* 24½"; brown human hair wig; dark brown eyes; open-closed mouth with teeth; bisque head, ball-jointed body; replacement clothes. Marks: **UNIS FRANCE / 71, 149 / 301** on head. *(Henson collection)*

FR-10.

FR-11.

FR-12.

FR-13.

FR-15.

FR-14.

FR-16.

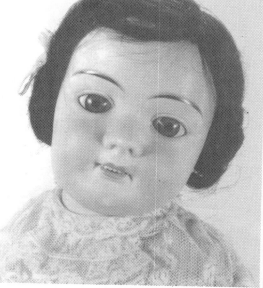

L̆:(FG):

Fig-FR-12.

FR-12. *Girl.* 17"; original red wig; brown eyes; open mouth with two rows of teeth; bisque head, ball-jointed body; pierced ears; old Chantung and cotton lace, long drawers, cotton knit socks. Mfr: Gaultier, 1860-1916. Marks: See fig. FR-12. *(Hutchinson collection)*

FR-13. *Bebe Jumeau.* 23"; new human hair wig; blue stationary eyes; open mouth with teeth; bisque head, ball jointed limbs, cloth body; pierced ears. Marks: **10** on head; **Bebe Jumeau / Diploma D'Or / DEP** stamped in blue on body. *(Hutchinson collection)*

FR-14. *Phoenix Babe.* 22"; human hair wig; stationary blue eyes; closed mouth; bisque head, ball-jointed body, pierced ears; old blue taffeta clothes. Marks: **Phoenix Babe /** (star) **93.** *(Hutchinson collection)*

FR-15. *Bebe Jumeau.* 19"; human hair wig; stationary blue eyes; open mouth with four teeth; bisque head, pierced ears; replacement dress. Marks: **Tete Jumeau** on head; **Bebe Jumeau / Diplome D'Honneur** on back. *(D. Hutchinson collection)*

FR-16. *Lady.* 22"; new human hair wig; blue eyes; open mouth with teeth; bisque head, ball-jointed body, pierced ears; replacement dress. Mfr. Paul Girard Bros. Marks: **CL / Depose / P 10 G** on head. *(Hutchinson collection)*

FR-17. *Girl.* 18"; original brown human hair wig; blue eyes; open mouth with four teeth; bisque head, ball-jointed composition body; pierced ears; redressed. Marks: **Tete Jumeau** on head; **Jumeau / Medaille d'Or / Paris** on body. *(Hutchinson collection)*

FR-18. *Girl.* 9"; human hair wig; sleep eyes; open mouth with four teeth; bisque head, ball jointed body; original handmade lace-trimmed silk dress, leather shoes. Marks: **UNIS FRANCE** in pointed oval on back. *(Hutchinson collection)*

FR-19. *Girl.* 28"; brown human hair wig; blue glass eyes; open mouth with six teeth; bisque head, papier mache body; all original clothes except shoes. Purchased in Canada, owner believes this doll to be French; verified by an authority on French dolls. *(Henson collection)*

FR-17.

FR-18.

FR-19.

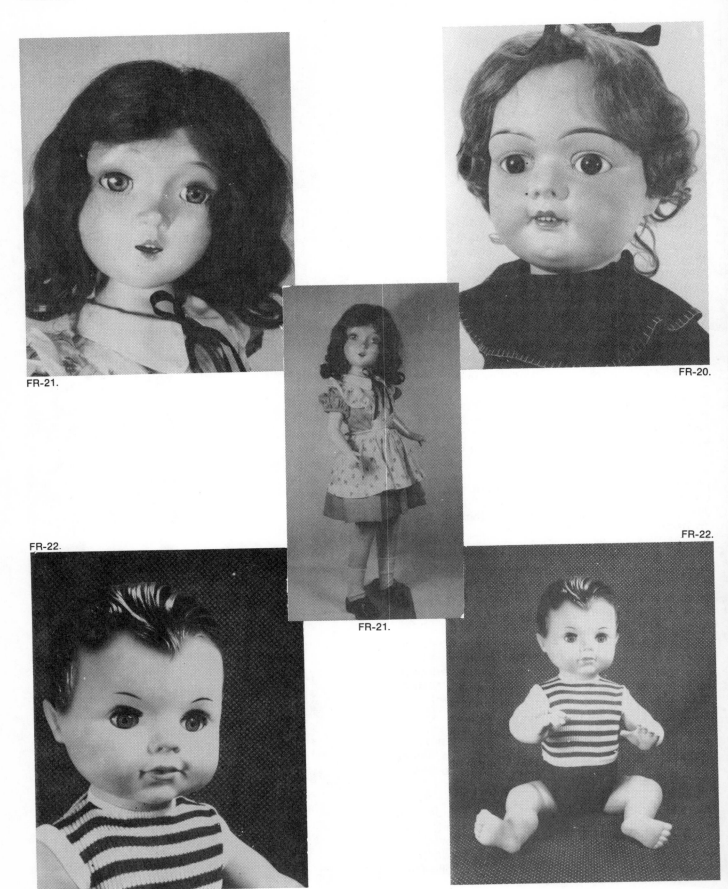

FR-21.

FR-20.

FR-22.

FR-22.

FR-21.

FR-23.

fig-FUL-1.

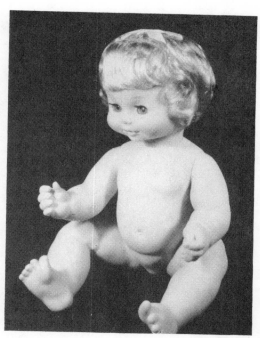

FR-24.

FR-20. *Girl.* 27"; red mohair wig; gray glass eyes; open mouth with five teeth; bisque head, papier mache body; black and red bathing suit. Purchased in Canada, see note on FR-19. Marks: **14** on head. *(Hutchinson collection)*

FR-21. *Girl.* Mohair wig; green metal sleep eyes with human hair lashes; open mouth with teeth and tongue; composition, fully jointed; original clothes. *(Wess collection)*

FR-22. *Baby Boy.* 19½"; molded-painted brown hair; brown sleep eyes with long lashes; closed mouth with dimpled chin; fully jointed high-color plastic with matte finish; original knit shorts and blue and white knit shirt. Note realistic bent baby legs. 1973.

FR-23. *Little Brother.* 20"; rooted brown hair; blue sleep eyes; open-closed mouth; fully jointed Polyflex, sexed; original shirt and pants. Marks: **MADE IN FRANCE / LAVABLE GRANT TEINT;** tag on shirt reads: **Introduced 1967 / MODELE DEPOSE / HAUTE COUTURE / CLODREY.** *(Potter collection)*

FR-24. *Little Sister.* 20"; rooted blonde hair; blue sleep eyes; open-closed mouth; fully jointed Polyflex; original yellow slip and panties; 1967. Marks: **MADE IN FRANCE.** *(Wardell collection)*

THE FULPER ART POTTERY

The Fulper Art Pottery was founded in Flemington, NJ, in 1805. It was not until the shortages of world war curtailed supplies of dolls that this works, ordinarily devoted to production of vases, bowls, can-

dle sticks, and other practical pieces, moved into the dollmaking field. For more of this story see HORSMAN.

FUL-1. *Baby.* 21"; replacement mohair wig; stationary blue glass eyes; open mouth with two teeth and tongue; bisque head, fully jointed papier mache body. Marks: see fig. FUL-1. *(Author's collection)*

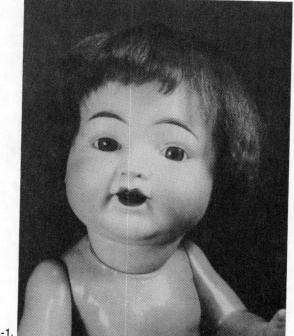

FUL-1.

FUL-2.

fig-FUL-2.

FUL-3.

FUL-4a,b.

FUL-5.

MAKERS OF THE
"Mother Goose" Dolls
Trademark Registered
Original in Conception—Lifelike in Expression—Light—Durable—Attractive—Artistic in Design and Dressing—Altogether Different.

It will surely pay you to call on SAML. GABRIEL SONS & COMPANY when next you visit New York. In the meantime, send for catalogue, giving terse descriptions and illustrations.
Liberal Discount to the Trade.

GAB-2a-d.

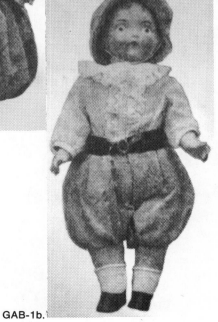

GAB-1a.

GAB-1b.

FUL-2. *Child.* 37"; human hair wig; stationary brown glass eyes; open mouth with teeth; bisque head, ball-jointed body; old child's clothes. Marks: see fig. FUL-2. *(Author's collection)*

FUL-3. *Girl.* 21"; replacement wig; blue tin eyes, painted lashes; open mouth, red tongue, two inserted teeth; bisque head, composition ball-jointed body. Marks: see fig. FUL-1. *(Author's collection)*

FUL-4a,b. *Two Fulper girls.* No description available. *(Courtesy Ralph's Antique Dolls)*

FUL-5. *Toddler.* 17"; replacement mohair wig; dark brown glass eyes; open mouth with two teeth and tongue. Adtocolite ball-jointed body, bisque head; ca. 1918. Marks: **FULPER** (in elongated oval) / **MADE IN U.S.A.** / **13** on head. *(Ortwein collection, photograph by Jackie Meekins)*

GAB-1a,b. *Mother Goose Dolls.* No description available. Mfr.: Sam'l. Gabriel Sons & Co. NY. *(Playthings, January, 1917)*

GAB-2a-d. *Mother Goose Dolls.* No description available. Mfr: Sam'l Gabriel Sons & Co., NY. *(Playthings, June, 1917)*

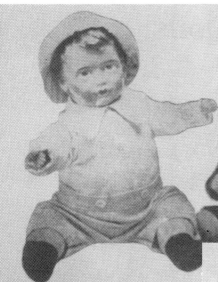

GEM-1a.

GEM-1b.

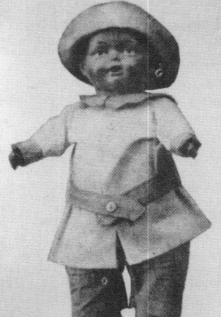

GEM-2a.

GEM-2b.

GEM-3a,b.

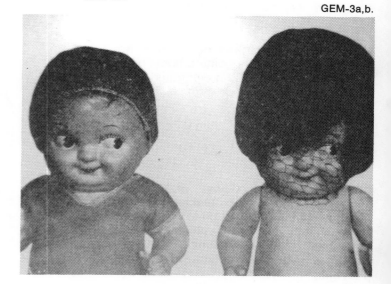

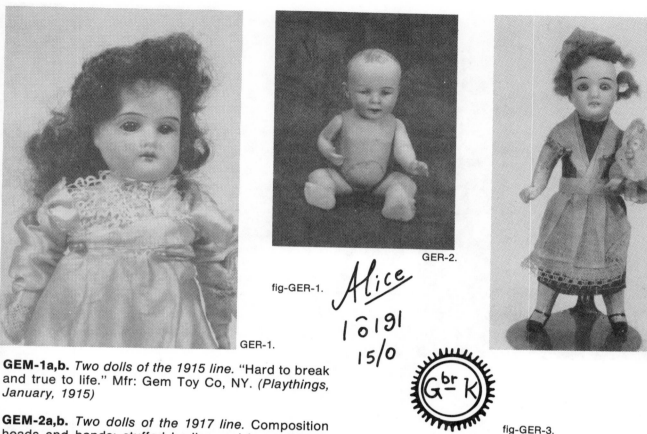

fig-GER-1.

Alice
1 ô 191
15/0

GER-1.

GER-2.

G br K

44-15

fig-GER-3.

GER-3.

GEM-1a,b. *Two dolls of the 1915 line.* "Hard to break and true to life." Mfr: Gem Toy Co, NY. *(Playthings, January, 1915)*

GEM-2a,b. *Two dolls of the 1917 line.* Composition heads and hands; stuffed bodies and legs; painted features. *(Playthings, December, 1916)*

GEM-3a,b. *"O-U-Kids".* With or without wigs; painted side-glance eyes; painted mouths. Jointed only at shoulders; legs are together and doll is on pedestal. Mfr: Gem Toy Co. *(Playthings, December, 1918)*

GER-4. *Girl.* 40"; synthetic red hair; brown glass eyes; open mouth, six teeth; bisque head, ball-jointed composition body. Marks: **478 / 10** on head. *(Griffin collection)*

GERMAN-MADE DOLLS

The German-made dolls have been divided into sub-categories defined by the material from which the head is made.

GER-1. *Alice.* 12"; replacement wig; stationary brown glass eyes; open mouth with four teeth; bisque head, kid body, cloth feet; old, possibly original clothes. Marks: See fig. GER-1. *(Hafner collection)*

GER-2. *Baby Boy.* 4"; brown feather stroke hair; painted blue eyes; painted open-closed mouth; bisque head and body, fully jointed bent baby limbs. Unmarked. *(Author's collection)*

GER-3. *Bisque-Head Girl.* 7"; mohair wig; glass eyes; open mouth, three teeth; bisque head, crude papier mache body and limbs; original clothes; holds 1½" Frozen Charlotte-type doll with molded-painted yellow center-part curls; original box states the two dolls came together. Mfr: Gebruder Krauss, Knoch or Kuhnlenz. Marks: See fig. GER-3. *(Hafner collection)*

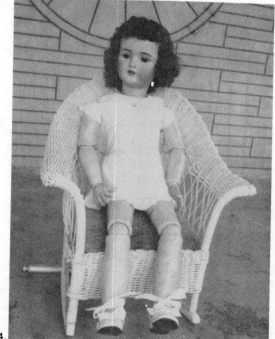

GER-4.

GER-5.

GER-6.

GER-7.

GER-8.

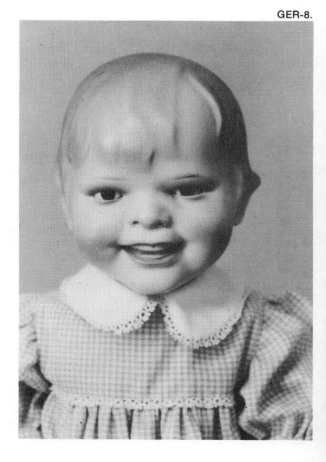

GER-5. *Girl.* 22"; replacement wig; brown glass sleep eyes with hair lashes; open mouth, four teeth; bisque head, ball-jointed body. Mfr: Probably Guttmann & Schiffnie. Marks: **G&S / Germany / 4** on head. *(Hafner collection)*

GER-6. *Phyllis.* Molded-painted hair; blue glass sleep eyes; open mouth with two teeth; bisque shoulder head, composition arms, stuffed muslin body and legs; all original clothes; 1923; trademark was registered in Germany by Schmidt and Ruchter. Marks: **Phyllis / Made in Germany / 711.15.** on shoulder head. *(Rush collection)*

GER-7. *Doll in Swing.* 7¾"; molded-painted yellow hair; blue eyes; closed mouth; all bisque; all original. Marks: **Germany / P-B** or **P-15.** *(Stroud collection)*

GER-8. *Gladdie.* 18½"; molded-painted blonde hair; brown glass sleep eyes; open-closed mouth, six teeth; red clay head, stuffed cloth body; 1929-1930. Marks: **Gladdie / copyrighted by / Helen W. Jensen / Germany.** *(Ortwein collection, photograph by Jackie Meekins)*

GER-9.

GER-9.

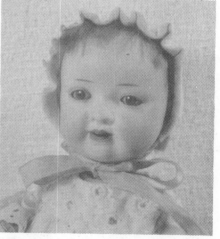

GER-11.

fig. GER-10.

GER-10.

GER-10.

GER-9. *Girl.* 25"; replacement wig; brown glass sleep eyes; open mouth with teeth; bisque head; ball-jointed body, molded bosom, note *deriere.* These dolls are found with heads by Simon-Halbig and Armand Marseille. Marks: **CM BERGMAN / Waltershausen / Germany / 1916 / 7a.** *(Courtesy Nita's House of Dolls)*

GER-10. *Toddler.* 9"; auburn wig; brown glass eyes; open mouth with teeth; pale bisque head, composition body and bent limbs; lawn and cotton lace dress, slip, hand crocheted hat. Marks: See fig. GER-10. *(Hutchinson collection)*

GER-11. *My Sweet Baby.* 10"; original mohair wig; blue glass sleep eyes; open mouth, two bisque teeth and tongue; bisque head, composition bent baby limbs; redressed. Marks: **Germany / My Sweet Baby / 4 / 0.** *(Courtesy Nita's House of Dolls)*

GER-12.

GER-13.

GER-14.

GER-15.

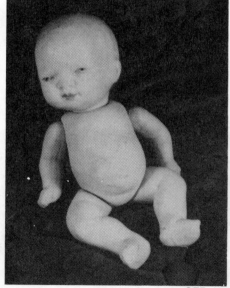

GER-16.

GER-12. *Edmund Steiner Girl.* 14"; original human hair wig; stationary blue glass eyes; bisque head, ball-jointed composition body; old dress not original. Marks: **E.U.ST.** (in diamond) / **Germany / 1.** *(Hutchinson collection)*

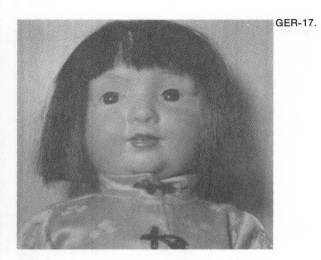

GER-17.

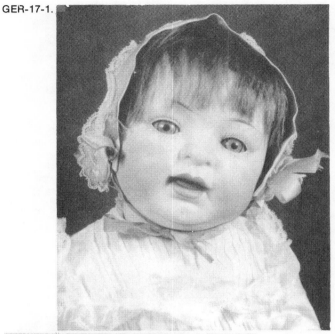

GER-17-1.

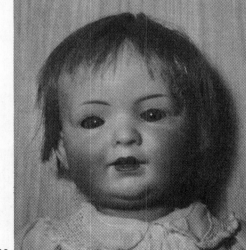

GER-18.

GER-19.

GER-13. *Otto Reinecke Baby.* 12', human hair wig; stationary blue glass eyes; open mouth, two teeth; bisque head, fully jointed composition baby body. Marks: **PM / 23.** *(Hutchinson collection)*

GER-14. *Girl.* 38"; human hair wig; glass eyes; open mouth with four teeth; bisque head; original clothes; used as a department store mannequin, given to woman for birthday in 1910. Unmarked. *(Cannon collection)*

GER-15. Bisque head on stick; stationary brown glass eyes; note holes where arms and legs apparently were fastened; belonged to present owner's mother. Marks: **1 (backwards 2) / 0.** *(Swift collection)*

GER-16. *Baby.* 6"; blue eyes; closed mouth; all fully jointed bisque. Marks: **682 / 14 / Germany.** *(Thompson collection)*

GER-17. *Oriental Child.* 17"; hair wig; brown glass sleep eyes; open-closed mouth with two teeth; bisque head, composition body; redressed. Marks: **B.P. / O** on neck. *(Cannon collection)*

GER-17-1. *Baby.* 15"; light brown human hair wig; painted gray glass eyes; open-closed painted mouth; bisque head, fully jointed composition body, bent baby legs; old clothes. Marks: **150 / 7** on head. *(Author's collection)*

GER-18. *Girl.* 15"; human hair wig; stationary blue glass eyes; unique open-closed mouth with tongue; bisque head, composition body, ball-jointed at neck, shoulders, hips, knees, elbows; redressed in Kate Greenaway clothes. Mfr: Armand Marseille. Marks: **G.B. / Germany / A O M / D.R.G.M 248 / 7.** *(Cannon collection)*

GER-19. *Baby.* 14"; human hair wig; stationary blue glass eyes; open-closed mouth with two teeth; bisque head, composition body and bent baby limbs, fully jointed. Marks: **585 / 6** on head. *(Cannon collection)*

GER-20a.b.

GER-23.

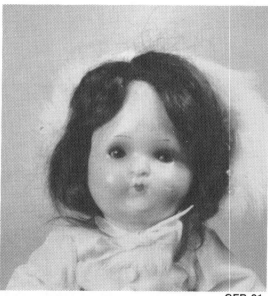

GER-21.

GER-22.

GER-22.

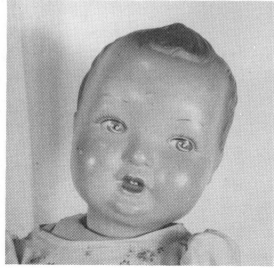

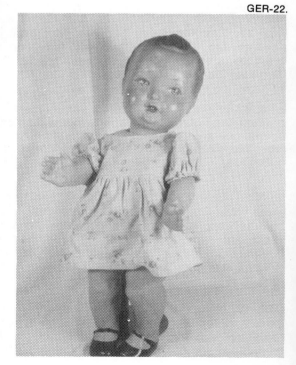

GER-23.

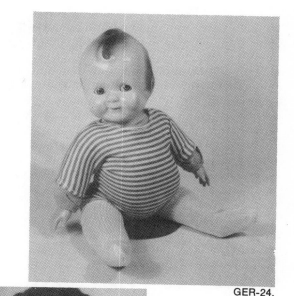

GER-24.

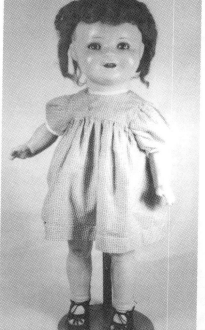

GER-25.

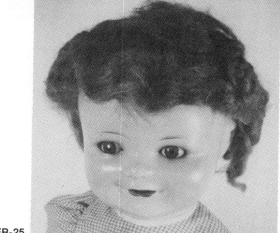

GER-25.

GER-20a,b. *Ski-boy and Swiss Girl.* 6¼"; boy has molded-painted hair; girl has glued-on fine synthetic blonde wig; painted blue eyes; closed mouth; plastic, jointed at shoulders, fat tummy; girl wears original Swiss outfit, painted shoes; boy wears original knit hat, scarf, shirt, pants, plastic skis and poles, painted shoes. Unmarked. *(Author's collection)*

GER-21. *Girl.* 12"; red mohair wig; blue sleep eyes; painted mouth; all composition, resembles painted bisque, jointed at shoulders and hips. Marks: **Germany / 8 / 0.** *(Courtesy Nita's House of Dolls)*

GER-22. *Girl.* 17½"; molded-painted brown hair; painted blue side-glance eyes; open-closed mouth with teeth; composition head, crude papier mache body, plaster composition limbs; possibly original clothes, molded-painted brown shoes. Unmarked. *(Gaylin collection)*

GER-23. *Girl and General Store.* 8"; molded-painted hair; painted eyes; composition head, carved wooden hands and feet, spring body; blue felt skirt, print blouse and apron, white hat, baskets nailed to hands. Came with wooden store shelves and counter with cans of food. *(Author's collection)*

GER-24. *Character Boy.* 13"; molded-painted hair; flirty blue tin sleep eyes; closed grin; composition head and gauntlet hands, fat stuffed cloth body and limbs; red and white knit romper. Marks: A very large circular mark on head, **Germany** is only legible word. *(Stewart collection)*

GER-25. *Girl.* 16"; original mohair wig; blue glass eyes; open mouth with four teeth and tongue; composition head and limbs, pressed cardboard body; original shoes. Marks: **502 / (triangle) / Germany / 5.** *(Gaylin collection)*

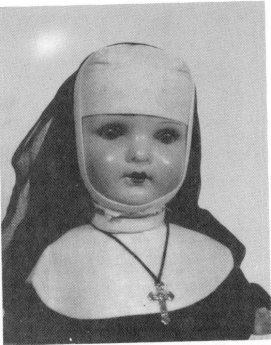

GER-26.

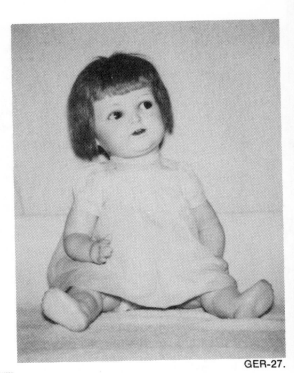

GER-27.

GER-29.

GER-28.

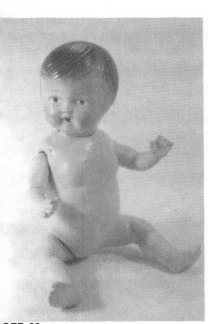

GER-30.

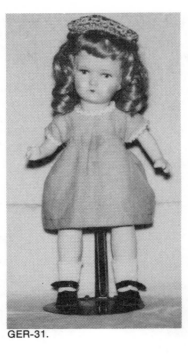

GER-31.

GER-32.

GER-26. *Nun.* Mohair wig; glass eyes; open mouth, two teeth; fully jointed composition toddler body with dimples in knees; all original. *(D'Andrade collection)*

GER-27. *Toddler.* 18"; glued-on wig; flirty blue glass sleep eyes; open mouth, two teeth, felt tongue; composition socket head, chubby limbs and body could be papier mache. Marks: **7400 / 73** on head, label inside original box reads: **D.R.P.Nr. / 443441,** outside label reads: **TAUSENDSCHONCHEN** in circle with **EMBLEM / HEN** on outside of circle **/ Primo Steh-U. / Sitzbaby / MADE IN GERMANY.** *(Warren collection)*

GER-28. *Geni.* 7½"; painted features; composition head and hands, spring bellows body probably made noise when pushed down, wooden stick legs and feet; flannel and cotton clothes. Marks: **78** on head. *(Gibbins collection)*

GER-29. *Baby.* 17"; soft mohair wig; flirty gray eyes; open mouth; composition swivel head; sculptured stockinette stuffed body jointed hips and shoulders, stitched fingers, toes, leg wrinkles; original white fleece three-piece snowsuit with blue trim, felt booties, cotton socks; purchased in Cuba in 1936. Note wig is loose and slipped back in picture of undressed doll. Unmarked. *(Photograph by Barbara McLaughlin, owner)*

GER-30. *Baby.* 11½"; molded-painted red-brown hair; painted blue eyes; painted open mouth, two inserted upper teeth; composition, fully jointed, fat tummy; original clothes. Marks: **Germany / Trademark /** (two illegible lines of marks), **W** on lower back. *(Author's collection)*

GER-31. *Our Pet.* 13"; replacement wig; painted blue eyes; closed mouth; composition socket head and body. Marks: **Our Pet / Germany / 5 / OX** on head. *(Warren collection)*

GER-32. *Heidi-type Girl.* 19"; original brown human hair wig; blue glass sleep eyes; open mouth, two teeth; light weight composition; all original felt, cotton, and gauze clothes, red and white oil cloth shoes, rayon socks. Marks: See fig. GER-32. *(Causey collection)*

GER-32.

H.

fig-GER-32.

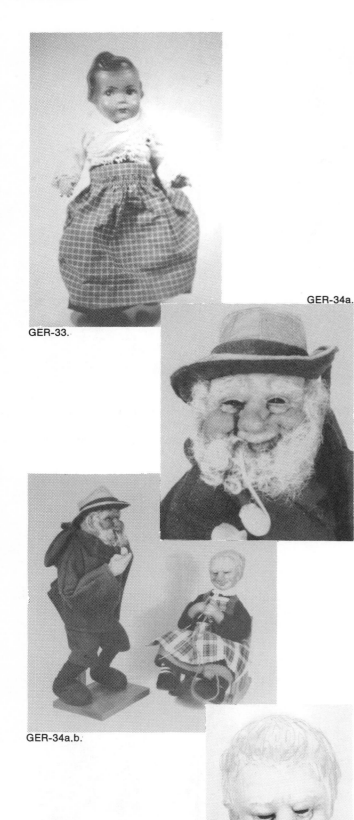

GER-33.

GER-34a.

GER-34a,b.

GER-34b.

GER-33. *Girl.* 8½"; molded-painted hair; painted blue eyes; closed mouth; all composition; all original clothes, painted Mary Jane shoes and socks. Marks: backwards **5** on back.

GER-34a,b. *Old German Couple.* 10¼", 13"; curly mohair wigs; needle sculptured, hand painted features; nylon stockinette stuffed with foam rubber over wire armature; felt clothes; ca. 1971. Unmarked. Made by private family in Germany. *(Rothert collection)*

THREE GERMAN CHARACTERS

The following three dolls were purchased from the original owner who believed them to be "over one hundred years old" since they had been brought from Germany by his parents. While recognizing the value of the dolls, the author was also convinced they were not as old as the owner believed them to be. When dolls are passed down in a family for many years their age tends to increase in unrealistic increments. For example, Grandmother's doll is often automatically assumed to be about 85 years old because Grandmother was that age when she died. Simple arithmetic will indicate that since Grandmother received the doll on her tenth birthday it must, therefore, be more nearly seventy-five years old, thus dating it around 1900 rather than 1890.

Dolls which could have been no older than 110 years have been presented to this writer as 200-year-old specimens. The point of all this is, of course, that great care should be exercised in dating dolls. As to the case before us, these three fat old Germans must be from the period after 1900 and before 1940. Other examples of this type may be found elsewhere in this volume.

GER-35. *Dutchman.* 20"; one curl on forehead; painted blue eyes; open mouth for pipe; papier mache head, excelsior-stuffed plush body; black pants, gold shirt, brown felt hat, green felt scarf, felt hands and feet, paper and wood accordian, wooden shoes and pipe. *(Author's collection)*

GER-36. *Chimney Sweep.* 20"; painted blue eyes; closed mouth; papier mache head, excelsior-stuffed velvet body and hat; gold flowers on front for buttons; felt hands and feet, black oil cloth shoes, belt, buckle, black smudges on face, heart on left shirt front reads: **"Ich bringe Gluck".** *(Author's collection)*

GER-37. *Sailor.* 18"; molded-painted hair; painted blue eyes; molded-painted open mouth; papier mache head, stuffed cloth and felt body, felt hands and feet; blue pants, collar, hat, anchor, black band on hat, gold flower buttons on shirt, wooden pipe. *(Author's collection)*

GER-35.

GER-36.

GER-37.

GER-35.

GER-36.

GER-37.

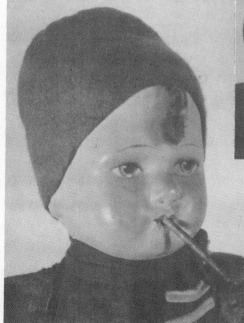

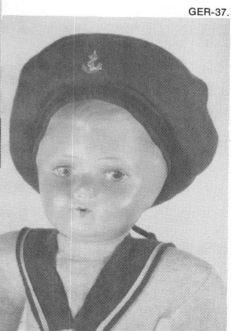

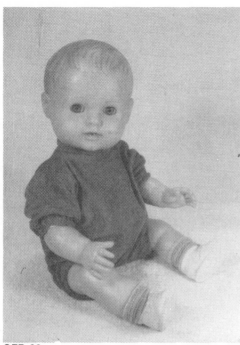

GER-38.

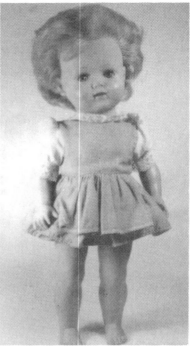

GER-39.

GER-40.

GER-41.

GER-42.

GER-38. *Baby.* 16"; molded-painted hair; sky blue sleep eyes; drink and wet mouth; fully jointed vinyl; redressed. Marks: (turtle in diamond) / **Schildkrot / Germany / 40** on shoulders; turtle in circle with **WASSERDICHT / WATERPROOF** around circle in middle of back. *(Mason collection)*

GER-39. *Girl.* 16"; rooted synthetic hair; blue sleep eyes; open-closed mouth with molded teeth; soft vinyl head, elastic strung vinyl body and limbs; original pastel chambray dress with white trim. Marks: **40 / 42 / MADE IN / W. GERMANY** on body. *(Author's collection)*

GER-40. *Girl.* 27"; human hair wig; pale blue sleep eyes; closed mouth; all hard plastic; ca. 1963. Marks: See fig. Ger-40. *(Campbell collection)*

GER-41. *Lilli, Barbie-type doll.* 11½"; rooted blonde hair; painted eyes; closed mouth; fine, early matte finish hard plastic jointed at neck and arms; brought from Germany in 1954. Marks: **Lilli** on stand, **"Made in Western Germany"** on bottom of stand. *(Siehl collection)*

GER-42. *Little Girl.* 7½"; molded-painted blonde hair; painted blue eyes; open-closed mouth; molded-painted vinyl body and clothes. Marks: **Made in W. Germany.** *(Bailey collection, photograph by Jackie Meekins)*

GER-43.

GER-44.

fig-GER-40.

GER-45.

GER-43. A collection of modern German-made dolls available in Canada. *(Campbell collection)*

GER-44. *Girl.* 6½"; synthetic blonde braided wig; inset glassine blue eyes; painted open mouth; vinyl body; knit sweater and hat, white shirt, panties; molded-painted shoes and socks. Marks: **MADE IN / WESTERN / GERMANY** on left shoe. *(Gibbins collection)*

GER-45. *Dancing Peasant Girl.* 7"; synthetic blonde hair; painted eyes; closed grin; fully jointed, vinyl head and hands, hard plastic body and legs; original clothes, painted shoes; key wind dancing mechanism. Marks: **Sweatheart / Dancing Doll / Germany** on head. *(Hartwell collection)*

GER-46a,b. *Boy and Girl.* 4"; mohair wigs; painted eyes; open mouths; plastic bodies; felt clothes, silk apron and cap; 1954. Marks: **90 / (clover leaf)** *(Rothert collection)*

GER-46a,b.

GOLD-1.

GOLD-1.

GIE-1.

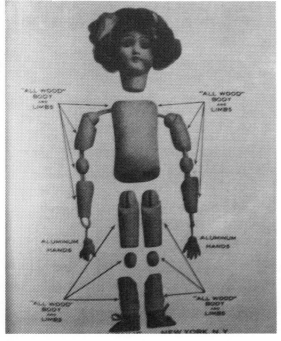

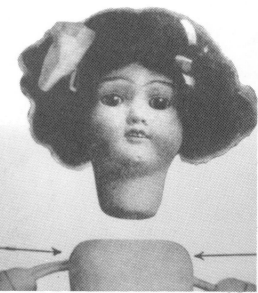

GIE-1.

GIE-1. *Gie-Fa Dolls.* Five sizes; moving eye screwed in place; aluminum heads and hands; featherweight hollow body, arms and legs of finest wood; *"The most sanitary doll in existence".* Mfr: Giebeler-Falk Doll Corp., NYC. *(Playthings, April, 1919)*

GOLD-1. *"Indian" Boy.* 11"; molded hair with remains of black mohair wig; painted black eyes; composition shoulder head and arms, cloth body and legs, disc-jointed; in original dress, missing shoes; 1930s. Marks: **GOLD DOLL** on shoulder head. *(Perry collection)*

GUND-1a.

GOTZ-1.

GUND-1b.

GRO-1.

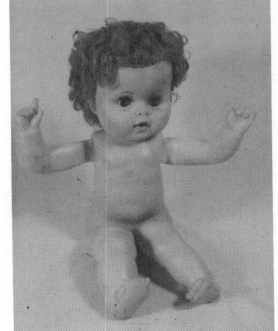

GOTZ-1. *Girl.* Rooted blonde hair; brown sleep eyes; closed mouth; all soft plastic; original clothes. Marks: **+4e / Gotz-Puppe** on head; tag on dress reads **MADE IN GERMANY, EINE / GOTZ / SPEEL-FREUNDIN.** *(Wardell collection)*

GRO-1. *Girl.* 13½"; blonde synthetic hair; blue sleep eyes; drink and wet mouth; all vinyl, note construction of limbs and joints. Marks: **17 / 14DM / U** on head; **1962© / GROMAN INC / BKLYN, NY. / PAT. PEND.** on back. *(Wiseman collection)*

GUND MANUFACTURING COMPANY

GUND-1a,b. *Tootsie Boy and Tootsie Girl.* "Large". "The Tootsie Dolls have jointed knees, unbreakable (composition) heads and hands, stockings, patent leather slippers, pretty, childish costumes."

"Tootsie dolls included *Marion, Wally, Brother, Sister,* and *"The Little Rogues."* Complexions are a delicate pinkish-red and faces are molded from real children. *(Playthings, February, 1912)*

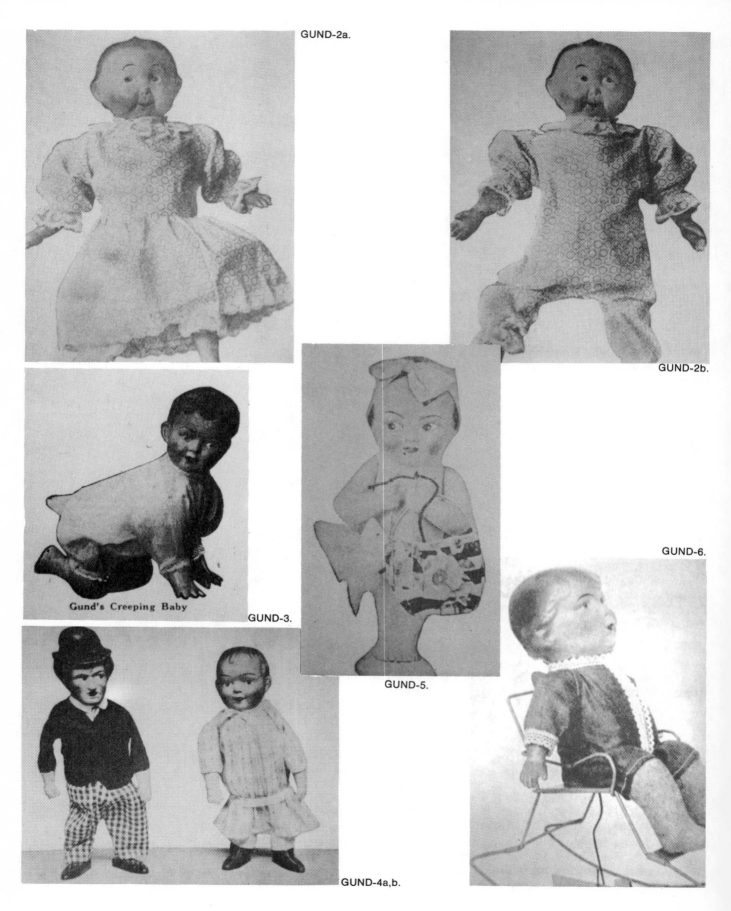

GUND-2a.

GUND-2b.

Gund's Creeping Baby

GUND-3.

GUND-5.

GUND-6.

GUND-4a,b.

Professor Pook   Marti   Mini

GUND-7.

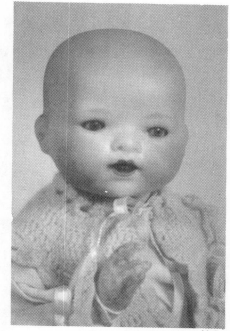

H-6.

GUND-2a,b. *The Flippety-Flop Kids.* "Character dolls that swing their arms and legs and cry out like real babies." Squeeze the doll with thumb and forefinger and arms and legs swing up and down and doll cries. Painted features; composition head and limbs, stuffed body; came with bare feet. *(Playthings, March, 1913)*

GUND-3. *Creeping Baby.* Composition head and limbs, stuffed body; mechanical; Gund also had walking animals of similar design. *(Playthings, January, 1915)*

GUND-4a,b. *Charlie Chaplin and Baby Doll.* Stuffed bodies, composition heads and hands; "Gund's mechanicals walk, waddle, tumble, dance, and creep." *(Playthings, April, 1917)*

GUND-5. *Nettie Knit "doing her bit".* 12"; doll is "busy" knitting for the soldiers with real steel needles and a bag of wool. *(Playthings, July, 1918)*

GUND-6. *Rocking Baby.* Composition head and hands, stuffed body; rocking chair of strong, bright colored wire, operated by clock work, runs about two minutes. Animals were also mounted on these rockers. *(Playthings, January, 1919)*

GUND-7. *Mini-Martians.* 4½"; created by Deet and Patti; included *Professor Pook, Marti, Mini, Bonnie, Meri,* and *Teenie;* extras included *Martian Star House;* "Carnaby Comet" clothes, *Jet Car* and *Space Scooter.* *(1967 Sears, Roebuck & Co. catalog illustration)*

H

H-6. *Baby.* 14"; sprayed hair; blue glass sleep eyes; open mouth with wobbly tongue; bisque head, composition body jointed shoulders, hips, hole in tummy with crier and push-bellows. Marks: **GERMANY / H&B.** *(Kaufman collection)*

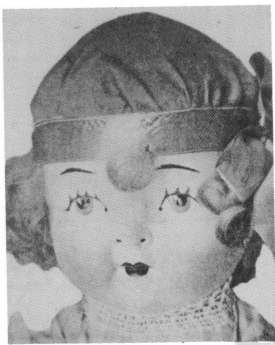

H-8.

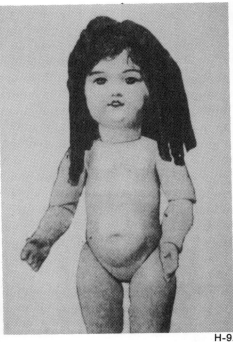

H-9.

H-10a.

(Copyright)

I am the Doll of Luckiness,
You know, I'm all the style;
A look at me when in distress
Will surely make you smile.

(Lucky Bill)
(Copyrighted 30367)

H-11.

H & Z DOLL & TOY CO.

H-8. *Dainty Marie.* 9"; mohair wig; painted features; all composition; lace-trimmed dress with huge satin bow, socks, tie slippers with buckle trim; design copyright 1919, C.B. Knight. Mfr: H&Z Doll & Toy Co. Inc., NYC. *(Playthings, January, 1919)*

H-9. *Zaiden Doll.* "Mr. D. Heyman wishes to announce that he has transferred his interests from the toy line, in which he was eminently successful, to the manufacture of dolls.

In co-operation with Mr. Heyman will be Mr. David Zaiden, known in Toyland as the patentee and designer of the famous ZAIDEN DOLL, now a Nationally famous article. The ZAIDEN DOLL is generally considered to be one of the very best and highest-class dolls in the market." Mfr: H&Z Doll & Toy Co. Inc., NYC. *(Playthings, December, 1918)*

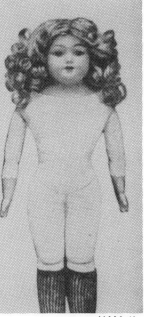

H-10b.

HAM-1a.

HAM-1b.

H-10c.

HAM-1c.

HAHN & AMBERG

H-10a,b,c. *Lucky Bill, Baby Blue, Sassy Doll.*

a. *Lucky Bill.*™ 10", 12"; white plush with composition head; sold for $4.20 and $8.50 per dozen.

b. *Baby Blue.* 10", 14"; blue felt with celluloid face; also came as Red Riding Hood in red felt.

c. *Sassy Doll©.* Assorted colors of silk and velvet with composition head; sold for $8.50 per dozen. Mfr: Hahn & Amberg. *(Playthings, July, 1909)*

H-11. *Lucky Bill.* 8½", 10", 11"; composition head, small dolls came in white, pink, blue, or red plush; 11" doll came in white plush only; $2.25, $4.20 and $8.25 per dozen. Mfr: Hahn & Amberg. *(Playthings, August, 1909)*

HAMBURGER AND CO.

HAM-1a,b,c. Three dolls from 1903 Import line of Hamburger and Co. *(Playthings, February, 1903)*

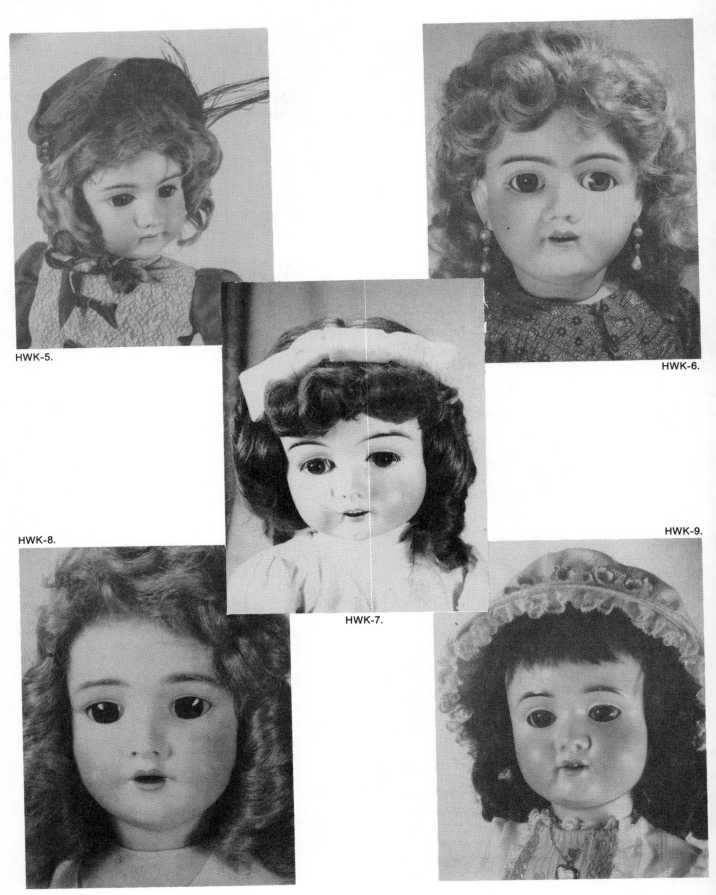

HWK-5.

HWK-6.

HWK-8.

HWK-7.

HWK-9.

HAP-3.

HAP-2a,b.

HAP-1a.

HAP-1b.

HWK-5. *Girl.* 33"; original wig; stationary brown glass eyes; bisque head, ball-jointed body; old clothes. Marks: **Germany / Heinrich / Handwerck / Simon & Halbig / 7.** *(Hutchinson collection)*

HWK-6. *Girl.* 27"; replacement wig; blue glass sleep eyes; open mouth with teeth; bisque head, composition ball-jointed body; pierced ears. Marks: **14 / GERMANY / 99 / DEP / HANDWERCK / 5½.** *(Courtesy Nita's House of Dolls)*

HWK-7. *Girl.* 27"; replacement wig; replacement brown glass eyes; hair lashes; open mouth with five teeth; replacement body, bisque head. Marks: **283 / 33 1 / MAX / HANDWERCK / Germany on head.**

HWK-8. *Girl.* 30"; replacement wig; brown glass eyes; open mouth; bisque head; composition ball-jointed body, pierced ears. Marks: **189-15 / DEP / Germany / Handwerck / HALBIG.** *(Hafner collection)*

HWK-9. *Viola.* 21"; replacement wig; brown glass sleep eyes; open mouth with four teeth; bisque head, composition ball-jointed body; ca. 1903. Marks: **Made in Germany / Viola / H & Co. / Hamburgert Co.,** body marked; **2¼ / Heinrich Handwerck / Germany.** *(Hafner collection)*

HAP-1a,b. *Happifats.* All bisque; two teeth showing; jointed only at shoulders; from the book by John Martin, designed by Kate Jordon; *"Happifats for Happiness".* *(Playthings, 1913)*

HAP-2a,b. *Happifats.* Painted features; composition head and hands, stuffed body; tag on clothes reads: **HAPPIFAT** with manufacturing information; probably made by K&K Toy Co. *(Playthings, January, 1917)*

HAP-3. *Happifats Dishes.* German-made, fine porcelain. *(Courtesy Ralph's Antique Dolls)*

HAS-5.

HAS-6.

HAS-6.

HASBRO
(Hassenfeld Bros)

Although Hasbro is primarily a toy manufacturer, their junkets into the doll field have been most interesting. Hasbro is quick to point out their GI Joe is not a doll but rather an action figure. Nevertheless such admonishment cannot deter doll collectors from including GI Joe and like figures in a special category of a collection.

In time to come this and other similar figures, along with their minutely detailed accessories, may present a rather unique picture of the development of military equipment as well as fashion. The latest of these have sprayed-on flocked hair, mustaches, and beards.

In addition, other adventure sets have been developed - camping, mountain climbing, and many others.

HAS-5. *Buddy Charlie.* 12"; molded-painted features; fully-jointed action figure; Army uniform; a little-recognized buddy of G.I. Joe. *(Montgomery Ward's 1965 Christmas Catalog)*
According to Mrs. Joseph T. Gregory, Buddy Charlie was made by Louis Marx. The doll is unmarked. For other Marx dolls see page 931.

HAS-6. *Peteena.* 9½"; synthetic fur wig; painted brown eyes with inset plastic lashes; painted closed mouth; all plastic with poodle head and tail; original chartreuse bikini and hat with yellow dots, yellow sandals. Marks: ©**1966 / HASBRO / JAPAN ® / PATENT PENDING** on back. *(Author's collection)*

HAS-7. *That Kid.* 21"; rooted tosca hair; blue sleep eyes with lashes; open-closed mouth with molded front teeth; soft vinyl head, rigid vinyl body and limbs; see photo for clothes; battery operated, pull string; says: "Put me down!", "You're funny looking!" and more. Marks: **HASBRO ® / 19®67** on head. *(Author's collection)*

HAS-7.

HAS-7.

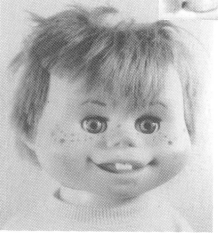

HAS-9c.

HAS-9a.

HAS-9b.

HAS-9d.

HAS-10.

HAS-8. *Aimee.* 16"; rooted hair; amber sleep eyes; fully jointed vinyl body; long dress and golden sandals, earrings; produced only in 1972. *(Photograph courtesy Hasbro Industries Inc.)*

HAS-9a-d. *Candy Babies.* 9"; rooted hair; painted eyes; open-closed grins; soft vinyl heads, each one different; vinyl hands, stuffed cloth bean bag bodies; sewn-on hats, nylon tricot outfits; 1972. *(Photographs courtesy Hasbro Industries Inc.)*

    a. *"Dots"* and **b.** *"Peppermint Pattie"* are trademarks of Sweets Candy Company, Inc.

    c. *"Baby Ruth"* is a product of Curtiss Candy Company, © 1973.

    d. *"Choo Choo Charlie"* © 1973 Quaker City Chocolate & Conf'y Co., Inc.

HAS-10. *Bewhiskered G.I. Joes.* Fully jointed vinyl action figures with new *"Kung Fu"* grip; synthetic hair and beards; available in black or white; note Peace symbols instead of dog tags; definitely a result of the Viet Nam war period; talking unit with pull ring. *(1974 Hasbro Catalog)*

HAS-8.

HAS-11.

HAS-12.

HAS-11. *Leggy.* 10''; rooted hair in assorted colors; painted eyes; closed mouth; vinyl, posable limbs, jointed at hips and shoulders; wardrobe available; produced only in 1973. *(Courtesy Hasbro Industries Inc.)*

Leggy Kate (#4630) Red head.

Leggy Nan (#4625) Brunette.

Leggy Sue (#4635) Black girl with Afro.

Leggy Jill (#4620) Blonde.

HAS-15.

HAS-13.

HAS-16.

HAS-14.

HAV-1.

HAS-12. *Flutterbyes.* 1½"; rooted pink, red, green, orange, yellow hair; painted features; one-piece vinyl bodies, four different faces, removable plastic wigs; new in 1974. *(Courtesy Hasbro Industries Inc.)*

HAS-13. *Sweet Dreams.* 17"; yarn hair; black felt eyes; button nose; embroidered smile; stuffed checked gingham body; eyelet lace trim night cap and print dress; *Annabel* wears pink clothes, has yellow hair; *Amanda* wears orchid clothes with pink hair; *Abigail* wears orange clothes with orange hair; new in 1974. *(Courtesy Hasbro Industries Inc.)*

HAS-14. *Sweet Cookie.* 18"; rooted blonde hair; painted eyes; open mouth with teeth; fully jointed plastic body with soft vinyl head; comes with battery operated portable mixer, bowl, drip bowl, spatula, kitchen counter, four spoons, measuring cup, napkins, cookbook, box of *Jello;* 1972. *(Courtesy Hasbro Industries Inc.)*

Jello® Brand Instant Pudding and Pie Filling, Jello ® is the registered trademark of General Foods Corp, White Plains, NY.

HAS-15. *The World of Love: Love, Peace, Flower, Soul, and Music.* 9"; rooted synthetic hair in various colors; painted eyes, inset lashes; closed mouths; all vinyl jointed at neck, shoulders, waist, hips, bendable legs; assorted costumes available; dolls also available in Deluxe set which included doll, dress-up outfit, and personalized tee-shirt; only produced for two or three years. Marks: **33 / HONGKONG / © HASBRO / U. S. PAT. PEND.** on lower back; box is marked: © **1971 Hasbro Industries, Inc.** *(Lynn collection)*

HAS-16. *The World of Love: Adam.* 9"; molded-painted brown hair; painted blue eyes; same construction as HAS-15; wears red knit shirt and blue denim jeans with metal nailhead trim. Marks: © **HASBRO / U.S. PAT PEND / MADE IN / HONG KONG** on lower back; tag on shirt reads: **THE WORLD OF / LOVE™ / BY HASBRO / MADE IN HONG KONG.** *(Author's collection)*

HAV-1. *The Teddy Doll.* Imported bisque heads; glass eyes; finest imported plush bodies. Mfr: Havana Novelty Co, NY. *(Playthings, September, 1907)*

HESS-1a.

HESS-1b.

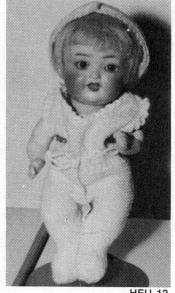

HEU-12.

fig-HEU-10.

fig-HEU-11.

HEU-10.

HEU-11.

HEU-13.

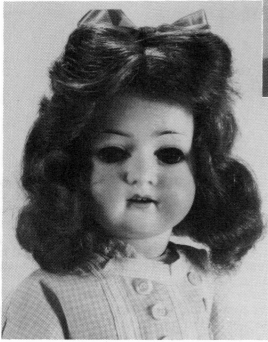

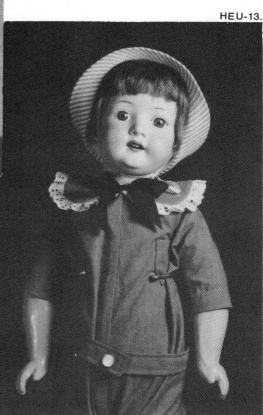

HEU-14.

HEU-15.

HEU-16.

fig-HEU-15.

3/0
91 HEU BACH e3
Germany

HESS-1a,b. Two dolls from the 1919 doll line of Theodore Hess & Co., NYC. 14"; curled wigs; sleep eyes; painted mouths; all composition with straight legs. *(Playthings, January, 1919)*

HEUBACH DOLLS

HEU-10. *Baby.* 10"; intaglio eyes; bisque head, composition or papier mache body. Marks: See fig. HEU-10. *(Campbell collection)*

HEU-11. *Girl.* 17"; replacement wig; brown sleep eyes with lashes; open mouth with teeth; bisque head, ball-jointed composition body. Marks: See fig. HEU-11. *(Hutchinson collection)*

HEU-12. *Boy.* 7½"; mohair wig; stationary blue glass eyes; open mouth with two teeth; bisque head, papier mache body; one-piece knit suit. Marks: **Heubach Koppelsdorf / 342-16 / 0 / Germany.** *(Hutchinson collection)*

HEU-13. *Boy.* 27"; human hair wig; stationary blue glass eyes; open mouth with teeth; bisque head, composition body with straight limbs; replacement clothes. Marks: **Huebach Koppelsdorf / Germany / 302 / 7.** *(Hutchinson collection)*

HEU-14. *Heubach type.* 18"; molded-painted hair with blue ribbon; painted blue eyes; open-closed mouth with two teeth; bisque head, composition ball-jointed body; redressed. Marks: **13 / 32 / 58.** *(Griffith collection)*

HEU-15. *Puss-in-Boots.* 6¼"; molded-painted green eyes; open mouth with teeth; bisque head, papier mache jointed body painted gray; original red cotton and lace dress; also sold as *"Three Little Kittens";* ca. 1920. Marks: See fig. HEU-15. *(Chaffin collection)*

HEU-16. *Girl.* 18"; molded-painted hair and ribbon; painted blue eyes; open-closed mouth with two teeth; bisque head, composition ball-jointed body. Marks: **13-32-58.** *(Griffith collection)*

HEU-17a,b,c.

HITT-1.

HIGH-1.

HIGH-2.

HEU-17a-c. Bisque heads, composition fully jointed bodies; all original clothes; all purchased in Cuba in 1936. *(McLaughlin collection)*

    a. *Hawaiian Girl.* 9"; brown sleep eyes; black mohair wig; open mouth. Marks: **S (PB in star) H / HANNA / 8 / 0.** Schoneau & Hoffmeister doll.

    b. *African Baby.* 8½"; painted eyes and closed mouth; post earrings, ring on left ankle. Marks: **Heubach-Koppelsdorf.**

    c. *Mexican Boy.* 10½"; open mouth with two teeth; sculptured black hair; post earrings in holes in ears. Marks: **Heubach-Koppelsdorf.**

HIGHGRADE TOY MFG. CO.

HIGH-1. *Girl.* Glued-on mohair wig; painted features; composition head and hands, stuffed body and limbs. Mfr: Highgrade Toy Mfg. Co., NY. *(Playthings, June, 1917)*

HIGH-2. *Girl.* Glued-on mohair wig; painted features; composition head and hands, stuffed cloth body and limbs. Mfr: Highgrade Toy Mfg. Co., NY *(Playthings, April, 1917)*

OSCAR HITT

HITT-1. *Snowflake.* 3¾"; molded-painted bisque; eyes are glass bubbles with bits of black metal for pupils which move freely in the glass domes. Marks: **SNOWFLAKE / Copr. By / OSCAR HITT / Germany.** *(Swift collection)*

HK-1.

HK-2.

HK-3.

HONG KONG DOLLS

HK-1. *Linda.* 14"; rooted tosca hair; painted blue eyes; closed mouth; fully jointed vinyl; original orange nylon dress, white trim, shoes and socks. Marks: **MADE IN / HONG KONG** on back, box reads: **LINDA / "material flame proofed" / MADE IN HONG KONG.** *(Author's collection)*

HK-2. *Hula Girl.* 9½"; long brown rooted vinyl hair; closed eyes with blue shadow; closed mouth; all vinyl with jointed arms; original print dress, flowers in hair. Marks: **HONG KONG** (in box). *(Quijas collection)*

HK-3. *Girl.* 11"; rooted brown hair; blue sleep eyes; lashes; painted closed mouth; fully jointed vinyl. Marks: **MADE IN HONG KONG** on back.

THE E. I. HORSMAN AND AETNA DOLL AND TOY COMPANY

According to an account in the June, 1912 issue of PLAYTHINGS magazine, the real inception of the American unbreakable doll had taken place in Russia several years earlier when a process for their manufacture was invented by one A. Hoffman. Although somewhat crude in its conception, the process proved to be the basic principle in development of the unbreakable doll made in America years later.

Although patents were obtained in Russia and the United States, great care was taken to keep secret the main features of the process. Hoffman came to America and began producing his *"Can't Break 'Em"* dolls in small quantities. The process

was then purchased by *The Aetna Doll and Toy Company* along with the tiny Hoffman factory. An association of Aetna with the *E. I. Horsman Company* proved vastly successful.

Aetna, under the management of Benjamin Goldenberg, manufactured the *Can't Break 'Em* heads while E. I. Horsman with his son, E. I. Horsman, Jr., produced and distributed the dolls. Since the Horsman name was already well known in the trade the new *American unbreakable character dolls* were off to a good start.

The younger Horsman, a talented artist and musician, improved the original formula and process. A patent was granted on November 28, 1911 causing considerable amazement in the manufacturing world since it was only seldom that anyone was able to invent a process of manufacture so original as to allow the inventor a patent on that process.

A description of the process used in production of the unbreakable heads was given in PLAYTHINGS, in January, 1907:

"The manufacture of the *"Can't Break 'Em Doll"* is extremely interesting. First there is a laboratory where the ingredients of a patented composition are mixed and made into a fluid. This fluid is then handled in kettles similar to large glue pots, and poured into hundreds of moulds. When the composition has settled and dried, the moulds are opened . . . to reveal dolls' heads and limbs of an almost colorless material and great elasticity. From this point the process involves drying which renders the heads perfectly hard, polishing, setting the eyes, coloring the heads and arms, and painting the faces.

While the heads are passing through this metamorphosis the fine hair-stuffed bodies are prepared in another department. The goods are then put together, and form a beautiful doll which is true to its name of *"Can't Break 'Em."* The wigs used are of mohair and range from the plain flowing hair variety to that of the first-class sewed curls.

EDWARD IMESON HORSMAN, JR.

HORS-33.

HORS-38.

HORS-34.

HORS-36.

HORS-35.

This factory also makes the *"White House" Teddy Bears* and *Bunnies* and several special dolls."

There began an era of American manufacture that was to last to the present day. From the Can't Break 'Em dolls such as Billiken, Baby Bumps, the Campbell Kids, Fairy, the Gold Medal Prize Baby, and the Jap Rose Kids, the company progressed to hard plastics, then soft vinyls and other modern materials.

A high point in the company's history is the story of the Horsman bisque doll. For years it had been a dream of the American toy industry to produce an all-American bisque head doll. Long before the indestructible doll was made in this country experiments were going on toward the production of bisque heads. As early as 1879 attempts had been made to produce satisfactory bisque doll heads in the Middle West of the United States, but for one reason or another these experiments were never successful.

A large amount of capital was necessary to underwrite the costs of actually producing such a head and it was not until the E. I. Horsman Company became interested in such a venture that the dream became a possibility. With the financial backing and trade know-how of the Horsman concern and the experience represented by the Fulper Pottery Company, Horsman was at last able to market a genuine bisque head doll made completely in the United States.

The Fulper Pottery Company was established in 1805 and for many years had been a leader in producing high grade pottery. Here were the kilns, the chemists, the potters, and the finishers who could produce a product that would rival the most beautiful European dolls. After the war, when markets returned to normal, imports were again available and continued production seemed unfeasible. The production of the Fulper-Horsman bisque head doll lasted only little more than two years and the dolls are considered quite collectible to the doll collector of today.

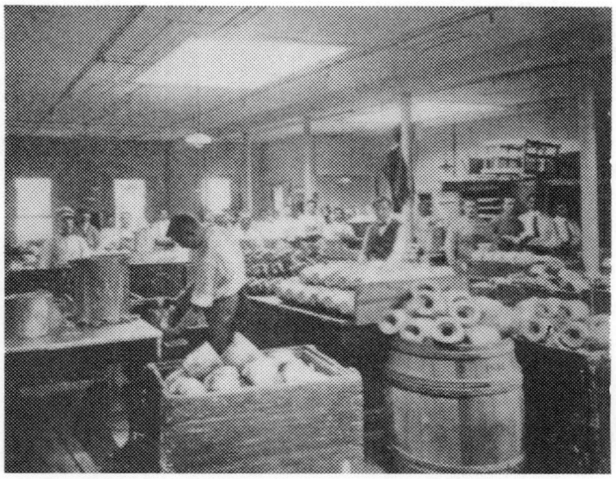
HORS-37.

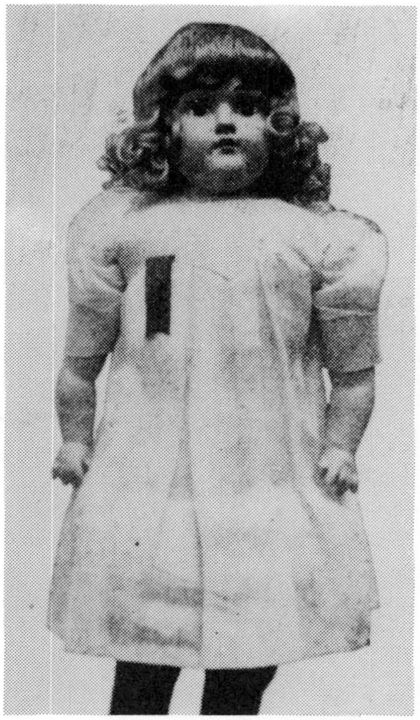
HORS-41.

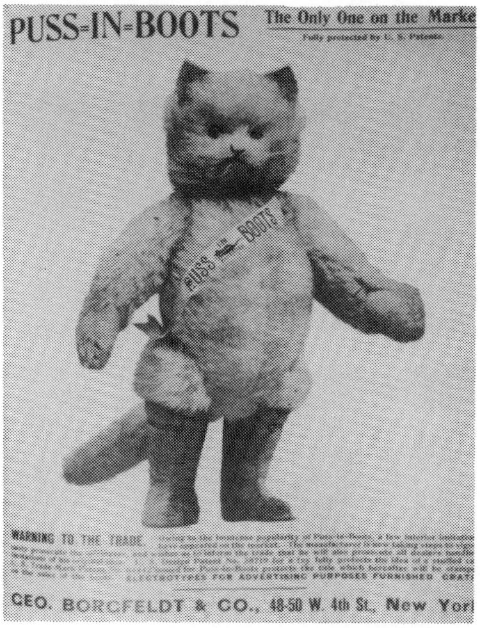

HORS-39.

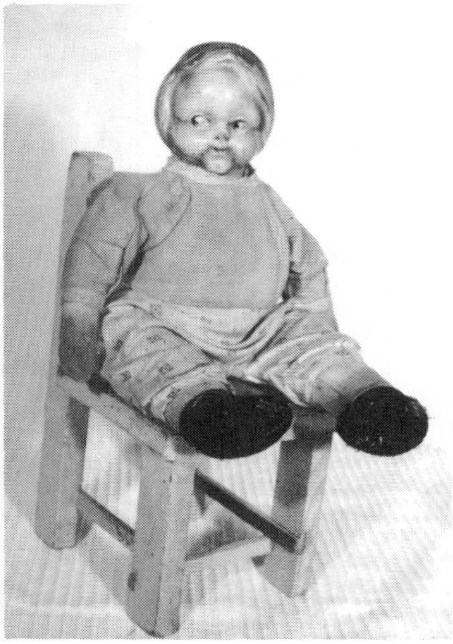
HORS-40.

HORS-33. E.I. Horsman, Jr. *(Playthings, 1918)*

HORS-34. *E.I. Horsman. (Playthings, 1918)*

HORS-35-37. Scenes in the manufacture of Horsman dolls. *(Playthings, 1912)*

HORS-38. "New factory of E.I. Horsman and Aetna Doll Co., Lafayette Street, NY, where the Horsman bisque dolls are made". *(Playthings, June, 1919)*

HORS-39. *Puss-in-Boots.* Stuffed synthetic fur body and limbs; ribbon reads: **PUSS / IN** (picture of a mouse with **AETNA) PATENTED / BOOTS.** Design patent #38719 applied for on 28 May, 1907, published 6 August, 1907, trademark #64442 applied for 28 February, 1907, published 11 June, 1907, held by Benjamin Goldenburg, New York, Certain Toy Clothing. *(Playthings, 1907)*

HORS-40. *Campbell Kid.* 9"; composition swivel head, stuffed cloth body; cotton two-tone suit. *(D'-Andrade collection)*

HORS-41. *Can't Break 'Em Girl.* With or without wigs; with or without sleep eyes; *Can't Break 'Em* heads, composition hands, stuffed bodies and legs; distributed by George Borgfeldt. Mfr: Aetna Doll & Toy Co. *(Playthings, 1909)*

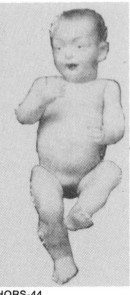

HORS-44.

HORS-45.

HORS-42.

HORS-46.

HORS-43.

HORS-42. *Can't Break 'Em Girl.* With or without wigs; with or without sleep eyes; *Can't Break 'Em* heads, composition hands, stuffed bodies and legs, distributed by George Borgfeldt. Mfr: Aetna Doll & Toy Co. *(Playthings, 1909)*

HORS-43. *Billiken.* Although Billiken has already been listed (ref. TCD, p. 225, HORS-1) it seemed good to show another in *original box. (Courtesy Ralph's Antique Dolls)*

A September, 1910, advertisement in Playthings announced a *"Revival of the Billiken"* and stated more than 200,000 were sold in the last six months of 1909. Many of the dolls were shipped to Australia, Asia, Africa, Europe, and South America. Copyright number 28790, March 20, 1909 by the Billiken Co. Came in 12", 15", and 25" sizes. *(Playthings, October, 1909)*

HORS-44. *Samson.* Same head as *Sambo* and *Dolly Strong;* called *"Uncle Sam's firstborn";* only made for two or three years; distributed by Amberg. *(Playthings, April, 1910)*

HORS-45. *Sambo, "The Nigger Baby"* ©. 12", 15"; composition head, spring-jointed body; "The first completely jointed doll ever made in the U.S."; sold for $8.50 and $13.50 per dozen. *(Playthings, April, 1910)*

HORS-46. *Girl.* Molded-painted hair and features, *Can't Break 'Em* head, composition limbs. Mfr: Aetna Doll & Toy Co. *(Playthings, May, 1910)*

HORS-47.

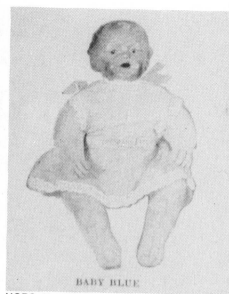

BABY BLUE

HORS-48.

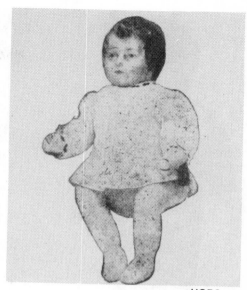

HORS-49.

HORS-50a.

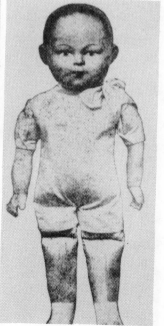

HORS-50b.

HORS-47. *Our Baby.* Probably same head as *Samson, Sambo* and *Dolly Strong;* velvet body; wears long infant dress, petticoats; white or black versions. *(Playthings, April, 1910)*

HORS-48. *Baby Blue.*© Painted blue eyes; *Can't Break 'Em* head, blue velvet body; guimpe with blue ribbons; in blue box; *"The Baby Beautiful™." (Playthings, April and June, 1910)*

HORS-49. *Character Baby. Can't Break 'Em* head; painted features; stuffed velvet body. *(Playthings, June, 1910)*

HORS-50a-c. Three models from the 1910 line. Includes: *Dutch Boy, Bellhop,* and *Baby; Can't Break 'Em* heads, stuffed bodies and limbs. *(Playthings, June, 1910)*

HORS-50c.

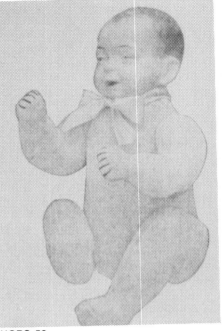

HORS-52.

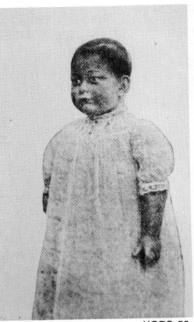

HORS-53.

HORS-51.

HORS-51. *Sister Billiken.* 12", 15"; mohair wig; kimona; © By the Billiken Co., copyright March, 20, 1909, trademark ©#28790. Mfr: E.I. Horsman Co., sole manufacturers of the Billiken doll. *(Playthings, January, 1910)*

An example of the Billiken craze extended. In addition there were memo holders, tape measures, stamp boxes, writing pads, bridge pads, blotters, paper weights, ink wells, calendars, clocks, post card albums, picture frames, savings banks in celluloid, leather, metal and china; also a celluloid roly-poly.

HORS-52. *Baby Bumps.* 12"; *Can't Break 'Em* head, pink velvet body. Another example, this one with paws for hands. *(Playthings, March, 1910)*

HORS-53. *Art Dolls.* Thirty characters now ready and others in preparation; all from models by eminent artists. *Can't Break 'Em* heads. Note modeling of head, arms, and hands. *(Playthings, March, 1910)*

HORS-54. *Campbell Kids and Friends.* Classical public relations stunt for doll and toy industry: Send a few pretty girls to promenade the boardwalk at Atlantic City carrying the latest product. *(Playthings, August, 1911)*

HORS-55. *Character Baby.* 11"; painted hair; painted blue eyes; closed mouth; *Can't Break 'Em* head, composition hands, fully jointed cloth body; original cotton shirt, tan overalls, felt shoes; probably one of the Art Dolls Series. Marks: Label on chest reads: © **1910 by / E.I. Horsman Co.** *(Burtchett collection)*

HORS-54.

HORS-55.

HORS-56.

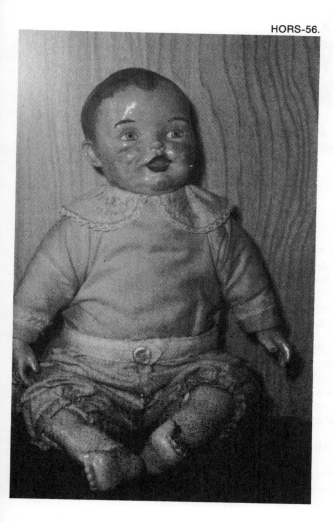

HORS-55.

HORS-56. *Boy.* 17"; molded-painted hair; intaglio side-glance eyes; open-closed laughing mouth, dimples, composition head and limbs, stuffed body; redressed. Marks: © **/ E.I.H. / 1911.** *(Cannon collection)*

HORS-59.

HORS-58a.

HORS-58b.

HORS-57.

HORS-57. *The Campbell Kid Chorus from the musical "Buster Brown".* Chorus girls are wearing Campbell Kid head masks. Another great promotional stunt often used was to tie-in a doll with a Broadway production and later, with movies. *(Playthings, October, 1911)*

HORS-58a,b. *The Jap Rose Kids.* Molded-painted hair; painted features; *Can't Break 'Em* heads, composition hands, soft bodies and limbs; companions to the Campbell Kids; made under special and exclusive license from Jas. S. Kirk & Co., Chicago. *(Playthings, January, 1912)*

HORS-59. *Fairy, of the Campbell Kid Family.* Molded-painted hair; painted features; *Can't Break 'Em* head, composition hands, soft body and limbs; made under special and exclusive license from N. K. Fairbank, Co., Chicago. *(Playthings, 1912)*

HORS-60.

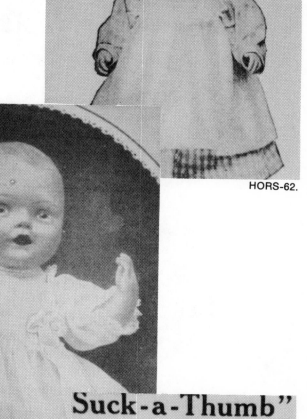

HORS-62.

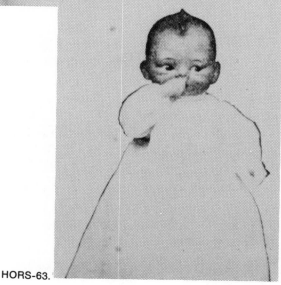

HORS-61.

HORS-60. *Dutch Kids.* Molded-painted hair; painted features; *Can't Break 'Em* heads, composition hands, soft body and legs; members of the Campbell Kid Family. *(Playthings, January, 1912)*

HORS-61. *Gold Medal Prize Baby.* Five sizes. Molded-painted hair and features; *Can't Break 'Em* heads and composition hands, soft bodies and limbs; ten styles of clothing; © **1911 by E.I. Horsman Co.** *(Playthings, 1911)*

HORS-62. *Sunbonnet Sal.* Mohair wigs; painted eyes; *Can't Break 'Em* head, composition hands, soft body and limbs. *(Playthings, July, 1912)*

HORS-63. *Suck-a-Thumb.* Molded-painted hair and features; *Can't Break 'Em* head, composition hands, soft body and limbs; infant style clothes; teething-age infant. *(Playthings, July, 1912)*

HORS-63.

HORS-64.

HORS-65.

HORS-67.

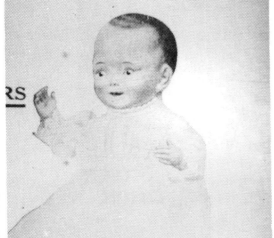

HORS-66b.

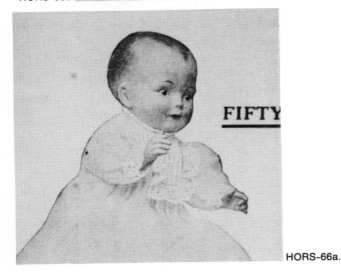

HORS-66a.

HORS-64. *Teddy Bull Moose. Can't Break 'Em* head, plush body, registered trademark; although not a doll, so interesting it is included here 'just for fun'. *(Playthings, 1912)*

HORS-65. *Polly Prue.* Molded-painted hair and features; *Can't Break 'Em* head, composition hands, soft body and limbs. *(Playthings, September, 1912)*

HORS-66. *Nature Babies, Serious Baby Bobby* and *Laughing Baby Peterkin. Can't Break 'Em* heads, composition hands, soft body and limbs; twenty different styles selling from 50¢ to $10.00. *(Playthings, September, 1912)*

HORS-67. *Schoolboy.* Molded-painted hair and features; *Can't Break 'Em* head, composition hands, soft body and legs. *(Playthings, July, 1913)*

HORS-68.

HORS-69.

HORS-70.

HORS-71.

No. 130
"CAMPBELL KID BABY"
Trade Mark

HORS-68. *Boy Scout.* Molded-painted hair and features; *Can't Break 'Em* head, composition hands, soft body and limbs. *(Playthings, July, 1913)*

HORS-69. *Carnival Baby.* Molded-painted features; *Can't Break 'Em* head, composition hands, soft body and legs. *(Playthings, July, 1913)*

HORS-70. *Camp Fire Girl.* Molded-painted features; *Can't Break 'Em* head, composition hands, soft body and limbs. *(Playthings, 1911)*

HORS-71. *Campbell Kid Baby.* Molded-painted hair with real ribbons; painted features; composition head and hands, soft body and legs. *(Playthings, July, 1913)*

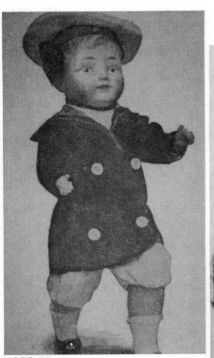

HORS-72.

HORS-73.

HORS-74.

HORS-75a.

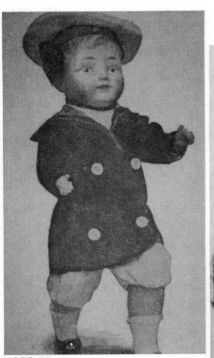

HORS-72. *Robbie Reefer.* Molded-painted features; *Can't Break 'Em* head, composition hands, soft body and limbs; red reefer coat, white sailor hat. *(Playthings, 1911)*

HORS-73. *Baby Premier.* Molded-painted features; *Can't Break 'Em* head, composition hands, soft body and limbs; twenty new infant models. Mfr: Aetna Doll & Toy Co. *(Playthings, August, 1913)*

HORS-74. *Black doll.* Molded-painted features; *Can't Break 'Em* head, composition hands, soft body and limbs. *(Playthings, June, 1913, November, 1914)*

HORS-75a,b. *Our Baby.* Two examples of the 1913 model. Painted hair; side-glance eyes, mouth; *Can't Break 'Em* heads, composition hands, soft bodies and limbs; long or short dress, bonnet, booties; bell on string around neck. This doll was probably on velvet body judging from the pictures. *(Playthings, August and October, 1913)*

HORS-76a-c. Three styles of *"Bauernkinder".* Molded-painted features; *Can't Break 'Em* heads, composition hands, stuffed bodies and limbs; "Real life studies of German peasant children", these dolls had olive complexions. A large line. (Playthings, April, 1914)

HORS-77a,b. Two *Campbell Kids.* Mohair wigs; painted features; *Can't Break 'Em* heads, composition hands, stuffed bodies and limbs. *(Playthings, July, 1913)*

HORS-77a,b.

HORS-75b.

HORS-76a.

HORS- 76b.

HORS-76c.

HORS-78a.

HORS-78b.

HORS-79.

THE GEE GEE DOLLY.

HORS-80.

HORS-78a,b. Two *"American Kids in Toyland"*. Molded-painted features; *Can't Break 'Em* heads, composition hands, stuffed bodies and limbs; 25 new styles, over 100 models. *(Playthings, December, 1913)*

HORS-79. *One example of the 1914 line.* Mohair wig; painted side-glance eyes; painted mouth; *Can't Break 'Em head*, composition hands, stuffed bodies and limbs. *(Playthings, January, 1914)*

HORS-80. *"The Gee Gee Dolly" "Designed by famous artist of childhood types, Mrs. Drayton, presented in boy and girl numbers, daintily dressed in blues, pinks and other pretty colors. The "Gee Gees" are indestructible dolls with flatish, moonshaped faces, merry upturned mouths, cute "snub noses" and wide open, laughing eyes. The artist presents her idea of the funny little "Flat" faces so common in childhood years. Their heads are sheeted with the famous "Can't Break 'Em" material." Two sizes available for $1.00 and $2.00. (Playthings, April, 1913)*

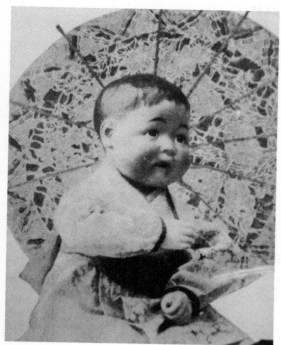

HORS-81.

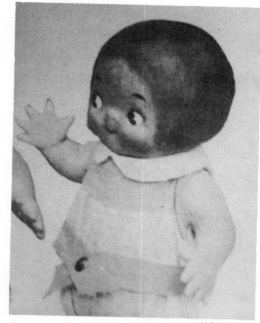

HORS-82a.

HORS-82b.

HORS-81. *Baby Butterfly.* Three sizes; composition head; painted features; kimona; Oriental baby; Patented November 28, 1911 and June 24, 1913; registered trademark. *(Playthings, January, 1914)*

HORS-82a,b. *Peek-A-Boo.* "Three styles are being offered, two of which are pictured on this page. One shows the cutest little girl doll one could wish to see dressed in polka dot costume that fades away at the knees to reveal the chubbiest little legs, and the pinkest little toes that a little girl ever shows when such prosaic things as socks and shoes go into the discard and the weather is fine for wading. Another "Peekaboo" shows a cunning barefoot little boy in a snappy summer suit, a doll quite as desirable as the little girl doll. The third of the series shows another little boy doll, a boy bather attired in a contrasting color stripe, one piece, bathing suit." Registered trademark, designed by Grace G. Drayton. *(Playthings, June, July, 1913)*

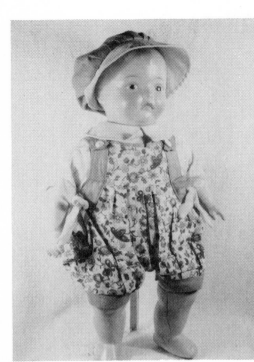

HORS-83.

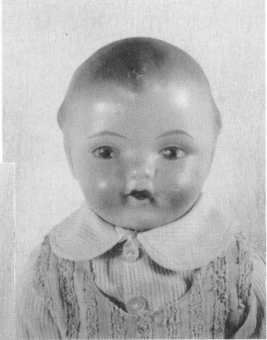

HORS-84.

HORS-83.

HORS-83. *Boy.* 19"; painted hair; painted blue eyes; closed mouth; composition head and limbs, stuffed cloth body; working cry voice; all original clothes; 1914-1918. Marks: **E.I.H.** © **A.D.C.;** tag on sleeve reads: **HORSMAN DOLL / VOICE PATENTED / BY B.E. LLOYD.** *(Author's collection)*

Sometimes fun bits of information pop up in researching dolls. In this case the author was told the doll had belonged to the mother of the woman who is secretary to Vincent Price, actor. The doll had been stored in a San Francisco warehouse until just a few years ago.

HORS-84. *Boy.* 16"; painted hair; painted blue eyes; open-closed mouth; composition shoulder head and gauntlet hands, stuffed cotton body and limbs; original cotton corduroy shirt, chenille type fabric suit; this is one of those dolls made with Horsman's marvelous composition (CBE) which rarely cracks; however, the paint *can* separate as though it were a covering of celluloid. 1914-1918. Marks: **EIH** © **1914.** *(Author's collection)*

HORS-85a,b.

HORS-87a.

HORS-86.

HORS-87b.

HORS-85a,b. *The Peterkins, Betsy and Tommy.* Molded-painted features; *Can't Break 'Em* heads, all composition bodies; registered trademark. *(Playthings, August, 1915)*

HORS-86. *Peterkin Boy #1012.* All Adtocolite composition; dressed or undressed. *(Playthings, October, 1918)*

HORS-87a,b. *Two dolls from 1919 line.* Mohair wig; painted features; all composition. Mfr: E.I. Horsman And Aetna Doll Co.
    "Announcement: In order to give our entire efforts to Horsman dolls we have discontinued all other lines." Horsman had been a distributor for other companies but turned to manufacturing dolls only in 1919. *(Playthings, December, 1918)*

HORS-88a,b.

HORS-88c.

HORS- 88a,b.

fig-HORS-92.

HORS-90.

Oliver Twist—16¼ in., large head, white waist with blue duck collar, blue duck knee pants, pearl button trim, attached stockings, leather slippers, each in box.

F8670—⅙ doz. in pkg.
Doz. **$10.00**

Peasant Boy—14 in., green overalls, white pique blouse, red piped green hood, attached stockings, felt slippers.

F8667—⅙ doz. in pkg. Doz. **$10.00**

HORS-88a-c. *The Velocipede Kids.* These dolls were variously referred to in Horsman's advertising as *The Irish Mail Kids, The Velocipede Kids, The Cycle Kids,* and *The Coaster Kids.* Boy, Monkey, Clown, and Negro were seated in handcar of solid wood painted bright red. Feet of dolls are fastened to pedals. *(Playthings, February, 1915)*

HORS-89a,b. a. *Oliver Twist,* **b.** *Peasant Boy.* See illustration for description. *(Butler Bros. 1918)*

HORS-90. *The Adtocolite* Doll™.* Two sizes; human hair and mohair wigs; sleep and stationary eyes; diagonal hip joint with ball-and-socket knee and elbow, all composition; dressed or undressed; *"The perfect American jointed doll at last!"* *Note—Name comes from **A**etna **D**oll & **To**y **Co.** - lite. *(Playthings, December, 1918)*

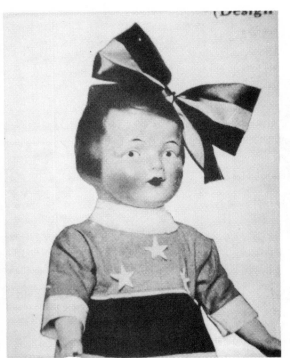

HORS-91a.

HORS-91b.

HORS-92a.

HORS-92b.

HORS-91a,b. *Uncle Sam's Kids, Miss Sam and Master Sam.* Painted features; *Can't Break 'Em* heads, composition hands, soft body and legs; dressed in red, white and blue; registered trademark. *(Playthings, April, 1917)*

HORS-92a,b. *Two dolls from the 1919 line.* Dolls are wearing the Horsman ribbon label which they announced in this ad would be on every doll henceforth, see fig. HORS-92. *(Playthings, December, 1918)*

HORS-93a.

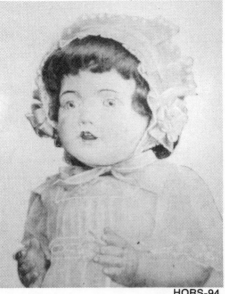

HORS-94.

HORS-93b.

HORS-95.

H.C.Q.
1916

fig-HORS-95.

HORS-93a,b. *Little Mary Mix-Up.* Name and design copyright by Press Publishing Co. (New York Evening World) from cartoons by R.M. Brinkerhoff; a booklet came with each doll. *(Playthings, 1919)*

    a. Actual cartoon drawing.

    b. Horsman doll rendering of character.

HORS-94. *The Horsman Bisque Line.* Bisque heads, wigs; five-jointed sitting babies and ball-jointed standing dolls; wore ribbon across chest for big advertising campaign about the American-made doll. Labeled "The World Standard" and "The Perfect Bisque Doll." *(Playthings, 1918)*

HORS-95. *Character Baby.* 11"; molded-painted blonde hair; painted black eyes; closed mouth; composition head and limbs, stuffed body. Marks: see fig. HORS-95. *(Perry collection, photograph by Jackie Meekins)*

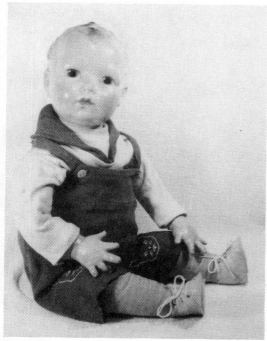

HORS-96.

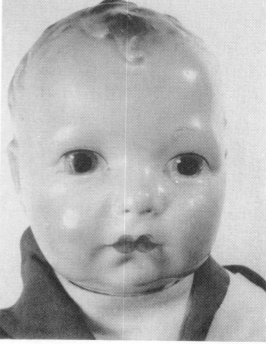

HORS-96.

HORS-96. *Boy.* 24"; molded-painted hair; large painted blue eyes with white highlights; painted cupid bow mouth; composition head and gauntlet hands; cotton stuffed body and limbs; redressed. Marks: **E.I.** © **H.C.** on head. *(Author's collection)*

The photograph at the right illustrates what can happen to a composition doll which does not receive the proper care. The author purchased this doll in California, brought it home to Missouri, and gave it a special place in a baby chair in a bedroom. Six months of being exposed to variances in temperature and humidity brought about the change shown here. The upper layer of paint seemed to lift and simply float away. Samples of cheek, eye and lip color were salvaged in the hope that somewhere, someday, someone will be able to repaint the doll with an approximation of the deft touch with which the doll was originally finished.

Reader Mrs. Leonard S. Lincoln writes that she has an identical doll, her childhood doll from 1923, which sold that year at $14.00. Her doll also has flaked badly, perhaps indicating an inherent flaw in the painting of these beautiful dolls.

HORS-96.

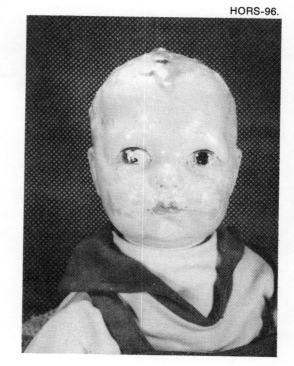

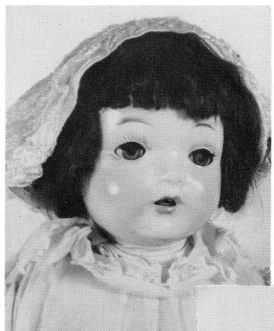

HORS-97.

HORS-98.

HORS-99.

HORS-100.

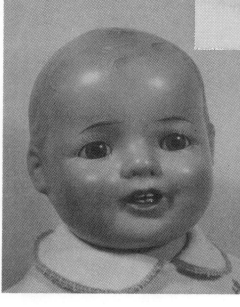

HORS-101.

HORS-102.

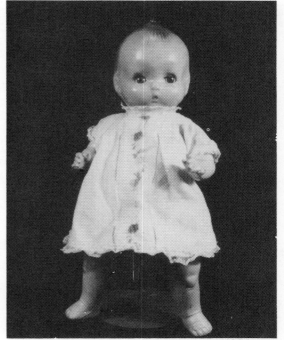

HORS-103.

HORS-97. *Girl.* 18"; reddish-brown mohair wig; blue sleep eyes; open mouth with teeth and tongue; composition head and limbs, cloth body; old clothes possibly original; ca. 1920. Marks: **E I H** © **A D C** written *backwards* on head. *(Wiseman collection)*

HORS-98. *Blue Bird Doll.* Wore Blue Bird cloak. Issued in commemoration of the visit to American of the Belgian poet, Maeterlinck. *(Playthings, 1920)*

HORS-99. *Heebee.* Mate to Shebee. 10½"; painted hair; painted blue eyes; all molded-painted composition; note molded booties with metal loops for big floppy bows; 1925. Unmarked. *(Author's collection)*

HORS-100. *Gold Medal Baby.* 21"; molded-painted tan hair; green sleep eyes with painted lashes; open-closed mouth with teeth and metal tongue; composition head and limbs, cloth body; redressed. Marks: **E.I.H. Co.** *(Wardell collection)*

HORS-101. *Laughing Dimples.* 20"; molded-painted yellow hair; tin sleep eyes; open-closed laughing mouth with painted teeth; composition shoulder head and limbs, cloth body, hands and body like *Dimples;* marks illegible. *(Stewart collection)*

HORS-102. *Key-Wind Mama Doll.* 21"; original blonde mohair wig; blue sleep eyes; open mouth with two teeth and tongue; composition head, soft sticky plastic limbs, cloth body; key-wind, cries when put down, stops when picked up. *(Hafner collection)*

HORS-103. *Jeanne Horsman.* 14"; molded-painted brown hair; brown celluloid and tin eyes; composition head and limbs, cloth body; redressed. Marks: © **JEANNE HORSMAN.** *(Gaylin collection)*

HORS-104.

HORS-104. *Naughty Sue.* 14½"; molded-painted top knot; brown side-glance sleep eyes; open-closed mouth; all composition. Marks: © **1937 HORSMAN.** *(Stewart collection)*

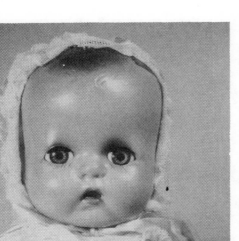

HORS-105.

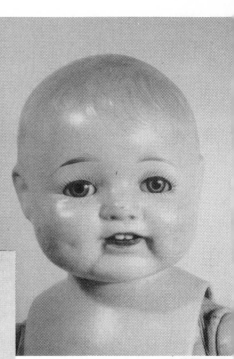

HORS-106

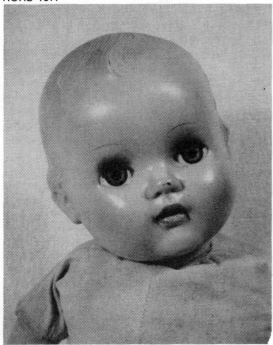

HORS-107.

HORS-106-1.

HORS-105. *Ma-Ma Papa Doll.* 18"; molded-painted brown hair; blue sleep eyes; open mouth; composition head and limbs, straight legs, cloth body; original clothes. Tag reads: **"I Say MA-MA I Say PA-PA"** / **HORSMAN / Super Quality.** *(Wardell collection)*

HORS-106. *Toddler Dimples.* 20"; molded-painted yellow hair; blue tin sleep eyes; open mouth with two teeth; composition head and limbs, cloth body; an older (toddler) version of *Dimples.* Marks: **DIMPLES** on head. *(Burtchett collection)*

HORS-106-1. *Dimples.* 19½"; to illustrate body construction.   Marks: © **/ E.I.H. / CO. INC.** *(Author's collection)*

HORS-107. *Baby.* 23"; painted hair; blue sleep eyes; open mouth with two teeth and felt tongue; hard plastic head, cloth body, soft sticky plastic limbs; ca. 1948. Marks: **HORSMAN.** *(Weeks collection)*

The GREAT DOLL SUCCESS!

CUTE TYPES...
MOST POPULAR IN BIG CITY STORES
TILTING HEADS
"MA-MA" VOICES
DARLING DRESSES

HORS-108. Illustration from 1931-32 Fall and Winter Catalog, Sears, Roebuck and Co.

I Say "Ma-Ma" I Go to Sleep

ADORABLE FACES

I Say "Ma-Ma" I Go to Sleep

"SALLY"

"DAINTY DOROTHY"

$2^{98} Post Paid **18F3048¼—20 inches tall.** Made especially for us by a leading maker under our own name. The value is most unusual. Dainty Dorothy is truly lovable and beautiful with her big almost real eyes that sleep, eyelashes and perfect girl-like features. Has the new type movable, tilting head that is so natural and girl-like. Charmingly outfitted in hat of latest style and her especially smart organdy dress with its scalloped hem. The head, arms and legs are of almost unbreakable composition. Says "Ma-Ma" clearly.

18F3049—19 in. tall. Sally is famous from Coast to Coast as one of the most popular and best liked dolls. Pretty as a picture, with her lovable real-like face, and her very cute dress and bonnet trimmed in net. Has go-to-sleep eyes, lashes, strong composition arms and standing legs. Says "Ma-Ma," too. **$3^{59}** Post Paid

18F3050—Sally, with jointed head, arms and legs. Painted features and a good looking dress. 12½ inches tall—(not illustrated) Shpg. Wt. 1 lb...................... **98c**

Horsman's Latest!
BIG DOLL SUCCESS

WASHABLE BODIES
EACH IN GIFT BOX

THEY SIT ALONE

ARMS AND LEGS CAN MOVE

HEADS TILT AND TURN

THE DOLL OF MANY POSES

NEW TYPE BODY

HELLO! MY NAME IS "BABS"

HOWDY I'm "SUE"

WHOOPEE! I'm "JANE"

AND I'm "NAN"

$1^{69} **18F3010—12 inches tall.** Babs is a cunning little imp entirely of strong composition. Tilting head, jointed arms and legs, sleeping eyes. Extremely sweet dress and bonnet. Shpg. wt., 1 lb.

$1^{95} **18F3011—14 inches tall.** Sue is strong for you—she's ever true. Has composition body, tilting head, movable arms and legs. Sleeping eyes with lashes. Smart dress of an excellent print material has a clever jabot. Stunning bonnet, to match. Shpg. wt., 1½ lbs.

$2^{98} Post Paid **18F3012—17 in. tall.** Jane is the kind of doll every little girl wants, so beautiful and cute. Has tilting head, movable arms and legs, go-to-sleep eyes, lashes, and all composition body which can be washed. Exceedingly pretty dress, with buttons and buttonholes. Bonnet to match.

$3^{98} Post Paid **18F3013¼—20-in. tall.** Nan is the largest and loveliest of these most popular Horsman dolls. Her charming dress with bonnet to match has hand embroidery on collar, buttons and buttonholes. Nan can be bathed. Made entirely of strong composition, with jointed legs and arms and tilting head. Her sleeping eyes that look almost real have eyelashes.

HORS-109.

HORS-108-2.

HORS-109.

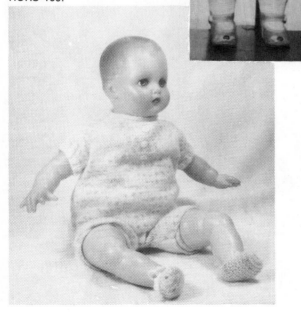

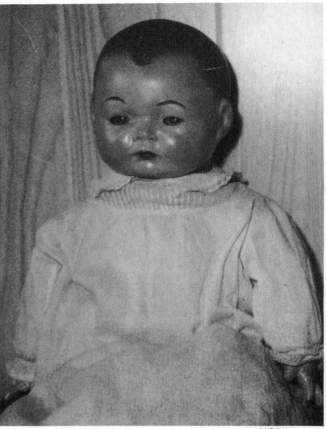

HORS-108-1.

HORS-108-1. *Tynie Baby.* 21"; molded-painted hair; blue metal sleep eyes; closed mouth; composition, stuffed cloth body. Marks: © / **E.I.H. / 1924.** *(Cannon collection)*

HORS-108-2. *Girl.* All original. *(Cannon collection)*

HORS-109. *Baby Boy.* 20"; molded-painted hair; blue sleep eyes; closed mouth; stuffed sticky vinyl head and limbs, cloth body; squeeker in head. Marks: **HORSMAN** on head.

HORS-110. *Baby.* 18"; rooted tosca Saran hair; blue sleep eyes; drink-and-wet mouth; fully jointed vinyl; original dress and bonnet were sheer white material with blue embroidery; ca. 1956. Unmarked. *(Lynn collection)*

HORS-111. *Cindy the Couturier Doll.* 16", 18"; rooted Saran hair; blue sleep eyes; hard plastic body jointed at neck, shoulders, waist, hips, and knees, soft vinyl head, high-heeled feet; original clothes; came with suitcase and wardrobe or in box; trademarked *Couturier Doll* in 1957; sold for $9.88 and $13.88. Marks: **HORSMAN / 88** on neck; tag reads: **HORSMAN'S / CINDY / WALKING DOLL** with walking instructions on inside of tag. *(Author's collection)*

HORS-110.

HORS-112.

HORS-111.

HORS-112. *Pretty Poser.* 8"; rooted hair; glassene sleep eyes; Super Flex limbs, fully jointed vinyl; original clothes, and trunk with extra outfits. (Spiegels Catalog, 1958)

HORS-113. *Ponytail Pam.* 17"; rooted hair; glassene sleep eyes; 'Super Flex' skeleton, fully jointed vinyl; red embossed nylon dress, pinafore, panties, shoes and socks; layette for doll sold separately. *(Alden Catalog, 1958)*

HORS-113.

HORS-113.

HORS-114.

HORS-115.

HORS-117.

HORS-118.

HORS-116.

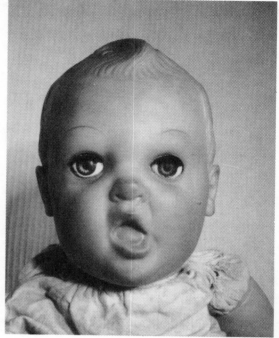

HORS-119.

HORS-114. *Tear Belle.* 16", 20"; rooted hair; glassene sleep eyes; fully jointed vinyl; cries tears; coos gently when squeezed. *(Alden Catalog, 1958)*

HORS-115. *Baby Evie.* 16", 20"; rooted hair; sleep eyes; fully jointed vinyl; dressed in nylon eyelet; retail $5.98 and $7.98. *(Alden Catalog, 1958)*

HORS-116. *Little Miss Moppet.* 16"; long rooted hair in ponytail; glassene sleep eyes; fully jointed vinyl; coo voice; wears dotted dress, pinafore, long stockings, shoes; "old fashioned toddler"; retail $6.98. *(Montgomery Ward's Catalog, 1958)*

HORS-117. *Pert'n'Pretty.* 21"; rooted hair; sleep eyes; fully jointed vinyl; wears brown straw hat, brown and white polka dot blouse; gold buttons and belt, tan polished cotton skirt with hankie in pocket, white gloves, hose, panties, slip, black sandals, earrings; sold for $7.98. *(Montgomery Ward's Catalog, 1958)*

HORS-118. *Cindy.* 25", 36"; rooted ponytail; sleep eyes; fully jointed plastic body, bendable knees, separate fingers may be entertwined to "pray", head moves from side to side, stands, sits, kneels; wears red and white rayon dress, starchy white nylon pinafore, panties, shoes, socks; retail $12.39 and $17.77. (Montgomery Ward's Catalog, 1958)

HORS-119. *Baby.* 23"; molded hair; blue sleep eyes; open-closed mouth; cloth body, early vinyl head and limbs. *(D'Andrade collection)*

HORS-120. *Girl.* 26"; rooted tosca wig; blue sleep eyes; closed mouth; pierced nostrils; good cheek color; stuffed vinyl, jointed at neck, one-piece body and limbs; all original rayon taffeta plaid dress, red pants, belt, shoes, socks; ca. 1950. Marks: **HORSMAN** on neck. *(Rothert collection)*

HORS-120.

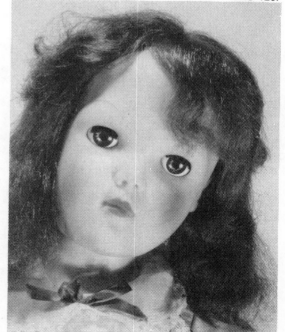

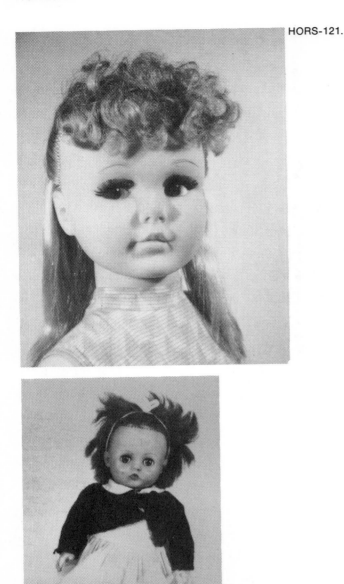

HORS-121.

HORS-122.

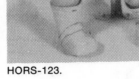
HORS-123.

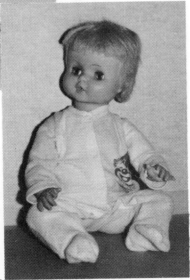
HORS-124.

HORS-121. *Girl.* 35"; rooted blonde hair; painted eyes; inset lashes; closed mouth; soft vinyl head, hard plastic body and limbs; original clothes. Marks: **HORSMAN DOLL INC.** *(Courtesy Nita's House of Dolls)*

HORS-122. *Girl.* 16"; blonde synthetic hair; blue sleep eyes; open-closed mouth; fully jointed hard plastic. Marks: **HORSMAN** on neck. *(Courtesy Camelot)*

HORS-123. *Much-loved Baby.* 14"; rooted red Saran hair; blue-green sleep eyes; closed mouth; stuffed vinyl one-piece body; cry voice; original blue knit sweater, yellow pleated cotton dress, yellow tam, panties; 1950s. Marks: backwards **21 / HORSMAN / 111** on neck. *(Lynn collection)*

HORS-124. *Baby.* Rooted synthetic hair; blue sleep eyes; drink-and-wet mouth; fully jointed soft plastic. Marks: **HORSMAN B200** on head. *(Campbell collection)*

HORS-125. *Life-size Infant.* 25"; molded-painted hair; blue sleep eyes with lashes; open-closed mouth; soft head, fully jointed hard plastic body; 1961. Marks: **HORSMAN** on head. *(Causey collection)*

HORS-126. *Baby.* 11"; molded-painted hair; blue painted eyes; open-closed mouth; fully jointed vinyl. Marks: **HORSMAN DOLLS MFG. CO. / 19-© / 12 / HORSMAN DOLL INC.** *(Terry collection)*

HORS-127. *Toddler.* 11"; rooted blonde Saran hair; brown side-glance sleep eyes; closed mouth; fully jointed toddler body. Marks: **H** on back. *(Bailey collection, photograph by Jackie Meekins)*

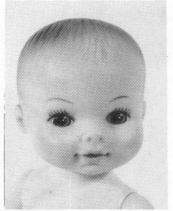

HORS-126.

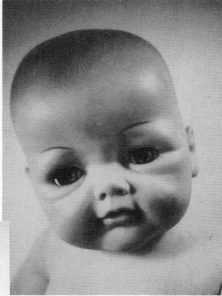

HORS-125.

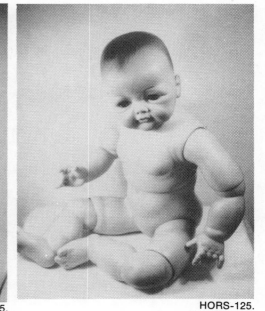

HORS-125.

HORS-128.

HORS-127.

HORS-128. *Girl.* 15½"; rooted platinum hair; blue sleep eyes; closed mouth; soft vinyl head and arms, hard plastic body and legs; original blue velvet dress. Marks: **19 / © HORSMAN DOLLS INC. / 6716** (last number illegible) on head; **HORSMAN DOLLS INC. / PAT. PEND.** on back; tag reads: (circle) **M** in center, **Mademoiselle Dolls** ™. and **Seal of Quality / M.** *(Hartwell collection)*

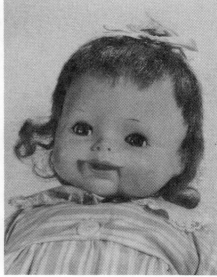

HORS-129.

HORS-130.

HORS-130.

HORS-128-1.

HORS-128-1. *Bootsie.* 13"; brown hair; blue sleep eyes; closed mouth; fully jointed vinyl body. Marks: **1** (in square) **4** (in square) **/ HORSMAN DOLLS INC. / 19©70.** *(Thompson collection)*

IRENE SZOR

Seldom is the name of the designer included in the marks on a doll. When the doll is found so marked, collectors refer to the doll as a 'signed doll' and seem to treasure it all the more.

Designer Irene Szor has been responsible for costume and doll design at Horsman since 1957. In addition, she has sculpted two dolls (HORS-129 and HORS-130) and created a large number of others which have been rendered by other artists. Although a very busy woman, she graciously made time in her schedule for the writer. The following information has been extracted from the tapes of that interview.

Tuffy (ref. HORS-29, TCD p. 241) is another example of a doll with an unusual face which was not accepted by the buyers. It was made only a short while.

Lil Charmer (ref. HORS-31, TCD p. 241) was designed in such a manner that it is able to stand on its hands, assume a crawling position, or sit. It is perfectly balanced and can also do back-flips.

The doll known to collectors as *Jacqueline Kennedy* (ref. HORS-24, TCD p. 239) was released as "Jackie"; however, Irene assures us it was not intended to represent the former first lady. The doll was one of Irene's concepts which was carried out by a mold maker.

The *Mademoiselle Dolls* (ref. HORS-128) were Horsman's venture into a deluxe line of dolls. Horsman's dolls are classified as a popular-priced line. The deluxe line was tried in 1967 and was carried only a short time. All the costumes were made in the Horsman factory and all the dolls were marked with standard Horsman markings. Boxes and paper wrist tags carried the *Mademoiselle* designation.

HORS-131a.

HORS-131b.

HORS-131a,b.

HORS-129. *Baby Precious.* 19"; rooted blonde Saran hair; blue sleep eyes; open-closed mouth with tongue, very large upper lip; vinyl head and limbs, cloth body; cry voice; original flannel panties, possibly original pink dress. Marks: © **1963 IRENE SZOR / HORSMAN DOLLS INC.** *(Author's collection)*

HORS-130. *Gloria Jean.* 16"; rooted blonde hair; blue sleep eyes; closed mouth; soft head and arms, fully jointed plastic body; original clothes. Marks: © **1969 / IRENE SZOR / HORSMAN DOLLS INC.;** box reads: **Gloria Jean by Horsman, An Irene Szor Creation.** *(Wardell collection)*

HORS-131a,b. *Hansel and Gretel.* 15"; rooted synthetic hair; blue sleep eyes; closed mouth; soft vinyl head, hard plastic body and limbs; original clothes. Marks: **MADE IN USA** on body; tag reads: **HORSMAN,** © **Michael Meyerberg, Inc., "Reproduction of the famous Kinemins in Michael Myerberg's marvelous technicolor production of Hansel and Gretel.** *(Courtesy Nita's House of Dolls, author's collection)*

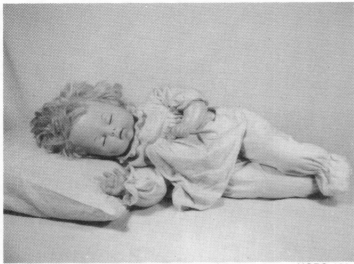

HORS-132.

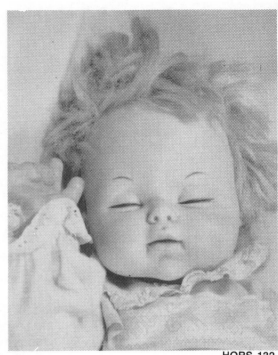

HORS-132.

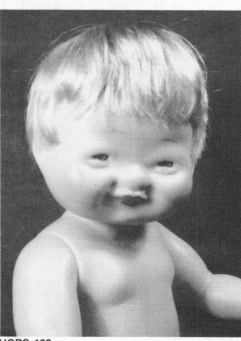

HORS-133.

HORS-134.

HORS-132. *Nitey-Nite Baby.* 24"; rooted blonde hair; permanently closed eyes; vinyl head and limbs, stuffed cloth body. Marks: **HORSMAN DOLL INC. / 1963 /** © on head. *(Wiseman collection)*

HORS-133. *Perthy.* 13", 16"; rooted synthetic hair; inset eyes; open-closed mouth; soft blurred features; all vinyl, separated toes and fingers; came in bathrobe and slippers; sometimes incorrectly referred to as *Happy Fella;* 1958. Marks: **HORSMAN / DOLL.** *(Author's collection)*

HORS-134. *Girl.* 16"; red rooted hair; blue eyes; closed mouth; fully jointed vinyl; original dress. Marks: **HORSMAN DOLLS INC. /** © **1963 G116.** *(Wiseman collection)*

HORS-135.

HORS-135.

HORS-137.

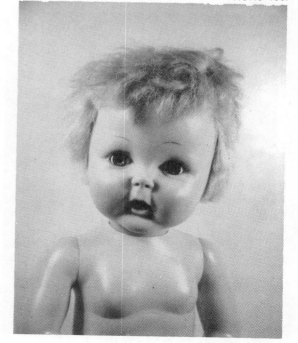

HORS-136.

HORS-135. *Alice.* 28"; rooted blonde synthetic hair; blue sleep eyes with lashes; closed mouth; soft vinyl head, rigid vinyl body and limbs; original blue cotton dress with white lace trim, white organdy apron, black patent slippers. Marks: **1 / HORSMAN DOLL INC. / ©** **1966 / 66271.** *(Author's collection)*

HORS-136. *Thirstee-Walker.* 26"; rooted blonde synthetic hair; blue sleep eyes; drink-and-wet mouth; fully jointed vinyl; holds bottle in hand. Marks: © **HORSMAN DOLLS INC. / 1962 TB26** on head. *(Wiseman collection)*

HORS-137. *Baby.* 12"; rooted blonde hair; blue sleep eyes with lashes; drink-and-wet mouth; fully jointed plastic and vinyl. Marks: **HORSMAN DOLLS INC. /** **19©64 / B144** on head. *(Author's collection)*

HORS-138a,b.

HORS-138c,d.

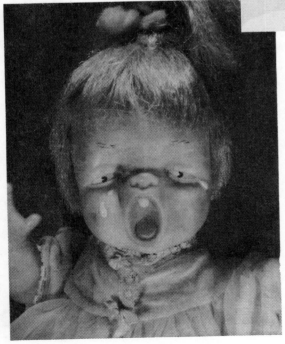

HORS-140.

HORS-139.

HORS-138a-d. *The Pip Squeeks, Singing Group.* 12";
rooted synthetic hair; painted eyes, lashes; open-
closed singing mouths; fully jointed vinyl; original
clothes; squeekers in arms; includes: a-*Cleo*, b-*Mark*,
c-*Anthony*, d-*Patty*. Marks: **6** (or 4,8,3 respectivly) /
HORSMAN DOLLS INC. / 19©67 / 6712 FF on head;
HORSMAN DOLLS INC. / T12 on waist. 1967 catalog
illustration. (Courtesy Sears, Roebuck & Co.)

HORS-139. *Bootsie.* 12½"; rooted black synthetic
hair; brown sleep eyes; closed mouth; soft vinyl head
and arms, hard vinyl legs and body; original clothes.
Marks: **2907 / 13EYE / T125 / 3 / © HORSMAN
DOLLS INC. / 1969.** (Wardell collection)

HORS-140. *Baby First Tooth.* Rooted blonde hair;
painted blue eyes; open-closed mouth with tongue
and one tooth; stuffed cloth body, vinyl head and
limbs; replacement clothes; molded tears on cheeks;
1960s. Marks: © **HORSMAN DOLLS INC. / 10141.**
(Author's collection)

HORS-141.

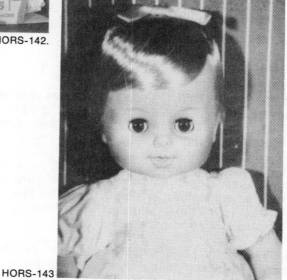

HORS-142.

HORS-142.

HORS-143

HORS-141. *Mary and Jerry.* Rooted synthetic hair; sleep eyes; drink-and-wet mouth; cries tears; fully jointed vinyl; came with cradle, stroller, rocking chair, layette sets; boy has same head with Dutch boy bob. *(Montgomery Ward's 1965 Catalog)*

HORS-142. *Re-issue Bye-lo Baby.* 14"; molded-painted hair; painted blue eyes; open-closed mouth; vinyl head and limbs, cloth body; original white nylon organdy bonnet and dress, cotton lining in dress, diaper. Marks: **3** (in square) / **HORSMAN DOLLS INC.** / © **1972** on head; cloth tag on body reads: **ALL NEW MATERIALS / CONTENTS / POLYURETHANE FOAM / AND COTTON / MFGD. BY / HORSMAN DOLLS, INC. / P.O. BOX 1390 / COLUMBIA, SOUTH CAROLINA / REG. NO. PA. 114.** *(Author's collection)*

Special note: The name Bye-lo Baby as applied to Horsman's 1972 offering is, to many doll collectors, a misnomer. It should be pointed out, however, that this is merely a new example of a longstanding practice in the industry of using old names on new models. We should, therefore, identify this doll as "Horsman's 1972 vinyl Bye-lo Baby" when referring to it in advertising or research.

HORS-143. *Train-a-Baby.* 15", 19"; rooted blonde hair; sleep eyes; drink-and-wet mouth; fully jointed vinyl; two-piece lace-trimmed outfit; drinks bottle and then wets diaper only when button on back is pushed. *(1973 Horsman Catalog)*

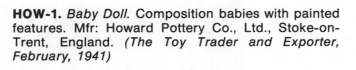

HOY-3.

HOY-2.

HOY-1a,b.

fig-HULES-1.

HOW-1. *Baby Doll.* Composition babies with painted features. Mfr: Howard Pottery Co., Ltd., Stoke-on-Trent, England. *(The Toy Trader and Exporter, February, 1941)*

HOY-1a,b. *Mary Hoyer's Brother.* 14"; fur wig; blue sleep eyes; closed mouth; fully jointed hard plastic; replacement clothes. Marks: **ORIGINAL / Mary Hoyer / DOLL** (in circle). *(Courtesy Nita's House of Dolls, Rebekka Anderton collection)*

HOY-2. *Mary Hoyer Nun.* 14"; brown mohair wig; brown glassene sleep eyes; closed mouth; fully jointed composition; authentic nun's habit is all hand stitched; 1938. Marks: **THE / MARY HOYER / DOLL** on back. *(Cannon collection)*

HOY-3. *Mary Hoyer.* 14"; original red-brown mohair wig; blue sleep eyes; closed mouth; fully jointed composition; replacement clothes. Marks: **THE / MARY HOYER / DOLL.** *(Edge collection)*

HOW-1.

HOWARD POTTERY
Co., L^TD.

NORFOLK ST.,
STOKE-ON-TRENT.

TERMS FOR
WHOLESALE

ENQUIRIES
WELCOME

LEADING MANUFACTURERS OF

DOLLS

DOLLS' HEADS

TOY TEA SETS

FOR HOME & EXPORT

RANGE FOR 1941
NOW READY.

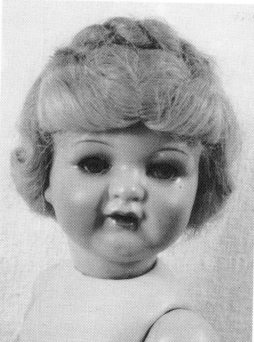

HULES-1

HULES-1. *Girl.* 18"; original blonde mohair wig with braids; blue glass sleep eyes with lashes; open mouth with two teeth; fully jointed composition. This composition head is sometimes mistaken for painted bisque. Often an inspection of the interior of the head is the only way to determine the type of material used in its manufacture. Marks: see fig. HULES-1. *(Author's collection)*

HUMMEL DOLLS

The Hummel dolls, which derived from Berta Hummel's charming illustrations of the children of her village, are considered interesting collectibles by most doll collectors. Following is an excerpt from a release furnished by W. Goebel, Porzellanfabrik which manufactures the dolls.

The Hummel dolls are signed on the head with the signature shown in (a) as well as with various parts numbers and the Goebel copyright symbols (b) and (e). Other dolls are also marked with (b) and (e) and, in the case of well-known designers, the artist's signature appears.

Clothes are often marked with sewn-in Goebel labels (d) and a triangular blue and gold metal tag (f) on a blue and gold cord hangs from a wrist of each doll. The reverse of the tag reads *"HUMMEL / WERK."* Some dolls arrive in acetate cylinders; however, those packed in card boxes are fastened with blue elastic cord secured with round blue and gold metal tags with the symbol (b) on one side and the words *"AUS DEM HUMMELWERK"* on the reverse.

All boxes are extremely well-marked with combinations of some or all of the symbols shown as well as color-lithographed illustrations of groups of dolls.

The Goebel dolls may prove to be among the best-marked lines of collectibles available today and may become real joys to future researchers. In the meantime, we can enjoy them as we add these charming "Kinderpuppen" to our displays of "moderns" or artist-signed dolls.

M.J. Hummel

"The artist was a Franciscan nun, Sister Maria Innocentia Hummel. One of six children, gifted from childhood in the art of painting, she was brought up in a home where music, art and religion were a matter of course. Blessed with a vivid imagination, Berta Hummel made delightful little cards and wrote verses, featuring those things dear to her little child's world, the flowers, birds, animals, school mates and playmates.

Berta Hummel entered the Munich Academy of Fine Arts in 1927. There she met two young Franciscan sisters who were also students at the school. On August 30, 1934, Berta Hummel took her final vows. Within the cloistered walls of the Sieben Convent near Saulgau (Wurttemberg), Berta Hummel as Sister Maria Innocentia continued sketching and painting. From her rich memories she drew the inspiration for these sketches, brought to life her friends who had made her childhood a "Heaven on earth". The warmth of expression, the touching simplicity and the impressive look of the sketches quickly enjoyed great popularity. They became so talked about that the W. Goebel china factory, a well-known manufacturer of porcelain and ceramics, approached the Sieben Convent to obtain the exclusive world-wide right for transposing the creations of M.I. Hummel into three-dimensional works of art.

The popularity of "Hummel" figurines as gifts, or as additions to private collections, has labeled them "The World's Best Loved Children". The warm and tender artist did not stand up to the rigours of the last years of war and the first post-war years. On November 6, 1946, Sister Maria Innocentia left to live in the "House of the Lord" forever."

All the dolls are made of polyvinylchloride (PVC), are of very high quality, and are beautifully costumed and accessorized. Over the years there have been

HUM-1.

HUM-2.

HUM-3.

(b)

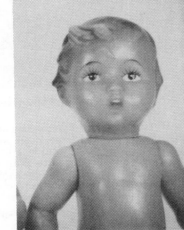

HUM-4.

(a)

M.J.Hummel

HUM-3,4.

characters too numerous to illustrate here; however, a good sampling is shown. Although rubber was the first doll material used, the PVC plastic seems to promise a longer-lasting doll; most of the rubber examples found today suffer a certain amount of chemical break-down of the rubber compound.

In addition to the Hummels, the W. Goebel, Porzellanfabrik has added to its doll line the work of a number of talented artists. These dolls are also shown under the Hummel classification since they are so often referred to by that name. The W. Goebel, Porzellanfabrik has become so closely associated with the Hummel name it is nearly impossible for collectors to separate the two.

HUM-1. *Mariandl.* 11½"; molded-painted hair and flowers; painted brown eyes; open-closed mouth with molded teeth; molded-painted rubber, fully jointed; original clothes. Marks: On head, no information available; tag reads: **MARIANDL / ORIGINAL / M.I. HUMMEL,** and **W-GOEBEL / OESLAU** with picture of a bee. *(Schulter collection)*

HUM-2. *Baker Boy.* 12"; molded-painted features; brown eyes; open-closed mouth with teeth; fully jointed rubber body; original clothes. Marks: **23 / M.I. Hummel / © W. Goebel** on head; tag on clothes reads: **MADE IN GERMANY.** *(Courtesy Nita's House of Dolls)*

HUM-3. *Rosl.* 10¾"; molded-painted light brown hair; painted brown eyes; open-closed mouth with teeth; all rubber jointed at shoulders and neck; original brown and white cotton dress. Marks: **1601 / M.I. Hummel / © W. Goebel** on head, (bee mark) / **1600** on back; dress tag reads: **M.I. Hummel.** *(Author's collection)*

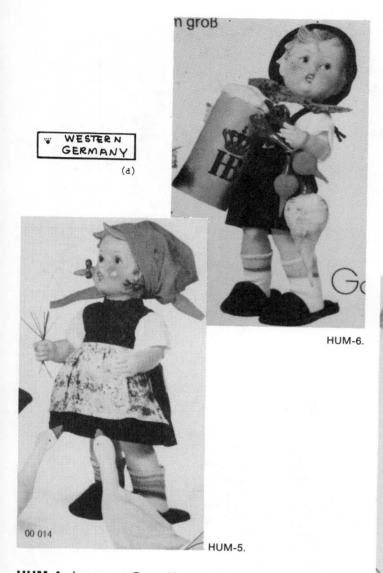

HUM-6.

HUM-8.

(f)

HUM-5.

HUM-7.

HUM-4. *Japanese Copy Hummel Boy.* 10¾"; molded-painted vinyl; open-closed mouth with teeth; fully jointed. Marks: **JAPAN / 67** on head. (On left is Rosl, HUM-3) *(Author's collection)*

HUM-5-8. These dolls are all 26 cm. tall; molded-painted hair; painted brown eyes; fully jointed polyvinylchloride (PVC); all wear felt and cotton character costumes and large brown felt shoes, a trademark of these dolls. *(W. Goebel Catalog, 1973)*

HUM-5. *Ganseliesl*
HUM-6. *Radi-Bub*
HUM-7. *Strickliesl*
HUM-8. *Wanderbub*

HUM-9a,b. *Hansl and Gretl.* 26cm.; molded-painted hair; painted brown eyes; fully jointed PVC bodies; felt and cotton costumes, large brown felt shoes. A smaller size series, 20cm., includes: *Vroni, Rudi, Seppl, Mariandl, Jackl,* and *Rosl* among others. *(W. Goebel Catalog, 1973)*

HUM-9a,b.

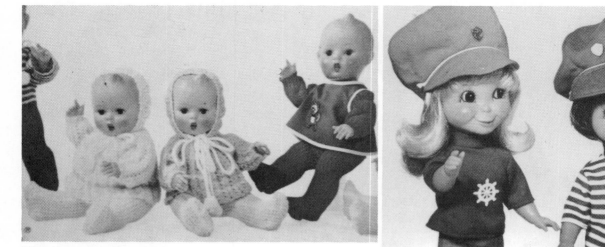

HUM-10.

HUM-11a,b.

HUM-12.

HUM-11c,d.

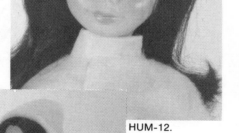

HUM-12-1.

HUM-13.

HUM-10. *Babies.* 26cm.; molded top knots; inset blue or brown stationary eyes; fully jointed PVC bodies; undressed or wearing red, white or blue knit suits, pink and blue suits and long pant stockings, or pink and blue fuzzy suits with long pant stockings. **(W. Goebel Catalog, 1973)**

HUM-11a-d. *Puppen designed by Michel Thomas.* 36cm.; rooted synthetic hair; painted blue-green side-glance eyes; molded-painted closed smile; fully jointed PVC bodies; wear character costumes of cotton, knit, and corduroy. *(W. Goebel Catalog, 1973)*

   a. *Jaqueline*
   b. *Gilbert*
   c. *Jeannette*
   d. *Pierre*

HUM-12. *Nina, the Fashion Doll.* 38cm.; rooted dark brown or blonde hair; blue sleep eyes with lashes; closed mouth; fully jointed PVC body; came in five different outfits with extra patterns for bride's dress, baby doll pajamas, maxi-cape, and skirt and blouse; 1972. *(Author's collection)*

HUM-12-1. *Hein.* 26cm.; rooted blonde hair; blue sleep eyes; closed smile; fully jointed PVC body; knit pants, shirt, hat and shoes; designed by Charlot Byj; 1972. *(Author's collection)*

HUM-13. *Sandmannchen (Sandman).* 17cm.; rooted beard, felt hair; painted eyes; closed line mouth; fully jointed PVC body; denim hat and pants, knit shirt, corduroy jacket, shoes; new in 1973. *(W. Goebel Catalog)*

HUM-14. *Pumuckl.* 27cm.; red synthetic wig; painted eyes; open-closed mouth with teeth and tongue; fully jointed PVC body; extra large hands and feet, jointed at wrists and ankles; carries a screw in one hand; knit shirt and pants with his name on the shirt. A German cartoon character. *(W. Goebel Catalog, 1973)*

HUM-15. *Vagabund.* 22cm.; synthetic fur wig, black mustache and beard; painted black eyes; molded open mouth for pipe; PVC head, hands, feet, wired foam body; blue felt pants, black felt hat with bird's nest; real wooden hobo stick; shoes with spats, no toes in shoes; designed by Charlot Byj; 1966. *(Author's collection)*

HUM-14.

HUM-15.

HUM-17e.

HUM-17a,b.

HUM-17c,d.

HUM-16.

HUM-18.

Note: The author has arbitrarily included all the dolls manufactured by the W. Goebel Porzellanfabrik under the Hummel classification. It is hoped that by so doing no one has been misled. *Only* the dolls depicting the works of Berta Hummel may be classified as *"Hummel Dolls."*

HUM-16. *Erbs-Puppen.* 26cm.; rooted blonde synthetic hair; painted eyes; closed mouth; fully jointed PVC body; original blue knit dress, panties; 1962. *(Rothert collection)*

HUM-17a-e. *Lore-Spatzchen.* 35cm.; rooted hair in various colors; blue sleep eyes; closed smiles; fully jointed PVC bodies; knit and synthetic fur costumes, vinyl shoes; five versions. *(W. Goebel Catalog, 1972)*

HUM-18. *Fratz.* 23cm.; rooted red hair; painted green eyes; closed smile; fully jointed PVC, bent baby legs and curled toes; red and white dotted shirt, white panties, wears lady bug on band on wrist; designed by Charlot Byj; 1962. *(Author's collection)*

Reader Editha Campbell reports finding an identical doll marked on both head and body: **REGAL TOY//MADE IN CANADA.** She also has a very similar doll with rounder eyes marked on head: **RELIABLE.** There have also been many reports of copies of many of the Goebel dolls being made in Japan and other Far Eastern countries.

HUM-19. *Jimmy.* 23cm.; rooted golden-brown hair; painted blue side-glance eyes; molded smile; fully jointed vinyl; overalls, shirt; designed by Charlot Byj in 1966. *(Author's collection)*

HUM-20.

HUM-21a-d.

HUM-19.

HUM-22.

HUM-22.

HUM-20. *Trine.* 26cm.; rooted red hair; painted green eyes; open-closed mouth with one tooth; fully jointed vinyl; original green checked dress and bandana; designed by Charlot Byj in 1957. *(Reeves collection)*

HUM-21a-d. *Cowboy and Cowgirl, Indianer and Indianerin.* 23cm, 26cm.; rooted black, blonde, platinum hair; painted side-glance eyes; fully jointed vinyl; dressed in suede cloth outfits with head bands and hats; Indians available in smaller size only. *(W. Goebel Catalog, 1973)*

HUM-22. *Affe Dombi.* 30cm.; molded head with brown synthetic fur wig; painted brown eyes; molded-painted monkey face; fully jointed vinyl body; synthetic fur suit snaps together at back like clothes, striped knit shirt; 1973. *(Author's collection)*

NUMERICAL MARKS INDEX